Real-time software systems

**JOIN US ON THE INTERNET VIA WWW, GOPHER,
FTP OR EMAIL:**

WWW: http://www.itcpmedia.com
GOPHER: gopher.thomson.com
FTP: ftp.thomson.com
EMAIL: findit@kiosk.thomson.com

WebExtra^{SM}
WebExtra gives added value online.

Point your web browser at:

        http://www.itcpmedia.com

A service of I(T)P ™

Real-time software systems

An introduction to structured and object-oriented design

J.E. Cooling

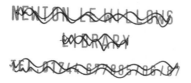

PWS Publishing Company

INTERNATIONAL THOMSON COMPUTER PRESS
I(T)P™ An International Thomson Publishing Company

London • Bonn • Boston • Johannesburg • Madrid • Melbourne • Mexico City • New York • Paris
Singapore • Tokyo • Toronto • Albany, NY • Belmont, CA • Cincinnati, OH • Detroit, MI

Real-time software systems: An introduction to structured and object-oriented design

Copyright © 1997 International Thomson Computer Press

I(T)P   A division of International Thomson Publishing Inc.
The ITP logo is a trademark under licence.

For more information, contact:

International Thomson Computer Press
Berkshire House
168–173 High Holborn
London WC1V 7AA
UK

PWS Publishing Company
20 Park Plaza
Boston
Massachusetts 02116–4324

http://www.itcpmedia.com

British Library Cataloguing-in-Publication Data
A catalogue record for this book is available from the British Library

Library of Congress Cataloging-in-Publication Data
A catalog record for this book is available from the Library of Congress

First printed 1997
Set by Columns Design Ltd., Reading
Printed in the United States of America
Cover Designed by Philip Goldfinch

ISBN (ITP edition)   1-85032-274-0
ISBN (PWS edition) 0-53495-492-8

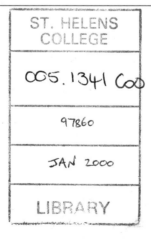

In memory of my parents Patrick and Kathleen Cooling
and
of Hugh and Teddy

Ar dheis De go raibh a nanamna

For my granddaughter
Eilish Siobhan Cooling

Contents

Preface

What is this book about?

This book shows how to develop software for real-time systems in a rigorous, systematic and professional manner using both structured and objected-oriented design (OOD) methods. It takes the reader through the complete design process, from a statement of requirements to the eventual source code. Example implementations of designs are given here using both Modula-2 and C++. However, the techniques used are not dependent on any particular language.

Who should read this book?

Those designing – or who intend to design – software for real-time systems. The central theme here is *design*, dealing with all aspects of the problem.

Why the emphasis on design?

There are few textbooks on the market which specifically deal, in depth, with software design. This book is intended to fill part of that gap.

Most books on software engineering include sections on design, but – even in the best – the treatment can be somewhat superficial. This only becomes apparent when you try to apply the principles in real situations. Other books integrate design aspects with a specific programming language. This approach has two disadvantages. The first, and obvious one, is that you may not wish to work with, or teach, that language. The second is that language features can distort the design approach.

Who will find this a useful text?

It is written for a wide audience, primarily those involved in producing software for 'real-world' applications. As such, it is applicable to many engineering disciplines:

electronic, electrical, mechanical, avionics, manufacturing and chemical, to name but a few. Two particular groups will find it of special interest:

- Those new to real-time software systems.
- Experienced designers who lack formal training in real-time design techniques.

As such it is suitable for both professional engineers and students.

At what level is this book pitched?

It assumes that the reader has experience of programming and program design – preferably in a modern high-level language. It would also be useful – though not essential – to appreciate the basics of digital electronics. This will help in understanding the many analogies made in the text between hardware and software design processes.

How is the text organized?

It consists of three distinct parts:
Introduction to real-time design – Chapter 1
Part One – Structured design – Chapters 2–10
Part Two – Object-oriented design – Chapters 11–16

Why this split into Parts One and Two?

The reasons are threefold:
1. Structured methods are mature, well established and widely used in the area of real-time software design. OOD is much newer, less well established and in a fluid state. Therefore the presentation of these techniques in the text is quite different.
2. It enables the material within each part to be well integrated.
3. The reader can concentrate on either structured *or* OO techniques if so desired.

What is the objective of Part One?

The purpose of Part One is to introduce all elements of structured design, a step at a time, using a bottom-up approach. It is based very much on the techniques devised by Michael Jackson, Ed Yourdon, Meilir Page-Jones, Paul Ward and Tony Mellor, together with influences of Derek Hatley and Imtiaz Pirbhai. The concurrency aspects owe much to the work of Ken Jackson and Hercock Simpson on MASCOT, Hassan Gomaa with DARTS and recent designs by Brian Kirk.

What is the objective of Part Two?

Part Two shows how object-oriented techniques can be applied to real-time systems, using a top-down approach. However, because the subject area is highly fluid, the material is presented with two specific objectives in mind. First, it aims to give a good, *broad* grounding in modern OO methods. Second, it sets out to show how to apply *selected* techniques for real-time design. Instrumental here has been the work of James Rumbaugh *et al.* (with OMT); Kent Beck and Ward Cunningham (CRC cards); David Harel; Sally Shlaer and Tony Mellor; Grady Booch; Ivar Jacobson; Brian Kirk; and the designers of HOOD.

How is Part One organized?

Part One starts with what the reader knows, namely:

- How to do program design
- What flow charting is

and builds on that knowledge, step by step. The gap between steps is kept as small as possible. Many 'mental hooks' are provided to bridge the gaps and make the learning process a straightforward one. Moreover, the reasons for, and advantages of, using several design stages are made clear. The relationship between the various stages is well defined, resulting in an integrated design approach.

At the outset (Chapter 2) the reader is introduced to the concept of using diagrams to define program structures (in effect a form of visual programming). The particular diagram used here is the Jackson program structure chart. From this it is only a small jump to modular design (Chapter 3), abstract software machines and the module structure chart.

The next stage brings in the concept of describing system *functionality* using data flow diagrams (Chapter 4). A simple small system is designed to illustrate this topic (Chapter 5). Moreover, it demonstrates the use, and integration, of data flow diagrams with structure charts.

At this point the second major attribute of embedded systems is introduced – dynamic behaviour. This is first discussed in terms of system behaviour (Chapter 6). Both diagram and text techniques are used to define such behaviour. These include the Mealy state transition diagram, state transition tables and state transition matrices. Next (Chapters 7 and 8) these ideas are applied to the software design process, by adding behavioural – *control* – information to the data flow diagram. The relationship between the data flow and state transition diagrams is clearly established.

The penultimate chapter of Part One deals with concurrency in a single processor system (here called *multitasking*). Independent and interdependent tasking is discussed, together with the rationale for this technique. Task control using coroutines, interrupts and schedulers is covered. Overheads related to multitasking are highlighted, together with the problems of task responsiveness and latency. It finishes by looking at the need for, and use of, communication components in multitasking designs.

Finally, to round things off, the reader is taken through the software design and implementation for a complete system (Chapter 10). For reasons of space many detailed items are omitted. However, *all* significant points are covered.

A full description of the example system – the *Chilled Water System* – is given in Appendix A.

How is Part Two organized?

Part Two opens (Chapter 11) with a general introduction to the concepts of object-oriented design – object, class, encapsulation, inheritance, relationships, communication and control. It assumes no prior knowledge on the part of the reader, expressing the ideas mainly in non-software terms.

These topics are then dealt with in detail in the following chapters. Chapter 12 looks at the object model, and shows how to derive this using two different techniques. The first is the data-driven approach, and the second is a responsibility-driven technique.

Chapter 13 is given over to the dynamic model, dealing with object communication and behaviour. It shows the need for external and internal modelling of OO systems, together with means to link these together. The use of the statechart method to implement finite state machines is covered in depth, as this is the basis for most OO state models.

Functional modelling (that is, a description of the processing performed in the system) is the topic of Chapter 14. This is a broad-based chapter, introducing the reader to a number of alternative techniques.

Chapter 15 is an important one in that it sets out to define techniques for object structuring, communication and control. In particular it deals with concurrency aspects, including interrupt handling. Many important implementation issues are discussed here, including:

- The need to consider system structure in terms of true concurrency (multi-processors) and quasi-concurrency (multitasking).
- Problems of mapping an abstract concurrent object model onto a practical sequential one.
- The need (or desire) to introduce object control structures.

Up to this point the approach has been one of demonstrating various OO design techniques. Chapter 16 now demonstrates how an OO design may be tackled using specific procedures. Here the reader is taken through the software design and implementation for a complete system (also the Chilled Water System). As with Chapter 10, many details are omitted, but all items of significance are covered.

Acknowledgements

First and foremost, I should like to thank all those who, by their advice, comments and criticism (and even a little praise) helped this book along into its final state. I would especially like to mention Andrew Collins, Joanne Cooling and Dr Jim Herd (of Heriot-Watt University). Andrew's review of the structured work was immense, detailed and very helpful. Thank you, Andy. Jo put in a massive effort to review the OO work (a task made all the more difficult by her being 8 months and two weeks pregnant). It proved to be extremely helpful, corrected some of my misapprehensions concerning OO, and helped smooth the rough bits in the first version of the text. Jim Herd's review was a significant one, as he combines qualities rarely found in this business: an academic with sound, practical real-time software experience. His assessment was thoughtful, constructive and detailed, and has resulted in a much improved book.

Next in line for appreciation are my commissioning editor, Samantha Whittaker, and her assistant editor, Nikki Vaughan. Sam has shown all the tenacity of a Yorkshire terrier in getting this project off the ground – her efforts have been recognized (by me, at least). Nikki has kept things running smoothly, responding quickly, efficiently and promptly to my whingeing. It's been a pleasure working with you both.

And finally a mention for those who contributed to my rest and relaxation during the writing of this book: Arthur Guinness and Sons Ltd, in conjunction with the Bull's Head, Markfield, Mistral Windsurfing, Rutland Water and Portland Harbour.

Jim Cooling
Loughborough

List of Abbreviations

ADC	Analogue to digital converter
ADFD	Action data flow diagram
CASE	Computer aided software engineering
CFD	Control flow diagram
CRC	Class, responsibility, collaboration
CSpec	Control specification
CT	Control transformation
DD	Data dictionary
DFD	Data flow diagram
DT	Data transformation
ERD	Entity relationship diagram
FIFO	First in, first out
HOOD	Hierarchical object oriented design
I/O	Input/Output
IC	Integrated circuit
ISR	Interrupt service routine
MUX	Multiplexer
ODFD	Object data flow diagram
OID	Object interaction diagram
OMD	Object message diagram
OMT	Object modelling technique
OO	Object oriented
OOD	Object oriented design
OOP	Object oriented programming
PCB	Printed circuit board
PSpec	Process specification
RTEX	Real-Time executive
S-H	Sample-Hold
SC	Structure chart
SP	Structured programming
STD	State transition diagram
STM	State transition matrix
STT	State transition table

1
Introduction

There are two major themes to this book. The first is the use of rigorous techniques for the design of real-time software. The second is the application of diagramming methods to support these techniques. Now, why are these important issues, and why should you be interested in learning about the topic? These are fair questions. This chapter sets out to answer them by explaining:

- what real-time systems are and how they may be categorized
- what design is
- the importance of design
- why you should learn how to design software
- what analysis is, and how it relates to design
- the power of visual methods
- the content and role of diagrams as part of the design process

1.1 Setting the scene

1.1.1 Real-time systems – an overview

The start of a busy day in the life of a computer professional:

> Radio alarm goes off: it's 6:30 a.m. Lights on, wash, dress, put make-up on. Only time for quick breakfast, so heat croissants in the microwave. Ring boss to confirm meeting arrangements. At last minute remember to set video recorder. Drive to airport. Arrive in a frustrated state as failure of local traffic light system has caused chaos around the airport. Booking arrangements confirmed, check in for flight. Relief: airborne at long last. Pleased to find that the aircraft is the latest type, has excellent in-flight entertainment facilities. ...

What has this got to do with software design? Directly, nothing. Yet this short account of the start of a working day tells us just how dependent we as people (and modern society in general) are on computers. Where are these computers, you may ask? Mostly they are 'invisible', in that they are integrated or *embedded* into a larger unit. The radio alarm, microwave oven and video recorder all contain a small micro-computer. Anti-skid braking systems in cars are again microprocessor controlled. Communication systems, traffic light control, airline booking systems, in-flight enter-tainment, aircraft flight control: all these rely on computers for their operation. And something else we often take for granted is the electrical power generating and dis-tribution system.

This book is concerned with the design and development of software for such real-time computer systems. In the broadest sense, they are systems where timeli-ness is important. Unfortunately, this is a rather limited definition; a more precise one is needed. Many ways of categorizing real-time systems have been proposed and are in use. One particular pragmatic scheme is shown in Table 1.1, the related attributes being those of Table 1.2.

Table 1.1 Real-time system categorization.

	Slow	Fast
Soft	Machinery condition monitoring	Man–machine interfacing
Hard	Missile point defence system	Airbag control system

Table 1.2 Attributes of real-time systems.

	Execution time	Deadlines	Software size	Software complexity
Hard–fast	****	****	*	*
Hard–slow	*	****	*→****	*→****
Soft–fast	****	**	***	****
Soft–slow	**	**	***	****

* Low weighting
**** High weighting

Hard, fast embedded systems tend, in computing terms, to be small (or may be a small, localized part of a larger system). Computation times are short (typically tens of milliseconds or faster), and deadlines are critical. Software complexity is usually low, especially in safety-critical work. A good example is the airbag deployment sys-tem in motor vehicles. Late deployment negates the whole function of the airbag protection mechanism (serious problems may also arise from late deflation).

Hard, slow systems do not fall into any particular size category (though many, as with process controllers, are small). An illustrative example of such an application is an anti-aircraft missile-based point-defence system for fast patrol boats. Here the total reaction time is of the order of 10 seconds. However, the consequences of fail-ing to respond in this time frame are self-evident.

Larger systems usually include comprehensive, and sometimes complex, man–machine interfaces (MMIs). Such interfaces may form an integral part of the total system operation, as for instance, in integrated weapon fire-control systems.

Fast operator responses may be required, but deadlines are not critical as in the previous cases. Significant tolerance can be permitted (in fact, this is generally true when humans form part of system operation). MMI software tends to be large and complex.

The final category, soft/slow, is typified by condition monitoring, trend analysis and statistics analysis in, for example, factory automation. Frequently such software is large and complex. Applications like these may be classified as *information processing* (IP) systems.

1.1.2 Design?

What is a *design*, and what do we mean by *designing*? Unfortunately we can't easily answer these questions: a precise, universally acceptable definition doesn't exist. For our purposes, however, the following extract from the *Oxford English Dictionary* sums up the processes covered in this text:

> Design (noun) – An outline or drawing for something that is to be made.
> Design (verb) – To produce a design.

Thus the end product of the software design process is a set of 'drawings' or 'plans'. These plans act as the defining documents for the production of source code. Please re-read and absorb the meaning of the last two sentences, because this is the core philosophy underlying *everything* that follows in the text. Simply put, diagrams define precisely how the software should be built.

All real design takes place incrementally, initial ideas being refined, elaborated and modified over time. That is, the first design goes through various development phases until the final version emerges. Hence software design *and* development are inextricably linked throughout the design phase.

1.1.3 The importance of design

Before making a product, is it important to first design it? The answer, of course, is yes. Even craftsmen who appear to just 'make' things do, in fact, work to plans. It just so happens that the plans are carried in their heads. Let us now, though, change the question. Is it important to carry out design using rigorous, organized and professional techniques? From the engineering community the answer will be a thunderous '*yes*'. But what of the software world? You *might* get a great yes vote. Regrettably, this is politico speak; the reality is quite dismal. And even more worrying is the culture which pervades many parts of the industry. The following article extract shows clearly what the problem is. Its premise is that getting a product out quickly, even though it contains bugs, is more important than getting it right. Underlying this is the author's view that products designed in a rigorous manner usually have poor (here meaning slow) performance.

> The bad news is that a product's poor performance might lose more customers than outright crashes or malfunctions! At least a user can report a crash with tangible symptoms and expect a fixed version of the code. Users can often avoid buggy features and still get use from the rest of the product.

This may be acceptable in, say, a word processing package. However, the application of such a philosophy to manufacturing systems, medical software, vehicle control and the like spells disaster. And on a personal level, how would you feel about 'flaky' software being responsible for your bank account?

What are the consequences of taking an 'up and at them' approach? The following lament by Robert Bliss very clearly answers the question:

> It sometimes seems that cost and schedule overruns are pandemic in software developments. It is hardly surprising that the term 'vaporware' was coined for the computer community. According to a recent report issued by the Standish Group International Inc., US companies waste $140 billion annually on failed or delayed software development projects. Around 31 percent of software projects are canceled altogether before they can be finished. And in a typical year in North America, software projects worth $81 billion are terminated without delivering *any* value. What other business has such a miserable track record … [organizations] milk projects for years beyond due dates, dribbling out minor features and bug fixes to a captive customer unwilling or unable to switch suppliers.

Enough said, methinks.

1.1.4 Why learn to design?

First, be clear on one point. Nobody can turn you into a designer by *teaching*; you have to learn how to do it. True, people can give advice. They can give guidance. They can evaluate your efforts. They can even teach design. But the reality is that you cannot be *taught* to be a designer. Furthermore, reading this book will not make you proficient. You have to get out and work at it, by turning ideas into practice.

So, why bother to learn to design software? The answers are essentially personal ones:

- It is a process of acquiring new – and useful – skills. This in itself is a highly satisfying activity for motivated people.
- Your professionalism and competence levels are significantly enhanced.
- The quality of your work (in the broadest sense) will be greatly improved. Most people get immense satisfaction from doing a job well.
- These factors will gain you respect from your peers. Again, this is something which is quite important to most professionals.
- It will open many new career paths.
- Lastly, a very personal opinion. Design is creative, challenging, exciting and stimulating (even fun?). Doing it well carries its own rewards.

Now that the commercials are over, we can begin our journey in earnest.

1.2   Design and the overall development process

Many models of the software development process have been produced. These range in structure and detail, but one that has frequently been referenced is the 'V' model. A somewhat simplified version of this is shown in Figure 1.1.

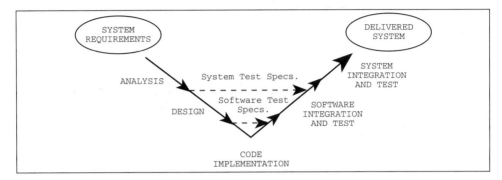

Figure 1.1 Simplified V-model of software development.

The diagram content and meaning is quite clear and should need no further explanation. But before launching into detailed discussion, it is important to understand one point: the meaning of *analysis*. In very simple terms, analysis is gaining an understanding of *what* is required of a system. More fully, for computer-based systems, it embraces:

- gaining a full appreciation of the user's system and its associated requirements
- establishing exactly what the computer system is supposed to do
- documenting these aspects in a clear and understandable way
- defining precisely the objectives of the (later) design activities

The relationship between analysis and design, as shown in Figure 1.1, would appear to be clear-cut. Implicit here is that there is a distinct split between the two activities. Such a view, for real-time systems, is somewhat simplistic (some would say naïve). Moreover, the V-model as given here is very software oriented. Reality is much more complex, as illustrated in Table 1.3.

The scenario it applies to is the overall development of a rapid transit system. It represents what one is likely to meet in practice – a layered process.

At the project outset, the most important player on the scene is the rapid transit system operator. Also, from the project point of view, the operator is the end client. Work begins with an analysis of the transport requirements which the system is required to meet. And this is probably the *only* stage in which pure analysis is carried out. Subsequently, analysis and design are carried out as an interlocking pair of operations. But there are a number of distinct sets of A/D (analysis/design) operations, each having a 'ceiling' (the input) and a 'floor' (the output).

For the operator, the floor of activities is the generation of the statement of requirements (SOR) for the complete system. This acts as the ceiling for the main

Table 1.3 The development process – a layered approach.

Rapid transit system operator	*Analysis* of the problem – Transport requirements	
	Analysis and design e.g. Analysis of service frequency Overall design of appropriate train systems *Output:* Overall system SOR	Floor
Main contractor	*Analysis* of system requirements and its overall design Design of the control and signalling (C&S) subsystem Elaboration of system specifications *Output:* Subsystem specifications	Ceiling Floor
Control and signalling subcontractor	*Analysis* of the C&S subsystem specifications *Design* of the C&S subsystem *Output:* C&S system, hardware and software specifications	Ceiling Floor
C&S software developer	*Analysis* of system and software specifications *Design* of the software *Output:* Design documentation and source code	Ceiling

contractor, whose first task is to analyse the requirements. Next, subsystem design is performed, using as input the information provided within the SOR. The floor activity of this work layer is the production of sets of subsystem specifications (one being the train control and signalling subsystem). Subsequent events are depicted in Table 1.3. For simplicity, only the software development phase is included at the bottom level. Also, bear in mind that for embedded systems, the process is somewhat more complex (Figure 1.2).

It is important to understand that you, as a software engineer, are likely to be involved in the bottom layer of work. Know your place in the scheme of things. And recognize that the computer is essentially a component within a complete system.

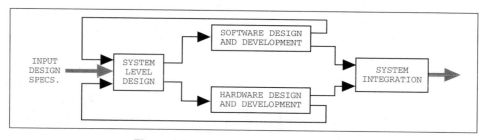

Figure 1.2 Embedded system development.

Thus system – not computer – requirements predominate. Also, be aware that Table 1.3 does *not* imply that the work packages are carried out in sequence. It may start out that way (and even that is problematic). But before very long *all* the players will be simultaneously engaged on the project. As a result you will find that the design is in a state of constant change. Needless to say, this presents many difficulties for the software developer. Thus your design approach *must* be able to deal with changing requirements.

A last point here is to consider how software development itself proceeds in real life. It does not occur in a 'big-bang' fashion. Rather, it takes place gradually, as illustrated in Figure 1.3.

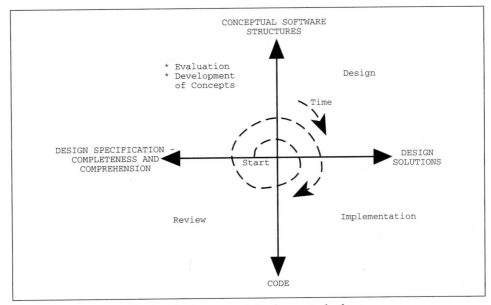

Figure 1.3   Incremental development of software.

The inputs to (the ceiling of) the design process are the software requirements specifications. Work proceeds by evaluating the specifications and then developing – in conceptual form – suitable software structuring.

Next is the design process itself, which translates concepts into design solutions. Following on is the implementation phase, the outcome being source code. This is not the finish, however. Generally, issues which come to light during the development lead us to review the design. In turn, this leads to a greater understanding of the problem; frequently it also results in changes to the design specification itself. At this stage we retread the path, using our new (or better) knowledge to improve the software product.

So far we have agreed what design is, why it's important and where it fits into the development cycle. Good. But just how should we approach the design process? How can we deal with design complexity? How can the design itself be represented, other than as lines of source code? The answer to these (and others) is the subject of the next section.

1.3   Diagramming techniques – or the world in pictures

1.3.1   Diagramming techniques and design – why?

Diagrams are an intrinsic part of our everyday life. We use them for countless reasons, for all sorts of applications. Just a few:

- showing the various displays produced on a TV screen when setting up a VCR
- illustrating foot positions when dancing the tango
- showing family trees
- guidance for filling in forms

Why use diagrams for these? Because the alternative, text, is a very poor option. Most of us would agree that diagrams are a much more effective way of conveying information (though in most cases text support is still needed). And one only has to look at engineering to see that diagrams are an integral part of the profession. So, why not apply the same ideas to software?

Now consider using diagrams for the following purposes:

- showing the correct way to stack boxes
- denoting danger
- indicating 'no smoking'

Here text would be almost as effective – provided you understand the language. In fact, the same comment applies to diagrams – you have to know what they mean. And this raises the need for defined syntax (the symbols and rules of the grammar) and semantics (the meaning). Nevertheless, there is no question that diagrams are much more powerful than text in conveying information. Thus they may be regarded as a higher-level language. Moreover, they can be made truly international with relatively little effort. Let us consider, in very general terms, their use within design, with reference to Figure 1.4.

First, diagrams enable clients to express more clearly their design requirements (Figure 1.4(a)). These act both as communication and specification documents. This specification has then to be turned into a design diagram, requiring:

- clarity of thought
- analysis of the problem
- formality and rigour
- identification of constraints
- explicit expression of the solution

The result of the process is the 'document' which acts as the manufacturing specification (here, Figure 1.4(b)). One can, at this point, evaluate the design against its original specification (preferably in conjunction with the client).

During the build phase, various design deficiencies are likely to come to light. The result is that the final product (Figure 1.4(c)) may differ somewhat from the original design. Again, diagrams help in identifying the changes (and the reasons for

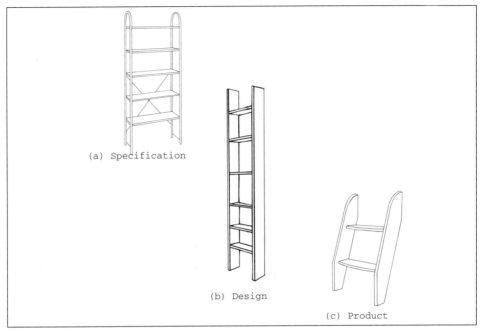

(a) Specification

(b) Design

(c) Product

Figure 1.4   Visual descriptions.

change). Further, the product can be assessed against the original requirements, taking into account functional, structural and performance features.

The result is that the delivered product not only works well; it also does what the client wanted in the first place.

1.3.2   Diagramming techniques and design – what?

Let us assume you are now persuaded that diagrams are good for you. Excellent. But this presents us with a new set of questions:

- What types of diagrams are applicable to the design process?
- What information should these diagrams contain?
- How, when, where and why will the diagrams be used?

To answer these we need to be clear what we, as designers, require of diagrams. We also need to be clear about our own role in the overall development process. Our job as software engineers working in real-time systems is to provide one component part of a system. Thus, at the beginning of design we need to know:

- what the system is supposed to do – its function
- what the system contains – the objects
- how the system is (or is to be) structured

These points are illustrated in Figure 1.5.

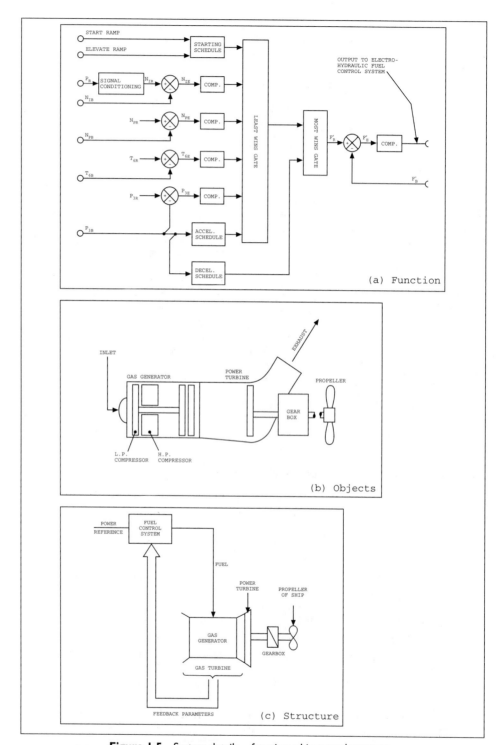

Figure 1.5 System details – function, objects and structure.

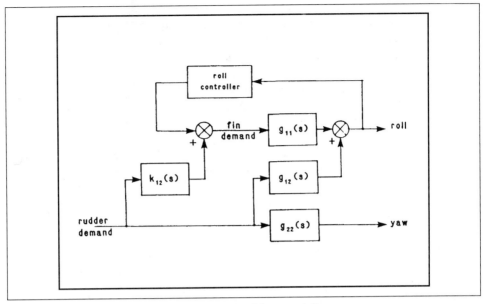

Figure 1.6   High-level functional diagram.

An important point – which diagram is the first to be produced? Almost certainly it will be a functional description, although initial diagrams are likely to be quite abstract (Figure 1.6).

In reality, the diagrams are so heavily interdependent that it is nonsense to take them in isolation. They *must* be seen as essential, interlocking parts of a bigger picture. To do otherwise is begging for trouble later in the project.

Having decided what diagrams are needed, how much information should they contain? Just how complex can a diagram be before it becomes unusable? Would you, for instance, consider Figure 1.7 to be helpful?

I doubt it very much. The reason is that people can only effectively handle a

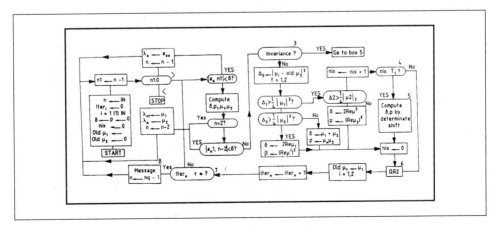

Figure 1.7   A complete diagram.

limited amount of information at any one time. This issue was investigated as a psychological problem in the 1950s by George Miller. His paper, 'The magical number seven, plus or minus two' is a landmark one – I recommend it to you. The conclusions are clear. Too much information (especially of the complex variety) is counterproductive. It merely confuses rather than enlightens. Thus simplicity is the order of the day.

Perhaps you can now begin to see the difficulty we face when using diagrams. On the one hand, there is a need to keep them simple and clear. On the other, the system we are dealing with is likely to be complex. The only sensible way to deal with this mismatch is to use *sets* of diagrams. Those produced first aim to give a large-scale (high-level) view of the system; later ones provide detailed (low-level) infor-

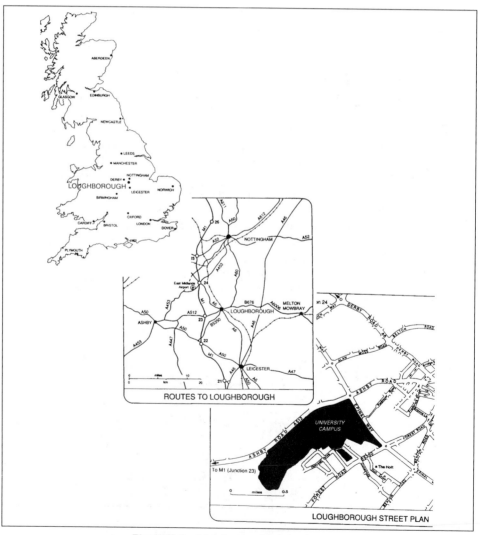

Figure 1.8   High-level and low-level views.

mation. In many cases these later diagrams are 'exploded' versions of earlier ones, as, for example, in the maps of Figure 1.8.

In such situations, there must be complete consistency across levels.

A final point to consider is the matching of diagrams to what they represent (rather grandiosely, their domain of application). What a diagram does is to abstract reality from a particular domain into a model. But the model has to be the right one for the domain. This point is very well demonstrated in Figure 1.9, giving two views of the London underground system (the tube). Figure 1.9(a) represents the system from the point of view of the traveller when underground (the train domain). In contrast, Figure 1.9(b) overlays the system on a normal map (the surface domain).

Same system, different views. Therefore it should be no surprise to find that we meet exactly the same issues in software development.

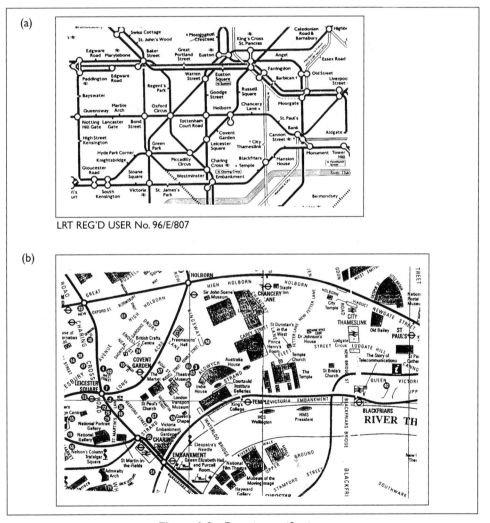

Figure 1.9   Domain-specific views

Review

Having completed this chapter you should now:

- understand the meaning and attributes of real-time systems, and how they may be categorized
- understand what design is, why it is important, and why it is desirable to become a proficient designer
- perceive the difference between analysis and design
- appreciate the role of design within the overall software development process
- understand the incremental nature of software development
- recognize that visual techniques are powerful tools for specification, communication and the expression of design ideas
- realize that systems need – at the very least – to be described in terms of function, objects and structure
- appreciate that these aspects can be clearly, comprehensively and unambiguously described using diagrams (with appropriate text support)
- understand the need for diagrams to have defined syntax and semantics
- see why there is a need for multi-level diagramming methods
- recognize that different problem domains require different diagram types

Part One:
Structured design

2
A pictorial description of programs:
The program structure chart

In keeping with the philosophy of 'from the bottom up', we shall first tackle the issues of program design. Fundamental to modern software design is the use of diagrams as a design tool – a 'picture'-based approach. This chapter introduces the diagramming technique which is closest to source code, *program structure charts*. It:

- explains why diagramming brings discipline and order to design
- reviews the ideas and implementation features of structured programming
- introduces the idea of defining program actions in terms of pre-conditions, operations and post-conditions
- introduces program structure diagrams
- describes in detail the symbols and rules of Jackson Structure Charts
- shows clearly how to translate a design from structure chart to source code
- defines a clear-cut set of translation rules
- shows how these translation rules make it easy to check ('trace') the design through its various stages
- reviews top-down design and stepwise refinement when used for program development
- extends the original Jackson notation

2.1   An introduction to structured programs

2.1.1   *Bringing discipline to programming*

You could be forgiven for thinking that engineering discipline and computer programming are mutually exclusive. This is especially true in the world of personal computing, the natural habitat (it would seem) of the ubiquitous hacker. But, for professional engineering programming, order and structure are essential. There are many good reasons for this, all hinging around one factor: program errors. In real-time systems such errors can produce effects ranging from irritating through expensive to catastrophic. So we can't afford to dismiss the situation with the comment 'what else can you expect of software?'. For our work we must use program design methods which:

- minimize the number of errors made in the initial programming
- make it easier to find errors
- make it faster to rectify the problems
- produce reliable, safe and correct software

These requirements were recognized some 30 years ago. As a result, one design methodology, *Structured Programming* (SP), emerged as a clear favourite. The rules of SP, updated in only a small way, say that:

- A very limited range of program control structures is needed.
- Programs should be built in a top-down manner.
- We should be able to prove that programs meet their specifications (program correctness).

For the moment we shall defer discussion on another important point:

- Programs should be constructed using software modules, these being organized in a hierarchical fashion.

Modular design is the subject of Chapter 3.

Structured programming had a major effect on the design of programming languages. What you now see as the normal features of high-level languages owe much to these concepts. But they also had a major influence in another area of software design: diagramming techniques.

Diagramming is nothing new to engineers. Go back thousands of years and you will find that they were widely used for civil engineering. In modern electronic engineering they are essential for developing abstract models of reality. After all, there isn't anything much more abstract than something you can't see, feel, hear, taste or smell (don't confuse electricity itself with its *effects*). Program code can also be somewhat abstract. When written in binary form, for instance, it is incomprehensible. Not the individual symbols, that is; there is nothing mysterious about binary notation. No, the thing which is 'invisible' is the *meaning* of the code: that is, what it's supposed to do and how – in the broader sense – it does it. Modern high-level languages, with their emphasis on good readability, have greatly improved the situation. But these are only part of the total answer to our needs. While they give us good *implementation* tools, they are not in themselves *design* methods. This is where diagramming comes in. Our design is expressed using 'pictures', and then implemented using a programming language.

So, having chosen to use diagrams, we then have to decide:

- How many types are needed?
- What is the purpose (or purposes) of these diagrams?
- What symbols (icons) should be used?

Is it likely that a single diagram type will meet our needs? Very unlikely. Experience from other branches of engineering says not, for one very good reason. Real systems have many different attributes. No single diagram type can show all these varied features simply, clearly and effectively. For instance, an electronic system will have circuit diagrams, circuit board layouts, block diagrams, timing diagrams and so on. Mechanical, civil and chemical engineering all have their own sets of diagrams. Why should software be different? The answer, of course, is that it isn't. It too needs a range of diagrams, all having a place in the overall design process.

In this chapter we'll look at the diagram which is closest to source code, the *Program Structure Diagram*. Before doing so, however, a number of basic ideas should be reviewed. These include:

- elementary diagramming using flow charting
- the control structures of structured programming
- the concept of control skeletons
- defining control skeletons using pictures
- control structure text
- inserting program operations into control constructs
- picture to code – a defined set of translation rules

These points are demonstrated in the context of the three basic program structures of SP: sequence, selection and iteration.

2.1.2 *Basic sequence structure*

This is the simplest program structure that can be used. It is nothing more than the execution of program statements in direct sequence, one at a time. The flow chart form is given in Figure 2.1, indicating that operation A is performed first, followed by B, then C, and so on.

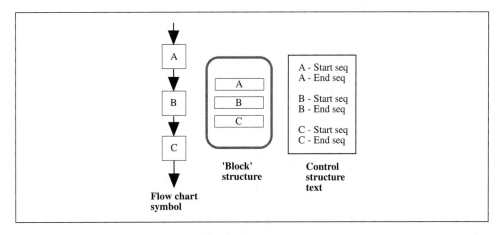

Figure 2.1   Basic sequence structure.

We use this 'box' symbol to define:

- what should happen
- when it should happen

Note very carefully that this does not say *how* these are to be implemented. What it does do is let us concentrate on what we want to do, not how we go about doing it.

In some instances each box might be implemented using a single line of code. In others, a number of code statements may be needed to achieve the desired result. Or it could be that we use subprograms to build the design. Use the best solution for each particular program problem. Thus it is useful to think of the program as being made up of a set of blocks (Figure 2.1). We can also define this block control structure using a structured text form. Finally we produce the source code, as shown in Figure 2.2.

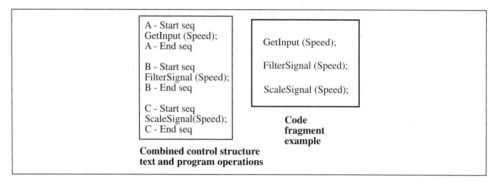

Figure 2.2   Sequence structure – translation to code.

These apparently simple figures illustrate some very important ideas:

- First we have clearly defined the structure of the program, not its implementation.
- Second, the program is structured as blocks. Each block has a specific purpose. The program structure is defined by the ordering of the various blocks.
- Third, this block structure is described using a control structure text diagram.
- Finally, each block is implemented as source code (Figure 2.2). Each block may be realized as a single line of code, multiple lines, a subprogram, multiple subprograms or any combination of these.

These figures also show another basic aspect of SP. Each block has a single input point and a single output point. What this means is that there is only one route into the code for this block; likewise there is only one exit from the code section.

What Figures 2.1 and 2.2 do is to define exactly how to translate the design diagram into source code *structure*. Note this well: the structure, not the actual code itself. The control structure text is a useful tool for the translation process. Treat it as a template for building the source code structure. As a result, the diagram-to-code translation rules are easy to use. They are not ambivalent, not ambiguous and not confusing. There is thus no 'magic' in generating the program code from the diagram design. In other words, the semantics are clear-cut and explicit.

Why are diagram semantics so important? Remember, the design methods used here are based almost entirely on diagramming techniques. If, in the final (build) stage, we don't have a precise set of translation rules, what then? How can we be sure that the program as built really meets our design objectives? This, I'm sure you'll see, is a rhetorical question.

2.1.3   Basic selection structure

The control structure for selection, as defined by SP, is shown in Figure 2.3.

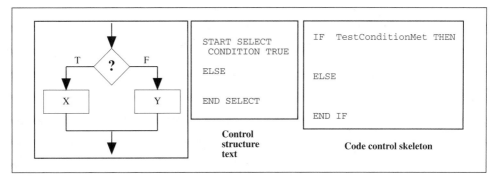

Figure 2.3   Basic selection structure.

As before, there is one entry point and one exit point. On entering the construct, a decision has to be made as to which internal route is to be taken (in this case, do either X or Y). This is further illustrated by the control structure text. From this text we can directly generate a code control skeleton, the example here using the IF THEN ELSE construct. Note that this isn't a one-to-one mapping. We could just as easily have used the CASE structure. And, of course, there is no barrier to it being written in assembly language code. The essential point of the figure, however, is that the code skeleton is defined by the diagram structure. In other words, there is a unique relationship between the design diagram and the code control skeleton (from now on called the control skeleton).

Taking this one stage further, the program operations can be combined with the control structure text (Figure 2.4). From this the combined control skeleton and program operations can be produced.

2.1.4   Basic iteration structures

There are three forms of iteration: pre-check, post-check and mid-check. Figure 2.5 gives the flow chart for the basic pre-check operation.

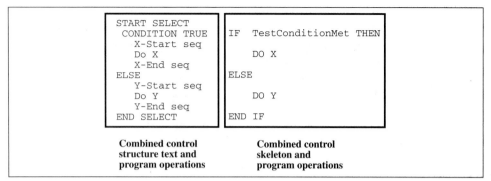

Figure 2.4   Selection structure – translation to code.

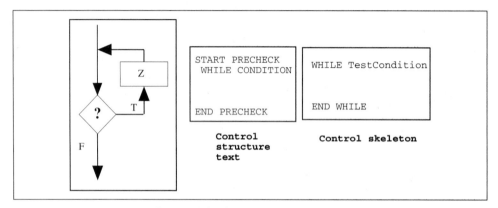

Figure 2.5   Basic pre-check iteration.

Also shown is the control structure text and a suitable control skeleton. To turn this into source code, the steps outlined in Figure 2.6 should be followed.

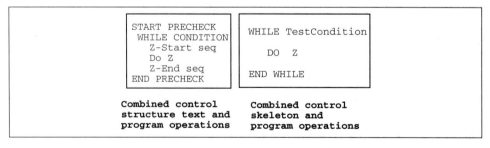

Figure 2.6   Pre-check iteration – translation to code.

By now you should be familiar with the notation and procedures used here. Observe once again the single entry and exit points.

Post-check iteration is shown in Figure 2.7.

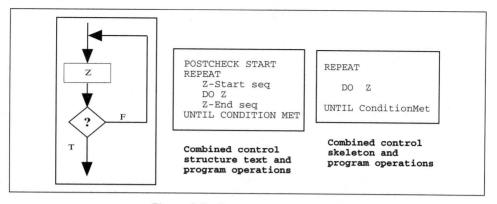

Figure 2.7 Basic post-check iteration.

You can see that we have moved straight to the combined control structure text and program operations diagram. Intermediate stages have been omitted. Similarly, the control skeleton and program operations have been combined in one step. In practice you will go directly from the design diagram to this final form in one move, as demonstrated in Figure 2.8.

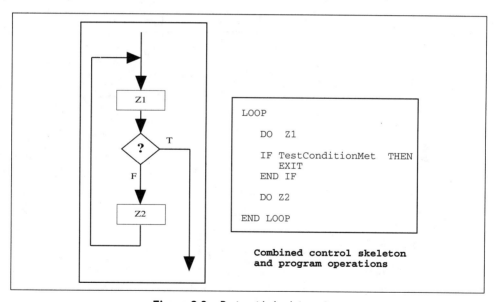

Figure 2.8 Basic mid-check iteration.

This illustrates the mid-check iteration. In this case only one test is made; in theory there is no limit to the number that can be made (in practice common sense should be used). But, no matter how many checks are carried out, the construct has only one exit point.

2.1.5 A last comment on control structures

You can see that a key feature of SP is that it calls for:

- a specific set of program control structures
- single entry and exit points for such control structures

What then is the value in adopting these rules? Let's take the second item to start with.

Any of the defined control structures can be drawn as in Figure 2.9.

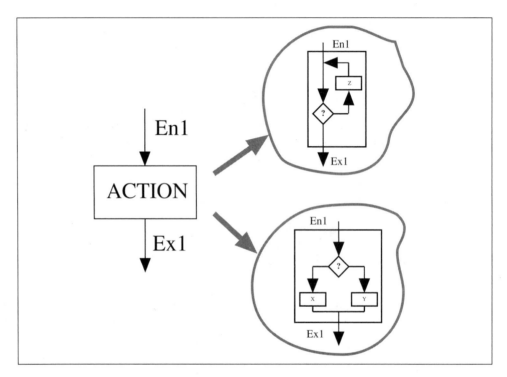

Figure 2.9 Block internal structure.

From the outside we have no idea how the operation is implemented. This allows us to take a quite abstract view of the problem. It can be reduced to three defining factors: pre-condition, operation and post-condition. Let us explain this using a very simple example. Suppose it is required to carry out square-rooting of an input signal (typically used with flowmeter systems). We decide that, as the signal always has a positive value, a simple algorithm can be used. It is also necessary to work within the number range of the computer. It is decided to use integer arithmetic, the maximum word size being 16 bits. Thus the complete specification for the operation becomes:

Pre-condition:	$0 \leq \text{InputSignal} \leq 65535$
Operation:	$\text{OutputSignal} = \text{Square root of InputSignal}$
Then	
Post-condition is:	$0 \leq \text{OutputSignal} \leq 255$

As a result we can test the actual program against this specification. If it fails to conform to it then clearly there is an implementation error. For most applications we are unlikely to test small fragments of code in this way. However, this approach is commonplace when hunting for bugs. Programs built using SP constructs can readily be split into individual sections. Such sections may then be tested separately, without reliance on other sections of the program. This is one of the fastest methods for tracking down algorithmic and logic problems, so why not make your life easier by using sensible control constructs?

Note also that the pre-condition highlights the need to work within a specified set of input conditions.

Now to return to the first point, using only a specified set of control structures. By limiting program constructs, *any* resulting program will, even at the highest level, be a structured one. This is demonstrated for a simple example in Figure 2.10.

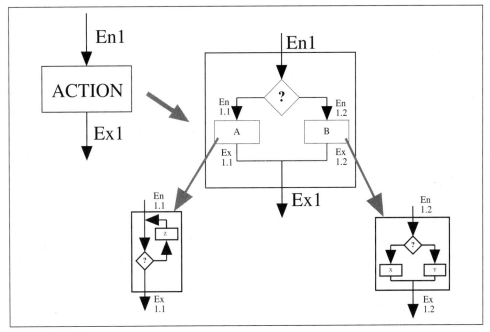

Figure 2.10   Analysis/synthesis of a structured program.

Therefore, not only is it possible to define the lowest level operations fully, this can also be done at the highest level. As a trivial example, suppose that we were simulating the behaviour of a data acquisition channel, made up of two blocks (Figure 2.11). Their specifications are shown in Table 2.1.

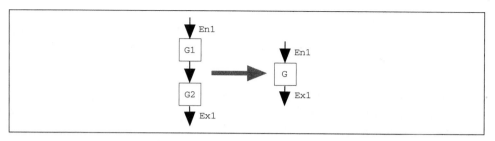

Figure 2.11   Cascaded blocks.

Table 2.1.

	G1	**G2**
Pre-condition	$0 \leq f \leq 0.01$	$0 \leq F \leq 10$
Operation	$F = 1000 \times f$	$FRate = \sqrt{F}$
Post-condition	$0 \leq F \leq 10$	$0 \leq FRate \leq 3.16$

Hence the end-to-end specification G is given as:

Pre-condition: $0 \leq f \leq 0.01$
Operation: $FRate = (1000 \times f)^{1/2}$
Post-condition: $0 \leq FRate \leq 3.16$

Consequently, we are now in a position to write an end-to-end test specification. Only in the event of test failure is there a need to delve into the innards of the algorithm.

2.2   Program structure diagrams – the structure chart

2.2.1   Introduction to the basics of structure charts

So far, flow charts have been used to illustrate the program constructs of SP. Now we shall meet its successor, the program structure diagram. Strictly speaking this is a generic term; many diagrams fall into this category. These include Jackson Structure Charts (SCs), Nassi–Schneidermann diagrams and Warnier–Orr diagrams (for further information see Cooling (1991) in Section 3 of the Bibliography). The various diagrams have two common aspirations:

- to replace flow charts
- to enforce the constructs of structured programming

But, you may ask, if flow charts can describe SP constructs, why replace them? Yes, flow charts do meet our needs. Unfortunately they also allow you to design disorganized, rambling and tortuous programs. Structure diagrams enforce a disciplined, structured and organized style of program design. Perhaps that's why only a minority of programmers use them.

In this text we will use Jackson Structure Charts to describe program structure. The basic notation has been extended in small, but (in our experience) useful ways. Some of the extensions have been provided by CASE (Computer-Aided Software Engineering) tool vendors. Others have come about with experience.

The simplest construct is, of course, sequential operation. In Figure 2.12 both the flow chart and structure chart forms are given.

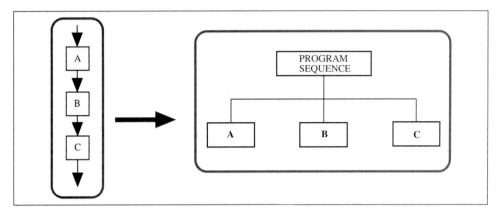

Figure 2.12   Program structure diagram – sequence.

However, they don't quite say the same thing. The flow chart tells us that we have three sequential operations, A, B and C. Their execution order is A followed by B followed by C. What the structure chart says is that:

• There is an operation called 'program sequence'.
• This is realized by performing actions A, B and C, in that sequence.

Thus the SC shows both sequence *and* decomposition. The example of Figure 2.13 fleshes out these points, the control structure text demonstrating them very clearly.

Here, the top-level operation is 'Process Speed Signal'. This is decomposed into three lower-level operations 'Get Input', 'Filter Signal' and 'Scale Signal'. Another way to look at this is to say that the high-level operation (the 'parent') is composed

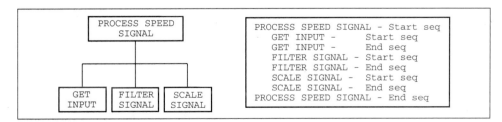

Figure 2.13   Sequence construct – structure chart and control structure text.

of three lower-level ones ('children'). Observe that decomposition runs top-to-bottom, while sequence goes left-to-right.

It is essential to understand fully the semantics of the structure chart (more precisely, the *program* structure chart). We use this to design our program by describing what is intended to happen. The most succinct description of our aims becomes the top-level one. Decomposition is used to define this in more detail – an elaboration process. Thus Figure 2.13 says that the operation to be performed is to process the speed signal. However, to do this, we actually first get the input signal, then filter it, and finally scale the filtered value. The wording used within the boxes describes the actions to be carried out; it is *not* source code. This aspect is shown clearly in Figure 2.14, where code statements have been inserted.

```
PROCESS SPEED SIGNAL - Start seq
    GET INPUT -        Start seq
    GetInput (Speed);
    GET INPUT -        End seq
    FILTER SIGNAL - Start seq
    FilterSignal (Speed);
    FILTER SIGNAL - End seq
    SCALE SIGNAL -    Start seq
    ScaleSignal (Speed);
    SCALE SIGNAL -    End seq
PROCESS SPEED SIGNAL - End seq
```

**Combined control structure
text and program operations**

```
GetInput (Speed);

FilterSignal (Speed);

ScaleSignal (Speed);
```

**Code
fragment
example**

Figure 2.14   Sequence construct – translation to code.

Note well that there is no code corresponding to the box 'Process Speed Signal'. Only the lowest-level boxes – called leaves – have associated code. The example here has one procedure call attached to each leaf, this being an implementation decision. Other solutions are quite acceptable. For instance, each leaf may be realized as:

• a single line of code
• multiple lines of code
• a subprogram
• multiple subprograms
• any combination of the above

Just as a point of interest, the structure chart of Figure 2.13 is called a *Tree* diagram. It has a *root* ('Process Speed Signal'), three branches, and a leaf at the end of each branch.

2.2.2 Decomposing the structure chart

It is very unlikely that a simple two-level SC will be sufficient to describe a real design. To demonstrate this, take the example of Figure 2.13. Suppose that we wish to describe the operation 'Filter Signal' more fully. Signal filtering consists of three distinct operations: checking the signal for validity, linearizing it, and then limiting its bandwidth. To show these, the structure chart can be elaborated as in Figure 2.15.

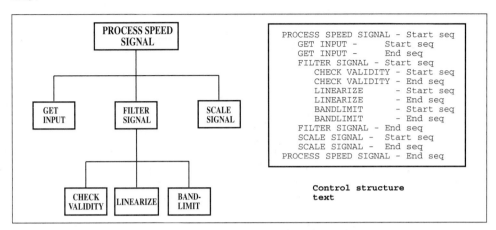

Figure 2.15 Program structure chart decomposition.

You should have no difficulty in understanding this diagram and the associated control structure text. However, it does raise a very important point: exactly how does the resulting source code relate to the diagram boxes? The rule is simple. Only *leaves* have corresponding code. To emphasize this, the combined control structure text and program operations have been written out fully in Figure 2.16.

Please look through this carefully. Make sure that you fully grasp the point being demonstrated. It can be seen that each leaf is implemented (in this case) by a single subprogram. Putting these together results in the source code fragment shown in Figure 2.16. This structure is defined to be 'flat code'.

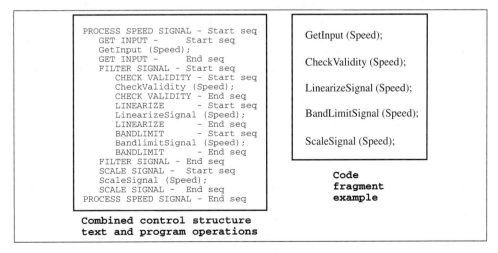

Figure 2.16 Program structure chart decomposition – translation to code.

2.2.3 Showing selection

Selection is shown on structure charts using the notation of Figure 2.17.

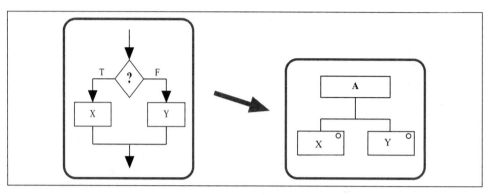

Figure 2.17 Program structure charts – selection (1).

The circles in the top-right part of boxes X and Y define that **A** is a selection – the choice is either X or Y. All possible alternatives are defined using the circle notation.

At first it may appear to represent exactly the same as its flow chart equivalent. This, emphatically, is *not* so. The interpretation of the flow chart is that either action X or action Y is carried out. In contrast, the interpretation of the SC is that an operation A consists of the operations X or Y. The essential difference? Here we have decomposed a higher-level operation (A) into a number of lower-level ones (mutually exclusive ones, true, but still children of A). The flow chart has no concept of decomposition. It is included here to act as a 'mental hook' into the semantics of the structure chart.

As shown, the SC is missing one vital component: the reasons – criteria – for selecting operation X or operation Y. Standard Jackson notation doesn't allow for this (one of the reasons for developing modified notation – see later). For the time being, however, the standard form will be used. With this you can visualize the structure chart as having the three-dimensional arrangement of Figure 2.18.

The selection criterion (or *test condition*) sits behind the parent box, and is an integral part of the structure. This is shown explicitly in the control structure text of

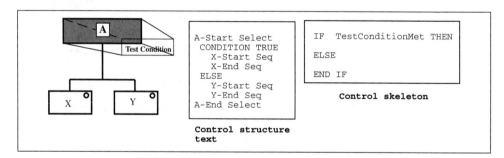

Figure 2.18 Program structure chart – selection (2).

Figure 2.18. Here the essential aspects of selection are brought together, the result being a formal definition of the structure. It tells us that the diagram states:

- An operation A is decomposed into two lower-level operations X and Y.
- A is a selection box; X and Y are sequential ones.
- Only one child operation – either X or Y – is carried out.
- The choice is made using some test condition.
- If the test condition is met, then X is selected. Otherwise Y is performed.

The result of this is a clear and unambiguous code control skeleton. Putting the program operations into the control structure text (Figure 2.19) reinforces these points.

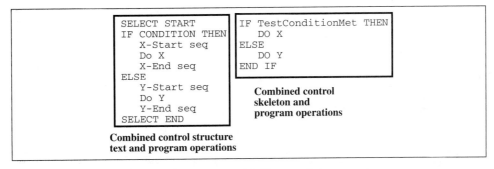

Figure 2.19   Selection SC (2) – translation to code.

This, then, explicitly defines the position of the executable statements within the control skeleton. Notice also that we have satisfied one of the basic rules of the structure chart: only leaves have associated code.

Three very important points are shown here:

- The structure chart defines the code control skeleton. Program operations play no part in this.
- There is a clear and defined set of rules relating the SC to the program code.
- There is complete traceability from the SC to the source code.

Of course, selection is not only a case of choosing between two alternatives – multiple choices are perfectly valid. But they have to be mutually exclusive. For the moment let us look at what is, in fact, the simplest form of choice – either doing something or choosing not to do it (Figure 2.20).

From the SC, two text structures have been directly generated – the code control skeleton and the combined control skeleton and program operations text. Intermediate stages have, for simplicity, been omitted.

You might ask whether it would make sense in Figure 2.20 to adapt the notation – omit the box for X and put a circle into **A**. However, this wouldn't make sense in terms of the way that selection is defined. What Figure 2.20 says is that **A** is the selection; we thus *always* make a check to see whether some action is to be

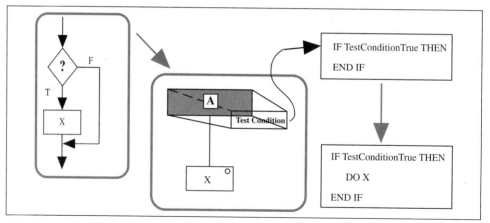

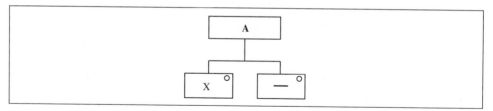

Figure 2.20   Program structure chart – selection (3).

performed. But X may or may not be carried out; it depends on the outcome of the check.

The notation shown in Figure 2.21 may be used as an alternative to that of Figure 2.20.

Figure 2.21   Program structure chart – alternative to Figure 2.20.

Here the THEN alternative is the null one; that is, no action is performed. At first sight there may seem to be little reason for this construct. Not so. With this the structure chart explicitly states that a null operation is called for – the designer's intent is quite clear. It reduces the likelihood of making mistakes. There is also another interesting aspect of this notation. For some reason it makes the reading and comprehension of SCs an easier task (a personal comment). It is strongly recommended that you use the notation of Figure 2.21.

Further decomposition of selection operations may, of course, be carried out. The first example, Figure 2.22, shows that operation B consists of three child operations, X, Y and Z.

Here the control structure text once again highlights the decomposition aspects of the design method. Observe that the code control skeleton is the same as that of Figure 2.18. This is not surprising: both diagrams depict identical selection operations. It is, though, well worthwhile studying and comparing the control structure

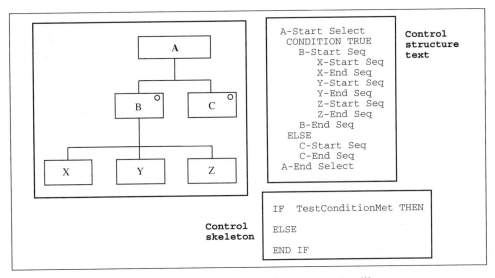

Figure 2.22   Decomposed selection operation (1).

text of the two diagrams. Doing this will help you to assimilate the semantics of the structure chart.

Generating the program source code is now a painless operation. It is produced by combining the control structure text and program operation diagram, as shown in Figure 2.23.

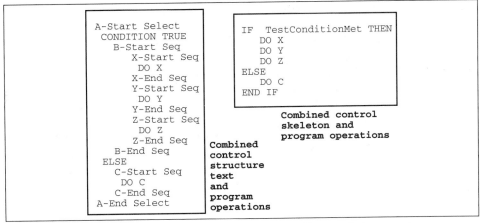

Figure 2.23   Decomposed selection operation (1) – translation to code.

This figure should be also be studied carefully. And just to restate a point: observe that there is no source code corresponding to boxes A and B.

Let us now look at a more complex selection structure (Figure 2.24).

What exactly does the diagram tell us? Writing out the control structure text is one

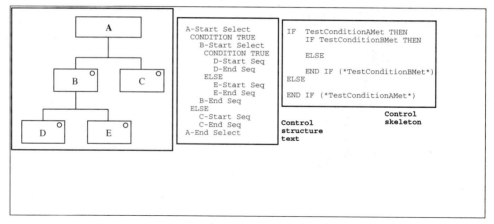

Figure 2.24 Decomposed selection operations (2).

good way to answer this question. This says that:

- The parent operation is **A**. This is a selection box.
- **A** is decomposed into two children, B and C. Either, but not both, is selected for actioning.
- B is a selection box, C is a sequence one.
- If B is selected, then a further selection takes place. Either D or E is chosen.
- Both D and E are sequence boxes.

From this we can deduce the structure of the code control skeleton. Notice how the decomposed selection operation translates into a nested selection construct. Now combine the control structure text with the program operations (Figure 2.25).

Once again, go through this in minute detail; make sure you understand it fully. You should now appreciate that this final stage – producing the source code – is essentially an automatic process.

```
A-Start Select
    CONDITION TRUE
    B-Start Select
        CONDITION TRUE
        D-Start Seq
            DO D
        D-End Seq
        ELSE
        E-Start Seq
            DO E
        E-End Seq
    B-End Seq
    ELSE
    C-Start Seq
        DO C
    C-End Seq
A-End Select
```

Combined control
structure text and
program operations

```
IF  TestConditionAMet THEN
    IF TestConditionBMet THEN
        DO D
    ELSE
        DO E
    END IF (*TestConditionBMet*)
ELSE
    DO C
END IF (*TestConditionAMet*)
```

Combined control
skeleton and
program operations

Figure 2.25 Decomposed selection operation (2) – translation to code.

2.2.4   *Iteration on the structure chart*

As pointed out earlier, iteration comes in two forms: pre-checks and post-checks. In Jackson notation one symbol only is defined (Figure 2.26).

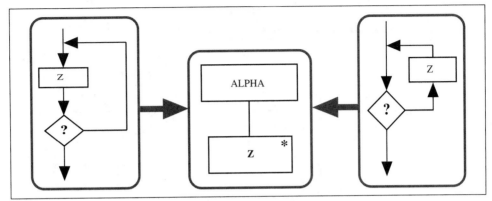

Figure 2.26   Program structure chart – iteration.

The star symbol in the upper right corner of the lower box indicates an iteration action. What the diagram says is that:

- There is an operation, ALPHA, which has an iteration structure.
- ALPHA is actually implemented by the execution of Z.
- More precisely, Z is the iterated component. It may be executed once, twice or as often as specified by the control conditions.
- Z, in some cases, may never be executed (this, of course, would have to be a pre-check iteration).

Strictly speaking, the original Jackson notation was used to specify pre-checks only. We, however, will use it to represent all iteration actions. While this is much more flexible, it does have one disadvantage. From the diagram it isn't possible to work out which check is to be performed. Extra information must be given somewhere. You will shortly see that this is not a problem.

Figure 2.27 gives the related control structure text and associated control skeletons.

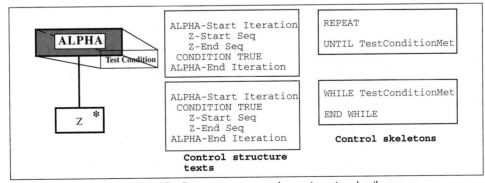

Figure 2.27   Program structure chart – iteration details.

The structure text makes clear that ALPHA is made up of iterations of Z. With this definition of the diagram semantics, the two boxes form a single unit. It would not make sense to draw a single box Z; no meaning could be given to this.

By combining the control structure text with the program operations, the overall program structure emerges (Figure 2.28).

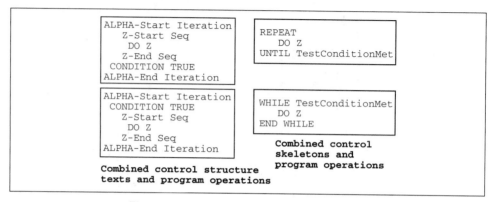

Figure 2.28 SC iteration – translation to code.

As before, the source code structure is generated by combining the control skeleton with the program operations.

In many instances the iterated component may itself need to be decomposed. There are no difficulties with this; we merely follow established decomposition rules. This is demonstrated in Figure 2.29.

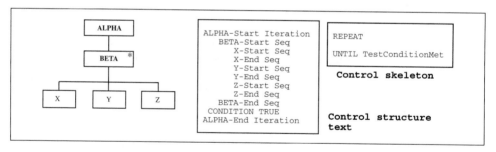

Figure 2.29 Decomposed iteration operation.

Here ALPHA is implemented using the iterated component BETA. BETA, however, consists of the child components X, Y and Z. Thus the actual implementation of ALPHA is an iteration of X, Y, Z. This point is made obvious by the control structure text of Figure 2.29. This has also made it explicit that a post-check is being carried out. Observe that the control skeleton is the same as that of Figure 2.27 (post-check only). We would expect this, as both have identical control structures. The combination of control structures and program operations (Figure 2.30) should also have no surprises.

```
ALPHA-Start Iteration            REPEAT
   BETA-Start Seq                   DO X
      X-Start Seq                   DO Y
         DO X                       DO Z
      X-End Seq                  UNTIL TestConditionMet
      Y-Start Seq
         DO Y
      Y-End Seq
      Z-Start Seq
         DO Z
      Z-End Seq
   BETA-End Seq
   CONDITION TRUE
ALPHA-End Iteration
```

**Combined control skeleton
and program operations**

**Combined control structure
text and program operations**

Figure 2.30   Decomposed iteration – translation to code.

Now for the final form of iteration – the mid-check. Few notations support this operation. Yet, in real systems, mid-checks are regularly performed. You *can* use a work-around solution using a post-check, but this is inefficient and unnatural. It seems to be a case of adjusting reality to suit the design notation – hardly a satisfactory solution. Therefore we have extended Jackson Structure Charts to denote the mid-check iteration (Figure 2.31).

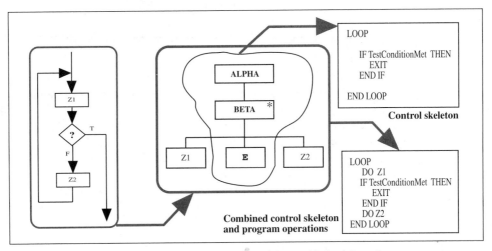

Figure 2.31   Program structure chart – mid-check iteration.

A box marked **E** shows where the exit check is made. The only restriction is that it *must* be the lowest level box in its branch. Its position within the control skeleton is illustrated in Figure 2.31, forming part of a LOOP construct. You can also see that the combination of control skeleton and program operations correctly implements the design.

Precisely how you implement this construct will depend on your programming language. Some, unfortunately, cannot exit from loops at mid-points (drat!), so make sure that your design can actually be built.

2.3   Top-down design and stepwise refinement – a review

A fundamental objective of SP is to describe (design) software in a top-down fashion. Consider, for example, the structure chart of Figure 2.32.

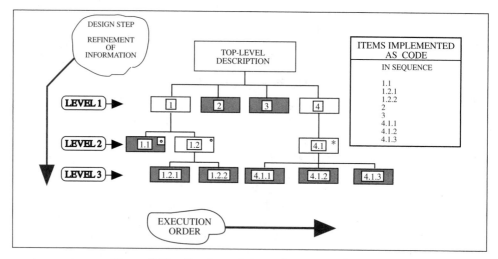

Figure 2.32   Top-down design and stepwise refinement.

First we have the highest, top, level (TOP-LEVEL DESCRIPTION) which gives the
design in its simplest form. This is then expressed in more detail at the next level
down, an elaboration process (boxes 1 to 4). The elaboration or decomposition
action is repeated until a satisfactory design structure is attained. Each decomposition is a design step, and represents refinement of information. Hence the expression 'stepwise refinement'. With the program structure chart design, only leaves
generate program (code) operations. A second basic rule is that the execution order
is from left to right. By combining these rules we can readily generate the source
code document.

Novices often find that structure charts are:

* apparently very easy to read
* frequently mis-read
* very difficult to design

Two factors are responsible for this. First, they just don't understand the semantics of
the diagram. We shall return to this in a moment. Second, design is rarely an easy
process. And you *cannot* produce a proper structure chart without significant design
effort.

You may well ask why it seems to be much easier to write code or produce flow
charts. Perhaps that should tell you something about the inherent design attributes
of these methods.

However, back to the first point: the semantics of the structure chart. It cannot be stressed strongly enough, or often enough, that you *must* understand how to:

- express your intention correctly and unambiguously
- check the precise meaning of your design

Treat the next few diagrams as being equivalent to an arduous physical training session: repetitive, boring (possibly) but, in the end, worthwhile.

Assume that our objective is to review the design presented in the SC of Figure 2.32. The way to tackle this is to take it a piece at a time, in this case level by level. Start, as in Figure 2.33, by placing a 'mask' over the lower level boxes of the structure chart.

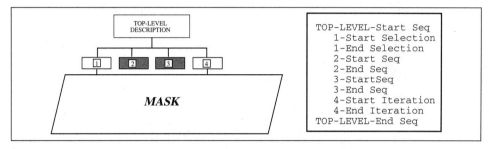

Figure 2.33   Top-down design – viewing the top two levels.

Alongside this, write out the control structure text relating to the visible boxes. Now check that the operations defined by boxes 1 to 4 do, in fact, meet the design objectives.

Move the mask down a level (Figure 2.34).

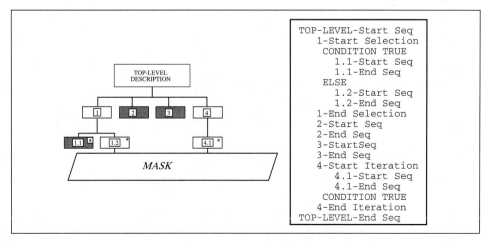

Figure 2.34   Stepwise refinement in action.

Update the control structure text. Ensure that the exposed boxes satisfy the objectives of their parents. Check that the test conditions are correctly specified.

When you are satisfied, view the complete diagram and update its control structure text (Figure 2.35).

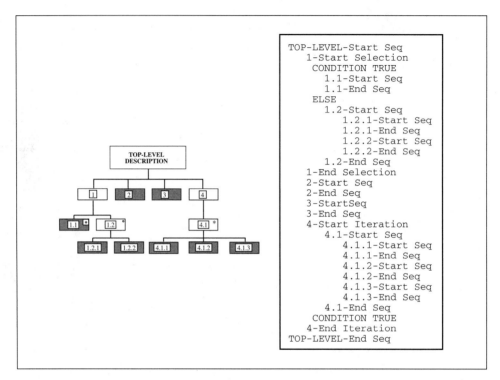

```
TOP-LEVEL-Start Seq
    1-Start Selection
        CONDITION TRUE
        1.1-Start Seq
        1.1-End Seq
        ELSE
        1.2-Start Seq
            1.2.1-Start Seq
            1.2.1-End Seq
            1.2.2-Start Seq
            1.2.2-End Seq
        1.2-End Seq
    1-End Selection
    2-Start Seq
    2-End Seq
    3-StartSeq
    3-End Seq
    4-Start Iteration
        4.1-Start Seq
            4.1.1-Start Seq
            4.1.1-End Seq
            4.1.2-Start Seq
            4.1.2-End Seq
            4.1.3-Start Seq
            4.1.3-End Seq
        4.1-End Seq
        CONDITION TRUE
    4-End Iteration
TOP-LEVEL-End Seq
```

Figure 2.35   Top-down design – reviewing the complete SC.

Repeat the specified set of checks. When you are satisfied, combine the control structure text with the program operations (Figure 2.36).

Check that program statements do actually go where intended – and that they correctly perform their required functions. Generate the program source code by combining the control skeleton with the program operations. Check that there is full consistency between all diagrams. Note one small but important consequence of the semantics of Jackson diagrams. When a parent box is decomposed, all its children must be the *same* type (think about it).

If you have successfully done all this, what have you achieved? You have shown that your design:

• matches its requirements (validation – producing the correct product)
• has been correctly translated into code (verification – producing the product correctly)

```
TOP-LEVEL-Start Seq            BEGIN (* TOP-LEVEL *)
   1-Start Selection              IF TestConditionMet THEN
      CONDITION TRUE                 DO 1.1
         1.1-Start Seq             ELSE
            DO 1.1                    DO 1.2.1
         1.1-End Seq                  DO 1.2.2
      ELSE                         END IF
         1.2-Start Seq            DO 2
            1.2.1-Start Seq       DO 3
               DO 1.2.1           REPEAT
            1.2.1-End Seq            DO 4.1.1
            1.2.2-Start Seq          DO 4.1.2
               DO 1.2.2             DO 4.1.3
            1.2.2-End Seq        UNTIL TestConditionMet4
         1.2-End Seq          END (* TOP-LEVEL *)
   1-End Selection
   2-Start Seq
      DO 2                    Combined control skeleton
   2-End Seq                  and program operations
   3-StartSeq
      DO 3
   3-End Seq
   4-Start Iteration
      4.1-Start Seq
         4.1.1-Start Seq
            DO 4.1.1
         4.1.1-End Seq
         4.1.2-Start Seq
            DO 4.1.2
         4.1.2-End Seq
         4.1.3-Start Seq
            DO 4.1.3
         4.1.3-End Seq
      4.1-End Seq
      CONDITION TRUE           Combined control structure
   4-End Iteration             text and program operations
TOP-LEVEL-End Seq
```

Figure 2.36 Translating Figure 2.32 to code.

Any errors from this point on will be due to code implementation details – by far the easiest to correct.

Control structure text, control skeletons and the various combined diagrams are intermediate stages between diagram and code. Once you become proficient in using structure charts these steps can be omitted. Generating the source code from the design diagram will become a one-step action.

2.4 Structure charts – extended notation

There are two reasons for extending structure chart notation. The first is to modify the basic ideas in order to put more information on the diagrams. This is here defined as the 'modified' form. The second is to introduce notation used in the larger design examples given later in this text. These examples have been produced using a CASE tool; the notation is specific to that toolset. For simplicity it (the notation) is called the CASE form.

The modified notation is given in Figure 2.37.

Take selection to begin with. Here the basic notation has been augmented by an extra box, showing the test condition. This information could, even using CASE tool

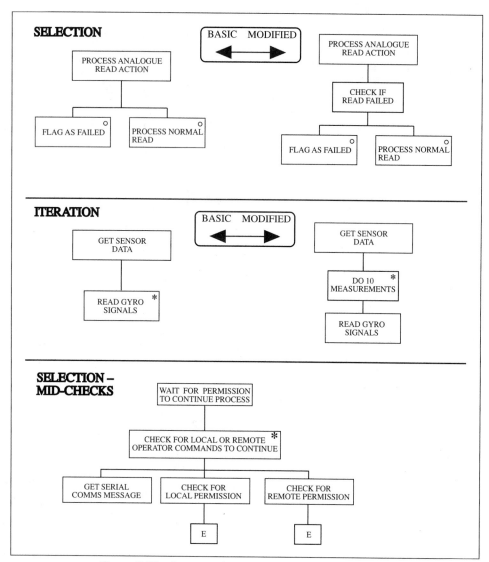

Figure 2.37   Structure charts – basic and modified notation.

technology, have been included on the diagram. Typically, a freeform text tool would be used. However, the advantage of using the modified method is that it forms part of the structure chart. Any omissions would be glaringly obvious. Moreover, it is unlikely to get lost during diagram modification. You will find that designing a structure chart is not a once-through straight-ahead activity. Like all design work, it is highly iterative. Many modifications may be made to the first solution. This is the time when items – such as text comments – can get lost. Keeping everything together (in this case, within the structure) minimizes such problems.

Much the same comments can be applied to the iteration construct. One particular point does require explanation – the location of the iteration symbol, the star. On the modified diagram it has been attached to the condition box 'DO 10 MEASURE-MENTS'. It could, of course, have been left in its original place. However, there is an advantage to be gained in making this change, as will be shown shortly. With this notation, at least three levels are required to define iteration. What the diagram says is that an action 'GET SENSOR DATA' is actually implemented using an iterated component 'READ GYRO SIGNAL'. The control condition is 'DO 10 MEASUREMENTS', that is, a predefined number of iterations.

The final iteration example in Figure 2.37 is the mid-check one. You should have no difficulty in following the diagram. Just one piece of advice, though. Use this construct only when it is needed, and do not hide it away in the detail of the diagram.

This example also illustrates the advantage of putting the iteration symbol within the condition box. That is, it allows us to use a multi-box structure below the condition box. The result is that it minimizes the number of levels needed to show iteration. Hence diagrams tend to be more compact and easier to read.

Figure 2.38 is an example of selection using both the modified and CASE notations.

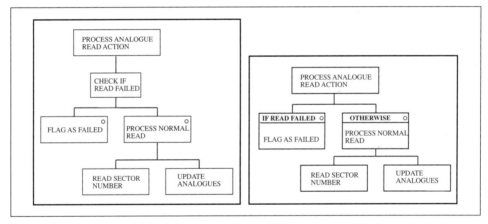

Figure 2.38   Selection structures – alternative representations.

The CASE form has a separate section in choice boxes to indicate the reason for choosing that particular route. This approach is neat, explicit and compact. Its only drawback lies with its compactness: condition descriptions are terse and may not be particularly meaningful to the casual reader.

Iteration is handled in a similar way (Figure 2.39).

Similar comments apply. Figure 2.40 has been included for completeness, to show decomposition of an iterated structure.

Is there any advantage in combining the two approaches (this, of course, could only be done if you have the CASE tool)? For iteration, no: use the standard CASE notation. But for selection, the answer is 'maybe'. Figure 2.41 shows how the two forms are combined for the example of Figure 2.38.

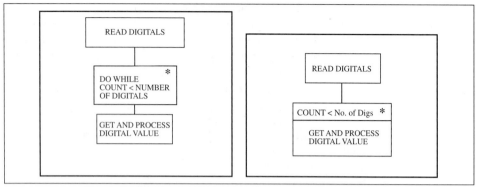

Figure 2.39 Iteration structures – alternative representations (1).

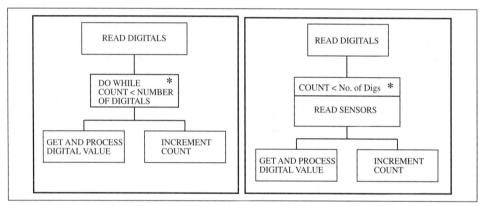

Figure 2.40 Iteration structures – alternative representations (2).

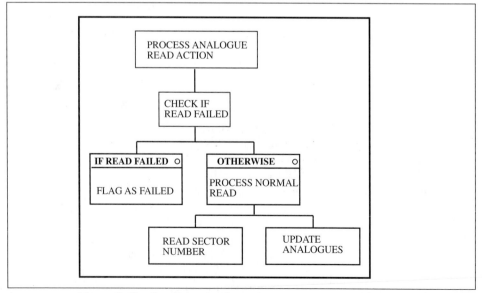

Figure 2.41 Combining the alternative representations – selection.

The advantage here is that the diagram carries more information, showing why particular decisions are made. The disadvantage is that it introduces an extra level into the hierarchy. Fortunately, it doesn't in any way change the diagram semantics. So in the end, the choice of notation may be safely left to the designer.

Review

Having studied this chapter you should now:

- understand why diagramming brings discipline and order to design
- appreciate the concepts of structured programming
- see how to define program actions in terms of pre-conditions, operations and post-conditions
- realize the rationale for the use of program structure diagrams
- fully understand the symbols and rules of Jackson Structure Charts
- know how to translate a design from structure chart to source code, using a defined set of translation rules
- see why these translation rules make it easy to trace a design through its various stages
- comprehend the use of top-down design and stepwise refinement for program development
- appreciate the value of the extension to the original Jackson notation
- feel confident enough to use structure charts for a real design

Three frequently asked questions are:

- When should we call a halt to the design of the structure chart?
- How many 'boxes' should there be at any one level?
- How many levels should my design have?

If you want cookbook answers to these, you'll have to look elsewhere – real design is much too complex for that. There is only one suitable reply – 'it all depends on your particular problem'. Not exactly very helpful, is it? Unfortunate, but true. However, some guidance can be given in these matters. Please, though, treat this for what it is: guidance, not rules. Let us consider each question in turn.

(a) When should we call a halt to the design of the structure chart?
    Three criteria should be used here. First, does the SC clearly and fully define the program design? Second, is the translation to source code a straightforward task? Third, is there clear traceability from SC to source code *and* vice versa? Only experience will bring home these points.

(b) How many 'boxes' should there be at any one level?
    It is better to consider how many child boxes each parent has rather than just counting the total. The reason for this lies in the design technique rather than the diagram itself. With good design, each branch tends to perform a

well-defined function (or functions). There is a high degree of decoupling between the various branches. Thus, when building and assessing designs, we find ourselves naturally running down branches, not across the diagram. So, how many child boxes? One cannot be dogmatic about this – treat the following as rough and ready rules. A single child box should only be used if you need to explain an action more fully (or to express it in a different way). If you end up with as many as seven boxes, look carefully at your design.

(c) How many levels should a design have?

Most of our designs seem to end up using between four and nine levels. Occasionally we have fewer, rarely more. However, this topic is closely tied up with that of modular design, the subject of the next chapter. We shall review program design on completing the section on module design.

Exercises

Produce Jackson Structure Charts for the various problems outlined below. Also produce the corresponding pseudo-code. It is assumed that data entry is done using a keyboard, all display information being presented on a screen.

2.1 Put out a text message and so acquire the length (L), width (W) and height (H) of a room. From this calculate the floor area (FA), wall area (WA) and room volume (V). Display all calculated values.

2.2 Obtain the L, W and H values as before. However, now give the user the choice of having either FA or WA or V calculated and displayed.

2.3 Modify Exercise 2.2 to give the user the facility to correct each entered value before proceeding to the calculation stage.

2.4 Extend Exercise 2.3 to allow the user to perform calculations for two rooms: a bedroom and a dining room.

3

Designing and building software machines:

The module structure chart

The design and diagramming techniques of Chapter 2 are powerful concepts. They are, though, intended essentially for program development – *programming in the small*. Unfortunately, they have distinct limitations when applied to software (that is, system) development – *programming in the large*. What this chapter does is extend these ideas, developing a rigorous software development technique. Central to this is the use of software machines (modules), and related diagramming issues. This chapter maintains the philosophy of the bottom-up approach, building on concepts already introduced. It:

- introduces the concept of the software machine
- shows why this is a powerful technique for software development
- describes the essential attributes of such software units
- compares aspects of top-down and bottom-up design
- describes the reason for, and approach to, the partitioning of software – *modularization*
- discusses packaging, structuring, coupling and cohesion aspects of modules
- shows how software may be built as a set of hierarchical machines
- defines how such hierarchical structures are illustrated using the module structure chart
- introduces the idea of partitioning software into application modules and service modules
- provides a descriptive set of rules for the structuring of modular software

3.1 Software machines – what and why?

3.1.1 The concept

The design techniques of Chapter 2 will, if used properly, lead to the production of high-quality programs. Although these are powerful concepts, they show their limitations when applied to larger software projects. They are fine for *program* development, but are much less so for *software* design. What we shall now do is look at a rigorous method, based on structure charts, for building reliable software. In doing so, many analogies will be drawn with the process of designing and developing electronic hardware.

Fundamental to our approach is the use of *software machines*. To show the ideas underlying this concept, let's use the analogy of the design and implementation of electronic hardware (Figure 3.1).

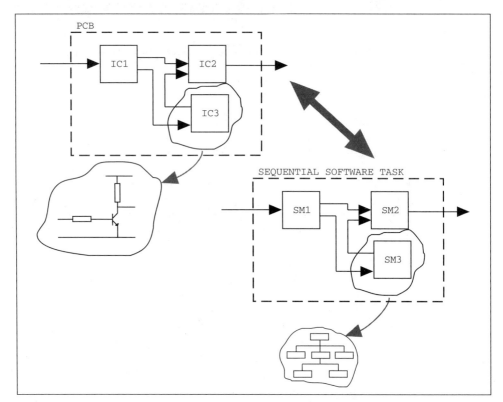

Figure 3.1 Hardware machines vs. Software machines.

Here we have a specific electronic function implemented on a single printed circuit board (PCB). The software equivalent to this is the sequential software task. To provide this PCB function, we connect together a set of integrated circuits (ICs): the hardware machines. What we wish to do here is to mimic this action in software using software machines (SMs). An IC is built from elementary electronic components, using wafer-level fabrication techniques. However, its *design* is shown using a circuit diagram of these components, without regard to the method of construction. In the same way, each software machine is built using elementary components – the source code statements. However, its design is described using the program structure chart. Therefore we can relate hardware and software in the way shown in Table 3.1.

Table 3.1.

Item	Hardware	Software
Major unit	PCB	Sequential task
Components of the major unit	ICs (the hardware machines)	SMs (the software machines)
Design description of the machines	Circuit diagram	Program structure chart

There are two distinct views of a software machine: its concept and its implementation (Figure 3.2).

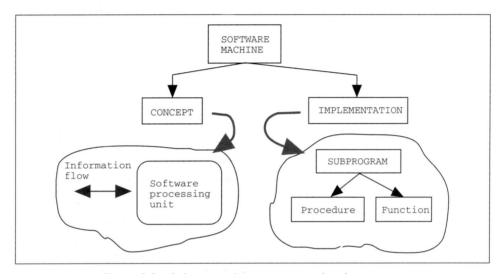

Figure 3.2   Software machine – concept and implementation.

This figure illustrates the essential features of the device:

- The SM is a self-contained unit.
- It carries out a defined processing function.
- We should be able to use it without any knowledge of its insides (its implementation).
- Information (data and/or control) normally flows between the machine and the external software environment.
- It is implemented as a subprogram (procedure, function procedure, function, subroutine and so on).

3.1.2   Multiple views of the design

What has been said in the preceding section seems quite plausible (and uses common sense). But you *do* need to ask yourself why we should bother to build software in this way (note: this is not 'why do we use subprograms?'. These, after all, are frequently used to build programs). To answer this you first have to think of software machines as being the building blocks of software – software 'Lego'. For example, study the situation depicted in Figure 3.3.

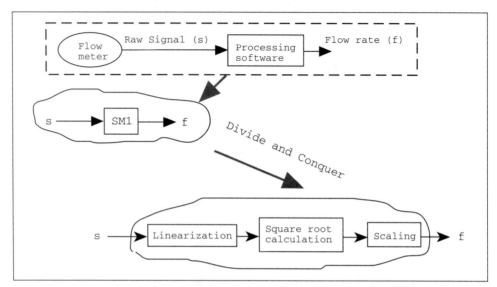

Figure 3.3   The software machine – a simple example.

This represents a signal-processing function, where the raw signal from a flow-meter is (somehow) transformed into a flow rate signal. Thus, in software terms, we can visualize this action as being provided by a software machine. Its input is 's', the operation is 'SM1' and the output is 'f'. This allows us to take a relatively abstract high-level view of the processing function. When the overall requirement is analysed, it turns out to involve three distinct sub-operations: signal linearization, square-rooting and scaling. But, at the higher level, we do not need to concern ourselves with the innards of the machine. Only three factors are important to us:

- what goes into the machine
- what the machine does
- what comes out of the machine

By concentrating on these factors, the overall software design problem is simplified. Specifically, it is easier to:

- ensure that the overall system design meets its specification
- build and test the software system
- track down errors in the finished software
- *manage* the design, build and test process

We can also, if we choose, implement the three internal building blocks as a set of software machines. Thus the design process is once more repeated, but now looking *within* SM1. Notice how this allows us to focus on the specifics of the problem: that is, linearization, rooting and scaling. It is a good example of the classical problem solution of Attila the Hun – divide and conquer. In fact, this divide-and-conquer policy is at the heart of the software machine design method.

3.1.3 Stability and portability issues

Suppose that, for the sensor signal of Figure 3.3, we were required to generate the linearization characteristic of Figure 3.4(a).

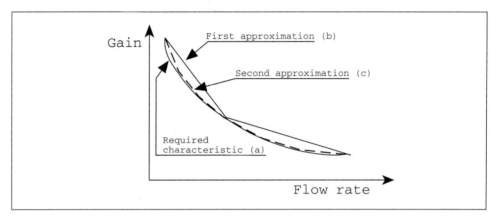

Figure 3.4 Required linearization characteristic.

Assume that it is decided to use a straight-line approximation – look-up table – technique to implement this. The initial solution, (b), is shown as a solid line. Now consider how we would deal with either (or both) of the following issues *after* the software has been built:

- inadequate system performance due to the coarseness of the straight-line approximation
- a change of sensor type, having a different non-linear response

For the first, a modified approximation would be used, (c). For the second, a completely new characteristic would be required. However, if these changes are contained entirely within SM1, there is no observable effect outside the machine (in software terms, that is). We say that the system is highly stable. All changes are localized – the overall software is free from ripple-through problems. Visualize once again SM1 as a software building block. We make the required changes by removing the existing block and fitting a new one. But it fits into the existing structure in exactly the same way as the old one did. Thus we do not distort our software framework, nor the total system functioning.

A second point to bear in mind is that particular functions may have more general use. For instance, square-rooting is not limited to signal processing; it is frequently applied in mathematical calculations. This leads to the idea of developing generalized software machines which can be used as templates. These general purpose or *generic* machines are tailored for specific applications using subprogram parameters – *parametrization*. This is the basis for reusable software.

Having reusable software leads naturally on to the idea of having a software library (Figure 3.5).

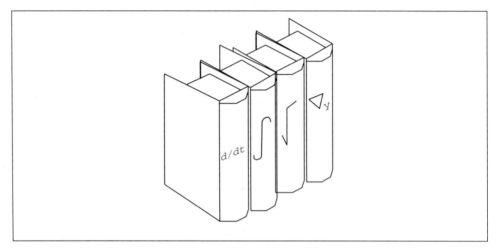

Figure 3.5   The software library.

We can reuse such generic machines either in the same system or in other systems. This saves effort and time, and hence cost. Further, as the software is proven, the number of mistakes made during development should reduce. But be careful: reusability is not without its problems. A number of key aspects have to be carefully managed, including:

- identifying suitable reusable software functions
- implementing these so that they are highly robust
- carrying out extensive proving tests
- providing adequate and correct documentation
- strictly controlling any software changes
- recording all such changes

3.1.4   *Performance evaluation*

Two important attributes of real-time embedded systems are:

- timing
- code size

How quickly will (or must) the computer respond to an event? What sampling rates can we achieve in our control loops? How long does it take for a signal to be processed? Questions like these arise time and time again in embedded applications. The second item, code size, tends to be less of an issue where general purpose processors are used. This, however, may be very important in the design of microcontroller-based systems. Memory is usually quite limited in the smaller single-chip devices. Designers have to ensure that their code and data will actually fit within the available memory space. Thus the two important questions are 'how fast?' and 'how large?'. Building software as sets of machines helps to answer these questions (Figure 3.6).

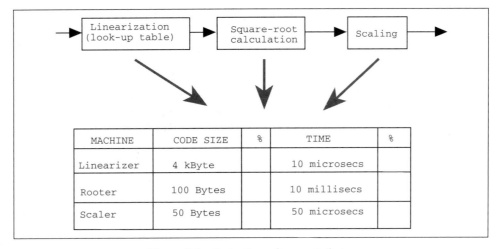

Figure 3.6 *Evaluating software attributes.*

Here the three separate functions of Figure 3.3 are shown as software machines. For each machine, estimates can be made of the required code size and execution time. Using this we can then build up an attribute table for the complete system software. In the early period of a project the figures will only be estimates (but that's the best we can do at that stage). These can be used for:

• prediction of memory requirements
• performance modelling

If your estimates suggest that your design objectives will be met, you can proceed – with some confidence – with the design. If not, you have a problem (an understatement, I might add). You could rely on hope, ignore the predictions, and plough on with design. This has been known to happen, but the outcomes have been entirely predictable. No, what is needed is design evaluation and improvement. For instance, in Figure 3.6, the software machine 'Linearizer' runs fast, but takes up a substantial amount of store space. Experienced designers will recognize that it is realized using a look-up table (given the other figures, that is). This is a simple example where hardware and software are combined to provide a single function – the technique of 'co-design'. It can also be seen from the table that the Rooter has quite different attributes. It uses only a small amount of code, but takes a long time to execute.

By clearly defining the attributes of the individual software blocks, we can identify potential problems. It also becomes clear where improvements can be made. For example, suppose that store space must be reduced. How should we tackle this? Provided processing time is available, the obvious solution is to modify the linearizer. Replacing the look-up table with, say, a polynomial curve-fitting routine will substantially reduce the code size. Of course, it will take much longer to execute. For the opposite case – no problems with memory but running out of time – it would make good sense to implement the Rooter as a look-up table. What we are doing here is, quite simply, making design trade-offs. And you can't do that with confidence without having a well-presented view of system attributes.

3.1.5 System partitioning, modularization and work sharing

In the early days of computing, programs tended to be developed as single items or entities. We now recognize that the most effective technique is to design *and* build them in a modular fashion. To do this, the total design must be split up into various work packages. But defining the design as a set of software machines is, in effect, partitioning the complete system. Thus it makes sense to group the software machines into sets of modules, even on a one-to-one basis (Figure 3.7).

Each unit can be developed and tested separately. Then the set can be integrated to form the complete software package.

Good partitioning is the cornerstone of developing software in an incremental fashion – a nice way of saying 'a bit at a time'. But it becomes even more important – in fact, essential – when software is produced by a team of designers. It isn't only

Figure 3.7 Software partitioning.

a case of defining the set of work packages. Integration and test plans are required. For this to be a (relatively) painless task the individual units must be designed to work together. This may sound like stating the obvious; why then do we meet so many problems of software incompatibility?

The key elements in this are the machine interfaces: how they slot in with other software units.

3.1.6   The outside view of a machine – its interfaces

What *should* the software machine look like on its outside? Well, go back to its hardware analogue, the integrated circuit. What features are important to the electronic designer when using an IC? First, it has a defined function (Figure 3.8).

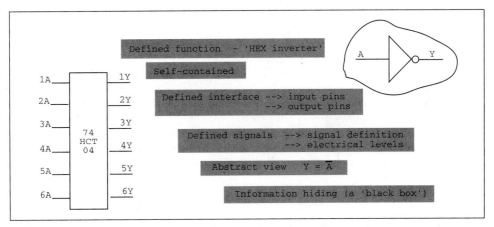

Figure 3.8   Outside view of a machine – IC example.

This shows the 74HCT04 HEX inverter IC as an example. The second point is that it is self-contained. We don't need another chip to do logic inversion. Third, the interfaces (pin connections) are clearly specified. Fourth, the individual signals are also specified, both in logic and electrical terms. Fifth, the function of the device can be expressed in abstract terms – implementation features are irrelevant. As a result, the IC can be treated as a 'black box' which hides all its implementation details. Taking these together, it is then possible to produce a test specification for the device.

Use these features to form a check-list when building a software machine:

- Has it a clearly defined function?
- Can its function be expressed in abstract terms?
- Has it a clearly defined interface (typically procedure parameters)?
- Does all information exchange with the machine go through the interface (use only parameter-passing methods)?
- Are the signals – parameters – well defined (number, in/out/inout, variable type)?

- Is it truly a black box (you don't care how it is implemented as long as it works correctly and reliably)?
- Can you test it out as an individual item?

3.1.7 Combining machines – bottom-up design

Good software structures don't come about by accident; they are *designed*. And engineering experience has shown that one of the most effective methods is a top-down approach. However, there are occasions when we need to build a specific component as part of a complete system. For such an operation a 'bottom-up' technique may be the best solution. Here we combine smaller machines to form the required component, a hardware example being given in Figure 3.9.

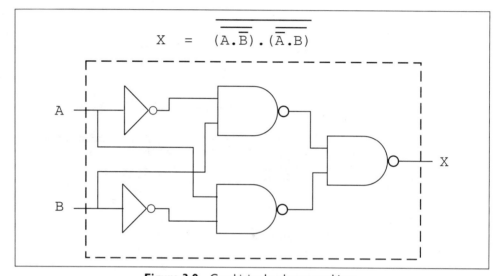

$$X \quad = \quad \overline{(A.\overline{B})}.\overline{(\overline{A}.B)}$$

Figure 3.9 Combining hardware machines.

The requirement is to build a machine which implements the logic equation of Figure 3.9. The solution is to use existing logic devices, combining them to produce the desired result (a 'super-machine'). We could, of course, have produced a device specifically for this application (using, for instance, programmable logic). The advantage of the bottom-up method, though, is that the devices, and their functions, are proven. If, however, a custom design is used, this isn't the case. Time and effort must be given over to device proving, which may turn out to be costly (especially if mistakes are uncovered).

We can apply exactly the same ideas to software. In fact, bottom-up techniques are the basis of Object-Oriented Programming (OOP). For 'software machine' read 'object'. These ideas work well for the building of specific machines. Moreover, some proponents of OOP advocate that complete systems should also be built in this way. Experience, though, has shown that major problems may be met when using a true bottom-up approach. For instance:

- While the individual objects may work perfectly well, the combination may not fulfil its function (a design error).
- The combination fulfils its function, but it also produces unexpected results (a design error).
- There are significant difficulties in integrating the super-machines.
- Changes in the design of a component machine (such as a software enhancement) may unwittingly modify the behaviour of the super-machine.

In reality, all design is a mixture of top-down and bottom-up (plus a little of what might be called middle-out). Generally you should use bottom-up design only where it makes sense – and with great care.

3.2   The partitioning of software – modularization

3.2.1   Modularization – what and how?

Modularization is the process of forming a complete software system from a set of individual units or 'modules'. Before getting into detail, we must be clear what a module is. It is unfortunate that this means different things to different people. Let *us*, however, be precise. The *Oxford English Dictionary* (*OED*) defines it as 'a standardized part or independent unit in construction'. In this text we follow the *OED*, defining it as 'a standardized part or independent unit in the construction of software'. From this, you can see that the thing called a software machine is also a module. Thus the question 'why modularize' has already been fully answered in the previous section. We shall now progress to looking at *how* software should be modularized.

A key point when building software as a set of modules is the partitioning of the complete system; that is, how we identify the modules in the first place. This problem is not just a software one: it applies to all systems. To illustrate some of the basic issues – and to bring a more general view to bear – let's consider partitioning the system of Figure 3.10.

This shows a small two-channel plant control system. Input signals are derived from sensors (transducers); control is exerted using actuators. A local display panel is fitted to the plant. Assume that the controller is to be implemented using non-

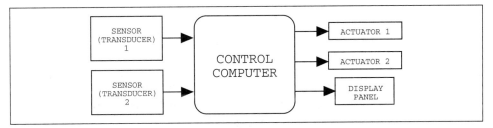

Figure 3.10   Example control system.

computer electronic technology (to get us away from the realms of software).

When the system requirements are analysed, four major functions are identified (Figure 3.11).

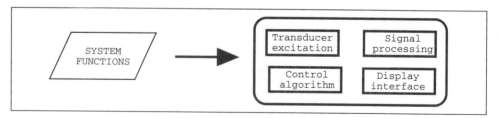

Figure 3.11

The question facing the designer is how to map these functions onto hardware. That is, what collection of hardware building blocks (modules) best matches system functions? In answering this question, it isn't sufficient to consider only the functions; we also have to assess the interaction of such functions.

Assume that our first design solution is that of Figure 3.12.

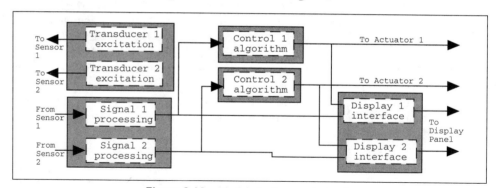

Figure 3.12   Modularization – solution 1.

Here, five modules (printed circuit boards) have been defined:

- transducer excitation
- signal processing
- display interface
- control algorithm computation (2)

Suppose now that an alternative design is proposed (Figure 3.13).

Here it has been decided to partition the system further by having a set of PCBs for each channel. As a result, eight PCBs are required in this design. Question: is this solution worse than, better than or essentially no different from the first one? Answer: it all depends; there is, regrettably, no 'right' answer. To arrive at a sensible conclusion, we need to assess the design against specific objectives. At a very

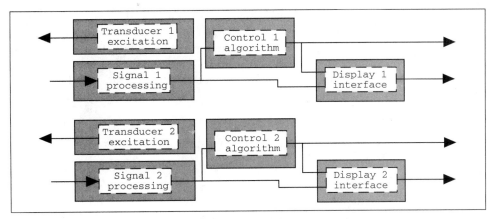

Figure 3.13   Modularization – solution 2.

general level, two particular criteria have been widely used for evaluating systems. Loosely speaking, these are the inside and outside views of the design.

The inside view is concerned with the partitioning of the overall system into individual modules. It helps in assessing the 'goodness' of the grouping of functions within these modules. In software terms this is called 'cohesion'. By contrast, the outside view looks at how modules are connected together *and* at how they interact (the reason for stressing this last point will be made clear later). Once again software has its own word to describe the outside view – 'coupling'.

Let us return to the two design solutions of Figures 3.12 and 3.13. What can we say about them from these two viewpoints? The grouping of solution 1 is very much dictated by system functions. The degree of grouping is higher than in solution 2, and results in fewer PCBs ('modules'). Further, the interconnection between modules is clear and obvious. In solution 2 the module interconnection is somewhat simpler, but not substantially so. So, solution 1 is the better one. Or is it? With this implementation, removing either an excitation or signal processing module will disable both channels. Removing the display module results in loss of information for the complete system. Hence the partitioning used has resulted in a very high degree of module interdependence. However, in solution 2, the two channels are essentially independent; they don't share any single-point failure mechanisms. For some applications this may be an essential requirement. Now take another point into account. Suppose that at some later time one of the transducer types is changed. Further suppose that this requires redesign of the excitation and signal processing electronics. With solution 1 the rework impacts on both channels. It may very well be that, in modifying one channel, layout changes affect the other one. Thus the stability of the design has suffered. With solution 2 this is a non-existent problem.

You should now see why you can't simply evaluate design solutions without taking into account system objectives. For some applications solution 1 is best. For others, solution 2 would be preferred. *The* most important point is to recognize that such decisions are made by the designer. This is where experience, intellect, knowledge and judgement come into play. You can't automate these qualities (as demonstrated by many dismal failures of artificial intelligence projects). If you have little design experience, you may, at first, find it difficult to apply these ideas. Just persevere. By applying rigorous methods your designs will, with time, become better and better.

Coupling, in terms of software modules, can be illustrated as in Figure 3.14.

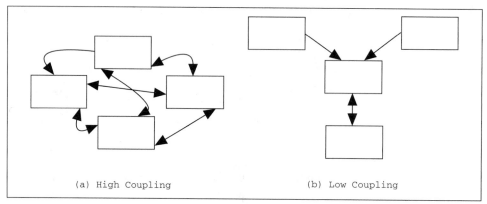

(a) High Coupling   (b) Low Coupling

Figure 3.14 Coupling – the outside view.

Where there are many, and complex, connections, coupling is high (Figure 3.14(a)). In contrast, where interfaces are simple, direct and well structured (Figure 3.14(b)), coupling is low. Our objective is to build systems which have low coupling. It is worth mentioning in passing that many object-oriented design methods produce results like Figure 3.14(a). One point is clear, though. Without expressing designs using diagrams, it is almost impossible to judge the coupling within a system.

Figures 3.15 and 3.16 bring out the essentials of cohesion.

Figure 3.15 shows the structure of a module – GetAnalogueData – designed to perform a data acquisition function. It consists of a set of sub-operations or functions: ReadADC, Filter and Linearize. The flow of information through the module is clear, while its translation to code is simplicity itself. The module is built as a single subprogram, this itself consisting of a sequence of three procedures. There is nothing superfluous here; all operations are necessary if the module is to work correctly. In other words, nothing more, nothing less, than that required is present. Now turn to Figure 3.16.

This shows the structure of a software module for the handling of an I/O subsystem. It is intended to control three devices: a serial comms unit (UART), analogue to digital converter (ADC) and a motor (MotorDrive). The rationale for this grouping is that all are I/O devices. As with the previous example, the module may be built as a subprogram, housing three procedures. However, it is significantly different from the module GetAnalogueData – it has low intrinsic cohesion. First, is it likely that we will always want to execute all procedures at the same time? Very unlikely. Thus, some method of selecting the desired procedure(s) will have to be provided. Second, suppose any one operation (procedure) is removed from the

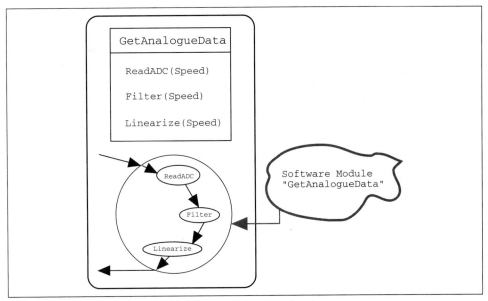

Figure 3.15   Example of high cohesion.

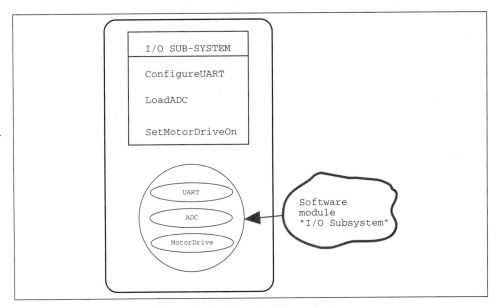

Figure 3.16   Example of low cohesion.

module. Does this affect the operation of the remaining components? No, it doesn't. This really is the telling point as far as cohesion is concerned.

All designs are a balance of coupling and cohesion. And, as the control system example brought out, they generally conflict. Our task is to produce software which:

- is based on the use of software machines (modules)
- has a good balance of coupling and cohesion

The way to achieve this is through good partitioning, packaging and structuring of the total system software.

3.2.2 Modules – packaging and structuring

At this point we need to define 'module' in a more restrictive sense: not its basic meaning as spelt out earlier, but rather its implementation. The original definition is extended by 'being implemented as a subprogram'. This definition is used to avoid confusion with higher-level packaging provided by some programming languages: the modules of Modula-2, packages of Ada and classes of C++, for instance. However, beware of turning this around: a subprogram is not necessarily a module.

Modules are used to package the software of our system – an encapsulation process. In fact we have two packaging requirements (Figure 3.17).

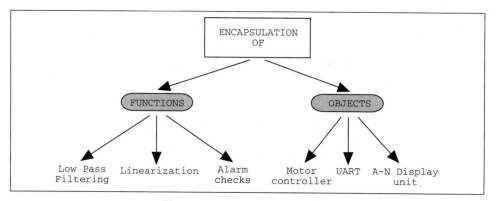

Figure 3.17 Packaging objectives.

The first is to encapsulate system functions, such as filtering, linearization and alarm checks. The second is to house objects such as device controllers and serial line interfaces. We are, of course, talking only of the software design. This conceptual view of a module is illustrated in Figure 3.18.

Its major attributes are as follows:

- The complete module is seen, on the outside, as a single unit.
- It has a well-defined function or purpose (*what* it does).
- It encapsulates both code and data to achieve that purpose (*how* it does it).
- There is distinct separation of 'what' from 'how'.
- Implementation aspects are hidden within the module.
- It has a well-defined, clean interface.
- The interface acts as the 'access window' of the module. Only this is visible to the outside world.

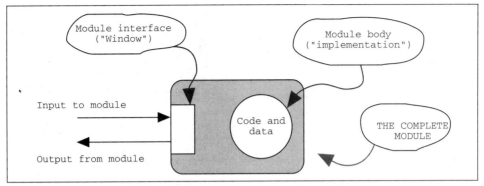

Figure 3.18   Module – conceptual structure.

- There should be no bypassing of the interface.
- It must not produce side-effects.

Side-effects are defined by the *Oxford Dictionary of Computing* as 'an effect of a program unit that is not apparent from its parameters, for example altering a non-local variable or performing input/output'.

This leads on to see how modules can be portrayed in diagram form. The chosen method must be able to show the following:

- the important features of the individual modules
- the interconnection of the set of modules

Bear in mind that we are dealing with sequential, not parallel, programs. Further, remember that subprograms have to be invoked (called) into action. This implicitly defines a hierarchical structure (Figure 3.19).

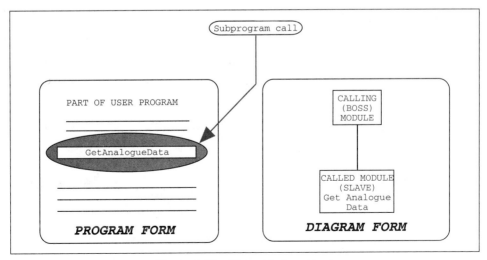

Figure 3.19   Hierarchical machines.

Look at the program form first. Assume that the user program is the top-level source code unit, built as a sequence of subprogram calls. One of these is `GetAnalogueData`. This relationship can be shown as a simple structure chart, containing a calling (boss) and a called (slave) module. What is shown here is a tiny system consisting of two software machines. Each machine has its own code; that is, it is a real software entity. Here we have the basis of the central point of this chapter, the *Module* structure chart.

This last point is so important that it is worth spelling it out again. Each box on the module structure chart represents a software machine. Each machine is implemented as a subprogram and has its own code. Thus every box is implemented as a section of code. The top level may, of course, be the main program unit; this is taken as implicit unless stated otherwise. Contrast this with the program structure chart.

As shown in Figure 3.19, the simplest subprogram structure has been used; a procedure without parameters. More generally, though, we need to transfer information to and from the subprogram. Take, for instance, the case where a procedure must be supplied with data when it is invoked (Figure 3.20).

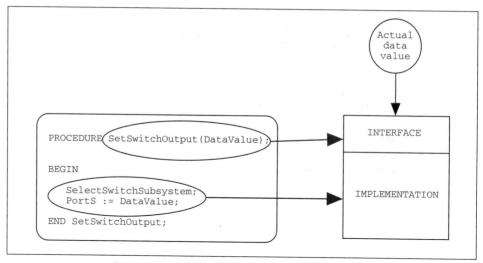

Figure 3.20   Building the module – simple input data.

Here we have a procedure `SetSwitchOutput`, having a single formal parameter `DataValue`. The procedure heading acts as the interface section: the piece that we can see. Its parameter forms the window through which the actual data value can be inserted at run time. Implementation details, the code between `BEGIN` and `END`, are hidden from the caller. Figure 3.21 demonstrates a call of this procedure within a main program, the actual parameter being `AllOn`.

This is an 'In' or 'Value' parameter, also called a data couple or data flag. The diagram, for clarity, shows only the slave module, together with the symbol for a data couple. The claimed advantage of the data couple is that data transfers can be

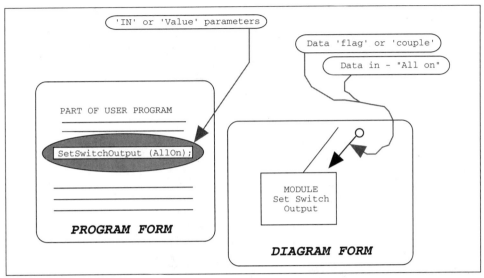

Figure 3.21   Data couples – input data to module.

shown on the diagram. Note that not all diagram notations support this feature; couples are included here for completeness.

Reversing the process – transferring data out of a module – is illustrated in Figure 3.22.

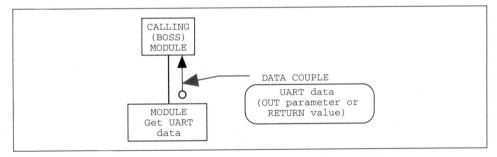

Figure 3.22   Data couples – output data from module.

Here the output data couple could be implemented as an OUT or VAR parameter; it could also be a subprogram return value. The most general case is that of two-way data transfer (Figure 3.23).

The use of subprograms leads fairly naturally to hierarchical structures, demonstrated with the simple program fragment of Figure 3.24.

The program (top-level) module, called GET OPERATOR SETTINGS, contains a procedure call ManageSerialComms. It has two actual parameters, RequestMessage and Reply. This procedure has corresponding formal parameters DataToLine and DataFromLine. The body of ManageSerialComms holds two procedures,

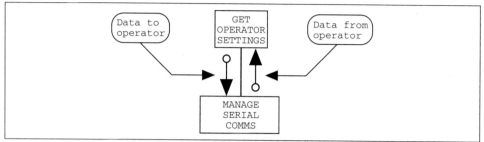

Figure 3.23 Data couples – two-way data transfer.

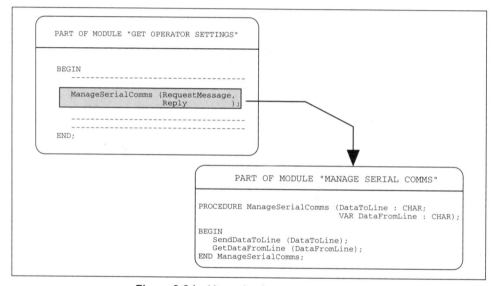

Figure 3.24 Hierarchical program structure.

SendDataToLine and GetDataFromLine. Both are parametrized. Thus GET OPERATOR SETTINGS invokes ManageSerialComms, which in turn invokes SendDataToLine and GetDataFromLine. Observe how the parameters are passed down through the levels.

Well, it took many words to describe this action. And I'm sure they needed careful and attentive reading. In contrast, Figure 3.25 – structure and content – is instantly understandable.

Here the top-level program module has a single slave module. This in turn can be regarded as the boss of the two lowest-level modules. All modules (apart from GET OPERATOR SETTINGS) are implemented as subprograms.

Up to this point we have concentrated on code/diagram relationships when developing modular software. Without a doubt the examples make the case for using diagrams to describe the source code structure. However, this is not the *primary* purpose of the module structure chart. No, its basic function is to *show the structure of the design* as a set of modules. Then, and only then, are these translated to code.

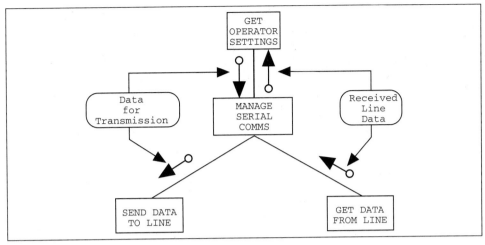

Figure 3.25 Data coupling in a hierarchical structure.

And, like all design work, this is an iterative process. In practice it is likely to take a number of attempts to get it right.

In these examples, data input to slave modules did not in any way define or modify their behaviour. Likewise, data sent back from the slaves did not affect the operation of boss modules. But, in real programs, we frequently find that we *do* want a module to control the behaviour of other(s) (Figure 3.26).

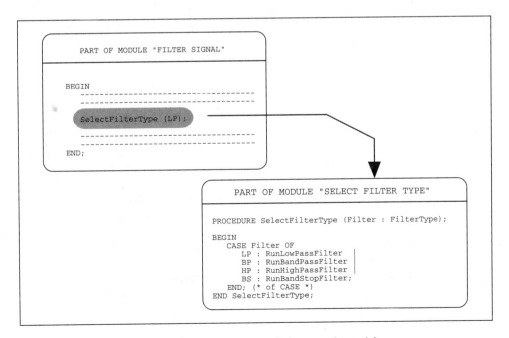

Figure 3.26 Controlling the behaviour of a module.

What we have here is a program module FILTER SIGNAL. Within this is a procedure `SelectFilterType`, having a single actual parameter `LP`. It can be seen from the code of the procedure that the corresponding formal parameter is `Filter`. Within the body of the procedure (the executable statements), `Filter` is used as the selector in a `CASE` statement. In this particular example, when `LP` is passed in at run time, `RunLowPassFilter` is executed. In other words, the actual parameter defines what happens within the module at run time.

This leads to the concept of the control flag or couple (Figure 3.27).

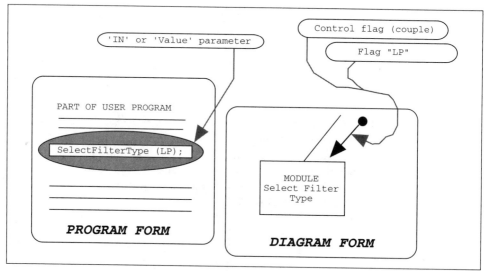

Figure 3.27   Control flags (couples) – input flag to module.

Here the structure and parameter passing of Figure 3.26 are shown in what is (or should be) familiar notation. Observe that a filled circle is used at the end of the arrow to denote a control couple. It is, of course, an In parameter type.

The reverse operation, transferring a control couple from a slave to its boss, is given in Figure 3.28.

A slave module, `CheckAlarmStatus`, has a formal Boolean parameter, `Alarm`. The boss module calls `CheckAlarmStatus`, using the actual parameter `LowOilPressure`. Its subsequent course of action is determined by `LowOilPressure`. If `TRUE` it shuts off the compressor motor; otherwise it passes on to the next module code statement.

In some systems the use of subprograms for building modules may lead to problems. To understand why, note what happens when a procedure is invoked. The program branches off from its position in the boss module to the slave code. On completion of the procedure it must return to the correct location in the boss module. To ensure that this happens correctly information must be provided. And the handling of such information takes time and requires RAM space. The problem is

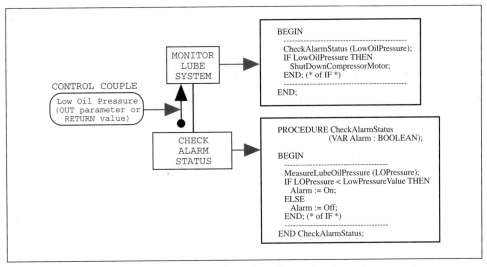

Figure 3.28   Control couple – slave to boss transfer.

further aggravated when parameter passing takes place. Parameters have to be set up prior to the procedure call. Likewise, returned items have to be handled on completion of the procedure. Both take time and need RAM store space. These, unfortunately, impose a time and store overhead which may not be acceptable. Therefore, procedurization may be a problem in:

- fast systems
- small systems (typically microcontrollers having limited RAM store)

It is almost sure to be a problem in small fast systems.

How can you deal with these issues? The first thing is to find out if you really have a problem. When you are told the system is 'fast', always try to get numbers for this. The answers may be most surprising (a regular reply is 'well, we don't quite know, but it's pretty fast'). Design your software using a modular approach, and see what emerges. If there are problems, look to see if you can 'in-line' the procedures; that is, make the compiler replace each procedure call with the actual procedure code. This eliminates the time and RAM overheads, but does, of course, produce larger programs.

3.2.3   More on coupling – data coupling

All module coupling shown in the previous examples was made using the most secure form of connection, namely:

- In (value) parameters
- Out (VAR or location) parameters

- In/Out parameters
- the return statement

Why are these secure, what are the advantages in using them, and which ones should be used? Each one is best used in a specific role, although this does depend somewhat on the programming language.

In parameters

All In parameters are named items (the actual parameters, that is. Formal parameters must, of course, be named). Therefore the source code shows explicitly what information is sent to the module. You can quickly and easily see what is happening, and hence check for code/diagram conformance. Further, the values used within the subprograms are copies, not the originals. Hence, if errors are made at run time, the originals are unaffected. In such circumstances it is possible to 'roll-back' through the program and safely reuse these items.

Some languages allow default parameters to be used. That is, you don't need to specify the actual parameters at the time of call: the compiler will automatically insert predefined (default) ones. This, in my view, should be outlawed, its practitioners being banished to work on program maintenance.

Out parameters

Here, too, parameters must be named. Strictly speaking, names used within a program designate a store location. Thus an actual Out parameter defines an address into which the output value is placed. Therefore we must be very sure that the correct parameters are specified on the call of the subprogram. We also need to be very aware of all uses of such items within the complete program.

In/Out parameters

These are used to handle two-way transfer of information. As such they denote the location or addresses where the actual parameters are stored – not the values themselves.

There are times when these are used instead of In parameters to transfer data into a subprogram. We lose security but save on the time and store overheads of copying. If you've ever computed matrix inversions you won't need telling just what savings can be made.

Return statement

With the return statement there is no named parameter. Instead, an explicit assignment statement is made, again a very visible action. It isn't always clear-cut whether to use the return statement or a parameter; much depends on program details. However, in most languages, only single simple variables can be returned. Structured types – arrays and records, for instance – thus require the use of parameters.

Just one point of clarification. In this text, both simple and structured types can be used for data coupling. However, the structures must be fixed and explicit (this would, for instance, exclude variant records).

3.2.4   *Coupling via structured data – stamp coupling*

Let us now investigate the situation where data structures aren't fixed or explicit. Suppose that modules are interlinked or coupled via such structures (*stamp coupling*). How is this done in practice, and what are its implications? To answer these, let us first see why such methods are used.

Suppose our system has a serial communications channel. We reserve a data area for storing incoming messages, say data area 1 of Figure 3.29.

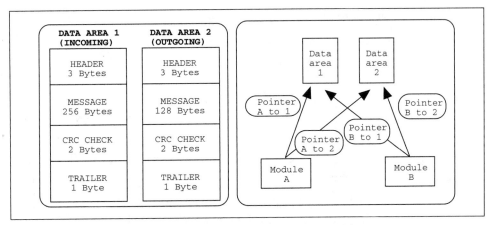

Figure 3.29   Stamp coupling between modules.

Likewise, a separate data store is set up into which outgoing messages can be deposited. Handling message information is complicated by the facts that:

- individual messages can vary in length
- the message structure can also vary
- we need to access different parts of the message structure at different times

The only things we can say with certainty are that:

- The maximum size of a message is predefined.
- The location of the start of the message is known.
- All other information must be derived from the message itself.

Suppose that module A is responsible for handling data transfers to and from the serial comms subsystem. Module B is part of the application program, using and generating such information. Further, suppose that Figure 3.29 represents the current situation within the data stores. So, what is an efficient way of accessing the data? One well proven – and widely used – method is that which uses *pointers*. For 'pointer' read 'address'. That is, we access the data area using its address, the datum point being the beginning of the store. Specific locations within the store are denoted using offsets from this point. Thus both modules can access the store area provided they are supplied with the pointers. However, they must both have *exactly* the same view of the data structures, or major problems may ensue. Take, for instance, a situation where B deposits data into area 1, this having a 3-byte header. For some reason A thinks the header size is a 4-byte one, so ... ? A second aspect is that modules cannot independently decide to change a structure; all users must agree. But that raises the problem of policing such changes – not a simple issue.

You will find little need to use pointers for the level of work covered in this text. Avoid them if at all possible.

3.2.5   Handling global data – common coupling

Common coupling occurs when modules have unrestricted access to a common data item(s) (Figure 3.30).

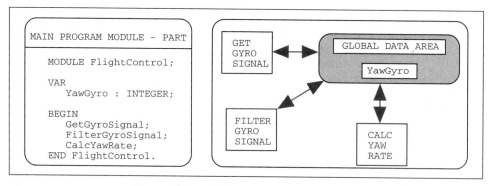

Figure 3.30   Common coupling – global data.

You can see within the source code a variable called YawGyro. From the position of its declaration it is both in scope and visible throughout the full program unit. Hence it can be accessed by the three modules GetGyroSignal, FilterGyroSignal and CalcYawRate. In other words, it is a common – global – item. The diagram makes this much more obvious than the source code – once again proving the value of pictures.

You may argue that global items make life simpler. We don't have to use parameter passing, with its attendant overheads. True – but that's about all that can be said for it. The real danger is that it can be used *anywhere* and by *anybody* within the program – without any semblance of visibility or control. The main program text gives no clues to where YawGyro is used, or, for that matter, whether it is even used at all. We are forced to investigate the contents of the three modules to find this information. And if by chance these invoke lower-level modules, this could turn out to be long, tedious and frustrating. The number of program errors caused by the abuse of globals is legendary. So avoid them like the plague unless you really have need of common data. Unfortunately, at some stage, you will come across the need to use global items. In embedded systems this tends to arise most often when dealing with:

- shared devices having absolute addresses in memory or I/O
- multitasking (concurrent) software

In these circumstances you must build safety and security into your software. Do three things. First, put all global items behind a protective shield. Second, make all accesses to them only through a defined control mechanism. Third, make this access controller an integral part of the shield. This, for the moment, is all you need to know about the use of globals. We shall return to this topic later in the text.

3.3   Organizing and structuring the software

3.3.1   Organizing the software

Before trying to structure software it is worth first organizing it into sensible groupings. But to do this it is necessary to define how this should be carried out. Different software design methods have different criteria – which can be somewhat confusing. The key point here is to recognize that, irrespective of the approach used, all jobs can be split into two parts. One is application-specific, the other application-independent (Figure 3.31).

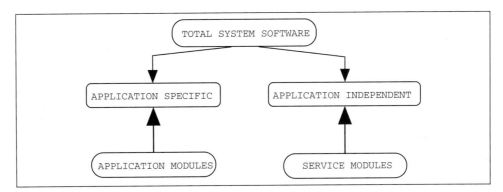

Figure 3.31   Organizing the software.

Modules designed to handle the application are here called 'application modules' (not exactly original, but at least the meaning is clear enough). Those independent of the application are termed 'service modules'. This name has been chosen to reflect their purpose – to provide a service to the application (more meaningful, in my view, than 'utility' module). How, though, do we distinguish between the two types? First take the service module.

It is defined here as 'a module which can be designed and built without reference to specific applications'. There are, in fact, two types of service module: general purpose and hardware-related. General purpose ones are those which are independent of the computer hardware. Typical of these are:

- mathematical functions (matrix inversion, Fourier transformation, Runge–Kutta estimation)
- control algorithms (digital PID function, pole-zero compensation methods, RLS identification)
- dynamic data structure handling (stacks, queues, lists)

Hardware-related service modules are those needed to manage the hardware of the computer system. These include functions internal *and* external to the computer itself, for example:

- programmable timers (internal)
- direct memory access (DMA) controllers (internal)
- serial communication devices (external)
- analogue to digital converters (external)

Such hardware-related modules will probably only work correctly on the computer for which they were designed. Thus this software, unlike that of the general purpose ones, is not portable. But, and this is a most important point, they are still application-independent. Nothing has actually been said about how or why these are used. Thus, once hardware has been designed, the corresponding service modules can also be developed (we will, at this stage, ignore hardware/software trade-offs). Moreover, service modules need be developed once only. They can then be used as many times as required (classic software reuse). The advantages of reuse have already been discussed; go back and review the salient points.

Compare this with the development of application software. Here it is impossible to begin software design without knowing what you wish to achieve – which is, in essence, to satisfy the project's statement of requirements. Now, by clearly separating out application aspects we are forced to focus on the broader (system) issues. At the same time it saves us from being distracted by highly detailed implementation issues. In real life it is rare to find projects that are identical. Thus application software tends to be unique, applicable to one system only. Seldom is such software, as a whole, reusable (although it may be possible to recycle specific parts). Service software, in contrast, is project-independent. Generally, given good design, it should be highly reusable.

3.3.2 Structuring the software

This section applies to both application and service modules, though the application is the more important one. A simple set of rules is given here, based on those for program design. Their objective is to help you to achieve quality software. Breaking these rules when developing service modules will lead to many and varied problems. However, such problems will be localized ones. You will probably eventually eliminate them by sweat and toil. But you cannot afford to take a blasé approach when designing application software. Doing so leads to the delivery of products that are incorrect, unreliable and unsafe.

First, a brief recap. The fundamental idea is that software is built as a set of indi-

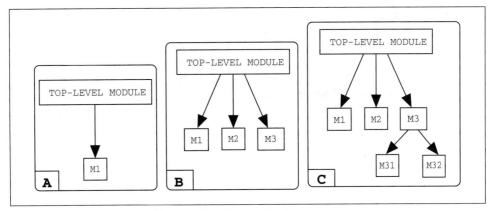

Figure 3.32   Structuring the software.

vidual software units. These are connected together in a hierarchical fashion, the simplest form being that of Figure 3.32(a).

Here we have a two-module system, consisting of a single boss and a single slave. The boss, or top-level module, calls on or invokes the slave M1 as and when required. When this happens, program control passes from the top module to M1. It then stays with M1 until this module returns control back to the top level. Now this is an important point. A boss cannot regain control once its subordinate is activated.

This, at first sight, may not seem all that important. In fact, it is *very* important. Suppose, for instance, that we program a loop operation which, under particular conditions, fails to find an exit condition. The result? The program gets stuck in M1 *ad infinitum*, and there is nothing that can be done about it. For embedded systems we are most likely to meet such problems when interacting with hardware. For example, suppose that the function of M1 is to acquire analogue data. Its first action is to start the conversion process. Following this, the 'data valid' flag is monitored until data is valid. Finally the data is read in by the processor. Which is fine – as long as the hardware works correctly. What, though, if 'data valid' is never signalled? Yes: yet again, an infinite loop.

This issue demonstrates yet one more reason for building software in modular fashion. It allows us to concentrate on individual units, looking carefully at their performance under abnormal conditions (*exceptions*). Where potential problems are found to exist, we need to show explicitly how to:

- detect problems if they do occur
- report their presence – transfer control – to an exception handling mechanism (exception raising)
- react to them (exception handling)

There are many flavours of exception mechanism, often being language-dependent. Little more will be said here, except to show how the data acquisition problem *could* be handled. Enclose the valid data check within a counting loop. Detect the fault when (if) the loop reaches a specific value. Raise the exception by transferring control back to the boss module. Handle the mechanism by code included within this module.

In Figure 3.32(a), there is no indication of how many times M1 is called. We shall continue to use notation based on Jackson structure diagrams; hence, as shown, M1 is invoked *once* only (this is quite different from Yourdon structure charts).

In Figure 3.32(b), a slightly larger four-module system is shown. Here the top-level module calls on the services of three subordinates. In keeping with Jackson notation, the execution order is M1, M2, M3.

This ordering is maintained in Figure 3.32(c), except that M3 is both a boss and a slave. M3 is invoked by the top-level module; it, in turn, invokes M31, then M32. Thus the complete sequence of operations here is:

- Program starts, top-level module (TL) begins to execute.
- TL invokes M1, control passes to M1.
- M1 completes, control passes back to TL.
- TL invokes M2, control passes to M2.
- M2 completes, control passes back to TL.
- TL invokes M3, control passes to M3.
- M3 invokes M31, control passes to M31.
- M31 completes, control passes back to M3.
- M3 invokes M32, control passes to M32.
- M32 completes, control passes back to M3.
- M3 completes, control passes back to TL.
- TL completes, program finished.

Notice that this is the best structure form, a pure tree. Unfortunately, life isn't always so obliging. Enter the *common* module (Figure 3.33).

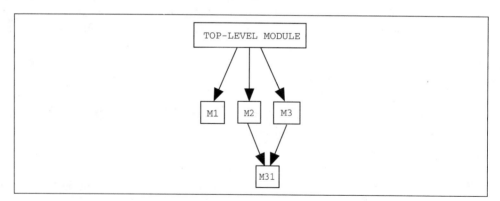

Figure 3.33 The common module issue.

As shown here, module M31 is invoked by M2 *and* by M3. It acts as a coupling mechanism between these machines, thus raising the overall coupling of the system. While this is not desirable, it may well be the natural outcome of our design approach. And, in fact, it frequently happens when application modules invoke service modules. For instance, M31 could be a screen-handling module. It is invoked by M2 to display, say, Artificial Horizon data; then later by M3 to display Gyro Compass status. There is nothing unusual in this, the result is quite reasonable. Thus it is flying in the face of reality to try to eliminate common modules. They are a predictable result of the use of service modules. Consequently, such modules must be of the highest design and build quality. However, for application modules, these should be avoided wherever possible; the aim is a pure tree structure. We shall return to this point, discussing it in more detail at the end of Chapter 8.

The notation of Figure 3.33 is used in Yourdon structure charts. With our Jackson-based notation, this is not allowed. Instead we show multiple calls of a module as multiple instances on the diagram (Figure 3.34).

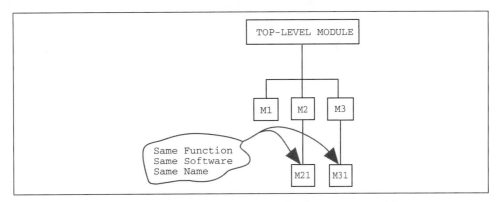

Figure 3.34 Jackson-based notation for the common module.

Be very careful when common modules are used. A good idea is to add special identification to highlight them. It also keeps the diagrams cleaner if service modules are *not* included on the structure chart. Show only the structure of the application. More will be said about this in a moment.

3.3.3 *Extended Jackson notation – module structure charts*

Here the basic Jackson notation is extended to take three factors into account:

(a) the need to handle both program structure charts *and* module structure charts
(b) the practicalities of programming languages
(c) CASE tool notation

As a result, some new symbols are defined, shown in Figure 3.35.

First, the top-level machine is designated a 'module'. The name isn't new, but here it has a very specific meaning (the semantics). In the context of extended notation, a module is viewed as a container. Thus the top-level machine is a container for all lower-level ones. This fits naturally into the way that programs are built.

Second, lower-level machines are defined to be procedures (here used as a general term for all types of subprogram).

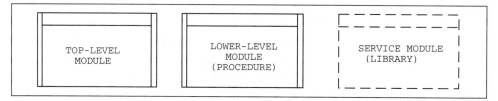

Figure 3.35 Extended Jackson notation for modules.

Finally, service modules are denoted as library units, the boxes having dotted lines. This makes them stand out on the module structure charts. Note, by the way, that service modules can be invoked at any level – and by any machine – in the hierarchy.

Let us apply this to a simple application (Figure 3.36).

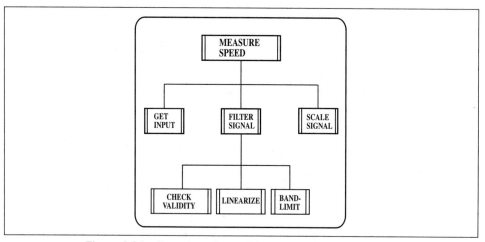

Figure 3.36 Describing the modular structure of the software.

Here the overall task – the top-level operation – is MEASURE SPEED. This is defined to be the program module. To perform this task, it invokes procedures GET INPUT, FILTER SIGNAL and SCALE SIGNAL. They are called in that order. However, when FILTER SIGNAL is activated, it calls CHECK VALIDITY, LINEARIZE and BAND LIMIT (in that sequence). Now let us see what the corresponding source code is (Figure 3.37).

It can be seen that the module MEASURE SPEED consists of three procedure calls: GetInput, FilterSignal and ScaleSignal. The procedure FilterSignal itself consists of three procedure calls: CheckValidity, Linearize and BandLimit. Information is passed using procedure parameters. Notice that, with the Jackson notation, data and control couples are not shown on the diagram.

Observe how the naming is consistent with the structure chart. Always try to do this, so making it easy to:

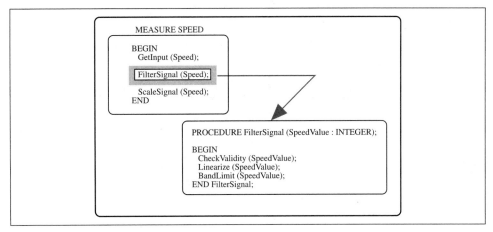

Figure 3.37   Program structure for Figure 3.36.

- understand the meaning of the code
- trace a design through its various stages

In practice, unfortunately, this isn't always possible. Diagram names may become rather too long to be used as program names. There are various reasons for this. For instance, some languages limit the length of identifiers. Others don't have a limit, but only check the name defined by the first few letters. And sometimes, even where there are no restrictions, names may be just too unwieldy. But, whatever you do, make sure that there is an obvious naming relationship between the two documents. And not only diagram to code. You also need to be able to go backwards – that is, code to diagram.

One further extension can be made to the module structure chart as shown in Figure 3.38.

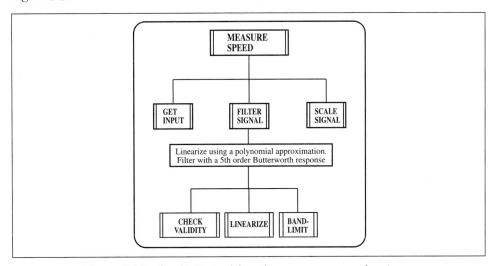

Figure 3.38   Combining module and program structure chart icons.

Here, the previous structure chart has been modified to include a *program* structure chart icon. The reason for doing this is to improve the level of information given by the structure chart. There is no code associated with this box. Thus both Figures 3.36 and 3.38 result in the same source code document.

In the combined structure chart – from now on simply called a module structure chart – such boxes can also be attached as leaves (Figure 3.39).

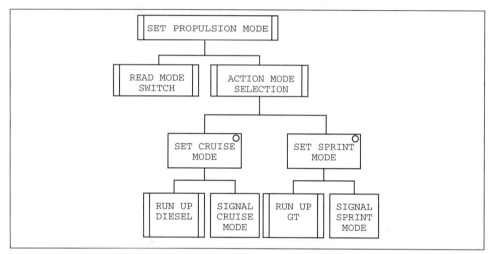

Figure 3.39 Combined SC – full format.

We apply exactly the same rule as before; that is, leaves have associated code. Thus the corresponding code for Figure 3.39 is given in Figure 3.40.

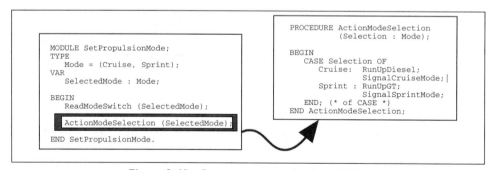

Figure 3.40 Program structure for Figure 3.39.

At this point you might feel that things are getting somewhat complex. Why not just stay with the original structure chart? Well, experience has shown that this combined chart:

- is much more expressive than the basic module chart
- is easy to design and use
- does not appear to cause any particular difficulties to first-time users

3.3.4 More on the service module

The service module is truly a piece of software Lego. We pick it up and plug it into the application as and when required. Naturally enough, we assume that it will fit into place, and will perform as specified. But, to meet these objectives, specific design criteria *must* be met:

- The module must be ultra-dependable.
- It must have a well-defined function.
- *What* and *how* need to be clearly separated.
- Its interfaces must be well defined, and preferably simple.
- Abstract naming should be used in the interface.

One feature that does warrant further discussion, however, is the encapsulation and interfacing aspects of service modules.

We use the service module to encapsulate functions and objects. In essence we wish to isolate the module user (client) from the nitty-gritty of the implementation. An excellent service module is one where internal changes produce no visible effects at the application level. Let's demonstrate this point with a simple example.

Assume that an embedded computer is used to collect data from two sensors (pressure and flow). At the beginning of the project both sensors are specified as having analogue outputs. To handle these signals, a two-channel data acquisition subsystem is designed (Figure 3.41).

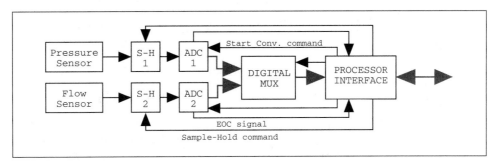

Figure 3.41 Two-channel data acquisition subsystem.

We decide to use a service module – GetSensorData – to hold the software needed to support this hardware. Its top-level module structure chart is shown in Figure 3.42.

Observe how the user is supplied with a very simple interface to this module.

Now suppose that much later into the project the flow sensor type is changed. The analogue (continuous) signal version is replaced by one having a pulse output. As a result, the hardware is redesigned to accept this alteration (Figure 3.43).

Naturally enough, the software must also be modified, the result being that of Figure 3.44.

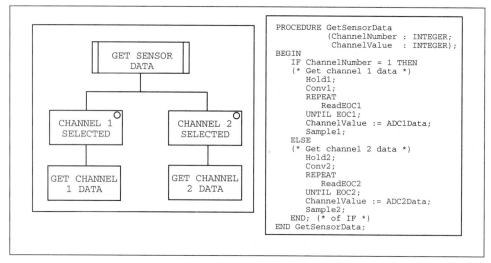

```
PROCEDURE GetSensorData
                (ChannelNumber : INTEGER;
                 ChannelValue  : INTEGER);
BEGIN
    IF ChannelNumber = 1 THEN
    (* Get channel 1 data *)
        Hold1;
        Conv1;
        REPEAT
            ReadEOC1
        UNTIL EOC1;
        ChannelValue := ADC1Data;
        Sample1;
    ELSE
    (* Get channel 2 data *)
        Hold2;
        Conv2;
        REPEAT
            ReadEOC2
        UNTIL EOC2;
        ChannelValue := ADC2Data;
        Sample2;
    END; (* of IF *)
END GetSensorData;
```

Figure 3.42 Structure chart – data acquisition service module.

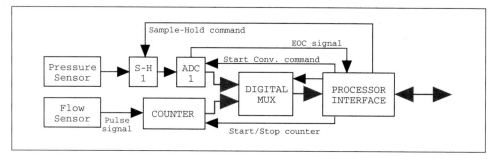

Figure 3.43 Modified data acquisition subsystem.

You can see how the interface is exactly the same as before. All changes are buried within the service module. Thus there is *no* impact on the design at the application level. Hence, if the design worked properly in the first case, it should still be correct after modification. Implicit here is that the new service module is fully tested and is satisfactory in all aspects.

This example also demonstrates how hardware design ideas can be very easily – and naturally – applied to software. The service module is the software analogue of the data acquisition subsystem. This subsystem encapsulates the acquisition function, and provides a clear interface to the processor. Moreover, a good hardware designer would make the processor interfaces of Figures 3.41 and 3.43 identical. Suppose, also, that the unit was implemented on a plug-in PCB. Then upgrading is merely a case of unplugging one board and replacing it with the new one. That's what we are striving for in software: plug compatibility, simplicity of replacement and consistent system behaviour.

```
PROCEDURE GetSensorData
         (ChannelNumber : INTEGER;
          ChannelValue  : INTEGER);
BEGIN
   IF ChannelNumber = 1 THEN
   (* Get channel 1 data *)
      Hold1;
      Conv1;
      REPEAT
         ReadEOC1
      UNTIL EOC1;
      ChannelValue := ADC1Data;
      Sample1;
   ELSE
   (* Get channel 2 data *)
      StartCounter;
      DelayCountPeriod;
      StopCounter;
      ChannelValue := CounterData;
   END; (* of IF *)
END GetSensorData;
```

Figure 3.44   Modified service module.

Review

In this chapter you have:

- been introduced to the concept, attributes and implementation of the software machine
- seen why this is such a powerful technique for software development
- met the application of top-down and bottom-up design techniques
- learned how to package and structure software in modular fashion, especially as a set of hierarchical machines
- learned how to show such hierarchical structures using the module structure chart
- seen that coupling and cohesion are good ways to assess modular structures
- observed the partitioning of software into application and service modules
- been given rules for the structuring of modular software

You should now feel confident to use a modular approach for the design of real software systems – 'programming in the large'.

Exercises

Produce Jackson module structure charts for the various problems outlined below. Also produce the corresponding pseudo-code. It is assumed that data entry is done using a keyboard, all display information being presented on a screen.

3.1 Produce a module structure chart which consists of three modules:

(a) get data
(b) calculate values
(c) display results

For each module – specified below – produce a program structure chart.

Module (a): put out a text message and so acquire the length (L), width (W) and height (H) of a room. Give the user the facility to correct each entered value before proceeding to the calculation stage.

Module (b): from the values acquired in (a), calculate the floor area (FA), wall area (WA) and room volume (V).

Module (c): display either FA or WA or V as calculated in (b).

3.2 Modify Exercise 3.1 to allow this to be used for specifically designated rooms (for example: dining room, kitchen, lounge, study). Use hierarchical structuring of modules wherever possible.

3.3 Modify Exercise 3.1 so that this operation can be used for any number of rooms (as defined by a user-entered value).

4

Introduction to data flow diagrams

The structure chart is a powerful way to implement visual software design – a form of 'software through pictures'. Remember, though, that its primary purpose is to define the structure of the software – without saying how this structure has been arrived at. In other words it is solution- not problem-oriented. As a result it has many limitations, though these are not at first all that obvious. This chapter introduces a higher-level technique, that of data flow design. It:

- explains the limitations of structure chart design
- introduces the concepts underlying data flow design
- describes the content and use of data flow diagrams (DFDs)
- explains how top-down methods are applied to DFD design
- describes a variety of methods for specifying functional operations
- shows how the data itself is specified
- explains the role of the data dictionary

4.1   Limitations of the structure chart

What, then, are the weaknesses of the structure chart? Let us examine these using a practical example.

Figure 4.1 is a top-level module SC defining the software of a missile control system.

First, what can we deduce from this? Even with no knowledge of the control system or the missile we can see that:

- The control loop runs continuously as long as power is on.
- The first operation is to read the telecommands, followed by reading the gyro signals.
- Following this the missile control orders are calculated.
- Next, depending on the flight time, the canards are either reset or deflected.

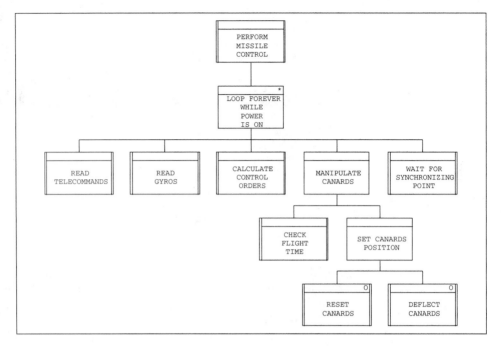

Figure 4.1 Module structure chart – missile control system.

- Finally, the software waits for a synchronization point, at which time the sequence is repeated.

But consider just some of the things that we *can't* deduce from the diagram:

- what the telecommands are
- what they specify
- how many gyros are fitted to the missile
- specifically, what data is used when calculating the control orders
- how many canards are fitted to the missile (in other words, how many output signals must be calculated)
- exactly how the flight time information is used (and where it is obtained from)
- what synchronization mechanism is used
- what precisely each processing function (software machine) is intended to achieve
- input, internal and output signals – what, when and why?
- what the attributes of all these signals are

You may even have a few questions of your own to add to this list.

So, the message from this is clear. The structure chart is a powerful diagramming technique for defining software structures. However, it is quite limited in the way that it handles system-oriented aspects of the design. Thus we require a diagramming method which, at the very least:

- allows us to express the design in terms of what is to be done (system functions)
- handles the design in a top-down layered manner
- provides information for the generation of the associated structure charts

Enter the data flow diagram.

4.2 Concepts and analogies

Our requirement is, in essence, to show the design from a functional point of view. We wish to put more emphasis on *what* is needed rather than *how* it is achieved. The result is a move to higher-level design descriptions of our systems. We can draw directly on electronic design methods to show what this means in practice (Figure 4.2).

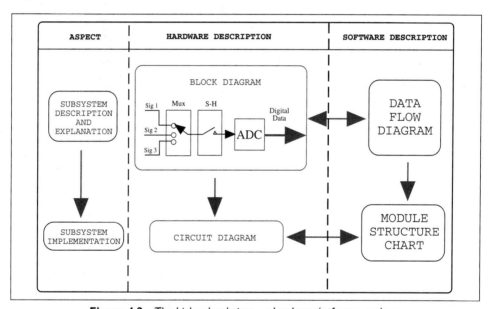

Figure 4.2 The higher-level view – a hardware/software analogy.

This shows the block diagram of part of a digital data acquisition subsystem. It consists of three input signals routed by a multiplexer (Mux) to a single sample-hold (S-H) module. The output of the S-H is digitized by an analogue to digital converter (ADC) to provide the required digital data.

Now, consider carefully what this diagram tells us – and also what it *doesn't* say. It shows us the major functional blocks in the data acquisition subsystem. It illustrates their function, either in picture or text form. It shows all signals within the subsystem, including inputs and output. Naturally such diagrams are accompanied by text explanations – we aren't expected to be psychic as well as clever. Diagrams and text, taken together, provide two essential pieces of information. First, there is a description of the structure and signal content of the subsystem. Second, there is an explanation of the way it works – its functioning. Note though that it doesn't define how these functions are implemented using electronic components. Circuit diagrams are used for this.

The software parallels to these diagrams are the data flow diagram and the module structure chart. Like their electronic equivalents these give us different, but complementary, views of the same system. Also, like their electronic counterparts, they must use an integrated approach. To appreciate this point, consider once more the hardware design diagrams. Here diagram integration means, for example, that:

- All signals on one diagram really do appear on the other one.
- Block diagram functions are actually implemented on the circuit diagram.
- Circuit implementations always have a corresponding block diagram description.

This point – an integrated method – is a most important one. It is *the* major driving force in defining the DFD-to-SC translation rules used hereafter.

To summarize: in simple terms, the primary purpose of a DFD is to show:

- what a system does (functional aspects)
- inputs to and outputs from the system
- what happens to the data within the system

4.3 Data flow diagrams – notation (syntax) and meaning (semantics)

4.3.1 Data transformations

Before looking into data flow diagrams in detail, consider the following question: why use design diagrams? The answer is simple: to express, convey and record design information. Unfortunately, not all diagrams manage to do this well. Problems arise from the symbols used and the meanings of such symbols. First, the notation used (syntax) must be rigorously defined. Second, having specified the symbols to be used, we must agree their meaning (semantics) – otherwise, how can we produce information which is neither ambiguous nor ambivalent? Thus both syntax and semantic rules need to be defined for a diagramming method to be useful and usable.

Let us begin by looking in detail at the issue of diagram notation. Once again electronic analogies are used (Figure 4.3).

Here we wish to show a functional operation (or transformation) which has inputs A and B and produces an output Y. The operation to be performed is the logical NANDing of the two inputs. One of the simplest methods would be to use a two-input single-output rectangular box (the 'icon'). However, if our diagram is to conform to MIL-STD-806B (the military standard for electronic logic symbols) for instance, this would not be acceptable. Instead the familiar NAND symbol must be used.

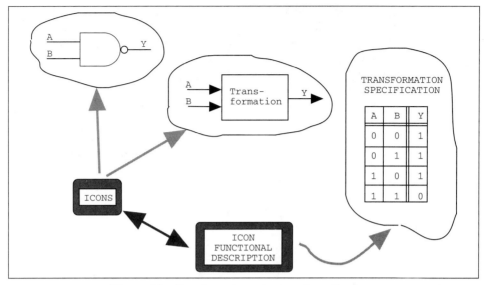

Figure 4.3   Transformations – icons and specifications.

So far, so good. We have agreed on the symbol to be used. But what is the *meaning* of this symbol? This also must be defined. In this case we use a *transformation specification*, this being given as a logical truth table. It defines clearly and unambiguously the inputs to, the output from, and the functionality of the transformation.

Our software diagrams must also be defined in a similar rigorous manner. The basic symbols of the DFD are data flows and data transformations (DTs) (Figure 4.4).

Note in passing that DTs are also called 'processes'.

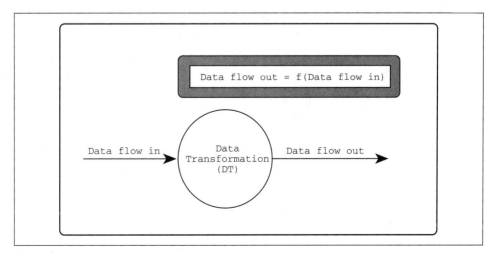

Figure 4.4   Data flows and transformations.

A data transformation – identified as a circle or 'bubble' – is a software operation. It takes in information (data), performs some function, and outputs information (data). Thus the output depends on both the operation performed and the input data. A complete data flow diagram consists of a set of DTs interconnected by data flows. However, before giving even a simple example, further aspects of the DFD must be looked at.

4.3.2 Data flows

Data flowing around a system can be grouped into four categories (Figure 4.5):

AMPLITUDE / TIME	CONTINUOUS	DISCRETE
CONTINUOUS	Thermocouple output	On-off switch
DISCRETE	Radar echo signal	Scanned switch pad

Figure 4.5 Types of data flow.

- time continuous
- time discrete
- amplitude continuous
- amplitude discrete

Thus it is quantized in terms of both amplitude and time. Yes, I know that within a processor system all items have discrete values. However, the grouping given here is based on a system – not processor – level view of data flow.

If you find it hard to distinguish between time continuous and time discrete data, the rule is simple. If the information is not always available, then the data is discrete.

Although there are four categories of data, most CASE tools support two only – time continuous and time discrete (Figure 4.6(a)).

Many rules relating to data flows are specific to a particular toolset. Hence, for the moment, only major features are discussed.

A data flow line may represent one item of data or a group of individual items. A most important point is that no two different flows are given the same name (Figure 4.6(b)).

A single data item may be used by more that one DT. To deal with this a single flow line can be split to show flow divergence (Figure 4.6(c)). Here, for example, a single input flow diverges to two outgoing ones (we are, of course, not limited to two – any number is valid).

Now consider where a data flow represents a grouping of data, say x and y of Figure 4.6(d). If we need to separate these out, exactly the same divergence symbol can be applied.

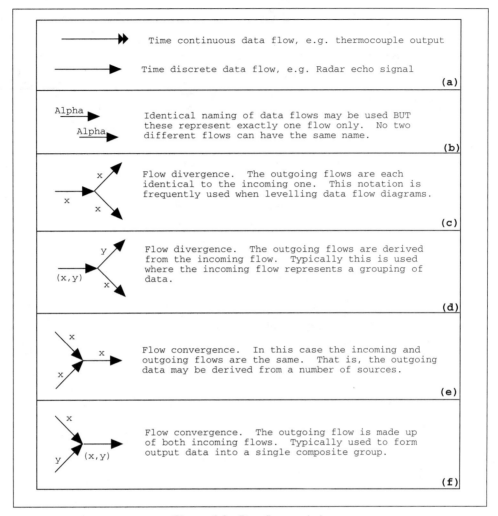

Figure 4.6   Data flow symbols.

The reverse operations, flow convergence, are shown and explained in Figures 4.6(e) and (f).

Note that the following names may be used as alternatives to 'data flow': *signal*, *command* and *variable*. The reason for this will be obvious from their context.

4.3.3   *Data stores*

Data storage is a small but important topic. The concept is illustrated in Figure 4.7.

In Figure 4.7(a), a sampling switch is inserted between incoming and outgoing signals. The outgoing signal appears only when the sampling command closes the switch. It disappears when the switch opens. Hence the outgoing data is available at sample instants only. Compare this with Figure 4.7(b), where a capacitor is connected

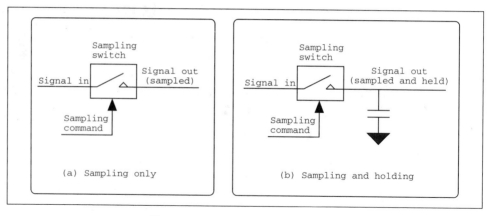

Figure 4.7   Unstored vs. stored data.

to the output signal line. This transforms the operation from sampling to sampling and holding. When the sample switch closes, the output signal charges up the capacitor. But, when the switch is opened, data is retained (held) by the capacitor. Thus the sampled value is available for use both at sample instants and at later times.

Software data items are stored in memory, this being represented as shown in Figure 4.8.

Read/write stores normally use random access memory (RAM); read-only data

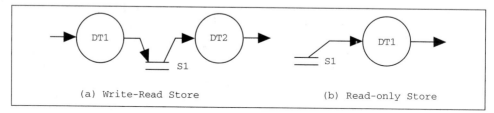

Figure 4.8   Data store symbol.

items are usually stored in erasable programmable read-only memory (EPROM). These could, of course, be held on disc.

The distinction between stored and unstored data can sometimes be confusing. You may argue that variables used in high-level language programming are normally stored in RAM. Does this make them a stored item? The answer is no (unless you specifically intend to store them). Using RAM store for variables is, at heart, a matter of implementation. The essential difference is quite simple. We store items to use them at some later time (examples will be given shortly).

4.3.4 External items

Items external to the software are sources and/or sinks of data. A flow sensor is a source, for instance, while a control valve is a sink. A data terminal or PC could be both a sink and a source of information. These items are defined to be terminators or external entities, shown diagrammatically as in Figure 4.9.

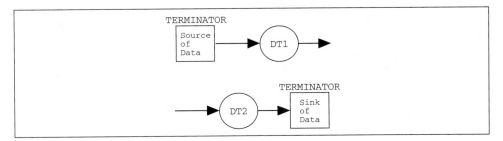

Figure 4.9 External entities (terminators).

4.3.5 Naming conventions for DFDs

The choice and use of names are important in DFD design. We have, at this stage, only four symbol types to name (Figure 4.10).

DATA TRANSFORMATION	◯	A DT operates on an input data flow to produce an output data flow
DATA FLOW	⟶⟶ ⟶	Time continuous Time discrete
DATA STORE	—	A data store is a place in which data is held for a period of time BECAUSE it is needed for use at a later time
EXTERNAL ENTITY	▢	An external entity is a sink or source of data

Figure 4.10 A review of DFD symbols.

There are good reasons for naming them in a particular way, as outlined in Table 4.1.

Always follow these rules. Further, make names meaningful. And, wherever possible, use names which make sense from the *system* point of view (for instance *Engine Fuel Valve* rather than *ADC Channel 1*).

Table 4.1 Naming conventions for data flow diagrams.

Item	Naming rule	Rationale	Example
Entity	Noun or noun phrase	An entity represents an object, a thing	Engine Fuel Valve
Data transformation	Verb or verb phrase – use *active* form	A DT defines an action, i.e. 'doing something'	Compute Fuel Signal
Data flow	Noun or noun phrase	A data flow represents a package of information, a 'thing'	JPT Temperature
Data store	Noun or noun phrase	The data store is a 'container' for data items	Engine Pressure Parameters

4.3.6 Putting it together

A very simple example of a data flow diagram is given in Figure 4.11.

This consists of three terminators, three data transformations, one read/write store and one read-only store.

The input signal to the system is obtained from a Jet Pipe Temperature Sensor, a source terminator. This is time continuous, and is identified as Raw JPT Temperature Signal. It is input to the DT Linearize JPT Temperature Signal. This produces two outputs, JPT Temperature and JPT Temp.

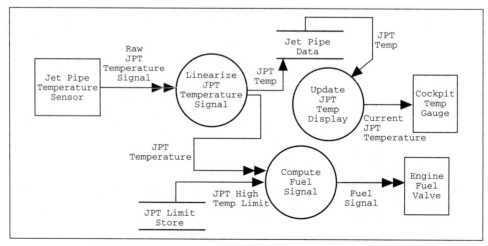

Figure 4.11 Data flow diagram – simple example.

JPT Temperature, together with JPT High Temp Limit, is input to the DT Compute Fuel Signal. Its output is the data flow Fuel Signal, being sent to the sink terminator Engine Fuel Valve. Observe that the High Temp Limit setting is obtained from the read-only store JPT Limit Store.

The data flow JPT Temp is written to the read/write data store Jet Pipe Data. By definition this must be a time-discrete item; it is written into the store at specific times. This information is used by the DT Update JPT Temp Display when it updates the cockpit temperature gauge reading.

One meaningful view of the DFD is that it acts like a snapshot of our system. It shows what items we have in our design, what data flows through it, and what we do with and to this data. But, like a snapshot, it is essentially a static description of the structure.

4.3.7   A brief review of DFD rules

It was pointed out at the beginning of this section that we have to have defined symbols and rules. So let us have a look at various valid and invalid DFD constructs. Let me make it clear that these rules are the generally accepted ones – but unfortunately there is no unique standard. You may well find variations on these in different methods and CASE tools.

In Figure 4.12 we have a set of valid DFD constructs.

For convenience of drawing, discrete flow symbols have been used throughout.

We have already met the situation depicted in Figure 4.12(a). Here an input signal is processed by DT1, its output being the input of DT2. This in turn performs a computation using this input, producing an output result. Because the code of this program is intended to run on a single processor, DT1 *must* be computed before DT2 (we have, remember, a sequential computing machine).

In Figure 4.12(b), the first DT, DT1, produces two outputs. One is the input for DT2, the other is sent to DT3. These, when executed, produce appropriate outputs. Now, here we have a slightly more complex situation compared with Figure 4.12(a). Which DT gets executed first? The answer is that we, as the reader of the diagram, don't know. It is a design decision. However, if the ordering is important, this information must be highlighted somewhere.

Figure 4.12(c) illustrates the case where a DT has two input signals, generating a single result from the computation. In this particular case, DT1 cannot execute until both inputs are present (as they are both discrete flows). Note, by the way, that a DT can have any number of inputs and outputs.

Connections to external entities (terminators) are shown in Figures 4.12(d), (e) and (f) – no surprises here.

In Figure 4.12(g) a data store is used to decouple two DTs, a situation already discussed. However, this same construct is also used in multitasking design (see later) to build communication 'pipes' or 'channels'. The store in Figure 4.12(h) is also used to decouple processes, here having two writer and one reader process. Figure 4.12(j) is similar to Figure 4.12(h). However, the intent here is not so much to decouple DTs as to provide a read/write 'pool' of data (we can, of course, have as many writers and readers as we choose to).

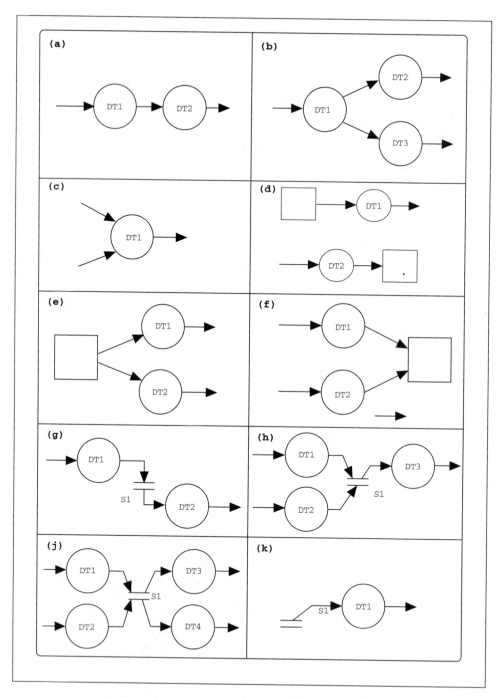

Figure 4.12 Examples of valid data flow diagram constructs.

Finally, Figure 4.12(k) illustrates a read-only store, normally used to hold constant values.

Various invalid DFD constructs are given in Figure 4.13.

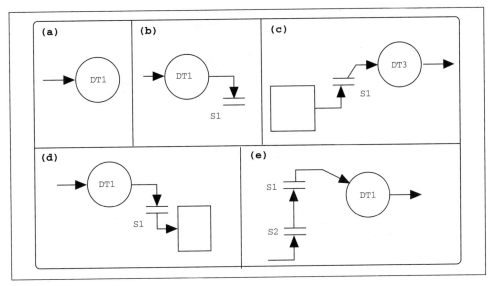

Figure 4.13 Examples of invalid data flow diagram constructs.

Here, in Figure 4.13(a), DT1 produces no output and therefore has no system function. Next, in Figure 4.13(b), data is written into the store S1, but is never used – a somewhat pointless action.

The next three constructs are invalid only because our rules say so. First rule: data from a terminator must be input to a DT. Therefore we need to insert a DT between the source terminator and S1 in Figure 4.13(c). Second rule: data to a terminator must be generated by a DT. Hence Figure 4.13(d) requires a DT between S1 and the sink terminator. Last, rule 3. Only DTs can write to or read from data stores. Thus, to make Figure 4.13(e) valid, a DT needs to be inserted between S1 and S2.

4.4 A systematic top-down approach to DFD design

4.4.1 General principles

All the good basic ideas of top-down design, hierarchical structuring and stepwise refinement apply to DFD design. And the starting point for our design? Where we show the total system as consisting of external entities connected to a software 'black box' (Figure 4.14).

In Figure 4.14 the single bubble – our black box – represents the complete set of software operations in this system. Connected to this via input and output data flows

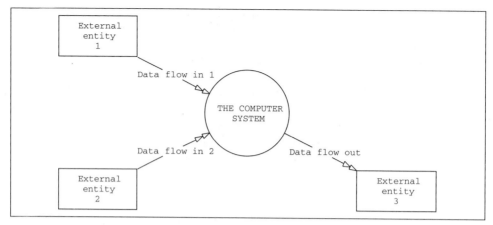

Figure 4.14 DFD design – context diagram.

are the external entities which use this software. Thus this diagram – the 'context' diagram – shows us:

- a single data transformation representing the complete software system
- the items which this software system interfaces to
- the data flows external to the software
- the type and direction of the data flows

This starting point is a crucial one. Why? Because it makes us focus on system, not software, aspects of the design. Further, it reinforces the point that the computer is just one component in a complete system.

The second step in the design process is to describe the functionality of the software system using DFD techniques. This diagram is called the *first-level DFD*, the process itself being defined as *levelling*. Loosely speaking, we level the context diagram to form the first-level DFD. Figure 4.15 is the levelled version of Figure 4.14 (more correctly, the levelled version of the DT 'THE COMPUTER SYSTEM' of Figure 4.14).

Observe:

- There is consistency between the external data flows of both diagrams – they are said to 'balance'.
- External entities are not shown at this level (this is more a convention rather than a necessity. However, it may be enforced by the rules of your CASE tool).
- All internal flows are hidden at the context level.
- The number of DTs, and their functions, are determined by the designer.
- The DTs are numbered as well as having names (for example, number 3 has been named DT3).
- When using CASE tool technology, numbering is normally done automatically. Names are defined by the designer.

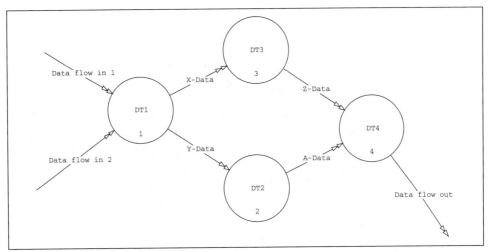

Figure 4.15 First-level DFD – general form.

The first-level DFD is said to be the 'child' of the context diagram. Likewise, the context diagram is the 'parent' of this DFD.

We can, if we wish, now level each DT, showing its function in more detail. For instance, the levelled version of DT2 is shown in Figure 4.16.

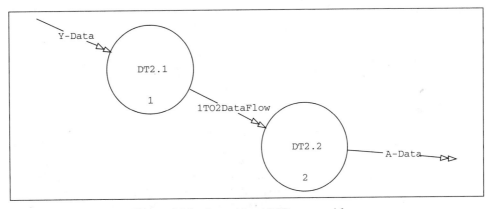

Figure 4.16 Second-level DFD – general form.

Once again there must be flow balance between a parent (DT2) and its child.

The outcome of the DFD design stage is a multi-level diagram showing, in layered form (Figure 4.17), the:

- function of the software, as a set of data transformations
- interrelationships of the DTs
- data flow of the software system, both external and internal

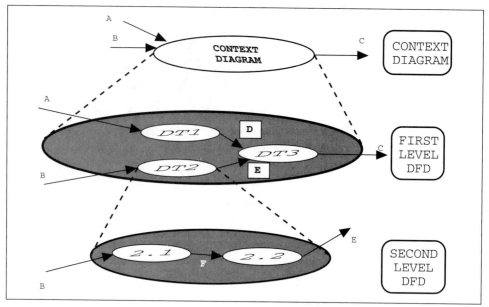

Figure 4.17 DFD levelling and balancing.

We could, of course, level any of the DTs of the first-level DFD. This applies also at second level, third level, and so on, until finally further decomposition is pointless. The lowest level DT is usually called an 'atomic' or 'primitive' process.

4.4.2 A simple illustration

Let us reinforce concepts of DFD design by looking at a simple but concrete example. The starting point is the system specification. From the information given in this we can produce the context diagram. For example, take the following part specification of a marine propulsion control system:

> The propulsion system contains within it one controller per shaft set. It (the controller) is required to set and control shaft speed and propeller pitch in accordance with bridge commands. Pitch control is achieved by issuing pitch demand signals to the propeller pitch actuator. Speed control is carried out by generating fuel demand signals for the propulsion gas turbine. Actual pitch (measured value) is obtained from a pitch sensor fitted to the propeller unit. Actual shaft speed is measured by a tacho fitted to the propeller shaft. The input command to the controller is demanded power. This is produced by a sensor fitted to the bridge power lever.

Using this we are in a position to produce the system context diagram (Figure 4.18).

The context diagram is a *most* important one; do not be fooled by its apparent simplicity. It gives you the opportunity to describe diagramatically the key aspects of the complete system. Now it is easy to pose essential questions, such as:

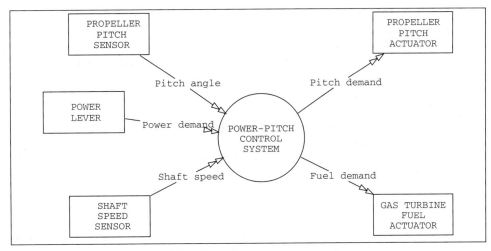

Figure 4.18 Example system – context diagram.

- Have any external items been omitted?
- Have any items been included which should not be present?
- Are all input and output signals present (and correct)?
- What are the attributes of the external devices?
- What are the attributes of the various signals?
- Precisely how does the software interact with the external devices?

It can be very useful to perform a design review on completing the context diagram. Misunderstandings and misconceptions are easily and quickly sorted out at this stage. And, after all, there isn't much point in designing and building the wrong software system.

Assuming that the context diagram is correct, the first-level DFD is designed (Figure 4.19).

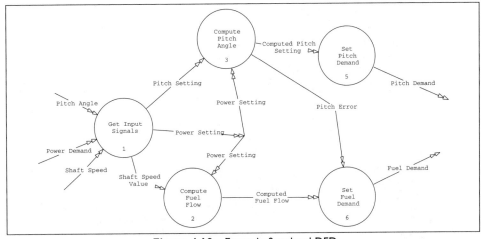

Figure 4.19 Example first-level DFD.

From this it can be seen that the child/parent flows are balanced. This particular diagram was produced using a CASE tool which automated the checking process. Such tools don't prevent mistakes being made, but they are very effective at flagging them up. One small point; the DT numbering has been done automatically by the case tool.

The leftmost DT, `Get Input Signals`, takes in `Pitch Angle`, `Power Demand` and `Shaft Speed` signals. Using these it computes `Pitch Setting`, `Power Setting` and `Shaft Speed` Values. These last two are input to `Compute Fuel Flow`, which generates the data flow `Computed Fuel Flow`. The DT `Compute Pitch Angle` generates `Computed Pitch Setting` and `Pitch Error` using the inputs `Pitch Setting` and `Power Setting`.

Study this diagram until you feel at home with the notation. Then try to decide exactly how the system should work. This example is not intended to explain how power–pitch control systems work. No, it sets out to show just how much information is carried on the DFD. Even with no knowledge of the system under study you should be able to deduce that:

(a) There are two major computing operations: `Pitch Demand` and `Fuel Demand`.
(b) There are five major computing functions. Three are concerned with input–output interfacing.
(c) There is a single data acquisition function, `Get Input Signals`.
(d) The pitch demand signal is a function only of pitch and power settings. It does not depend on speed values.
(e) The fuel demand signal depends primarily (it would appear) on shaft speed and power setting. However, it is modified by the pitch system via the `Pitch Error` value.

Observe how clear naming makes it so much easier to understand a diagram. Any extra typing pays for itself many times over in the life of a project. Also, it is recommended that a functional description is produced for each and every DT (quite different from other mainstream methods which do this only for the primitives). More on this in a moment.

The design of Figure 4.19 is not unique. Give the same problem to three designers and the results are unlikely to be the same. This comment is made to highlight that DFD design is a creative process, something that can't be automated. So if at times you find yourself struggling to arrive at a satisfactory solution, don't worry. Design is rarely easy. Moreover, you can't design software for embedded systems without having a good understanding of the system itself.

It is a good rule always to complete each diagram before performing any levelling. You don't *have* to do this of course, but then you don't *have* to wear car seat belts.

The whole point of the levelling technique is to let us apply top-down stepwise refinement to the design. Here we decide to level the DT `Compute Fuel Flow`, producing its child DFD (Figure 4.20).

Once again parent/child data flows must be balanced. Observe here an example of a split flow, `Power Setting`. This same flow is used by two DTs, `Compute Fuel`

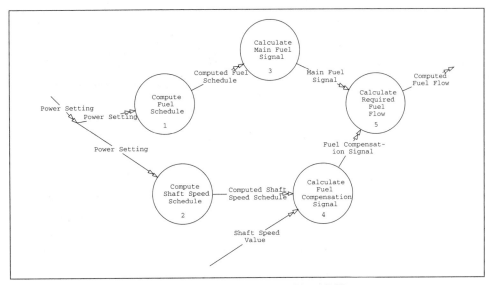

Figure 4.20 Example second-level DFD.

Schedule and Compute Shaft Speed Schedule. Study the DFD to see how much sense you can make of it. Decide for yourself just how much good naming helps this process (there are always those who prefer cryptic comments, but then masochism is still fashionable in some circles). You should find that you end up with a good overall understanding of the design. However, specific and/or detailed points remain unclear. For instance, exactly what computation is carried out by the DT Compute Fuel Schedule? How and why do we calculate the fuel compensation signal? And so on. It should be obvious that a DFD must be supported by extra information: the data transformation description or *specification*.

4.5 Describing data transformations – the PSpec

4.5.1 *The essential pairing*

A data transformation symbol and the description (specification) of its function form an inseparable pair (Figure 4.21).

As pointed out earlier, a DT without a corresponding specification leaves us with much incomplete information. And a specification without a corresponding DT is somewhat nonsensical. Note in passing that 'DT specification', 'process specification', 'PSpec' and 'mini-spec' all mean the same thing when applied to a primitive transformation. However, in this text, PSpec only will be used, for consistency and simplicity. Further, *any* DT at *any* level in the DFD structure can have an associated PSpec. Another view of the topic: a PSpec is to a DT what a data sheet is to an integrated circuit.

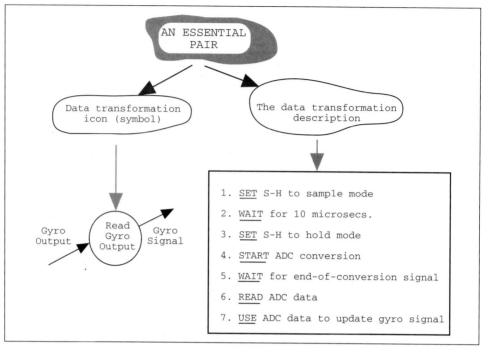

Figure 4.21   The DT and its specification – textual style.

4.5.2   Text descriptions

In Figure 4.21, the DT Read Gyro Output computes Gyro Signal, the input being Gyro Output. A straightforward way to describe the function of the DT is simply to write it out – a text specification. Text style is a matter of personal choice, frequently (in the early stages) being quite informal. In some situations it may be better to substitute or augment this with a more formal format. Some form of structured English should be used, structures being limited to:

(a) sequence (Figure 4.21 is a good example)
(b) selection:
    IF Temperature is greater than Set Point
    THEN Increase Flow
    ELSE Decrease Flow
(c) iteration (repetition):
    Activate master alarm UNTIL accept button is pressed

The purpose of this is to make the PSpec clear, unambiguous and complete.

You may also wish to define explicitly what conditions must be met for a transformation to be valid. This is especially important where mathematical operations are involved. Further, it can be very useful to specify conditions after a transformation has executed. These are called *pre-conditions* and *post-conditions*. What we say with the pre-condition is that 'these conditions must be satisfied before starting the computation. Otherwise it won't work correctly'. What the post-condition says is that 'provided the pre-conditions were met, and the computation is completed, these results are guaranteed'. The following is a simple example:

PSpec for `Compute Flow Rate`

Input:	Differential Pressure (DP)
Output:	Flow rate (Q)
Calculation:	$Q = K_1 \sqrt{DP}$
Pre-condition:	$0 \leq DP \leq 100$
Operation:	$Q = K_1 \sqrt{DP}$
Post-condition:	$0 \leq Q \leq 10$

Integration of the DT and its specification is highly desirable (in our view, mandatory). This is yet one more area where CASE tools come into their own.

Whatever format is used, the key questions are:

- Is the function clearly expressed?
- Are there any ambiguities in the specification?
- Is the PSpec ambivalent?
- Is it complete?

If the answers to these are satisfactory, then you've done a good job. Unfortunately, there are many specifications which are near-incomprehensible in text form (insurance policies, perhaps?). Take the DT and transformation specification of Figure 4.22, for example.

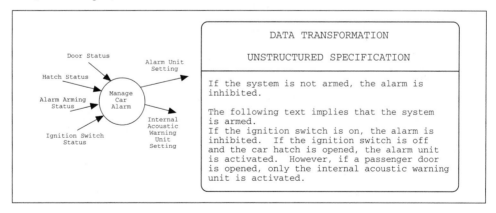

Figure 4.22   Example of a complex DT specification.

This is part of the DFD design for a car alarm system. The DT has four inputs and two outputs, together with a rather complex specification. Is it easy to understand this? Well, it does take very careful reading. Is it easy to misunderstand the specification? Yes, if you aren't fairly careful. The basic problem is that we have a number of items which have a complex relationship – the brain has difficulty in coping with this.

Using a formal metalanguage will ease the problem, but only up to a point. A better solution is to define the transformation using diagrams or/and tables.

4.5.3 The decision tree

A decision tree is a pictorial way of describing condition(s) – and associated results or consequences – in complex logic-type problems (Figure 4.23).

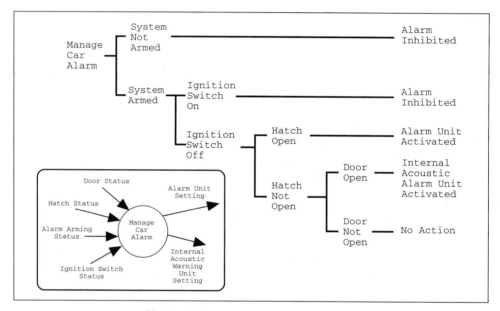

Figure 4.23   A decision tree specification.

This is the tree equivalent of the text specification of Figure 4.22. To read this diagram we start at the root, the point identified as `Manage Car Alarm`. Two branches run out from this, denoted by the conditions `System Not Armed` and `System Armed`. The diagram shows that these are mutually exclusive; only one route can be traversed. Here we have a decision point: which branch should be taken? If the condition is that the system is not armed, then the consequence is that the alarm is inhibited. However, if the system *is* armed, then yet another decision must be made. Is the ignition switch on or off? If it is on, the alarm is to be inhibited. If not? Well, I'm sure you can work the rest out for yourself. This, in itself, will demonstrate how effective decision trees are, and also how easy they are to use.

It can be seen that the input signals to the DT are used in the decision-making process. Output signal values are determined by the results of such decisions. What we have here, then, is a graphical description of a combinational logic machine. We are used to specifying combinational logic devices using truth tables. Now for their software counterpart.

4.5.4   *Decision tables*

The information of Figure 4.23 can be given in tabular form, the so-called decision table (Figure 4.24).

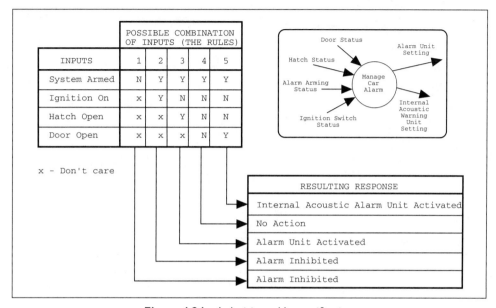

Figure 4.24   A decision table specification.

Here all inputs are listed on a row by row basis. They are organized so that the first decision corresponds to the first row, next decision to the second, and so on. Be aware that there isn't a unique layout for decision tables; you will find many variations in use. In this example all questions require a Yes/No answer – they are binary valued. This keeps the example simple. Of course, in practice inputs may be multi-valued.

Every possible valid combination of inputs is shown, organized as a set of columns. Each combination (column) is called a rule. When the rule is confirmed (the conditions are satisfied) an appropriate response is generated. In the example here for instance, when the system is armed, all other conditions are irrelevant ('don't care'). Rule 1 is satisfied, and the response is Alarm Inhibited. Read through the table carefully, checking to see that it is correct and makes sense.

You will see from Figure 4.24 that there are four inputs and five valid rules. If we were to form a table which considers *all* possible combinations, this would have 16 columns (for n binary-valued items, there are 2^n possible rules). This makes for a more complex table, one which is more difficult to understand. It does, however, make the designer consider the effects of invalid combinations. Generally it is most useful to do this when analysing and defining system behaviour. Then it can be reduced to hold only valid combinations when specifying DTs during software design.

Table 4.2 Compact form of decision table.

Inputs	Possible combination of inputs (the rules)				
	1	2	3	4	5
System Armed	N	Y	Y	Y	Y
Ignition On	X	Y	N	N	N
Hatch Open	X	X	Y	N	N
Door Open	X	X	X	N	Y
Actions					
Internal Acoustic Alarm Unit Activated					✔
No Action				✔	
Alarm Unit Activated			✔		
Alarm Inhibited	✔	✔			

A more compact form of the decision table is shown in Table 4.2.

Here the word 'ACTION' has the same meaning as 'RESPONSE' in Figure 4.24. The table is straightforward to use. When a particular rule is met, the resulting action is noted by ticking the rule/action intersection.

Which to use – tree diagram or decision table? Without having an integrated graphics editor, producing tree diagrams is a problem. And they may become rather large. In contrast the decision table is compact and easy to produce using modern word processors. Unfortunately, its very compactness makes it quite 'dense', and thus more difficult to follow. In the end it's a matter of personal choice.

4.5.5   Graphs, diagrams and maths

In engineering, information is produced and recorded in many forms. One very widely used way to show relationships between variables is to draw a graph. There is no reason why these shouldn't be used as part of the PSpecs. In fact, where appropriate, they should be positively encouraged. Consider Figure 4.20, for instance, where we have the DTs Compute Fuel Schedule and Compute Shaft Speed Schedule. Such schedules are best described in graph form, as in Figure 4.25. The value of this figure is self-evident.

Now don't forget that we are involved with the design of embedded systems, and that each area of technology uses diagrams and notation specific to that particular area. For example, Figure 4.26 is part of a control loop diagram as used by a control engineer.

If a single DT implements this function, then use the diagram as part of its PSpec.

There are many times in engineering and scientific applications that we express our requirements mathematically. So, if a DT implements such a requirement, put the details in the PSpec (Figure 4.27).

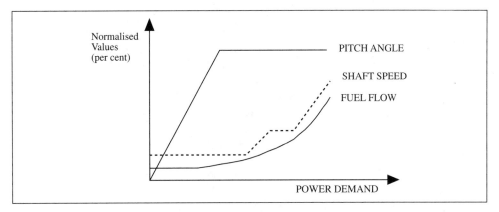

Figure 4.25 Graphical specification.

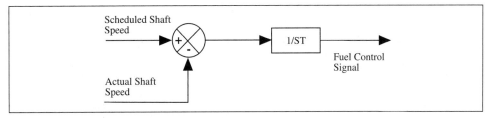

Figure 4.26 Control diagram specification.

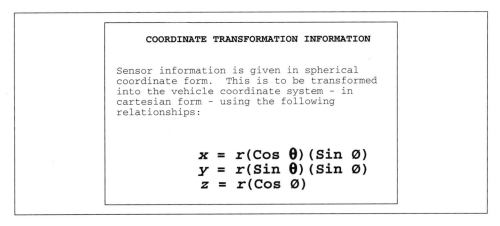

Figure 4.27 Mathematical specification.

4.5.6 PSpecs – a last comment

The PSpec is an integral part of DFD design. It defines precisely (we hope) what the application software is supposed to achieve. How can we ever hope to check the validity and performance of the final code without having objective test data?

You have seen here a variety of ways to specify DTs. Different problems require different solutions; pick the most appropriate one. And bear in mind these are not mutually exclusive. Use any combination that makes sense. If possible, define (and then use) a rigorous format for the overall structure of PSpecs. You may find that your CASE tool provides the basis for such a structure. And don't start nit-picking on detailed points. That's merely counterproductive.

So far, so good. We've built a DFD (levelled as desired), specified all DTs, and named all data flows and data stores, which is fine. However, essential information is still missing: the meaning and make-up of the data itself.

4.6   Describing the data – the data dictionary

4.6.1   Introduction

Part of a DFD for a robotic controller is shown in Figure 4.28.

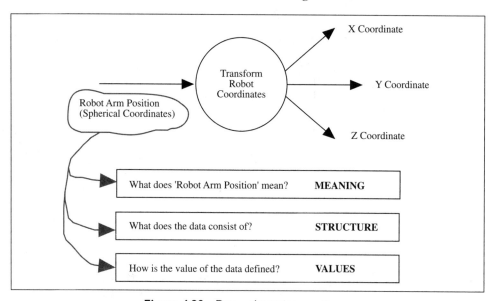

Figure 4.28   Data – the major questions.

The DT, Transform Robot Coordinates, takes in the input signal Robot Arm Position. It carries out the required computation (defined in the PSpec), and produces outputs X Coordinate, Y Coordinate and Z Coordinate. That's clear enough. But what precisely does Robot Arm Position mean? What does it consist of? What values can it take? Thus any piece of data has three essential qualities:

* meaning
* structure
* values

It is impossible to complete a design unless all three are known.

Now we have to decide:

- how to describe the data and its attributes
- where to put this information

Let us first deal with the second question – where to put the information. Describing the data is covered in the next section.

If you wanted to find the meaning of a word, where would you look? In a dictionary, of course. What we do in DFD design is to use exactly the same concept by having a 'data dictionary'. All data items are recorded in our data dictionary, together with their attributes. This means, of course, that each project has its own data dictionary. This also means that, at the start of a project, it is empty. At the end of a project it should list all data used within the design. Moreover, we would expect a CASE tool to automatically link a DFD to its related data dictionary.

4.6.2   Data – meaning, structure and values

How should data be described? Like the PSpec, a mix of formal and informal techniques can be used. There is no unique way of specifying data. However, the notation given here (or close cousins) is widely used. It has its roots in the Backus–Naur form (BNF) metalanguage and the work of Tom DeMarco.

The set of symbols used in the data dictionary of this text is given in Table 4.3.

Table 4.3 Data dictionary notation.

Symbol	Meaning
* *	Comment delimiters
=	Is made up of
+	Together with (concatenation)
[|]	Select one of
{ }	Iteration
( )	Option
" "	Literal

First there are the comment delimiters. Any text written within these is treated as informal information. It isn't part of the formal description of the data. However, in practice, it can be one of the most useful parts of the data dictionary entry. An example is shown in Figure 4.29.

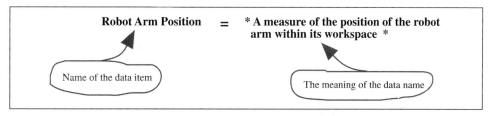

Figure 4.29   Specifying the meaning of data.

Normally we are free to include comments anywhere in the dictionary entry.

Some examples illustrating how data structures may be described formally are given in Figure 4.30.

```
Robot Arm Position  =  r  +  θ  + φ

                    r  =  Radius
                    θ  =  Azimuth angle
                    φ  =  Elevation angle


    Nitrogen Pressure    =[Main Tank Pressure | Reserve Tank
                                                Pressure    ]

    Shaft Torque         =1{Strain Gauge Output}100

    Serial Data = Receiver Address + Data Word + (Sender Address)

    Hydraulic Alarm = "ALARM - Loss of CPP Hydraulic Pressure"
```

Figure 4.30   Specifying the structure of data – typical examples.

These demonstrate that the basic data description structures are those of sequence, selection or iteration.

The first entry defines `Robot Arm Position` to consist of three individual items, that is it is a composite data unit. It can be read as 'Robot Arm Position is made up of (consists of) r and θ and ϕ'. The following three lines then explain what these items are.

The second entry states that `Nitrogen Pressure` consists of *either* Main Tank Pressure *or* Reserve Tank Pressure.

In the third entry we see that `Shaft Torque` consists of a number of items defined as `Strain Gauge Output`. The minimum number is 1, the maximum being 100. This is a shorthand way of writing:

```
Shaft Torque = Strain Gauge Output + Strain Gauge Output + ...
```

Entry four shows that `Serial Data` consists of `Receiver Address` and `Data Word` and, optionally, `Sender Address`. This construct may seem redundant; after all it could be written as `0{Sender Address}1`. We use it to show clearly that it is something which may be present or absent; it is not merely an iterated item.

The final entry is frequently used, for instance, to define information which will be displayed. Here it specifies that `Hydraulic Alarm` consists of the literal text `Alarm – Loss of CPP Hydraulic Pressure`.

At this point the meaning and structure of the data has been described. We are now left with the final task, defining its value. Value specifications consist of a number of components (Figure 4.31).

It is important to recognize that the actual make-up of a value specification will depend very much on the application.

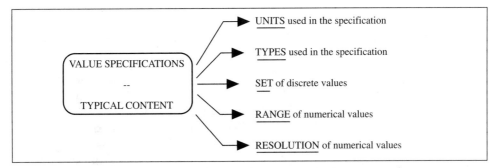

Figure 4.31   Value specifications – general content.

Let us put all these aspects together. A (part) example for the `Robot Arm Position` is given in Figure 4.32. This should be self-explanatory.

```
Robot Arm Position = * A measure of the position of the
                       robot arm within its workspace *

                    r + Θ + Φ

r = * range value: units - metres
                   range - 0 to 1
                   resolution - 0.001
                   Numerical type - floating point *

Θ = * Azimuth value: units - degrees
                     range - 0 to 180
                     resolution - 0.1
                     Numerical type - floating point *

Φ = * Elevation value: units - degrees
                       range - 0 to 360
                       resolution - 0.1
                       Numerical type - floating point *
```

Figure 4.32   Specification example 1.

A quite different system is shown in Figure 4.33.

This is a liquid storage tank which is fitted with a number of float switches. The output from these is fed into a computer-based data collection unit. This produces and transmits an output signal `Main Tank Level`. The data dictionary explains what this output signal is (the commented text), defining it to be a data byte. It shows that `Main Tank Level` consists of one of five items, `Extra Low` OR `Low` OR `Normal` OR `High` OR `Extra High`. Each item is further described in terms of its bit pattern.

Now, this last aspect warrants further discussion. Bit patterns are very detailed features. Therefore it is highly unlikely that we would define this at the early stages of a design. The initial entries are more general, more system-oriented. As the design progresses this information is elaborated and refined. Thus the data dictionary must be kept up to date at all times for maximum benefit.

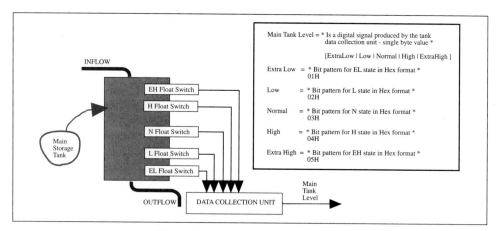

Figure 4.33   Specification example 2.

4.6.3 Stored data

Data which is stored must also be defined. Strictly speaking, we detail the *contents* of the stores. The data items will, of course, already have dictionary entries derived from the DFD data flows. It is important to ensure that the contents listing and the input–output flows balance up. This is yet another action which is child's play to a CASE tool.

4.6.4 Data dictionary entries – comment

It is surprising how large the data dictionary can become by the end of a design. Trying to deal with this manually is extremely difficult. Don't even think about doing it. If you haven't got a CASE tool, then at least use a database package. However, the integration facilities of the CASE tool make it a far better choice. It should, for instance:

- automatically link the DFD to the data dictionary
- provide a standard template for data entries
- allow you to check that all data items are entered in the dictionary
- enable you to browse through the dictionary, searching for particular items or specific data groups
- check from the dictionary where the data items are used
- prevent you from defining an item more than once
- check that formal definitions comply with the metalanguage rules

The rest is up to you.

Review

After studying this chapter you should now:

- recognize the strengths and weaknesses of structure charts
- understand what DFD design methods set out to achieve
- understand the basic rules for the building of DFDs
- know the role of data transformations, data flows, data stores, terminators, PSpecs and the data dictionary
- know how to specify data
- know how to specify a data transformation
- appreciate the ways by which PSpecs can be expressed
- feel confident to tackle a DFD design, starting with the context diagram, using a top-down approach
- understand that levelling is an essential part of this approach

Three particular questions are frequently raised by newcomers to DFD design:

- How detailed should a design be?
- How many DTs ('bubbles') should there be at any one level?
- How many levels should a design have?

Like structure chart design, these have no simple answers – distrust highly prescriptive rules. It all depends on your application. But, to get you going, here is some general guidance.

How detailed should a design be?
Your DFD design should emphasize what the system does and how it works – not how the software itself is structured. Check that your solution *does* fully describe the software system. Make sure that it is complete – that there are no missing bits that have to get 'magicked' in at a later stage – and verify its correctness by talking a colleague through the design itself.

How many DTs ('bubbles') should there be at any one level?
Coupling and cohesion are good guides here, as it isn't just a matter of numbers. Ask yourself the following questions. Have the DTs clear, well-defined and sensible functions (cohesion)? Do the DT interconnections, the data flows, remind you of a spider's web (coupling)? Is it easy for others to quickly grasp the content and function of the design? The famous 'magical number 7±2' is a good guide here (there should be between 5 and 9 bubbles), but please use common sense.

How many levels should a design have?
The overall design approach here uses DFDs and SCs as complementary techniques (more of that shortly). As a result, highly detailed aspects can be deferred until the module structure chart is designed. This is quite different from traditional DFD design. Experience (of small to medium-size embedded systems) shows that few

designs have fewer than four levels. Rarely do we exceed seven.

Let us assume that you understand all the ideas laid out in this chapter. Let us also assume that you have successfully completed a DFD design. But where do you go from here? Good question. The answer to that is the subject of Chapter 5.

Exercises

For the scenarios listed below, produce context diagrams and DFDs as appropriate.

4.1 A jet-pipe temperature (JPT) control system on a gas turbine engine protects against excess temperature by:

- measuring JPT temperature
- linearizing the signal
- checking signal validity
- filtering the signal
- comparing the result with a preset upper limit
- reducing engine fuel flow if this is exceeded (the reduction is proportional to the excess temperature)

4.2 A car is fitted with an automatic cruise control system. It operates by:

- measuring the desired cruising speed (set by the driver)
- measuring the actual speed
- comparing the actual and desired speeds to form an error signal
- changing engine fuel flow in response to the error signal so as to eliminate the error (and so hold speed at the desired value)

4.3 A trip computer on a vehicle can calculate various journey parameters. It:

- measures fuel flow rate (gallons per hour)
- measures speed (miles per hour)
- computes total fuel used
- computes distance travelled
- computes fuel consumption
- keeps a note of maximum speed attained on the journey

5

Design using DFD techniques:

Simple input–compute–output systems

In this chapter all design features discussed so far are brought together in one example. This system is based on a real application. Although it is a simple one, it is large enough to demonstrate the power of a professional design approach. It includes the use of:

- system diagrams and specifications
- context and data flow diagrams
- process specifications (PSpecs)
- the data dictionary
- module structure charts

At this stage we shall limit ourselves to a relatively straightforward software structure, the 'input–compute–output' type. More complex ones are left until later.

5.1 Basic objectives and methods

Systems having the fundamental structure of Figure 5.1 are here described as 'input–compute–output' types.

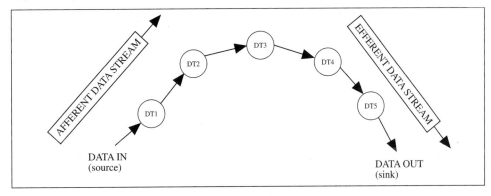

Figure 5.1 Simple input–compute–output system.

As shown, data generated by some source is acquired by the computer system, being input by DT1. Computations are performed within the machine, final results being output by DT5. The input data stream is often called the *afferent* flow, the output being the *efferent* flow. Note that all input and output flows are here designated as 'data', irrespective of their actual system function.

One of our basic objectives is to develop a rigorous DFD–SC–Code transformation strategy. Now, SC–code transformation has already been dealt with. But we still need to define how module structure charts can be developed using DFD design information. Moreover, the approach used must be:

- logical
- consistent
- traceable

The method defined here has a number of clearly defined steps.

1. Each DT maps across to a module, this being implemented as a subprogram (Figure 5.2).

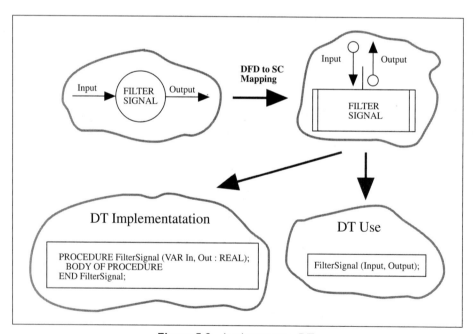

Figure 5.2   Implementing a DT.

Inputs and outputs normally translate to data or control couples. These in turn are realized as subprogram parameters. Strictly speaking, the subprogram fulfils the requirements of the PSpec.

2. The top-level DFD generates levels 0 and 1 of the structure chart (Figure 5.3).
3. Each level of a decomposed DFD generates a set of modules (Figure 5.4).

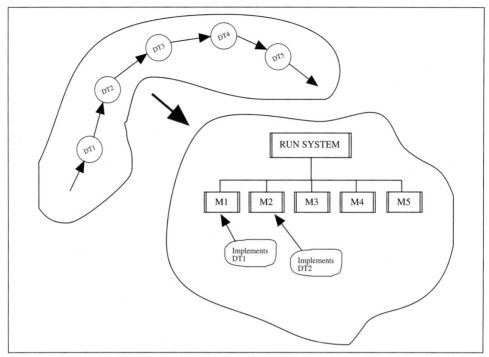

Figure 5.3   From DFD to module SC – top level.

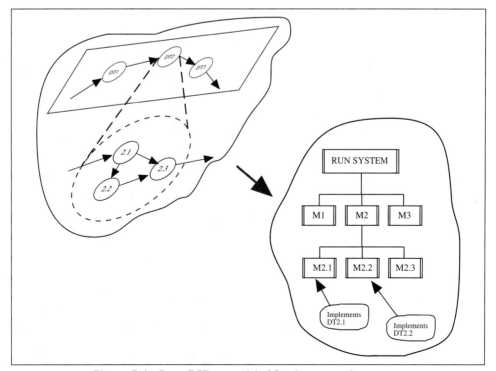

Figure 5.4   From DFD to module SC – decomposed structures.

4. The resulting modules are children of the higher-level module generated by the parent DT.
5. Module ordering is defined by the DFD ordering. If necessary, the designer must specify the ordering of modules using the structure chart (see Figure 5.4). In effect, the major purpose of the SC is to add structure to the functional description of the system.

One word of warning: be consistent in applying these guidelines. They *are* prescriptive, and hence may well affect your design decisions. But the benefits of using this method far outweigh its disadvantages. Now let us see how these rules can be applied to a real system.

5.2 The design objective – valve actuator test unit

5.2.1 Introduction

One component of a gas turbine engine is a fuel modulating valve driven by an electro-mechanical actuator (Figure 5.5).

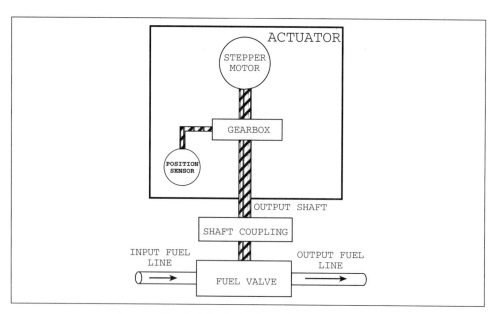

Figure 5.5 Fuel valve and actuator.

The purpose of this unit is to set the amount of fuel delivered to the engine, and thus its power output. It forms part of the computer-based control system of the engine. One function of this system is to control engine power automatically in response to operator demands. It does this by modulating the amount of fuel supplied to the engine.

From the point of view of the electrical system the actuator consists of a drive motor and a position sensor (Figure 5.6).

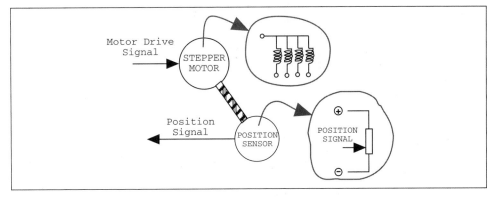

Figure 5.6 Actuator – electrical components.

The motor drives the output shaft via a mechanical gearbox, the shaft position being measured by an attached sensor. Motive power is provided by a stepper motor; position sensing is done using a rotary potentiometer.

It is required to develop a PC-based test unit for the valve actuator (Figure 5.7).

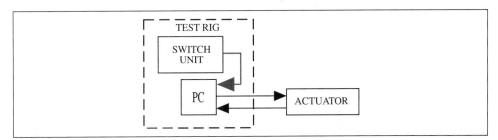

Figure 5.7 Actuator test system.

The test unit is to provide automatic closed-loop position control of the actuator. Position commands are input via a switch unit, this emulating a parallel data interface of the real system. Starting the test program is done by the operator via the PC's keyboard. The current actuator position is to be displayed on the PC's monitor. After this all functions are carried out automatically until the system is powered down.

This, then, is the bare bones of the requirements specification. Much system-level work remains to be done before detailed design commences. Systems design forms an essential part of real-time systems development, defining the objectives of the embedded computer. As an engineer you must design software which meets such system requirements. It is rarely acceptable to do it the other way round: that is, to change system objectives to cater for inadequate software (though this has been known to happen).

5.2.2 Actuator and rig specification

(a) Actuator

Valve closing: shaft downward travel
Valve opening: shaft upward travel
Travel (stroking) time: 5 s
Travel distance: 50 mm
Run-out speed (slew rate): 5 mm/s
Large signal bandwidth: 0.032 Hz
Small signal bandwidth (approx.): 3 Hz

(b) Motor

Drive: 4 phase stepper motor
Voltage: 12 V d.c.
Current: 500 mA per phase

(c) Position sensor

Type: rotary potentiometer, geared to shaft
Rotation: clockwise for shaft downward travel; anticlockwise for shaft upward travel
Total angular travel: 3600 degrees (10 turns)
Signal: Fully clockwise → 10 V d.c.; fully anti-clockwise → 0 V d.c.

(d) Switch unit

Switch type: on/off
On: set input to logic 1
Off: set input to logic 0
No. of switches: 8
Switch function: define demanded position
Note: external circuitry allows the operator to first set the demanded position and then feed it to the PC.

(e) Hardware (PC) interfacing

A standard plug-in board is available for use in this project. It houses the required set of interfaces.

(f) Software interfaces

(i) Stepper motor drive

Motor speed and direction	Data bit pattern
Maximum clockwise	1001 1111
Stopped	0000 0000
Maximum anticlockwise	0001 1111

Bit 7, the most significant bit (MSB), sets the direction. Bits 0–5 set the speed. There is a linear relationship between the value defined by these bits and the speed of the motor.

(ii)   Position sensor
   Fully clockwise (valve closed): 1111 1111
   Fully anticlockwise (valve open): 0000 0000
   Coding: straight binary
   The signal is linear over the range of sensor movement.
   Max. rate of change of signal = 256 bits in 5 s = 1 bit in 19.5 ms
(iii)   Switch unit
   Valve demanded position:
   fully closed: 1111 1111
   fully opened: 0000 0000

Coding: straight binary

5.2.3   *Control system specification*

The basic control loop function is illustrated in Figure 5.8.

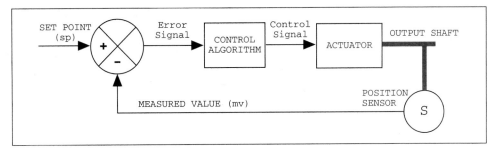

Figure 5.8   Basic control loop.

Here the actuator's demanded position (set point – sp) is compared with its actual position (measured value – mv). Any resulting error is processed by the control algorithm to produce the actuator control signal. This signal drives the actuator so as to reduce the error to zero (and so move the actuator to its demanded position). Initial studies have indicated that a simple non-linear 'bang-bang' controller is good enough for this application. Thus the control algorithm has the form specified in Figure 5.9.

Here the error signal produces no output control signal until it exceeds an upper threshold (T_u) value. At this point full output signal is switched on. This causes the motor to run at full speed, so reducing the error. When the error falls to the lower threshold (T_l) point, the motor is switched off.

The difference between the positive and negative upper switching points is called the dead zone (dz); that between the corresponding upper and lower switching points is the hysteresis (hys).

Studies of the engine installation have predicted that mechanically induced sensor noise may be encountered. This is likely to fall in the range 5–10 Hz. Thus a digital plant noise filter is to be incorporated in the feedback (data acquisition) path.

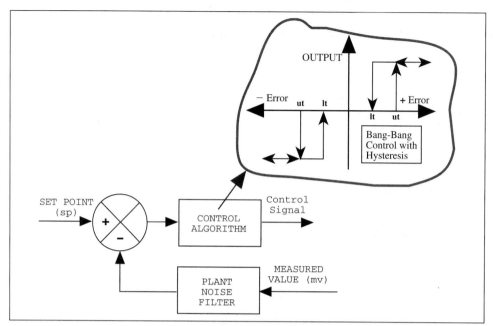

Figure 5.9   Controller function.

From a control point of view, the system must meet the following specifications:

(a) Control law
    On–off switching
    Switching points:
    Initial settings are dead zone = ± 5% of travel (± 13 bits approx.)
    Hysteresis on switching = 1% of travel (rounded to 3 bits)
(b) Noise filter
    Attenuation at 3 Hz: 0 dB
    Attenuation at 5 Hz: 20 dB minimum
    Attenuation at 10 Hz: 20 dB minimum
(c) Sample rate: initially 50 Hz

5.3   Design – the opening stages

5.3.1   DFD design

Preliminary DFD design begins with the context diagram (Figure 5.10). By now this should be a familiar item.

In this chapter all design diagrams have been produced using the SELECT Yourdon CASE tool. This tool also generates associated documentation, including data dictionary entries (Listing 5.1).

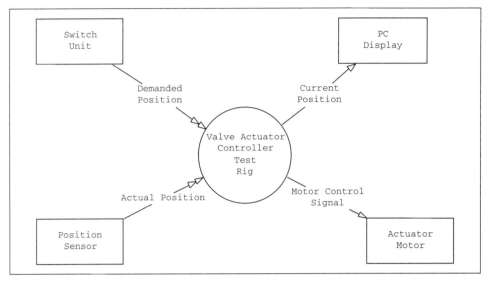

Figure 5.10   Valve actuator system – context diagram.

This shows the dictionary information which has been derived (automatically) from the context diagram. It is now up to the designer to complete this document. Information such as that shown in Listing 5.2 is entered for all relevant items.

Access to the dictionary editor is made from the CASE tool working environment.

The next stage in the design process is to develop the first-level DFD (Figure 5.11).

There are many possible design solutions; this is one offering. Note that it is driven strongly by the system functionality as depicted in Figure 5.9. Thus the DFD model is very closely related to the system processing model. Such an approach is highly recommended, as it leads to low coupling and high cohesion. Further, an essential part of the process is BASE – brain-aided software engineering (a term which, I believe, was first coined by Tim Lister).

Before going much further, one extremely important point needs to be made relating to DFD design. Yourdon and Ward–Mellor techniques (see Bibliography) view data flow diagrams as 'a graphical table of contents for the primitive PSpecs'. Thus, with their approach, the PSpecs drive the code, not the DFDs. In contrast, the philosophy here is that each level of a DFD:

- *does* have meaning
- generates related code

Therefore a full functional description of each level should be provided, as in Listing 5.3.

These two, the DFD and its functional description, should clearly, completely and unambiguously define the required software functions.

Newcomers to the subject often find two aspects of DFD design quite confusing:

```
Project: C:\SELECT\SYSTEM\SENG2\
Title  : Chap 5 design
Date: 24-Oct-94 Time: 16:11

Report: Item Interface

This report contains an alphabetic list of dictionary
items which have inputs and/or output flows.

Name: Actuator Motor
Type: Terminator
Inputs:
      Motor Control Signal [Discrete flow]
Outputs:
      ** None **


Name: PC Display
Type: Terminator
Inputs:
      Current Position [Discrete flow]
Outputs:
      ** None **


Name: Position Sensor
Type: Terminator
Inputs:
      ** None **
Outputs:
      Actual Position [Continuous flow]


Name: Switch Unit
Type: Terminator
Inputs:
      ** None **
Outputs:
      Demanded Position [Continuous flow]


Name: Valve Actuator Controller Test Rig
Type: Context node
Inputs:
      Demanded Position [Continuous flow]
      Actual Position [Continuous flow]
Outputs:
      Current Position [Discrete flow]
      Motor Control Signal [Discrete flow]


—— End of report ——
```

Listing 5.1   Data dictionary – initial entries.

```
Report: Item Details (Brief)

This report contains an alphabetic list of all dictionary
items and any details which have been filled in.

Name: Actual Position
Type: Continuous flow
Bnf:  \Valve actual position signal\
Units: Degrees (volts)
Range: 0-360 (0-10)
Rate: 720 degrees/sec (2 volts/sec)
Accuracy: Better than 9 bit resolution
Comment: This signal is digitized using an 8 bit ADC.   The
accuracy of the sensor does not degrade the performance of
the ADC.
```

Listing 5.2   Data dictionary item – elaborated information.

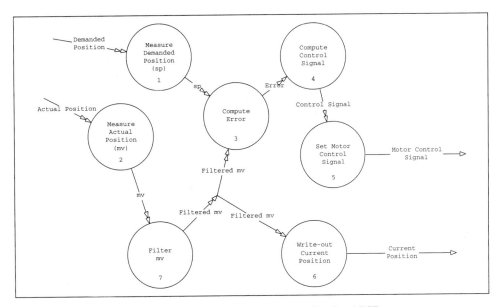

Figure 5.11   Valve actuator system – first-level DFD.

data flow types and the use of data stores. First, how do we distinguish between continuous and time-discrete flows? Second, when do we need to use data stores? Both issues, surprisingly, have their roots in the same problem – the blurring of design and implementation aspects. We know that the software will be implemented on a processor. We also know that a processor is fundamentally a discrete machine. So, logically, from an implementation point of view all internal signals are discrete ones. Further, if they are stored in RAM (which they usually are), there is no need to show data stores.

To deal with these points we need to adjust our thinking, taking a more abstract

```
@IN  = Actual Position
@IN  = Demanded Position
@OUT = Current Position
@OUT = Motor Control Signal

@PSPEC Valve Actuator Controller Test Rig

The Actual Position of the actuator is read in by the DT 'Measure Actual
Position (mv)'.   Its output, 'mv', is fed to the DT 'Filter mv', which
produces a filtered version of this signal.

Demanded Position is acquired by the DT 'Measure Demanded Position
(sp)'.  Its output, 'sp', together with 'Filtered mv', form the inputs to the
DT 'Compute Error'.  This calculates the error between the two values,
producing an output 'Error'.

'Error' is processed by 'Compute Control Signal' in accordance with a
predefined control algorithm.  The result of this is the output 'Control
Signal', being input to the DT 'Set Motor Control Signal'.  From this the
DT generates the appropriate Motor Control Signal to set actuator motor
speed.

The filtered version of the measured value, 'Filtered mv', is fed to the DT
'Write-out Current Position'.  Using this information, the DT produces
screen display information Current Position
```

Listing 5.3   Functional description of the first-level DFD.

view of the design. Concept must be separated from implementation. The solution is quite a simple one. Pretend that the controller is a continuous, not a discrete, one. Each DT is implemented using an analogue rather than a digital computer. Now it becomes simplicity itself to distinguish between continuous and discrete flows. Moreover, the reasons for employing data stores will emerge naturally as design progresses.

For this example, no further decomposition of the DFD will be made. Each individual DFD is considered to be a primitive transformation, thus requiring a PSpec. That for the DT MEASURE DEMANDED POSITION (sp) is given in Listing 5.4.

Further, the data dictionary needs to be completed, taking into account the additional (internal) data flows. However, no more will be said concerning these aspects, important as they are. Here our primary purpose is to concentrate on design and implementation features.

5.3.2   Structure chart design

It can be seen (Figure 5.11) that even this simple system has a more complex structure than that of Figure 5.1. Decisions have to be made concerning the execution of particular DTs. For instance, should Demanded Position be read before Actual Position (or vice versa)? It is up to the designer to resolve such points. They must, of course, be taken into account when designing the module structure chart (Figure 5.12).

```
@IN  = Demanded Position
@OUT = sp

@PSPEC Measure Demanded Position (sp)

1. Informal description:
The purpose of this DT is to read-in the actuator Demanded Position
as set by the operator.  It is obtained by reading the test rig
switch unit setting, a parallel binary value (one byte).  Its
attributes are:

  Coding: Straight binary
  Demand for fully open: 0(H)
  Demand for fully closed: FF(H)
  Memory address location of the switch device: TBA

The DT output, sp, represents this value as a real number.


2. Structured specification.

  2.1 Get input signal Demanded Position from operator.
  2.2 Apply rate limiting to the signal.
  2.3 Convert the signal (a byte) to floating point form.
  2.4 Define this value as sp.

Comment: This structured specification is extremely simple because it
does not describe detailed low-level operations.
@
```

Listing 5.4 PSpec for the DT 'MEASURE DEMANDED POSITION (sp)'.

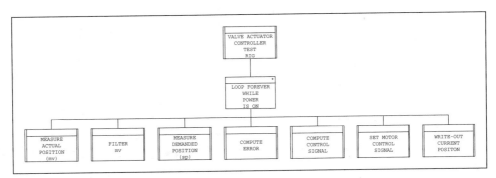

Figure 5.12 Valve actuator system – structure chart.

In fact, the SC enables the designer to define the order of DT execution explicitly. Remember: the design here will eventually be implemented as a *sequential* program; there are no concurrent (parallel) software operations.

What we have in Figure 5.12, then, is the module SC for the first-level DFD. If required, each individual procedure can be extended using SC techniques. In this example we choose to do this to the procedure MEASURE DEMANDED POSITION (sp) (Figure 5.13).

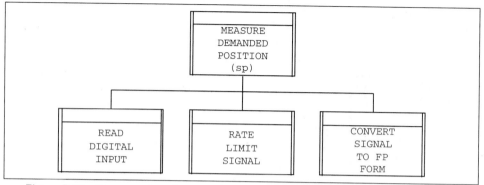

Figure 5.13 Structure chart for procedure MEASURE DEMANDED POSITION (sp).

Here the set point value is read in by the subprogram Read Digital Input. The input signal is then rate limited. Following this it is converted to floating point form.

5.3.3 Code – general structuring and identification of service procedures

The organization and structuring of the code units should be defined *before* writing any source code. However, in doing this you need to take into account the programming language which is to be used. This may (usually does) have a major bearing on subsequent decisions. In this example, the implementation is done in Modula-2. Thus the complete program is built in modular fashion, using program and library modules as appropriate (Figure 5.14).

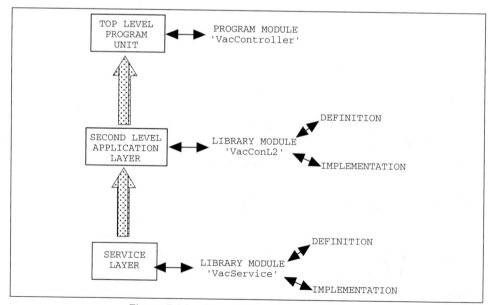

Figure 5.14 Organization of source code units.

To avoid confusion, the word 'module' will, in this section, be taken to mean a Modula-2 module. Software 'machines' will be referred to as procedures.

The highest level, the *top-level* program unit, implements the top level of the structure chart. Sitting below this is the *second-level* layer module, which holds all the procedures used by the top-level module. Feeding into this from the service layer module are the service procedures. All modules apart from the program one are Modula-2 library types. Thus each consists of two parts: Definition and Implementation.

By inspection of the structure chart, the program module is defined to consist of the procedure calls shown in Listing 5.5.

```
MeasureActualPosition
FilterMV
MeasureDemandedPosition
ComputeError
ComputeControlSignal
SetMotorControlSignal
WriteoutCurrentPosition
```

Listing 5.5 Program module procedure calls.

At this stage the actual parameter values are yet to be defined. And this leads to one very important point: parameters of procedures which interact with real-world devices. Take the data transformation Measure Actual Position of Figure 5.11. This has an input data flow Actual Position, its output being mv. It is implemented by the procedure MeasureActualPosition. The question is, what are the actual parameters of this procedure? At first sight the answer would appear to be Actual Position and mv. However, it is impossible for Actual Position to be a parameter. The signal comes from the outside, not the software, world. Thus the complete procedure call in the program module becomes:

MeasureActualPosition (MV);

Likewise, for the DT Set Motor Control Signal, the data flow Motor Control Signal cannot be a parameter. It too represents a signal which interacts with the real (external) world of the processor system.

Hence the basic code of the program module becomes that shown in Listing 5.6.

```
MeasureActualPosition (MV);
FilterMV (MV, FilteredMV);
MeasureDemandedPosition (SP);
ComputeControlSignal (Error, ControlSignal);
SetMotorControlSignal (ControlSignal);
WriteoutCurrentPosition (FilteredMV);
```

Listing 5.6 Basic code of the program module.

Now for the task of defining the service procedures. Here it can be seen that there are two distinct groups: I/O and control-related. As usual, naming is important. However, here we are designing general purpose building blocks. Therefore the names chosen must reflect this property. They *must not* be application-dependent. We use our knowledge of the system to identify the procedures, in this case arriving at the set given in Listing 5.7.

```
(* I/O SERVICE PROCEDURES *)
GetDigitalInput
ReadAnalogueInput
SetMotorSpeed
WriteToScreen

(* CONTROL SERVICE PROCEDURES *)
DoBangBangControl
FilterNoise
```

Listing 5.7 List of service procedures.

These usually have to be parametrized. In doing so, appropriate names must be selected for the formal parameters, as for instance, in Listing 5.8.

```
PROCEDURE GetDigitalInput (VAR DigitalValue : BYTE);
PROCEDURE ReadAnalogueInput (VAR AnalogueValue : BYTE);
PROCEDURE SetMotorSpeed (MotorSpeed : BYTE);
PROCEDURE DoBangBangControl (InputData : REAL;
                            VAR ComputedOutput : REAL);
PROCEDURE FilterNoise (NoisyInput      : REAL;
                       FilterType      : FilType;
                       FilterOrder     : FilOrder;
                       VAR CleanOutput : REAL);
```

Listing 5.8 Parametrized service procedures.

Note that no service procedure has been specified for screen writing activities. In this case we choose to use standard compiler-supplied functions.

5.3.4 Program development

Opening moves

The first stage of the development is the writing of:

- the program module `VacController`
- the second-level module – the definition module `VacConL2`

These are shown in Listings 5.9 and 5.10.

```
MODULE VacController;
FROM VacConL2 IMPORT MeasureActualPosition, FilterMV,
                     MeasureDemandedPosition, ComputeError,
                     ComputeControlSignal,
                     SetMotorControlSignal, WriteoutCurrentPosition;
VAR
    MV                 : REAL;
    SP                 : REAL;
    FilteredMV         : REAL;
    Error              : REAL;
    ControlSignal      : REAL;
BEGIN
    MeasureActualPosition (MV);
    FilterMV (MV, FilteredMV);
    MeasureDemandedPosition (SP);
    ComputeError (SP, FilteredMV, Error);
    ComputeControlSignal (Error, ControlSignal);
    SetMotorControlSignal (ControlSignal);
    WriteoutCurrentPosition (FilteredMV);
END VacController.
```

Listing 5.9   Program module source code.

```
DEFINITION MODULE VacConL2;

PROCEDURE MeasureActualPosition (VAR MV1 : REAL);
PROCEDURE FilterMV (MV1 : REAL;  VAR FilteredMV1 : REAL);
PROCEDURE MeasureDemandedPosition (VAR SP1 : REAL);
PROCEDURE ComputeError (SP1, FilteredMV1 : REAL; VAR Error1 : REAL);
PROCEDURE ComputeControlSignal (Error1 : REAL; VAR ControlSignal1 : REAL);
PROCEDURE SetMotorControlSignal (ControlSignal1 : REAL);
PROCEDURE WriteoutCurrentPosition (FilteredMV1 : REAL);

END VacConL2.
```

Listing 5.10   Second-level definition module source code.

The follow-up – preparing for incremental development

Stage two involves writing a preliminary version of the second-level implementation module VacConL2. The purpose of this is to:

- ensure that the program module can be tested for logical correctness
- check that all second-level procedures required by the program module are present and are used correctly
- provide a starting point for the use of incremental development techniques

The code for this module is given in Listing 5.11.

Observe that each procedure is in effect a dummy operation (a 'dummy test stub'). The code has no relationship to the required operation, it merely generates a text message. Moreover, we aren't yet using any service procedures. This comes

```
IMPLEMENTATION MODULE VacConL2;

FROM SYSTEM IMPORT BYTE;
FROM InOut IMPORT WriteString, WriteLn;

PROCEDURE MeasureActualPosition (VAR MV1 : REAL);
BEGIN
    WriteString ('Measure Actual Position  - DUMMY STUB');
    WriteLn; WriteLn;
END MeasureActualPosition;

PROCEDURE FilterMV (MV1 : REAL; VAR FilteredMV1 : REAL);
BEGIN
    WriteString ('Filter MV  - DUMMY STUB');
    WriteLn; WriteLn;
END FilterMV;

PROCEDURE MeasureDemandedPosition (VAR SP1 : REAL);
BEGIN
    WriteString ('Measure Demanded Position  - DUMMY STUB');
    WriteLn; WriteLn;
END MeasureDemandedPosition;

PROCEDURE ComputeError (SP1, FilteredMV1 : REAL; VAR Error1 : REAL);
BEGIN
    WriteString ('Compute Error  - DUMMY STUB');
    WriteLn; WriteLn;
END ComputeError;

PROCEDURE ComputeControlSignal (Error1 : REAL; VAR ControlSignal1 : REAL);
BEGIN
    WriteString ('Compute Control Signal  - DUMMY STUB');
    WriteLn; WriteLn;
END ComputeControlSignal;

PROCEDURE SetMotorControlSignal (ControlSignal1 : REAL);
BEGIN
    WriteString ('Set Motor Control Signal  - DUMMY STUB');
    WriteLn; WriteLn;
END SetMotorControlSignal;

PROCEDURE WriteoutCurrentPosition (FilteredMV1 : REAL);
BEGIN
    WriteString ('Writeout Current Position  - DUMMY STUB');
    WriteLn; WriteLn;
END WriteoutCurrentPosition;



BEGIN
    WriteString ('THIS MODULE UNDER DEVELOPMENT AND TEST');
    WriteLn; WriteLn; WriteLn;
END VacConL2.
```

Listing 5.11   Second-level implementation module – version 1.

later. Observe also the naming of the formal parameters of the procedures. The convention adopted is for a formal parameter to have the same name as its corresponding actual parameter – but with the addition of a '1'. Hence:

Actual parameter: `Error`
Formal parameter: `Error1`

We could, of course give the corresponding actual and formal parameters *exactly* the same name. However, the method used here eliminates any ambivalence during traceability checks (see later). Furthermore, it is especially helpful should the programmer use global items to eliminate parameter passing (a most dreadful unprofessional practice).

It should be pointed out that this naming technique should be used only at the application level. Remember, the purpose here is to develop major software building blocks which are application-related. The procedures are specialized, not general purpose, ones.

After compiling and linking these three modules the program module may be executed. In this particular example it generates the screen display of Listing 5.12.

```
THIS MODULE UNDER DEVELOPMENT AND TEST
Measure Actual Position   - DUMMY STUB
Filter MV   - DUMMY STUB
Measure Demanded Position   - DUMMY STUB
Compute Error   - DUMMY STUB
Compute Control Signal   - DUMMY STUB

Set Motor Control Signal   - DUMMY STUB

Writeout Current Position   - DUMMY STUB

```

Listing 5.12   Screen display after first test run.

This demonstrates clearly that the program, at the top level, complies with the structure chart design.

Another stage of incremental development
Incremental development can be dealt with in many ways. There are, though, two extremes:

- Extend level by level on the structure chart.
- Take each top-level procedure in turn as a root. Develop the related software by extending from the root down its branches.

Hard and fast rules cannot be laid down; it is very much a matter of personal choice. However, our own experience has shown that development branch by branch is highly effective and easy to handle. To demonstrate this method, the branch having the root `Measure Demanded Position` (Figure 5.13) is now implemented. This leads to a modification of the second-level implementation module to include the procedures:

- `ReadDigitalInput`
- `RateLimitSignal`
- `ConvertToFPForm`

The necessary changes to Listing 5.11 are shown in Listing 5.13.

Here the three procedures listed above are implemented (by declaration), and then used within `MeasureDemandedPosition`. You can see that, at this stage, each one is merely a dummy module. Observe also changes to the text messages of both the module itself and the procedure `MeasureDemandedPosition`. Once the

```
IMPLEMENTATION MODULE VacConL2;


(* * * * * * * * * * * * * * * * * * * * * * * * * * * * * * * * * * * * * * * * * * * * * * * * * * * * * * *)
PROCEDURE ReadDigitalInput (VAR DigitalSetPoint1 : BYTE);
BEGIN
   WriteString ('   Read Digital Input  - DUMMY STUB');
   WriteLn;
END ReadDigitalInput;

PROCEDURE RateLimitSignal (DigitalSetPoint1    : BYTE;
                           VAR LimitedSetPoint1 : BYTE);
BEGIN
   WriteString ('   Rate Limit Signal  - DUMMY STUB');
   WriteLn;
END RateLimitSignal;

PROCEDURE ConvertToFPForm (LimitedSetPoint : BYTE;
                           VAR SP12        : REAL);
BEGIN
   WriteString ('   Convert Signal to FP Form  - DUMMY STUB');
   WriteLn;
END ConvertToFPForm;
(* * * * * * * * * * * * * * * * * * * * * * * * * * * * * * * * * * * * * * * * * * * * * * * * * * * * * * *)


PROCEDURE MeasureDemandedPosition (VAR SP1 : REAL);
BEGIN
   WriteString ('Measure Demanded Position - STARTING');
   WriteLn;
   ReadDigitalInput (DigitalSetPoint);
   RateLimitSignal (DigitalSetPoint, LimitedSetPoint);
   ConvertToFPForm (LimitedSetPoint, SP1);
   WriteString ('Measure Demanded Position - ENDING');
   WriteLn; WriteLn;
END MeasureDemandedPosition;
```

Listing 5.13   Changes to the second-level implementation module.

required recompilation and relinking are carried out, the program may again be executed. In this case the resulting screen display is that shown in Listing 5.14.

```
THIS MODULE UNDER DEVELOPMENT AND TEST
SECOND STAGE OF TESTING


Measure Actual Position  - DUMMY STUB

Filter MV  - DUMMY STUB

Measure Demanded Position - STARTING
   Read Digital Input  - DUMMY STUB
   Rate Limit Signal  - DUMMY STUB
   Convert Signal to FP Form  - DUMMY STUB
Measure Demanded Position - ENDING

Compute Error  - DUMMY STUB

Compute Control Signal  - DUMMY STUB

Set Motor Control Signal  - DUMMY STUB

Writeout Current Position  - DUMMY STUB
```

Listing 5.14   Screen display after second test run.

To continue the branch development, each of the three procedures must now be completed. Before doing that, however, our service procedures must be in place. To do this we form a library module `VacService`, the definition module being given in Listing 5.15.

The information is now becoming quite detailed. However, its meaning should be clear to designers capable of working at such a detailed level. We will not go into implementation details. Let us assume that the implementation code is now written, then compiled, tested and debugged. This enables us to use it in the application program (Listing 5.16).

As before, only the changes to this module are shown. We are now in a position to run the next set of tests, but now using real input data. Of course, some changes must be made to the test scenario, but these are minor.

You might feel that using two procedures, `ReadDigitalInput` and `GetDigitalInput`, is somewhat wasteful. As shown we don't need both; the first merely invokes the second. But there is good justification for this. First, it clearly separates out the application and service aspects of the design. Second, it allows later extension of `ReadDigitalInput` without affecting the existing service procedure. Third, it minimizes the impact on the application if changes are made to the service facilities. These last two points will be demonstrated shortly.

```
DEFINITION MODULE VacService;

FROM SYSTEM IMPORT BYTE;

TYPE
   FilType = (Bessel, Butterworth, Chebyshev);
   FilOrder = (First, Second, Third, Fourth, Fifth,
               Sixth, Seventh, Eight);

(* I/O SERVICE PROCEDURES *)
PROCEDURE GetDigitalInput (VAR DigitalValue : BYTE);
PROCEDURE ReadAnalogueInput (VAR AnalogueValue : BYTE);
PROCEDURE SetMotorSpeed (MotorSpeed : BYTE );

(* CONTROL SERVICE PROCEDURES *)
PROCEDURE DoBangBangControl (InputData       : REAL;
                             VAR ComputedOutput : REAL);
PROCEDURE FilterNoise (NoisyInput    : REAL;
                       FilterType    : FilType;
                        FilterOrder   : FilOrder;
                       VAR CleanOutput : REAL);

END VacService.
```

Listing 5.15   Service procedures – definition module.

```
IMPLEMENTATION MODULE VacConL2;

FROM VacService IMPORT GetDigitalInput,
                       ReadAnalogueInput,
                       SetMotorSpeed,
                       DoBangBangControl,
                       FilterNoise,
                       FilType,
                        FilOrder;

(*********************************************************)
PROCEDURE ReadDigitalInput (VAR DigitalSetPoint1 : BYTE);
BEGIN
   WriteString ('   Read Digital Input  - STARTING');
   GetDigitalInput (DigitalSetPoint1);
   WriteString ('   Read Digital Input  - ENDING');
   WriteLn;
END ReadDigitalInput;

(*********************************************************)
```

Listing 5.16   Second-level implementation module – update 2.

5.4 Modifying the design

5.4.1 Introduction

All real designs will, at some stage in their lives, be modified. Some changes have to be incorporated even before the programs are completed. Others may arise many years after the equipment has entered service. It is well known that these are very time-consuming and costly activities – mainly because so many designers completely ignore upgrading aspects. Software, sadly, is rarely devised with maintenance in mind (it has been suggested that 70% of all software costs are due to maintenance. Moreover, about 50% of this cost is incurred in trying to understand precisely what the existing software does). However, if the original work is well organized and structured, design modification is much easier to deal with.

The purpose of this section is to demonstrate how our approach to software development aids the modification process. It shows how three types of change can be accommodated:

- changes at the service level
- enhancements at the application level – extending application procedures
- major alterations at the application level

5.4.2 Change of service function

Suppose that there is a need to produce a variant on the actuator controller – one where the set point is derived from a two-digit binary-coded decimal (BCD) switch. This, naturally, means that the switch hardware interface has to be redesigned. The question of interest to us, though, is how should this be dealt with in software?

With our present structuring, the modification is quite straightforward. The existing service procedure `GetDigitalInput` is replaced by a new one, `GetBCDdigitalInput`. However, it is very important to have the same interfacing (that is, the procedure parameter) as the original one, as for example:

```
PROCEDURE GetBCDdigitalInput (VAR DigitalValue : BYTE);
```

Then, *at the application level*, replacement is merely a simple exchange (Listing 5.17).

Implementation code for the new service procedure has, of course, to be produced. Before it is used by an application it must be fully developed and tested. Provided the interfaces of the old and new are identical, we shouldn't have problems with the application software (but you can never be 100% certain, of course).

5.4.3 Extending an application procedure

A new operational requirement is added to the specification at a late stage of the project. Limits must be applied to the actuator set point demands to prevent mechanical damage. A review of the design shows that this can be implemented in software. It is decided to modify the procedure `ReadDigitalInput` by putting limit checks within it (Listing 5.18).

```
IMPLEMENTATION MODULE VacConL2;

FROM VacService IMPORT GetBCDdigitalInput,
                       ReadAnalogueInput,
                       SetMotorSpeed,
                       DoBangBangControl,
                       FilterNoise,
                       FilType,
                       FilOrder;

(************************************************************)
PROCEDURE ReadDigitalInput (VAR DigitalSetPoint1 : BYTE);
BEGIN
   WriteString ('  Read Digital Input  - STARTING');
   GetBCDdigitalInput (DigitalSetPoint1);
   WriteString ('  Read Digital Input  - ENDING');
   WriteLn;
END ReadDigitalInput;

(************************************************************)
```

Listing 5.17   Second-level implementation module – update 3.

```
(************************************************************)
PROCEDURE ReadDigitalInput (VAR DigitalSetPoint1 : BYTE);
BEGIN
   WriteString ('  Read Digital Input  - STARTING');
   WriteLn;
   GetBCDdigitalInput (DigitalSetPoint1);

   (* Now applying limits to the input signal *)
   IF ORD(DigitalSetPoint1) < 10H THEN
      DigitalSetPoint1 := 10H;
   ELSIF ORD(DigitalSetPoint) > 0F0H THEN
      DigitalSetPoint1 := 0F0H;
   END; (* of IF *)

   WriteString ('  Read Digital Input  - ENDING');
END ReadDigitalInput;

(************************************************************)
```

Listing 5.18   Extending an application procedure.

From this it can be seen that the demanded position must lie within the bounds 10H and F0H. Note also that this is a rather poor way to write the code; literal values should have been avoided. It is much better practice to use named constants such as LowerLimit and UpperLimit. However, the example illustrates that, if you really feel masochistic, you *can* work at a highly detailed code level.

You should be able to see from this example that our software has a very high degree of stability. Moreover, the modification is not only highly visible; it is also highly localized (and thus much easier to test).

5.4.4 An operational change to the software

At present, our software, if executed, will run in a continuous loop. Unfortunately, there is no control of the timing of the loop (its period – originally specified as 100 ms). Let us assume that precise timing is not required; a few milliseconds jitter in 100 ms is acceptable. In such cases we can use the internal timer of the PC – via simple read and set actions – to control the loop sample time. This item, a fairly detailed one, can be readily included in the design at the SC stage (Figure 5.15).

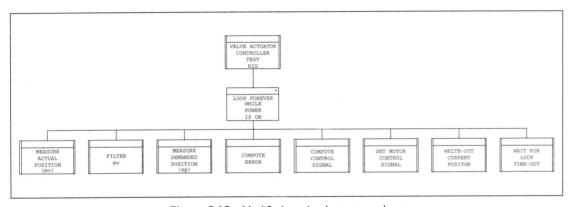

Figure 5.15 Modified top-level structure chart.

It is then a relatively simple task to insert this as a procedure in the program level module.

5.4.5 A major change to the application

During testing it is found that the dynamic response of the actuator is unsatisfactory. Simulation indicates that the problem can be solved by changing the closed-loop control strategy. The bang-bang control function should be replaced by a digital three-term PID controller. A review of Figure 5.11 indicates that one DT only is affected – Compute Control Signal. As a result it is levelled to show more detail (Figure 5.16).

From this it can be seen the control function consists of three sub-functions. These, Compute Derivative Action, Compute Proportional Action and Compute Integral Action, are cascaded together (a series connection). The corresponding structure chart extension for Compute Control Signal is given in Figure 5.17.

As a result the structure of procedure ComputeControlSignal is modified to align it with the SC (Listing 5.19).

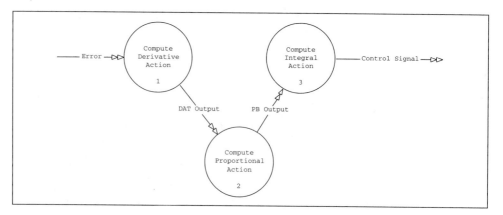

Figure 5.16 Levelled DT Compute Control Signal.

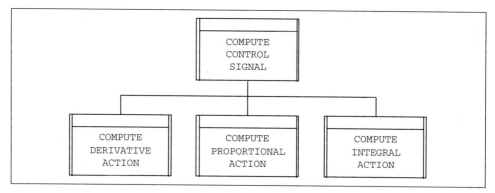

Figure 5.17 SC extension for COMPUTE CONTROL SIGNAL.

Included in Listing 5.19 is the declaration of the three new procedures. You can also see that the import list has been modified. The service procedure DoBangBangControl has been removed as it is no longer used by the application.

Implementation of the three control procedures is, logically, the next stage in the modification process. We, however, will stop at this point in the example. The way forward is clear-cut and doesn't need further explanation.

You may have noticed that the structures of Compute Control Signal and Measure Demanded Position are similar. Yet the example here chose to level the latter one only on the DFD. This is deliberate; it has been done to highlight some important design aspects.

First, all decisions regarding levelling and decomposition should be made by the designer. Some software design methods are based on a set of rigid prescriptive rules. Following these slavishly will eventually lead to trouble. You will find that their downfall is their sheer inflexibility: such rigidity cannot deal with all real design problems.

Second, the depth of levelling of the DFD can be kept to a sensible amount. Very detailed expansion can be done on the SC. Please always keep in mind that the

```
FROM VacService IMPORT GetDigitalInput,
                       ReadAnalogueInput,
                       SetMotorSpeed,
                       FilterNoise,
                       FilType,
                       FilOrder;

VAR
   DAToutput        : REAL;
   PBoutput         : REAL;

PROCEDURE ComputeDerivativeAction (Error2 : REAL; VAR DAToutput1 : REAL);
BEGIN
   WriteString ('  Compute Derivative Action  - DUMMY STUB');
   WriteLn; WriteLn;
END ComputeDerivativeAction;

PROCEDURE ComputeProportionalAction (DAToutput1 : REAL; VAR PBoutput1 :
REAL);
BEGIN
   WriteString ('  Compute Proportional Action  - DUMMY STUB');
   WriteLn; WriteLn;
END ComputeProportionalAction;

PROCEDURE ComputeIntegralAction (PBoutput1 : REAL; VAR ControlSignal23 :
REAL);
BEGIN
   WriteString ('  Compute Integral Action  - DUMMY STUB');
   WriteLn; WriteLn;
END ComputeIntegralAction;

PROCEDURE ComputeControlSignal (Error1 : REAL; VAR ControlSignal1 : REAL);
BEGIN
   WriteString ('Compute Control Signal  - STARTING');
   WriteLn; WriteLn;
   ComputeDerivativeAction (Error1, DAToutput);
   ComputeProportionalAction (DAToutput, PBoutput);
   ComputeIntegralAction (PBoutput, ControlSignal1);
   WriteString ('Compute Control Signal  - ENDING');
END ComputeControlSignal;
```

Listing 5.19 Second-level implementation module – update 4.

objectives of the two diagrams are very different. The DFD shows how the problem is tackled; it is system-oriented. In contrast, the SC defines the structure of the required code implementation; it is solution-oriented. As descriptions become more detailed, you will find that we gradually move from system aspects to implementation issues.

Third, extra levelling of the DFD increases the visibility of the design. This helps considerably at the code implementation and test stage.

5.5   Design traceability

Design traceability is the process of checking that the final code really does implement the required design. It looks for complete consistency across the design, from the first-level DFD to source code via the related DFDs and SCs. Here a CASE tool is extremely helpful, as DFD consistency checking is a standard inbuilt feature. However, DFD to SC tracing is likely to have to be done manually. And, without automated code generators, the SC–code translation checks will also have to be done by hand.

The following steps are given for guidance; no formalized technique is imposed. Further, it assumes that DFD consistency checking is done automatically by your CASE tool.

Check 1
Compare top-level DFD (Figure 5.11), top-level SC (Figure 5.12) and top-level program module (Listing 5.9).

- Is each DT translated to a procedure box on the SC?
- Is the SC procedure ordering correct?
- Is the DT/SC naming consistent?
- Is each SC procedure box translated to a procedure in the program module?
- Is the SC/program module procedure naming consistent?
- Are the procedures in the program module organized as defined by the SC?
- Are all external real-world data items absent from the program module?
- Are all internal (that is, software) data flows of the DFD declared in the program module?
- Are they the correct types?
- Are they used only as procedure actual parameters?
- Are they input to and output from the correct procedures?

Check 2 – Levelled DT
Only one DT, Compute Control Signal, was levelled in this example. Hence the check can only be applied to this one. However, the technique can be applied to any levelled DT. Once again we assume the DFD levels are consistent.

Compare the following:

- levelled DT Compute Control Signal (Figure 5.16)
- SC extension for Compute Control Signal (Figure 5.15)
- program and second-level code modules (listings 5.9 and 5.11, final version)

For simplicity, only part of the design is checked out, the related code being that of Listing 5.20.

- Is each DT translated to a procedure box on the SC?
- Is the SC procedure ordering correct?
- Is the DT/SC naming consistent?
- Is each SC procedure box translated to a procedure in the code module?

```
ComputeControlSignal (Error, ControlSignal);
```

```
PROCEDURE ComputeControlSignal (Error1 : REAL; VAR ControlSignal1 : REAL);
VAR
   DAToutput       : REAL;
   PBoutput        : REAL;

BEGIN
   ComputeDerivativeAction (Error1, DAToutput);
   ComputeProportionalAction (DAToutput, PBoutput);
   ComputeIntegralAction (PBoutput, ControlSignal1);
 END ComputeControlSignal;
```

```
PROCEDURE ComputeDerivativeAction (Error2 : REAL; VAR DAToutput1 : REAL);
BEGIN
   WriteString ('   Compute Derivative Action  - DUMMY STUB');
   WriteLn; WriteLn;
END ComputeDerivativeAction;
```

Listing 5.20   Traceability exercise.

- Is the SC/program module procedure naming consistent?
- Are the program procedures organized as defined by the SC?
- For procedure `ComputeControlSignal`:
  - Are all data flows declared?
  - Are all data flows which come from the parent diagram declared as the procedure formal parameters?
  - Are these correctly named (for example, `Error` on Figure 5.11 becomes the formal parameter `Error1`).
  - Are formal parameter names based on those of the actual parameter (for example, formal parameter $\Rightarrow$ `ControlSignal1`, actual parameter $\Rightarrow$ `ControlSignal`)?
  - Are all internal data flows (`DAToutput`, `PBoutput`) declared?
  - If these are dynamic variables, are they declared local to the procedure?
- For procedure `ComputeDerivativeAction`:
  - Are all data flows which come from the parent diagram declared as the procedure formal parameters?
  - Are these correctly named (for example, `DAToutput` on Figure 5.16 becomes the formal parameter `DAToutput1`).
  - Do the names correspond to the actual parameters (for example, formal parameter $\Rightarrow$ `Error2`, actual parameter $\Rightarrow$ `Error1`)?

Review

This chapter has both consolidated and extended your knowledge. Now that you have finished it you should:

- feel confident to tackle a small but real design
- see clearly the use of and relationship between Context, DFD and SC diagrams and source code
- understand the basic translation rules for going between DFDs and SCs and the program code
- understand the role of the PSpec, and know how to produce one for a data transformation
- appreciate the reason for, and the value of, the data dictionary
- see how to develop software incrementally
- recognize the advantages in using incremental development
- realize that the design method used here leads naturally to design visibility, quality software and program stability
- see how this method leads to extensive procedurization. This, by its very nature, extends program execution time and requires extra data storage (usually RAM)
- realize that such overheads can be attacked by the use of in-line compiler directives (pragmas)

The methods shown here are sound, rigorous and powerful. Using these you are in a position to produce first-class software. Unfortunately, you will find that such a disciplined approach has its detractors. A very typical response by inexperienced (and also, unfortunately, by some supposedly knowledgeable) programmers is that it is a waste of time. Just get in there and cut the code. Don't bother with all this faffing about! All I can say is give it a try; you'll be surprised at the discipline and rigour it brings to the development process. Yes, you will need to spend more time on the initial phases of program development. And you will generate a great deal of documentation. But later you will reap the benefits in terms of quality code, low error rates and minimal debugging efforts.

Exercises

5.1 In what situations would you expect to find service modules written before the application software? Would this affect the way in which you approach the design of your software?

5.2 How can separating software into interface and implementation units be put to good use for debugging purposes?

5.3 In this text, dummy stubs generated screen messages for test purposes. How could you adapt this technique for the development of target system software – in the target itself – when there is no screen?

5.4 What guidelines would you suggest would help in deciding on the execution order of DTs?

5.5 Section 5.4.2 deals with the need to update service modules. Here the replacement module has been given a name which is different from the original. An alternative approach is to keep the same name, but to have a different implementation module. What are the pros and cons of the two techniques?

5.6 What features or software aspects could reasonably be introduced when designing the structure chart? And why would you want to do this in the first place?

6

Defining system dynamic behaviour:

Introducing the state transition diagram

By now you should be able to see just how effective the DFD is for describing system functions. It gives us what you might call a 'snapshot' of the system. But, like a snapshot, a DFD always looks the same, no matter what is going on in the design. In other words, the view it gives is a static one. And yet many, if not most, real-time systems change their behaviour with time. That is, they exhibit dynamic behaviour. The question is, how can we show such changes in system operation? The answer is – the state transition diagram (STD).

The purpose of this chapter is to introduce the state transition diagram within the context of system operation. It:

- gives various examples of dynamic functions
- introduces the state transition diagram
- shows how the STD is used to define dynamic modes of operation
- describes tabular alternatives to the STD
- explores the STD in detail, including diagram decomposition
- discusses timing and sequence issues in dynamic systems, and highlights their relationship to the STD

6.1 Dynamic behaviour – an introduction

All the following statements have been extracted from system specification documents for real-time applications:

The autopilot will have three ride modes – soft, medium and hard.

The shaft brake is to be released when the engine is running and the throttle is moved past the idle position.

At (T+2.5) seconds IPN is injected into the starter and the ignition is switched on. If flame is not detected by (T+2.75) seconds initiate an emergency shutdown of the starter system.

The Sonar range gate is to be opened 300 microseconds after pulse transmission.

From these it can be seen that the behaviour of such systems varies over time. That is, we have dynamic, not static, operation. At any instant in time each system has a specific mode of behaviour: its 'state' (the state of a system is defined by its behaviour). For example, a propulsion motor could have the following states: standby, starting, running-up or driving. Or a student in a lecture could be writing, reading, day-dreaming or sleeping.

Exactly what has this got to do with software? The answer is *everything*. Software requirements are completely bound up with system requirements. Thus, before launching into detailed design we need to describe, clearly, completely and unambiguously, *system* behaviour. However, in describing such behaviour, two important restrictions are applied. First, the systems we deal with are considered to have definite, discrete states. Second, the number of states is finite.

Note, by the way, that in this text *mode* and *state* have the same meaning.

6.2   Describing system dynamics – the state transition diagram

It has been pointed out that dynamic systems can be described in terms of their states. However, it isn't enough just to define the states. There is also need to explain why *changes* of state take place. Such information *could* be given in text form. We, however, choose to use diagrams.

Diagramming methods which show such information have their roots in directed graph theory. Here we limit ourselves to one technique, the state transition diagram (STD).

A method widely used in electronics and communications to describe state behaviour (for example, sequential logic operation, network mode changes) is the Mealy machine. The fundamentals of this machine are shown in Figure 6.1.

Each state is denoted using a circle. In this case the system has only two defined states, state 1 and state 2. The connecting arrowed lines are transition arcs or simply

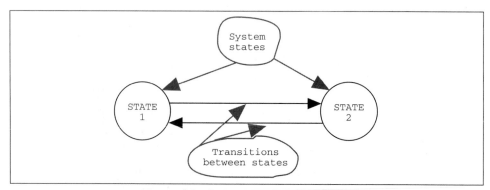

Figure 6.1   Basic state transition diagram.

transitions. As shown the system moves (makes a transition) *from* state 1 *to* state 2, then back to state 1 (hence the origin of the name *state transition diagram*). Note that these two states are mutually exclusive. What we have here then is a graphical model of a finite state machine (FSM).

When it comes to software-based systems, the circle notation may be confused with DFD transformation symbols. To avoid this, the circle is replaced by a rectangle (Figure 6.2). The meaning of the diagram is unchanged.

Figure 6.2   Modified state transition diagram.

At this point the states of the system have been defined, together with the relevant transitions. But we don't yet know why such transitions take place. Take, for instance, the situation depicted in Figure 6.3.

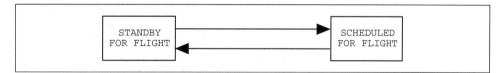

Figure 6.3   Simple state description.

This represents the state of a passenger waiting in an airport check-in area (a very simplified situation, of course). The traveller has a standby ticket. Hence, on arriving at the desk, she is placed into the standby queue. Her state is STANDBY FOR FLIGHT.

At some stage it is decided to include her in the flight schedule – a transition to the SCHEDULED FOR FLIGHT state. But then the unfortunate passenger loses her place on the flight and is put back on standby. Why the changes? We really don't know – the information at hand is incomplete. What needs to be done is to define the causes of, or the events leading to, such changes. This we do as shown in Figure 6.4.

It can be seen that, with each transition, an *event* is shown. Thus the transition from STANDBY FOR FLIGHT to SCHEDULED FOR FLIGHT is caused by the event Seat Becomes Available. The next state change occurs if a Priority Passenger Arrived, leading to a return to the standby mode. Observe that event information is written alongside the associated transition, in this case above a horizontal bar (for some diagrams the bar is optional).

In this example an event produces a state change. But that's all it does. Nothing else happens in the system. No action is generated as a result of the event taking

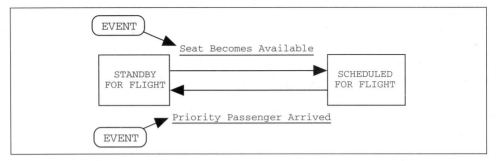

Figure 6.4   Events or conditions.

place. Now for a new scenario. Suppose that, when a seat becomes available (the event), the passenger is checked in (Check Passenger In – the corresponding action or response) (Figure 6.5).

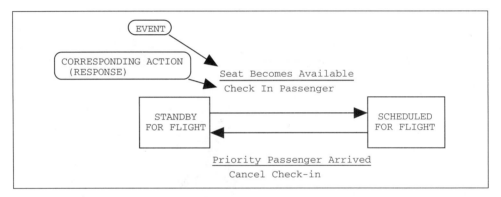

Figure 6.5   Actions or responses.

After this, should a priority passenger arrive (event), then the check-in is cancelled (the action or response). Recognize that these actions are responses to events; they are *not* consequences of the states. Note also that the transition takes place as a result of an event; it has nothing to do with the response. On the STD, actions are written below the events which generate them.

To reiterate: these last two examples make the point that a transition takes place as a result of an event. But there may, or may not, be resulting actions or responses.

It is possible that a number of events may have to occur to produce a state change. This point is illustrated in Figure 6.6.

Here events Start Button Pressed and Interlocks Clear must both occur for the transition to take place. The corresponding response is that the start relay gets energized. Note that we do not define event order, merely the logic conditions that must be satisfied. Hence the word *condition* is sometimes used instead of event in such situations (more generally they are taken to be synonymous).

It is also possible for an event to generate not one, but multiple, responses (Figure 6.7).

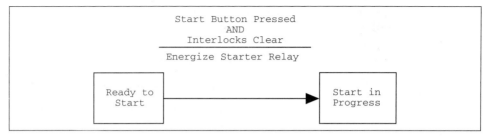

Figure 6.6 Multiple events or conditions.

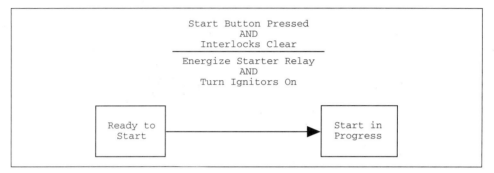

Figure 6.7 Multiple responses.

In this case the result is that the starter relay is energized and the ignitors are turned on.

These last examples are fairly straightforward. In some systems, particularly logic sequencers, much more complex events and responses may be encountered. Even so, the STDs must correctly and fully describe how such systems behave. Thus many and varied combinations of logical ANDs, ORs, NOTs and other logical operations may be used. Further, such systems often have numerous states and complicated transition patterns. As a result, their state transition diagrams also become complicated and difficult to use. In such cases other methods (discussed in the following sections) may prove to be better than the STD.

6.3 Alternatives to the STD – tabular notation

When defining dynamic behaviour, four items are relevant. These are:

- the current state
- the next state
- the event (or events) which causes the transition from the current to the next state
- the action (or actions) which the event (or events) produces

As pointed out earlier, actions may or may not take place. However, when describing software systems, events almost always generate responses.

In some instances we might not be interested in all four aspects. Take the case where we wish to highlight *transitions*, as in the

State 1 → Event → State 2

relationship. To do this we can put this in tabular form, the so-called *state* table (Figure 6.8).

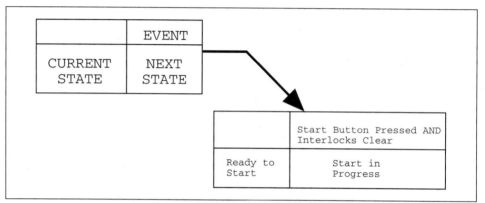

Figure 6.8   Emphasizing transitions – the state table.

Similarly, to put the spotlight on *actions*, that is the

State 1 → Event → Action

relationship, the *action* table can be used (Figure 6.9).

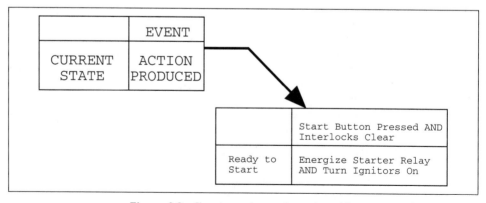

Figure 6.9   Showing actions – the action table.

These are fine, but it makes life easier to use as few tables as possible. It is possible, fortunately, to combine both state and action tables into a single composite table. There are, in fact, two common approaches: the state transition table and the state transition matrix. And note: there are no agreed standards for these tables. So don't be surprised to find variations in use.

One common form of the state transition table (STT) is given in Figure 6.10.

CURRENT STATE	EVENT	ACTION	NEXT STATE
Ready to Start	Start Button Pressed AND Interlocks Clear	Energize Starter Relay AND Turn Ignitors On	Start in Progress

Figure 6.10   The state transition table (STT).

If you are mainly interested in events and actions related to specific transitions, this is a most useful table. We first look for the row which holds the current state *and* the relevant next state. Sitting between these, on the same row, are the related events and actions.

An alternative form of the STT is shown in Figure 6.11.

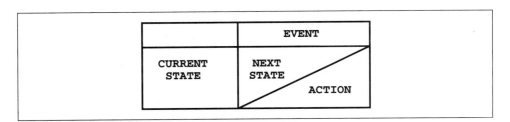

Figure 6.11   State transition table – alternative form.

The state transition matrix (STM) comes into its own when our primary interest centres on events (Figure 6.12).

Here a matrix of states and events is formed. For each state of the system there is a row in the matrix. Likewise, for each event or condition there is a corresponding

	EVENT	EVENT
CURRENT STATE	ACTION ——— NEXT STATE	ACTION ——— NEXT STATE
CURRENT STATE	ACTION ——— NEXT STATE	ACTION ——— NEXT STATE

Figure 6.12   The state transition matrix (STM).

EVENT / CURRENT STATE	Start Button Pressed AND Interlocks Clear	Idling Speed Reached
Ready to Start	Energize Starter Relay AND Turn Ignitors On ----- Start in Progress	
Start in Progress		De-energize Starter Relay AND Turn Ignitors Off ----- Engine Running
Engine Running		

Figure 6.13 Example state transition matrix.

column. At each row/column intersection point the related action(s) and next state are defined. This is illustrated in more detail in Figure 6.13.

Here, for instance, if the current state is Start in Progress, only the event Idling Speed Reached affects the system. Should the event arise, a transition is made to the state Engine Running. The response to the event is that the starter relay is de-energized and the ignitors are turned off.

It should be no surprise to find that different forms of the STM are in use.

It can be seen that tables and matrices can show much information in relatively little space. Thus, for systems which have complex dynamics, they are much more compact than the corresponding STDs. Unfortunately, this compactness makes it difficult to see clearly the overall behaviour of the system. Their particular forte is the ability to highlight specific, not overall, system attributes. STDs, in contrast, are very good at showing the big picture of system behaviour. Moreover, our experience is that engineers generally prefer to work with STDs rather than STTs/STMs.

The STD is a powerful way to describe system behaviour. As you will see in Chapter 7, this also applies to software behaviour. Do not, however, neglect other methods. Treat them as complementary, not as alternatives, to the STD. In particular, the STM is especially useful where events and their effects need to be fully assessed.

6.4 More on the state transition diagram

Let us now look at some other aspects of the STD. It is implicit in our design approach that there is always a well-defined, unique initial state. We identify this (Figure 6.14, Initializing the Processor) by drawing an entry transition which does not start in another state – a 'hanging' transition.

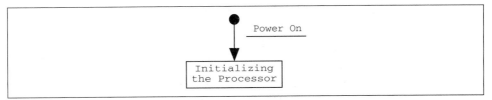

Figure 6.14   Showing the initial state.

There clearly has to be a reason to enter this state, caused by a particular event or events. As presented here the system goes into its initial state when power is switched on. This is shown in the usual way on the STD. In this particular case no actions are generated by the event. However, other applications may well call for specific actions to be carried out during initialization.

Now that the start-up state has been identified, what about the final state of the system? It might seem logical that where power-on leads to the initial state, power-off should lead to the final state. This may very well be true, illustrated in Figure 6.15.

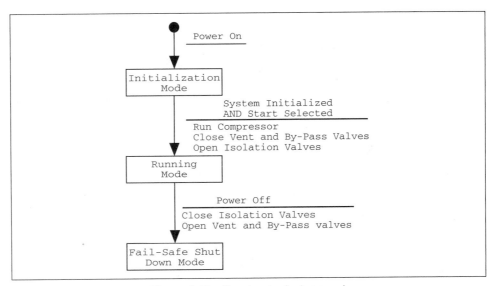

Figure 6.15   Showing the final state – 1.

Here, when the power goes off, it leads to the system entering the power failure shutdown mode. The resulting actions are that the isolation valves are closed and the vent and bypass valves are opened (clearly the valves must be designed to do this when they are de-energized). We recognize the shutdown mode as being the final state because it doesn't have an exit transition.

Now, though, let us look at this in a different, but very specific, context. Suppose the STD is used to define the operational behaviour of a computer-controlled system. Loss of power in such a system leads to loss of control. Should this situation be shown on the STD? In general, no. Why? Because loss of power is an abnormal condition, an *exception*. Exceptions should generally be kept off the normal STD (we shall return to this point later). Only normal modes of operation should be shown, as in Figure 6.16.

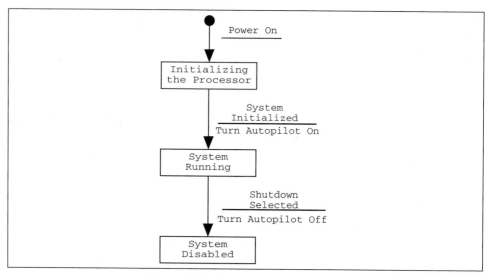

Figure 6.16   Showing the final state – 2.

There are also cases where there is no defined final state. One such situation is shown in Figure 6.17, which is very typical of small embedded control systems.

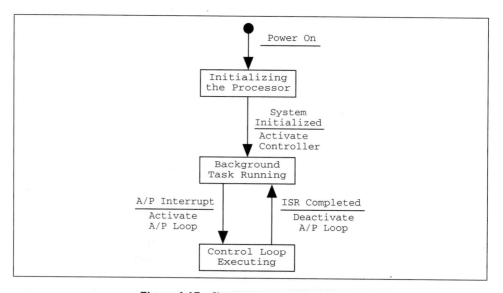

Figure 6.17   Showing continuous operation.

Here, on power on, the processor goes into the initialization state. When the system is initialized a transition is made to `Background Task Running` state. The response to `System Initialized` is `Activate Controller`. The system remains in this mode of operation until an A/P interrupt arrives. This results in a transition to the state `Control Loop Executing`, the response being that the A/P loop is activated.

Return to `Background Task Running` occurs when `ISR Completed` is signalled. At this point the A/P loop is deactivated. Once again the system remains in this mode until the interrupt next appears. Consequently the above-noted sequence is repeated. The result is that the system operates continuously, having a two-state circular mode of operation. There is no end state – it will continue like this until the power is switched off. At this point the STD has no meaning – the computer is deactivated.

Up to now, all examples have shown events leading to a change of state – to a new state, that is. Yet it can happen that the 'new' state is in fact the original one, as shown in Figure 6.18.

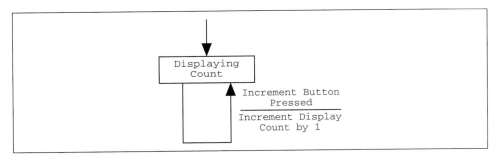

Figure 6.18   Return to current state (no state change).

Suppose this represents (in part) the operation of a digital counter used to record the number of visitors to an exhibition. Assume that it starts with a count of zero. Then, as the first visitor enters the exhibition, the increment or count button is pressed. This increments the count by one, the display now showing the number '1'. A second visitor arrives, the process is repeated, and we end up with a count of '2'. This continues until the end of viewing, at which time the display shows the visitor total. Thus there have been many events (more precisely many instances of the event `Increment Button Pressed`), many actions and many transitions – but no state change.

Moving on, let us now deal with multiple transitions to and from a state. You will see that, in Figure 6.17, there are two transitions into `Background Task Running`. It is obvious that only one of these can be taken at a time. So obvious, in fact, that it didn't need a special mention. But what of transitions leaving a state (Figure 6.19)?

This STD describes the dynamic behaviour of a cassette tape player. Assume that at this instant it is in the play mode (`Playing`). By making the appropriate selections we can stop, fast forward or rewind the tape. It is clear that only one of these should be selected. That is, all actions should be mutually exclusive. And that is precisely

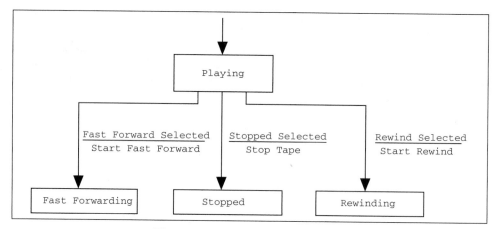

Figure 6.19 Multiple exit transitions.

how we interpret the STD. All exit transitions from a state are mutually exclusive – only one route can be taken.

What happens if both FF and REW are pressed simultaneously (yes, it will happen at some time). The STD does not take this into account, this being an undefined illegal condition. This doesn't mean that we can neglect illegal or abnormal operations – far from it. The problem must be dealt with at some point in the design phase. We could, for instance, check the selections in turn, responding only to the first active one. Such decisions, though, are made by individual designers; we really can't generalize.

As it stands, the STD is a powerful aid in evaluating abnormal behaviour. We *could*, of course, incorporate exceptions and illegal events into the diagram. But the resulting complexity would, for most practical systems, make the diagram almost unusable. A more useful approach is to produce an extra STD which shows only exceptional behaviour. This should be augmented by text, defining system responses to abnormal and illegal conditions.

Following on from the last item, how can we keep STDs simple? One way is to use the ideas of top-down design, decomposition and stepwise refinement (Figure 6.20).

The highest level view of the system is a three-state one: Standby, Starting and Running. However, Starting has many sub-states, four as shown here.

The STD of Figure 6.20 tells us that the system starts up with an initial state Standby. It then makes a transition into Starting, the final state being Running. However, the transition from Standby actually takes it into the (sub)state Checking Interlocks. From there it enters Priming Fuel System, eventually reaching Igniting Fuel. This is the final sub-state; transition from this is to Running. The event which causes this last transition is given on the top-level diagram. You can see that, by hiding the sub-states, the top-level diagram is uncluttered and clear.

STD decomposition is not a well-defined topic; different methods are in use. Moreover, you may find that your CASE tool does not support automatic levelling. In that case:

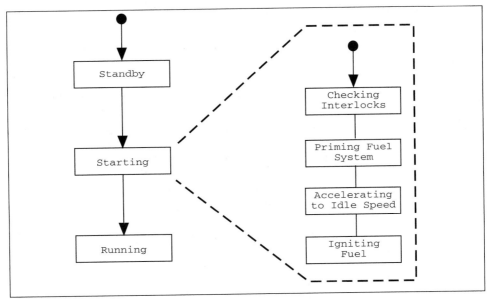

Figure 6.20   Decomposing (levelling) an STD.

- Define fully your decomposition method.
- Define appropriate manual checking procedures.
- Define your documentation standards.

Fortunately, the design method used in the real-time DFD (Chapter 7) implicitly takes decomposition into account. So, from a software point of view, we don't have a problem.

When we come to deal with anything other than small systems, we run into a problem (from the STD point of view, that is). Such systems usually consist of several cooperating subsystems. For example, in a burger bar a number of employees have to cooperate correctly for you to get your burger; there are the cooks, the packers, the counter staff and so on. We can, using an STD, describe what each individual job involves. But what about the overall system? Can we produce an STD for that? The answer is 'yes', but only with much extra effort. Our problem is that the number of possible combinations of sub-states can become rather large. For instance, given:

> Task a, with two states, 1 and 2
> Task b, with three states, 1, 2 and 3

then the potential combinations are:

> a1   a1   a1   a2   a2   a2
> b1   b2   b3   b1   b2   b3

Now add a third task, C, which also has three states. This brings the total number of possible combinations to 18. Of course, it may be impossible for some of these to occur in practice. Even so, we can easily end up with a quite complex situation.

Our difficulties are further compounded by subsystems which at times cooperate but at other times act independently. Take, for instance, computer control of aircraft systems. During landing the flaps and flight control surfaces may be interlinked via the flight control system. However, at other times they may operate quite independently. The STD techniques described here are not very good when faced with such situations. Methods *have* been developed to handle such problems. These, though, are beyond the scope of this text, so no more will be said on the topic.

One final point for discussion: naming. By now you should be aware that states, events and actions have been named in a consistent manner. The rules are simple:

- For states, the name should show what is happening while the system is in that state; for example, Running, Halted, Accelerating.
- Events and conditions define things which have happened. Use positive wording, based, where appropriate, on an active verb phrase, past tense. It *must* include a verb to denote the event/condition.
- Actions and responses should be expressed in a similar way. However, these should be written as reactions to a command.

These are for guidance only. Use your common sense when applying them. Don't be dogmatic.

6.5 Timing and sequence issues

6.5.1 *Timing aspects*

The whole point of using STDs is to show how system behaviour changes with time. Yet time itself hasn't been explicitly mentioned. The reason is that our STD model of reality shows that:

(a) Systems have a set of discrete, unique states.
(b) Each state exists for a time determined by system events or conditions.
(c) Transitions between states take zero time.

We can demonstrate this using a form of time-line diagram (Figure 6.21).

Assume that this is part of a complete STD for a turbo-generator (TG) unit. The first state shown indicates that the generator is off-line. When the event Generator On Selected happens, the main contactor is closed, and the generator comes on-line. This sequence is further depicted on the time-line diagram of Figure 6.21.

Now take another aspect of TG operation: running up the engine which drives the generator. Let us suppose that the engine is running at idling speed, and we then select normal generating speed. As a result, the engine speed gradually increases (an acceleration phase), eventually reaching its normal running speed. It therefore seems sensible and reasonable to define acceleration as one of the system states. The STD and time-line diagrams for this are shown in Figure 6.22.

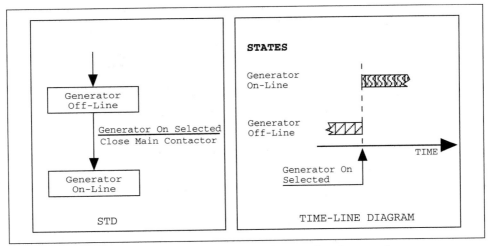

Figure 6.21 STD and corresponding time-line diagram – 1.

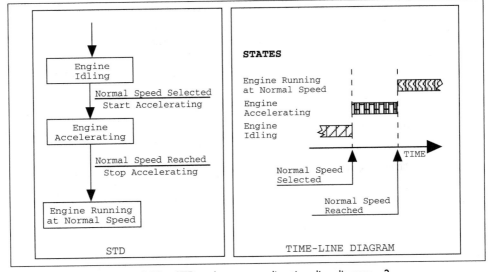

Figure 6.22 STD and corresponding time-line diagram – 2.

Here we can validly show the transitions taking place instantly; acceleration time is accounted for.

Now return to Figure 6.21. Suppose that there is a requirement to check that the main contactor actually closes when ordered to do so. An auxiliary contact is used to provide a switch input signal to the control computer. Thus, the close command is issued, and the auxiliary contact status is read in. And this is where we can get into trouble. It has been assumed so far that contact closure is instantaneous. This, of course, is impossible – but it didn't seem to matter before. Assume that the worst-case closure time is 200 ms. To allow for this the time-line diagram must be modified (Figure 6.23).

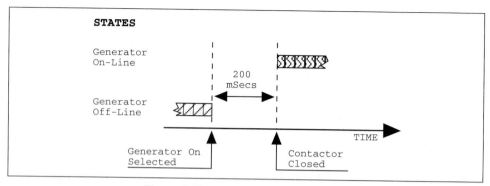

Figure 6.23   Modified time-line diagram.

Here the two defined states (as per the STD) are now separated by an undefined region. We cannot say precisely what the situation is while the contactor is energizing. But it (the undefined region) does have a definite upper time-bound. Only after this time has passed can the auxiliary contact signal be treated as a valid one. However, 200 ms is extremely long in processor terms. It *must* be taken into account when designing the software. Otherwise the auxiliary contact is likely to be read within microseconds of sending the close command. This will undoubtedly produce a software malfunction – which will come to light only on system trials. Red faces all round, chaps.

6.5.2   Sequence aspects

Suppose a condition becomes true only when a set of individual signals goes true (for example, Low Oil Pressure AND Engine Running). Does the order (the sequence) in which they arrive matter? Generally, no. What we have is a combinational logic machine. But what of the responses? If the STD defines an action to be 'Close Hydrogen Valves AND Open Oxygen Valves', does the order matter? Mostly not. But there are times when the sequence must be correct.

For the example here, assume that if both valves are open simultaneously, then oxygen and hydrogen will mix (a disastrous combination). Therefore we *must* always close one valve before opening the other one – the correct sequence must always be maintained. Make sure this is recorded with the design documentation.

With many systems, getting the order right is good enough. In others, we have to make sure that *all* actions are carried out in an unbroken sequence. Suppose in this example that the computer has just issued a command 'close hydrogen valve' – and an interrupt arrives. How long is it going to be before we signal the oxygen valve to open? We don't know. It depends on the interrupt service routine. Now our system is in an undefined state, one that it was not designed to deal with. This could be a serious problem. So, if we run into such situations, always make sure that the action set is an indivisible one.

So far, so good. The order of commands is correct, and they are grouped as an indivisible set. But we may still have problems, owing to the response times of the controlled items (this is to show that getting the order right may not, in itself, be sufficient).

Suppose that the valve specification is as follows:

Valve opening: $50 < T_{open} < 70$ ms
Valve closure: $50 < T_{close} < 70$ ms

The hydrogen valve is closed and the oxygen valve opened, as per specification. But in this case both valves may actually be open for up to 20 ms: highly undesirable. Yet another example which shows the importance of timing aspects.

The moral of this story is that you can't produce safe and reliable software without knowing how the system operates.

Review

On completing this chapter you should now:

- appreciate why many real-time systems have a changing pattern of behaviour
- see how the state transition diagram allows you to model such operations
- understand the STD attributes of states, transitions, events (conditions) and actions (responses)
- understand the rules and notation of the Mealy finite state machine
- know how to deal with multiple events and/or actions
- appreciate that an event is required to cause a state change
- realize that an action is not necessarily produced
- also realize that, when an action is generated, it is a response to an event
- see that responses are related to transitions, not states
- perceive how STTs and STMs can be used together with, or in place of, STDs
- know how to show initial and final states on an STD, and how to decompose one if necessary
- understand that detailed timing aspects may sometimes be neglected, but at other times must be taken into account
- see why the same comments can be made concerning the sequencing of multiple responses
- know how to use time-line diagrams

Exercises

6.1 Your bathroom light is operated by a pull-action switch. If the light is off, a single pull puts it on. If it is on, operating the switch puts it off. Draw the STD for the system.

6.2 A car is fitted with an electrically operated window. To control it there is an UP button and a DOWN button. Pressing a button causes the window to move in the appropriate direction until:

- the button is released or
- the window hits an end-stop

If both buttons are pressed simultaneously, and the window is stationary, the window does not move. Both buttons must be released before the system reverts to normal operation. If the window is already moving and the second button is pressed, the window stops. Both buttons must be released before the system reverts to normal operation.

Produce the STD for the window operation.

6.3 Draw the STD for the following application.

A simple time display has a four-digit digital display (two for hours – H digits, and two for minutes – M digits). It also has four push-buttons: Inc (I), Dec (D), Accept (A) and Set (S). When it is powered up, all digits flash, showing a random value. The only button it responds to is A. Pressing and then releasing ('depressing') A causes the display to first go steady, and then begin its normal mode of operation.

To set the time, S is depressed. This causes the H digits to flash, and allows them to respond to the D or I buttons. Pressing D decreases the displayed value, pressing I increases it. Releasing the button (D or I) leaves the display showing a fixed value (but still flashing). Now depressing A sets the H digits steady but sets the M digits flashing. Again using the S, D or I buttons, the M display can be set as required. At the end of this operation the M digits will be flashing.

If the user is satisfied with the set value, the A button is depressed. The M digits go steady and the timer begins its normal mode of operation.

However, if the user wishes to carry out further changes, then the S (and not A) button is depressed. The M digits go steady and the H digits flash. Time setting can now be carried out as described earlier.

7
The real-time data flow diagram:
Control plus data

By now you should be in a position to clearly and fully describe *system* dynamic behaviour. But how can we show the dynamic aspects of a *software* design? One thing is clear. The data flow diagram, as it stands, isn't much help. As described so far, it shows only static, not dynamic, features of the design. We could, of course, introduce new types of design diagram to deal purely with behaviour. However, a better approach is to build on existing knowledge by extending the DFD to take dynamics into account. That is, to integrate dynamic behaviour with the existing non-dynamic DFD model. The result of doing this is the *real-time data flow diagram*.

The purpose of this chapter is to establish the basic concepts, notation and use of the real-time data flow diagram. It:

- introduces the control flow diagram
- shows the components used on this diagram: control transformations, control flows, prompts and control stores
- describes the function and use of the control transformation
- explains how to specify the function of a control transformation
- shows that the real-time data flow diagram is essentially a combination of two models of the system software: the control flow model and the data flow model
- explains how these two models interact
- describes the reason for, and use of, Enable/Disable, Trigger and Activator prompts
- shows how multiple control transformations may be used

7.1   Introducing the control flow diagram

Let us start by looking at the system shown in Figure 7.1(a).

This consists of a motor, motor controller, control computer and control switches. The computer accepts signals from the control switches and, using this information, generates control commands. These points may be represented on a 'control' diagram which includes a finite state machine (FSM) (Figure 7.1(b)). Inputs to the computer

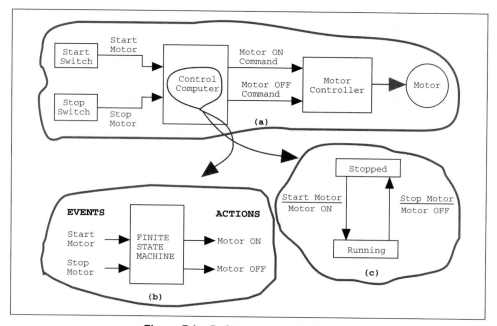

Figure 7.1 Defining computer behaviour.

are equivalent to FSM events. Likewise, computer outputs, being responses to the inputs, are equivalent to FSM actions. The diagram shows these events and actions, but gives no indication as to how the machine itself behaves. Such information must be provided separately, in this case using a state transition diagram (Figure 7.1(c)). These three diagrams, taken together, define the total system behaviour. To recap, the 'control' diagram shows:

- that the system has dynamic behaviour
- the events (inputs) which drive the FSM
- the responses (actions) produced by the FSM

Note that it does not *define* the behaviour of the state machine itself; that is the function of the STD.

Now let us introduce the equivalent diagram as used in software design: the control flow diagram (CFD) (Figure 7.2(b)).

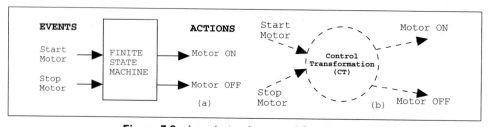

Figure 7.2 Introducing the control flow diagram.

The two diagrams in this figure have exactly the same meaning. Only the notation is different. Observe that dotted lines are used, direction of flow being indicated using arrows. Both input and output flows are here, for simplicity, called *control flows*. Thus control inputs represent events, control outputs being actions. The control transformation (CT) of Figure 7.2(b) is equivalent to the FSM of Figure 7.2(a).

It is still necessary to specify the dynamics of the control transformation (the CT shows that dynamics exist, but not what they are). Once again we can call on the state transition diagram (Figure 7.3) to perform this role.

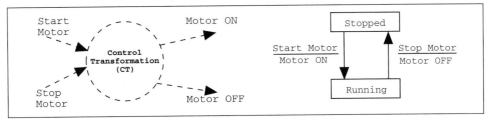

Figure 7.3   The control transformation and its specification.

In general terms, the CFD tells us that:

- The software of our system performs a dynamic function.
- The inputs to the software are Start Motor and Stop Motor.
- The software reacts to these inputs to produce outputs Motor ON and Motor OFF.

Its associated STD defines:

- that the dynamic function may be shown as a two-state machine which runs in an endless loop
- the transitions of the system
- the events which produce these transitions and their related responses

In essence, an STD is the specification for a CT. Note that any valid alternative to the STD (for example, STM) could be used here as a control specification (CSpec). However, for simplicity and consistency, we shall assume hereafter that the software dynamics are defined using an STD.

These two, the CFD and the STD, are an essential pairing. From this it is clear that:

- Each CT input must appear as an event on its related STD.
- Each STD event must have a corresponding CT input.
- Each CT output must appear as an action on the STD.
- Each STD action must have a corresponding CT output.

These are called 'balancing checks', and are an essential part of the design process. What is not quite so obvious is that all control flows are two-valued (binary) ones.

That is, an event is present (Start Motor, for instance) or it is not. Responses, similarly, are binary.

It would make sense to present control aspects in the form of Figure 7.4.

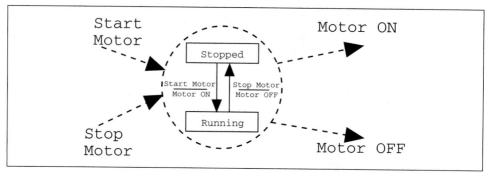

Figure 7.4 The complete control description.

This makes the point that a complete control description consists of a CFD *and* its associated specification. Unfortunately, for most applications, the STD is too large to include within the CT. In practice it is attached to the CT but not displayed on the CFD. Using CASE tool technology this CT–STD pairing is maintained automatically, together with support for balancing checks.

The next chapter deals in great depth with the implementation of control transformations and associated activities. We shall defer detailed discussions until then. However, just to give a feel for the topic, let us see how the STD of Figure 7.4 *could* be implemented. Using pseudo-code, the result is:

Comment: Assume initial state is Stopped

LOOP

    WAIT for Start Motor signal

    SEND Motor ON command

    WAIT for Stop Motor signal

    SEND Motor OFF command

END LOOP

Control transformations may also define the combining of events, as in Figure 7.5.

This shows that before the command Raise Undercarriage can be generated, two events must have occurred. The aircraft weight switch must have operated and undercarriage up must have been selected. Note that the order in which the events arrive is irrelevant; this is purely a combinational machine.

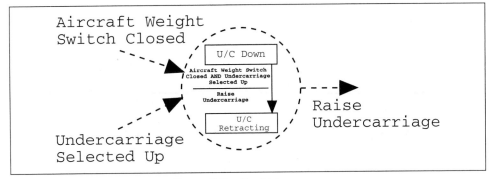

Figure 7.5   Combining events.

It is also possible for a single event to generate multiple responses (Figure 7.6).

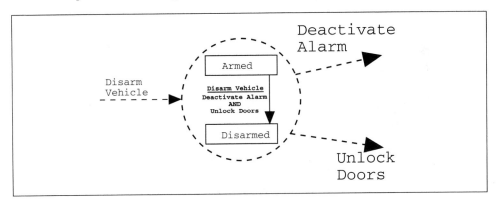

Figure 7.6   Multiple responses.

Here the event `Disarm Vehicle` produces two responses (actions): the doors are unlocked and the alarm is deactivated. It is assumed that both actions are generated simultaneously.

An important issue not addressed by this notation concerns ordering of events and/or responses. If ordering *is* important, this must be defined explicitly by the designer. An alternative approach is to introduce more states into the design (but this complicates the diagram).

7.2   The real-time data flow diagram – a CFD/DFD pairing

7.2.1   *Introduction*

The previous section set out the basic ideas, syntax and semantics of the control flow diagram. Using this approach a system's software function could be defined using only a CFD (as illustrated by Figure 7.4, and its associated pseudo-code).

There is no requirement for a DFD. However, for reasons which will be made clear in Chapter 8, this method is *not* adopted here. A DFD is always included.

Where systems have dynamic modes of operation, two factors need to be taken into account:

- *what* the system does (its functionality)
- *when* its functions are performed (its dynamics)

Functionality is best described using a data flow diagram. Dynamics, it has been shown, may be clearly expressed using control flow diagrams. What we do here is to combine both the DFD and the CFD into a single diagram. This is called the real-time data flow diagram (Figure 7.7).

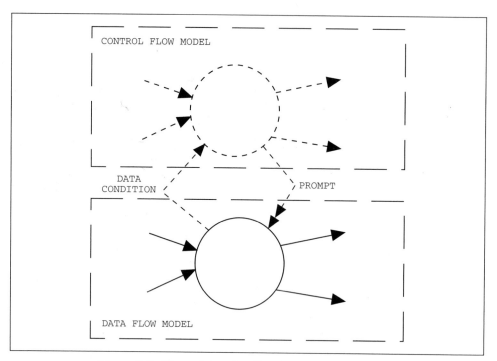

Figure 7.7 The real-time data flow diagram – basic concept.

It shows that:

- The design incorporates two system models – function and behaviour.
- There is interaction or signalling between the two models.
- Signals from the CFD to the DFD model are called *prompts*.
- Signals from the DFD to the CFD model are called *data conditions* (and act as events for the CT).

Prompts come in three flavours: Enable/Disable pairs, Triggers and Activators. In contrast there is only a single event type. Let us now look into these in more detail.

7.2.2 The Enable/Disable prompt

To show how the Enable/Disable prompt is used, consider an extended version of the system given in Figure 7.1: Figure 7.8.

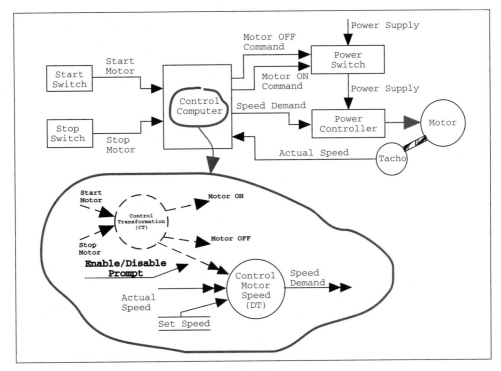

Figure 7.8 CT to DT signalling – the enable/disable prompt.

Here the simple on/off motor control has been replaced by a variable speed unit. The control computer now incorporates a closed-loop speed control function. Its purpose is to maintain the actual motor speed at a preset set speed value. This it does by first comparing the actual speed with the set speed. Using this information it then computes an appropriate speed demand signal which is sent to the power controller. To represent the software design aspects of this, a data flow diagram is used. Here, in Figure 7.8, the related DT is `Control Motor Speed`.

A control flow diagram is (as before) used to define the dynamic mode of operation; that is, switching the motor on and off in response to input signals (Figure 7.8). However, there is a design requirement that the control loop should only be activated when the motor is switched on. To deal with this, the DT is controlled (turned on and off) by the CT. The link between the two is the prompt, in this case an Enable/Disable (E/D) one.

Thus, what we have in Figure 7.8 is a small but complete real-time data flow diagram. The prompt is the link between the CFD and DFD models – there is no DFD–CFD event signalling in this example. DFD status is illustrated in Figure 7.9.

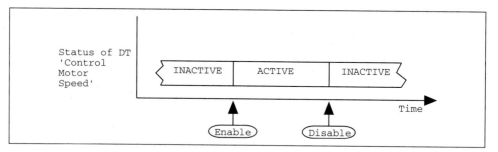

Figure 7.9   DT status – enable/disable prompt control.

Until the DFD receives an Enable prompt, it is inactive. That is, no processing is carried out. Once enabled, it carries out the processing defined by its process specification. In this case it performs closed-loop speed control of the motor. This continues until a Disable prompt is received, at which point it ceases to operate (we talk about the DT being 'enabled' and 'disabled'). To become active again it once more needs to be enabled. It can be seen that its behaviour is similar to a bi-stable memory device. Enable is equivalent to the set operation, Disable to reset.

As shown here, the E/D pairing has been grouped together into a single prompt. However, if desired, they may be separated into two distinct prompts, one being Enable, the other Disable.

The CFD of Figure 7.8 doesn't give any indication as to why or when the E/D prompts are produced. To do this we once again call on the STD associated with the CT (Figure 7.10).

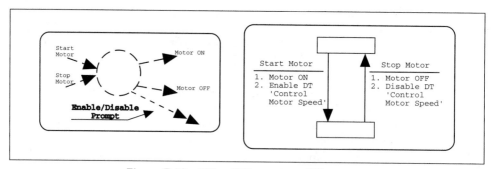

Figure 7.10   CT to STD mapping – E/D prompt.

You can see that we define explicitly when the DT is enabled and disabled. These are listed as actions (responses) on the STD, the diagram being self-explanatory. Once more we can apply balancing checks to the diagrams. In addition to those already defined, the following should be made:

• Each Enable and Disable prompt must have a corresponding action entry on the STD.

• Each Enable and Disable action entry must have a corresponding prompt on the CFD.

These may seem somewhat trivial and of limited value, but wait until you have to deal with a real design. Then you'll appreciate the value of carrying these out (and in having automated tools to help you).

It is important to recognize that enabling and disabling are related to events, not states. That is, once a DT is enabled, it will remain so, irrespective of the number of state changes which take place (Figure 7.11).

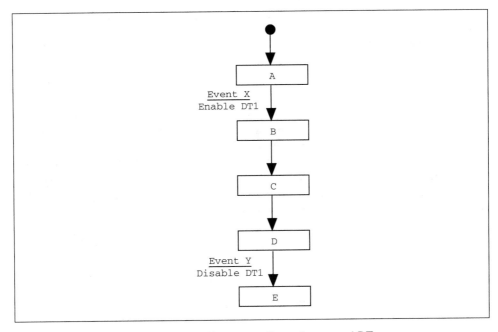

Figure 7.11   Memory attribute of prompted DT.

Assume that the system is in the initial state A. Event X occurs, leading to a state change to B and also the enabling of DT1. DT1 remains active during states B, C and D, only becoming deactivated when event Y arrives. This event causes the necessary disabling prompt to be generated.

7.2.3   The Trigger prompt

Now to meet a second, widely used, prompt – the Trigger (T). The need for and use of triggers is demonstrated in the example of Figure 7.12.

This is a small temperature measuring system. It consists of four devices: a temperature sensor, control switch, data acquisition computer and a remote display. The computer inputs the sensor temperature signal, processing the raw signal as appropriate. It then transmits the measured temperature signal to the display for viewing by the operator. When this information is received by the remote display, the unit transmits an acknowledgement response. However, it is a design requirement that the computer only performs these operations when given a measure command.

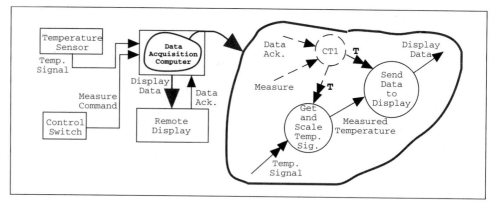

Figure 7.12   CT to DT signalling – the trigger prompt.

Further, only one measurement is made for each measure command.

The software design, in terms of the real-time DFD, is given in Figure 7.12. Here a single CT acts as the controlling mechanism for the system. Its inputs are `Data Ack.` and `Measure`, the outputs being two Trigger prompts. When a DT is prompted by a Trigger it becomes active and performs its defined function – *once* only. It then reverts to the inactive state; that is, it self-suspends (Figure 7.13).

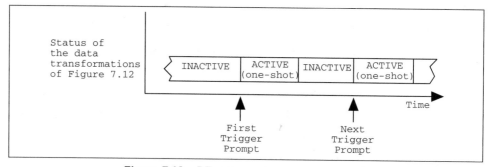

Figure 7.13   DT status – trigger prompt control.

It can be seen that its behaviour is similar to a monostable (one-shot) memory device. The behavioural aspects are defined in the STD of Figure 7.14.

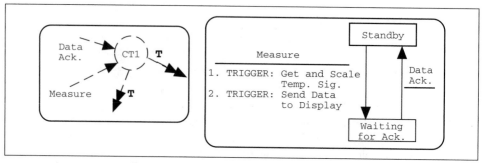

Figure 7.14   CT to STD mapping – triggers.

There are no surprises here; in fact, the Trigger prompt is the easiest one to understand and to implement.

7.2.4 The Activator prompt

We now come to the final prompt, the Activator (A). To illustrate these, let us replace the triggers of Figure 7.14 with the Activators of Figure 7.15.

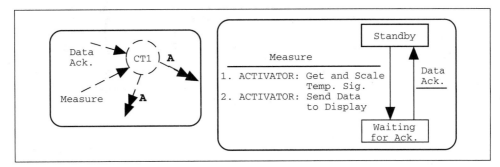

Figure 7.15 CT to STD mapping – activators.

At first sight this appears to be almost identical to the Trigger. However, it is significantly different in operation. When a DT receives an Activator prompt it becomes active. It stays active until another state transition takes place, at which point it reverts to being inactive. This is illustrated in Figure 7.16 for the system operation defined in Figure 7.15.

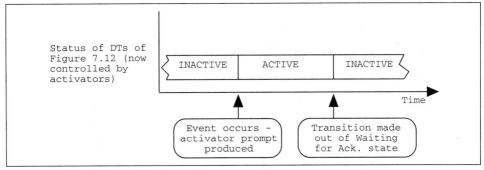

Figure 7.16 DT status – activator prompt control.

Observe that emphasis is placed on transition *from* the state Waiting for Ack., not *to* Standby. To reinforce this aspect, consider Figure 7.17. Here, when event X occurs, DT1 is activated and the system enters state B. The DT remains active until a transition takes place from B, either to state C or State D.

You might argue that the Activator is unnecessary, as its function could be implemented using the E/D prompt. True; however, there are good reasons for employing the Activator, discussed in detail in the next chapter.

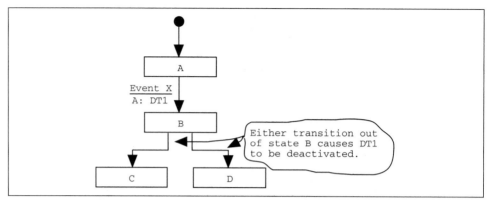

Figure 7.17 Activated DT behaviour.

7.2.5 DT to CT signalling

There are many occasions when system behaviour is affected by the result of a processing operation. Consider, for instance, the system shown, in part, in Figure 7.18.

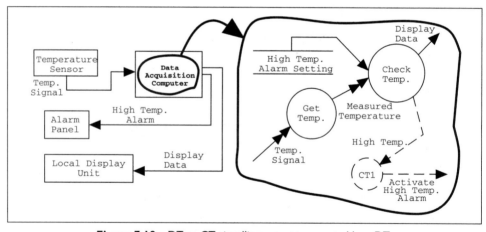

Figure 7.18 DT to CT signalling – event generated by a DT.

Here, a data acquisition computer measures the temperature of a device, generating an alarm should high-temperature conditions occur. It can be seen from the DFD that the temperature signal is acquired by the DT Get Temp. The output from this, Measured Temperature, is input to the DT Check Temp. In turn, its data output is sent to a local display. Now, should the measured temperature exceed the high alarm setting, the DT sends a signal to CT1. This responds by producing an output Activate High Temp. Alarm. As far as the CT is concerned, this input is merely another event. It makes no difference that it has come from a DT.

7.3 Multiple control transformations

Up to now we have used only one CT at a time. There are times, however, when it might be an advantage to employ a number of CTs. Where a system is a distributed multiprocessor one, this makes much sense. However, here we will restrict ourselves to a single processor installation. For some applications it may be that the logic operations of a single CT become complex and confusing. In this case the problem might be more easily handled by splitting these problems across a number of CTs (Figure 7.19).

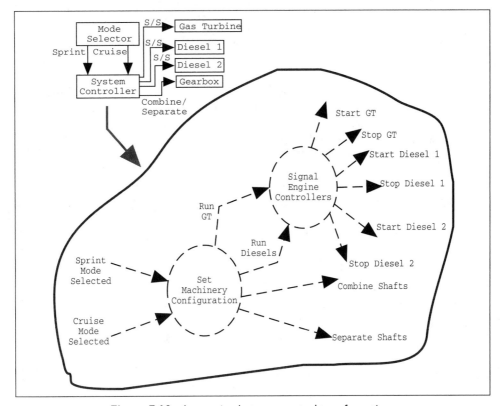

Figure 7.19 Interaction between control transformations.

This shows part of a propulsion control system, consisting of engines, gearbox unit, system controller and mode selector switch. The system operates in either cruise or sprint mode. For cruise operations the shafts are separated, each one being driven by a diesel engine. In sprint mode, both shafts are combined in the gearbox, being driven by the gas turbine.

It has been decided to split the dynamics across two control transformations, Set Machinery Configuration and Signal Engine Controllers. It can be seen that two of the outputs of the first CT act as inputs to the second one. Each CT has an associated STD (Figure 7.20).

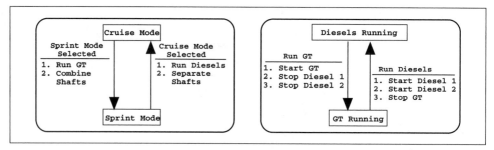

Figure 7.20   STDs for Figure 7.19.

Splitting the problem makes it fairly easy for the reader to assimilate system behaviour. This, of course, is a very simplified version of the real system, used to bring out the essentials of the topic. In practice we would find many extra signals, and much more complex logic, in use.

One last point: there is no reason why signals shouldn't go from the second CT to the first one if so desired.

7.4   Control stores

The function of a control store is to store control information for use at some later time. In this way it performs a similar role to the data store. Figure 7.21 shows the notation used for the control store.

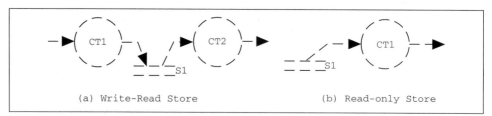

(a) Write-Read Store   (b) Read-only Store

Figure 7.21   Control store symbol.

Note that, *in this text*, the following rules are the default ones:

- The control store may be read/write or read-only storage.
- For a read/write store, new information overwrites the old version.
- Writing into the store is performed by a CT.
- Reading from a store is also carried out by a CT.
- The information content of read-only stores is defined by the programmer. Normally it is set up at initialization time.

Review

You have met the symbols defined in Figure 7.22 in this chapter.

CONTROL TRANSFORMATION	(dashed circle)	A CT takes in event (control) flows and produces output controls or prompts
CONTROL FLOW – EVENT, RESPONSE OR DATA CONDITION	— →	All are time discrete, binary valued. EVENT – Input to a CT. RESPONSE – Output from a CT. DATA CONDITION – DT to CT signal.
CONTROL FLOW – PROMPT	E/D ⇒ —T⇒ —A⇒	Enables/disables a DT Triggers a DT Activates a DT
CONTROL STORE	– – – – – –	A control store is a place in which information is held for a period of time BECAUSE it is needed for use at a later time

Figure 7.22   CFD symbols.

You should now:

- fully understand the meaning of these symbols
- know their function as part of a complete control flow diagram
- appreciate the purpose of the control flow model of software
- understand how the control flow and data flow models are combined to form the real-time data flow diagram
- see why and how prompts are used
- recognize the difference between Enable/Disable, Trigger and Activator prompts
- know why DT to CT signalling is used
- understand clearly the distinct roles of the CFD and the STD
- feel confident to carry out CFD/STD balancing checks
- appreciate how multiple CTs can be used on a single CFD

One final point. From here on, the real-time data flow diagram will merely be called the data flow diagram.

Exercises

For the situations described below, produce appropriate real-time data flow diagrams. Show for each control transformation its related state transition diagram.

7.1 Simple battery-powered kitchen weighing scales contain:

(i)   a sensor whose output is proportional to weight
(ii) a control switch, normally open, momentarily closed by pushing on the display panel of the unit
(iii) a digital display to show weight

In standby mode the unit is permanently powered up, but the display is normally off. When the display panel is pushed it enters the operational mode. The following occurs:
(i)   The display digits flash.
(ii) The weight sensor output is measured.
(iii) The weight is calculated.
(iv) The result is displayed.

Items (ii) and (iii) are repeated continuously.

To return the unit to standby, the display panel is again pushed.

7.2   A car is fitted with an automatic cruise control system. It has two states: OFF and AUTO. In OFF it does nothing, while in AUTO it controls vehicle speed to a preset value.

When the system is powered up (ignition switched on), it enters the OFF state. On AUTO being selected (a push-button on the driver's control unit), the speed control loop is activated. At any time it can be turned off by:
(a) selecting OFF on the driver's control unit, or
(b) kicking the accelerator pedal, so operating a micro-switch on the pedal unit

7.3   The operation of the weighing scales of Exercise 7.1 is modified as follows:

If at any time the weight goes to zero, a timer is started. Provided a weight is placed on the unit within 10 seconds the unit continues with normal operation. Otherwise it automatically returns to the standby mode.

8

Implementing controls:

From DFD to code via the structure chart

You have seen how important (no, essential) it is to define system behaviour and dynamics. We do this in structured design methods using control transformations and their associated descriptions – state transition diagrams and control specifications. It takes time and experience to become proficient in the design of the real-time DFD. However, the next stage – translating these designs into structure chart and source code form – can be quite a difficult one. Rarely is this topic well covered in textbooks. What this chapter sets out to do is to establish a workable, sensible and consistent set of translation rules. It also extends, and elaborates, a number of important aspects of data flow design techniques.

When you have completed this chapter you will:

- understand, in general terms, the steps involved in going from the real-time DFD to source code via the structure chart
- know, in detail, two techniques for implementing control transformations, centralized and distributed control
- more fully appreciate the use of control transformations to control and interact with data transformations
- have a better understanding of Enable, Disable, Trigger and Activator prompts
- be familiar with methods for implementing prompts
- realize how dynamics are defined within levelled DFDs
- see why control flows cross DT boundaries, and know how to implement such flows
- be able to handle interfacing to external signals in a consistent and clear manner
- appreciate what the common module issue is, and learn how to live with it

8.1 How to implement a control transformation

8.1.1 Introduction

We now come to a topic which probably causes more difficulty than any other design aspect. That is, how do we translate a control transformation into source code?

It's important to keep in mind two factors:

- the role of the CT within the DFD
- the definition of the behaviour of the CT

These, taken together, fully define the control aspects. You *cannot* ignore either one when implementing the CT.

Let us take as our starting point the example shown in Figure 8.1.

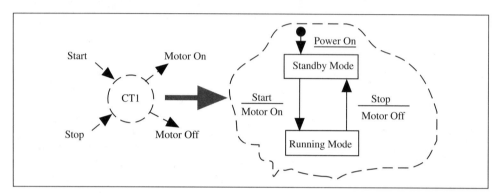

Figure 8.1   Example CT/STD pairing.

Here, input control signals Start and Stop are fed into CT1. This, in turn, generates output signals Motor On and Motor Off. Where these control signals come from and go to is shown on the DFD; the effects produced by the input signals are defined in the state transition diagram. Full balancing *must* be carried out between the two diagrams before trying to implement the CT. If we do this properly, then the STD acts as the main driving force in the building of the software.

The translation method described here is a prescriptive one. It is strongly recommended that you stick with this, for one quite simple reason: to make it easy to trace the progress of the design through its various phases.

Translation takes place in two steps:

- from the STD to a structure chart module(s)
- from the structure chart to source code

Note the first point well: the CT is built using the software machine (module) approach. How this relates to the modules defined by data transformations will be discussed shortly.

Two methods can be used to define the SC modules (Figure 8.2). (I'm sure other variations can be made.)

The first option is to house all control activities within a single module – *centralized* control. Alternatively, we can use a set of modules, working together, to achieve the same result – *distributed* control. In that case, each mode (as defined by the STD) has its own manager module. Coordination and control of the mode managers is performed by an overall supervisor module. Before looking into these in

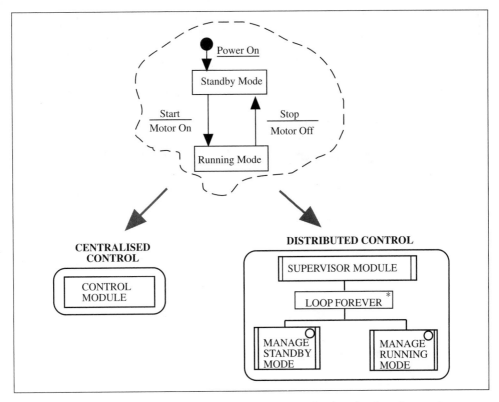

Figure 8.2 CT to module structure chart – centralized vs. distributed control.

detail, we need to set out the basic translation rules for

STD → SC → Code Structure

First, take the situation described by the STD of Figure 8.3.

This describes an endless loop: from Standby Mode to Running Mode to Standby Mode and so on *ad infinitum*. Events and responses have been deliberately left off the diagram; they cannot change the basic behaviour pattern. In SC terms, an endless loop is specified as an endless iteration (a 'forever' loop). The code structure

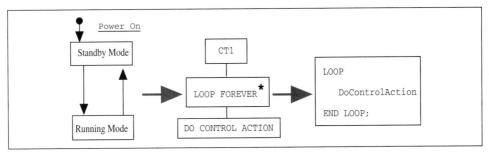

Figure 8.3 STD–SC–code translation (1).

can be done in a number of ways; here the LOOP-END LOOP construct is used.
Now let us add an event (condition) to the STD (Figure 8.4).

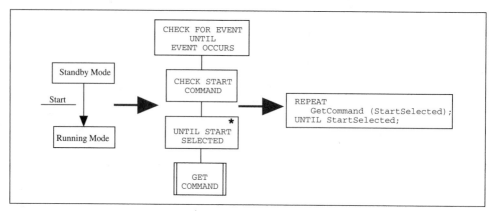

Figure 8.4   STD–SC–code translation (2).

Just for the purposes of explanation, assume that there is (are) no associated
response(s). The change from Standby Mode to Running Mode takes place only
when the event 'Start' occurs. Now, in a normal sequential program, there is only
one way to get such an event – read it in (interrupt-driven systems are left until
later). Hence the structure chart shows a repeated reading in of the Start command
until Start is selected. In code terms, the procedure GetCommand is repeated until the
control Boolean value StartSelected goes true (a 'busy-waiting' condition).
    The next stage is to add the response(s) (Figure 8.5).

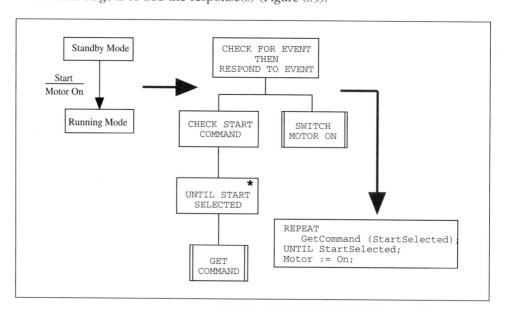

Figure 8.5   STD–SC–code translation (3).

The interpretation of the STD is that 'when Start occurs, the response "Motor On" is generated'. This requirement is illustrated in the resultant SC as a single procedure box. It can be seen that the resultant code implementation is simple and clear.

8.1.2 Centralized control

With a centralized control approach, the whole CT is implemented as a single composite unit or module. It is, of course, perfectly acceptable to use procedures (software machines) as component parts of the module. For our example here, the SC derived from the STD is that of Figure 8.6.

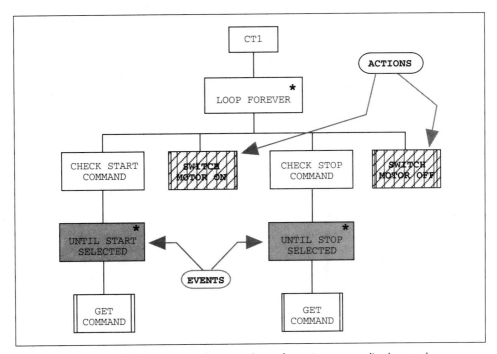

Figure 8.6 Implementing the control transformation – centralized control.

From the earlier discussion on transformation mechanisms, this should need little explanation. However, observe carefully how events and actions are depicted on the structure chart. The alternative meaning of *event*, that is *condition*, is probably a more apt one here. Two particular aspects of the diagram should be noted. First, it doesn't explicitly define the states (modes) of the system. Second, we have used it to expand on the basic information contained within the STD.

The SC, when translated to code, gives the source program of Figure 8.7.

As pointed out already, the control skeleton is unique. There must be a one-to-one mapping between the SC and the source code skeleton. However, the *actual* source program form can vary.

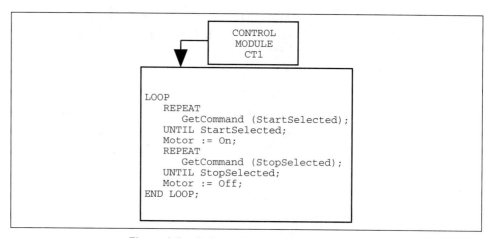

Figure 8.7 Code implementation for Figure 8.6.

8.1.3 Distributed control

Here we break the implementation into two distinct parts:

- a supervisor module – the state machine controller
- a set of mode (or state) managers, controlled by the supervisor

The concept of the supervisor module is outlined in Figure 8.8.

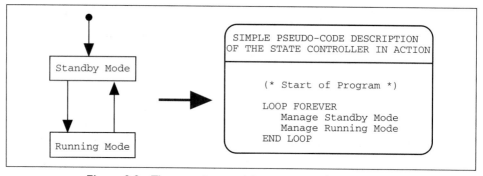

Figure 8.8 The supervisor module – a state machine controller.

There are only two system modes (states): Standby and Running. The function of the supervisor is to define which mode manager is to be activated – and when this is to take place. It can be seen from the pseudo-code that the supervisor sets each manager into action. However, it does *not* stop the mode manager executing; this is entirely the responsibility of the manager itself. So, as shown here, the supervisor runs as an infinite loop. On start-up it first activates the Standby Mode manager. This runs until it reaches a termination point, whence control is returned to the supervisor. Now the Running Mode manager is started. When *it* terminates, control is once more returned to the supervisor, the Standby Mode manager activated, and so on (until the power is turned off).

The most important point to note here is that the supervisor is concerned only with the handling of the mode managers; that is, it implements mode switching. However, it couldn't care less about system events and responses. These are the concern of the mode managers.

In this quite simple example the supervisor's job is very straightforward. There are only two states, and the mode changes are totally predictable. Now, as you might guess, this is the exception rather than the rule. Generally the supervisor has to select one mode for activation from a number of possibilities. The question is: how does it choose the correct one? We do this here through the mode managers. These return a control flag `NextState` to the supervisor, defining the *next* state to be entered (Figure 8.9).

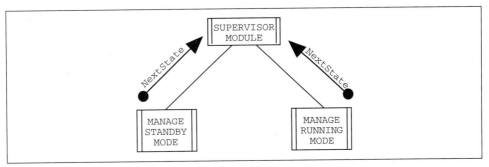

Figure 8.9 Control flags from the mode managers to the supervisor.

The future course of action of the supervisor is set by the flag value. This point is shown clearly in Figure 8.10.

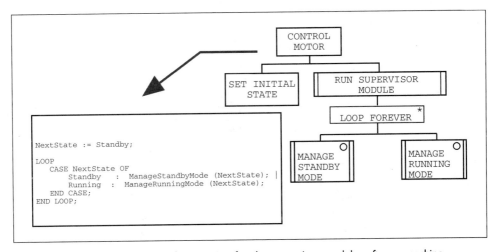

Figure 8.10 Code implementation for the supervisor module software machine.

The code section, apart from being small and obvious, is also complete. Correct operation hinges on the use of the control flag NextState. In this example it is used as a parameter of the two mode manager software machines. When the program is first run, the flag is set to Standby. This ensures that the system entry (initial) state is correct. The module then goes into a continuous loop, the first operation being a call of the Standby Mode manager. When this finishes executing it sets its parameter (the flag NextState) to Running. As a result, the next actioning of the CASE construct activates the Running Mode manager. On completion of ManageRunningMode, the NextState flag is set to Standby, and the cycle repeats.

Just to reiterate a point: such simple applications do not require the use of flags. If anything, they complicate rather than simplify the situation. And they also impose a parameter passing/handling overhead. However, practical systems are rarely described by *simple* two-state machines as given here. Further, it is only in the more complex state systems that distributed control is used. For these, state control using control flags is effective and efficient (more will be said about this in a moment).

Let us stop and review current progress. The supervisor module has been completed. However, the two manager modules have yet to be built – our next task. The approach is, if anything, simpler than that used in the centralized control technique. What we have is the structure defined in Figure 8.6, but now divided into two distinct operations (Figure 8.11).

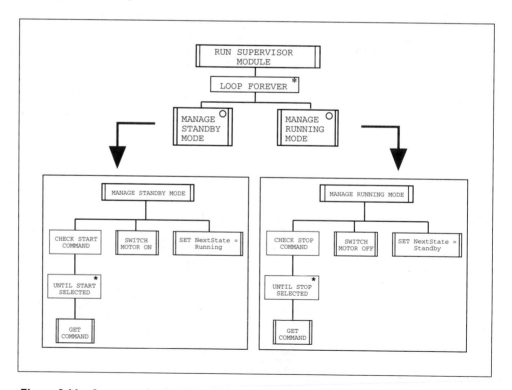

Figure 8.11   Structure of software machines 'Manage Standby Mode' and 'Manage Running Mode'.

It is yet another case of 'divide and conquer'. That is:

- First break the complete task into a set of simpler sub-tasks.
- Ensure that sub-tasks have little reliance on each other (low coupling).
- Implement each sub-task in turn.

Observe that the coupling mechanism here is the NextState flag. This has – as shown in Figure 8.11 – increased somewhat the complexity of the structure charts. It is, though, only a minor (almost trivial) issue. The related code aspects are illustrated in Figure 8.12, which needs no explanation.

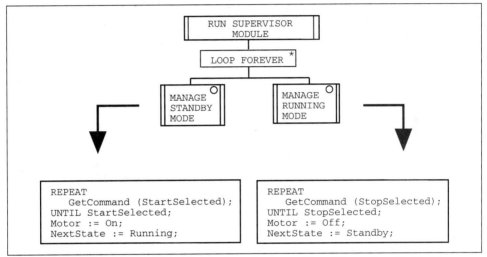

Figure 8.12 Code implementation for software machines 'Manage Standby Mode' and 'Manage Running Mode'.

Therefore, to implement the control transformation CT1 we combine the code of the supervisor and manager modules. There isn't a unique way to do this; one common approach is shown in Figure 8.13.

Do not regard the solution as *the* definitive method. Any sensible solution is acceptable.

Now, to conclude this section, let us look at another example control transformation. This will further illustrate the advantages of implementing CTs using decentralization plus control flags. Figure 8.14 is the STD for a three-state autopilot system.

The information displayed has been kept to a minimum to allow us to concentrate on essentials. The structure chart for the corresponding mode supervisor module is shown in Figure 8.15.

In this case there are three mode managers, corresponding to the three states of the state transition diagram. What we wish to define is the decision-making process of the supervisor module.

On power-on, the autopilot is put into the soft ride mode. It then responds to pilot switch selections, these being 'Hard', 'Soft' or 'Medium'. All permissible transitions are shown in Figure 8.14. You can see how each state *must* know what the

```
(* PROCEDURE ManageRunningMode *)
REPEAT
   GetCommand (StopSelected);
UNTIL StopSelected;
Motor := Off;
NextState := Standby;
(* END of procedure ManageRunningMode *)


(* PROCEDURE ManageStandbyMode *)
REPEAT
   GetCommand (StartSelected);
UNTIL StartSelected;
Motor := On;
NextState := Running;
(* END of procedure ManageStandbyMode *)

(* START OF MAIN PROGRAM *)
BEGIN
   NextState := Standby;

   LOOP
      CASE NextState OF
         Standby  :  ManageStandbyMode (NextState); |
         Running  :  ManageRunningMode (NextState);
      END CASE;
   END LOOP;
END .
(* END OF MAIN PROGRAM *)
```

Figure 8.13   Outline code implementation for the complete control transformation CT1.

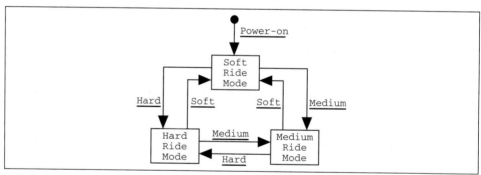

Figure 8.14   Example three-state system.

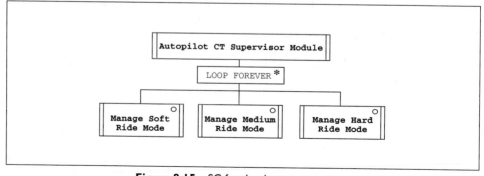

Figure 8.15   SC for the three-state system.

next transition will lead to. For instance, when in medium ride mode, transitions can take place to either soft ride or hard ride. The transition selection (which `NextState`) is based on information gathered during the medium ride mode. Thus, when the medium ride mode manager finishes executing, it can explicitly define the next system state. In this case it does it – as shown earlier – by using the control flag `NextState`. It therefore should be no surprise to find that the supervisor module is structured as in Figure 8.16.

```
BEGIN
    NextState := SoftRide;

LOOP
    CASE NextState OF
        SoftRide   : ManageSoftRideMode(NextState) |
        MediumRide : ManageMediumRideMode(NextState) |
        HardRide   : ManageHardRideMode (NextState)
    END CASE;
END LOOP;
END.
```

Figure 8.16 Supervisor module code example – three-state system.

The clarity, simplicity and ease of understanding of this should be obvious. What perhaps is not so obvious is that even very complex state machines can be implemented like this. You will find this out for yourself when you put this design method into practice.

A complete demonstration program for this example is shown in Listing 8.1.

8.2 Controlling data transformations

8.2.1 Brief recap

One of the major uses of CTs is for the control of data transformations. For 'control' read 'on/off control'. We can use a CT to define when a DT should begin executing; likewise it can decide when to shut the DT off. There is also a third scenario. Here a CT triggers a DT into action, but termination is the responsibility of the DT itself. The controlling signal generated by the CT is called a prompt; this name *always* has that meaning.

Chapter 7 introduced the various types of prompt:

- Enable (E)
- Disable (D)
- Trigger (T)
- Activator (A)

You will find that Enables and Disables are usually paired up.

In many cases you may find that a particular requirement can be satisfied in two (or sometimes more) ways. From an abstract point of view the choice may be

```
MODULE AutoStab;
FROM InOut IMPORT WriteLn, WriteString, Write, Read; TYPE
    RideMode = (Hard, Medium, Soft);
VAR
    RideSelection : CHAR;
    NextMode      : RideMode;
PROCEDURE GetRideSelection (VAR Selection : CHAR);
BEGIN
WriteString ('Make ride selection - H, M or S'); WriteLn; WriteLn; Read
(Selection); WriteLn;
    Selection := CAP (Selection);
    WriteString ('The selection is  ');
    Write (Selection); WriteLn;
END GetRideSelection;
PROCEDURE ManageHardRideMode (VAR NextState : RideMode); BEGIN
    REPEAT
        GetRideSelection (RideSelection);
    UNTIL RideSelection <> 'H';
    IF RideSelection = 'M' THEN NextState := Medium
    ELSE NextState := Soft;
    END; (* of if *)
END ManageHardRideMode;
PROCEDURE ManageMediumRideMode (VAR NextState : RideMode); BEGIN
    REPEAT
        GetRideSelection (RideSelection);
    UNTIL RideSelection <> 'M';
    IF RideSelection = 'H' THEN NextState := Hard;
    ELSE NextState := Soft;
    END; (* of if *)
END ManageMediumRideMode;
PROCEDURE ManageSoftRideMode (VAR NextState : RideMode); BEGIN
    REPEAT
        GetRideSelection (RideSelection);
    UNTIL RideSelection <> 'S';
    IF RideSelection = 'M' THEN NextState := Medium;
    ELSE NextState := Hard;
    END; (* of if *)
END ManageSoftRideMode;
BEGIN
    ManageSoftRideMode (NextMode);
    LOOP
        CASE NextMode OF
          Soft   : ManageSoftRideMode (NextMode); |
Medium : ManageMediumRideMode (NextMode); |
 Hard   : ManageHardRideMode (NextMode);
        END; (* of CASE *)
    END; (* of LOOP *)
END AutoStab.
```

Listing 8.1   Demonstration program for Figure 8.15.

immaterial. However, in practice it may have profound effects. When deciding what to use, we need to look at how the DT is implemented. This can be done in one of two ways:

- as a subprogram – a sequential software unit
- as a task – a concurrent software unit

Subprograms are familiar items. Here the term is a generic one, which includes procedures, functions and function procedures – call them what you will. Tasks, however, may well be new to you. Concurrency is covered in detail in Chapter 9. For the moment you don't need to know a great deal about the topic; the following will suffice. Each task:

- is a complete software unit
- is built as a single sequential program
- can execute at the same time as ('concurrent with') other tasks
- needs a system facility to control its execution
- will usually interact with other system tasks

Mechanisms which support tasking include interrupts and real-time executives. Here we will limit ourselves to interrupts.

8.2.2 The Enable/Disable prompt

Consider the situation depicted in Figure 8.17.

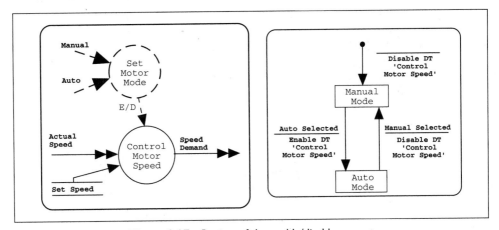

Figure 8.17 Review of the enable/disable prompt.

Here the behaviour of the CT is that of a two-state machine. Its input signals are Manual and Auto, being derived, say, from some sort of control selection. Only a single output is generated, the E/D prompt. This starts and stops the DT Control Motor Speed. We, at this point, have no interest in the innards of the DT. Strictly speaking, an STD should never be concerned with the details of a DT. Only its control is important, this being spelt out on the STD. However, now that implementation decisions have to be made, we cannot ignore how the DT is built. It must be clearly spelt out whether the DT will be a task or a subprogram.

First consider how the task construct is used. As stated earlier, this will be limited to interrupt-driven operations. To distinguish between concurrent and sequential programs, extra DFD notation is needed. Figure 8.18 shows one method, the zig-zag line being a common way of denoting interrupts.

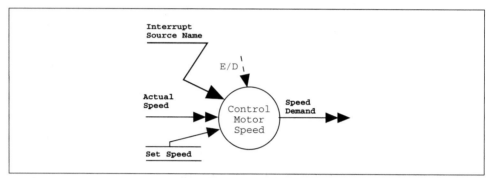

Figure 8.18   Interrupt driven DT (task).

You may, of course, find that your CASE tool does not let you do this. In that case (no pun intended), use your initiative. Remember, though, to make sure that any home-brewed notation is consistent throughout your design. And it should also be defined in your design documentation. Moreover, it is essential that the diagrams have only one meaning; the semantics must be clear-cut. Readers must not be able to interpret them in different ways.

The semantics of Figure 8.18 say that here there is an interrupt-driven DT Control Motor Speed. The code of the DT is executed when an interrupt Interrupt Source Name arrives – but subject to the interrupt being enabled. Thus the E prompt enables the interrupt; the D prompt disables it. The E/D prompt acts as a switching signal; there is no direct connection between the code of the CT and that of the DT.

From the information given in the STD/DFD pair the structure chart for the CT (Figure 8.19) can be generated.

A useful analogy is to view a structure chart as being the offspring of an STD/DFD pairing.

You can see from the corresponding code fragment where and when the switching of the DT takes place. The first operation is to disable the interrupt, then enter the continuous loop of the CT program. In this particular design a single subprogram GetCommand is used to interrogate the command settings. Its parameter is used to denote which setting is to be checked. Until the check condition AutoSelected is met, the program loops. When this occurs, the interrupt is enabled. Thus the DT will execute under interrupt control (typically a timer-generated interrupt signal). This will continue until the interrupt is disabled in response to the command

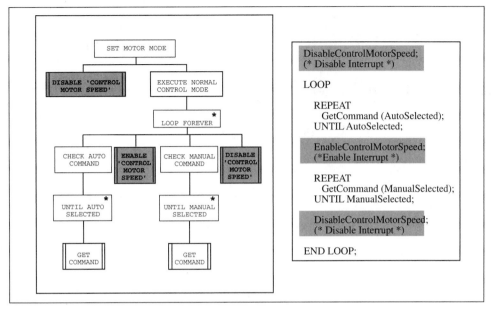

Figure 8.19   Structuring and implementing the Enable/Disable prompt – DT as task.

`ManualSelected`. At this point the program reverts to checking for `AutoSelected`, and so repeats the cycle.

Now let us see how the CT would be constructed if the DT was formed as a subprogram. The example given here uses a centralized control approach, as the state machine operation is clear-cut. Before getting into detail it is worth restating some well-known attributes of subprograms:

- They have to be called into action ('invoked').
- Once called they normally run to completion (exceptional conditions are beyond the scope of this design work).
- They run *once* only on each invocation.

These factors significantly affect the implementation of the E and D prompt mechanisms.

First, take the Disable action. Subprograms naturally terminate; thus there is no need to produce an explicit Disable command. Disable is the default state.

Now for the Enable action. This is equivalent to a 'switch-on' command. The subprogram is commanded to run repeatedly until it is disabled. However, left to its own devices it will run once only, terminating naturally. One way to keep it running is to enclose it within a loop (Figure 8.20(a)).

In the SC fragment, the subprogram `Control Motor Speed` represents the controlled DT of Figure 8.18. As implemented, it is fine for switch-on. Unfortunately this implementation is an infinite loop, with no mechanism for turning it off. What we now need to provide is a loop terminating condition to mimic the Disable prompt.

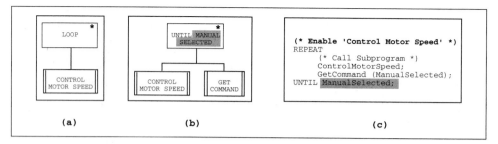

Figure 8.20   Enabling and disabling subprograms – basic idea.

This is done in Figure 8.20(b) by checking for the command Manual Selected, and terminating when the condition is true. The corresponding code fragment is shown in Figure 8.20(c). For our example system, the CT implementation is shown in Figure 8.21.

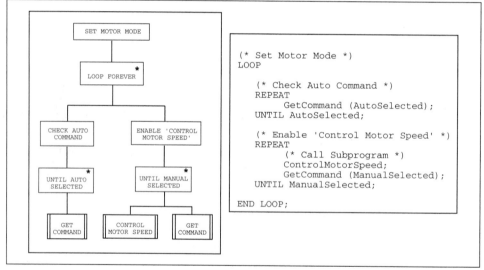

Figure 8.21   Structuring and implementing the Enable/Disable prompt – DT as subprogram.

The complete program, once started, runs as an infinite loop. Before entering this loop there is no need to disable the DT Control Motor Speed. By default it will be inactive. Command checking is done as in the previous design; nothing new here. However, when Auto is selected, the subprograms ControlMotorSpeed and GetCommand are invoked, running within a controlled loop. Termination occurs when Manual is selected, and the whole process is repeated.

In summary then, the E/D pair is implemented as a controlled loop. Starting the loop is equivalent to Enable, terminating to Disable. Note, by the way, that this applies even if we use flat code (no subprogram calls) to implement the DT.

8.2.3 The Trigger prompt

The Trigger prompt is the easiest one to implement. We can use the design shown in Figure 8.22 to quickly review its meaning.

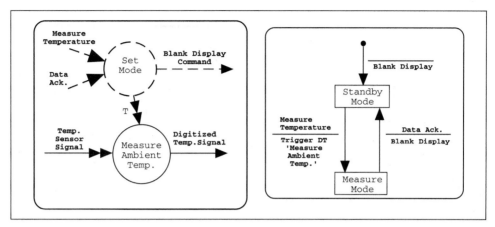

Figure 8.22 Review of the Trigger prompt.

Here the CT SetMode produces two outputs. One is a control signal, the other is a Trigger prompt. This prompt is used to trigger the DT Measure Ambient Temperature into action. The dynamics of the CT are shown on the attached STD. Triggering, remember, is a one-shot activity. When a DT is triggered into action, it executes *once* only. Therefore, when the signal Measure Temperature arrives, the DT is kicked into action to carry out a single measurement. When this is completed – and while the system is in the Measure Mode state – the DT does nothing.

From the DFD/STD information we can derive the structure chart of Figure 8.23.

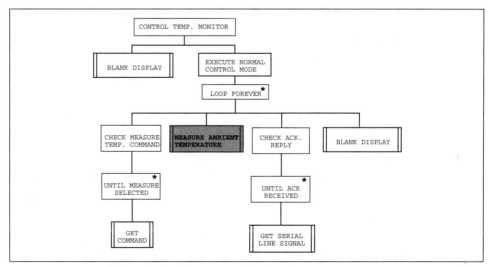

Figure 8.23 Structuring of the Trigger prompt example.

This begins with a call to blank the display, after which the system enters a continuous loop. At this point it (the system) is in Standby Mode. It remains there, checking the `Measure Temp.` command, looping until the command is received. The result of this event is to:

- change the system state to `Measure Mode`
- call `Measure Ambient Temperature` (the response to the event)
- check continuously for the event `Data Ack` (check `Ack Reply`)

When the `Data Ack.` signal arrives the check loop is exited. The next operation is to blank the display, the system reverting to Standby Mode within the continuous loop of operation.

Implementation of the structure chart is an easy process, as demonstrated in Figure 8.24.

```
BlankDisplay;

LOOP

    REPEAT
        GetCommand (MeasureTempSelected);
    UNTIL MeasureTempSelected;

    (* This is the triggering of the operation *)
    MeasureAmbientTemperature;

    REPEAT
        GetSerialData (AcknowledgeReply);
    UNTIL AcknowledgeReply;
    BlankDisplay;

END LOOP;
```

Figure 8.24 Implementing the Trigger prompt.

Only one further point deserves a mention. You might argue that there is no need to have two separate calls to `Blank Display`. By putting this as the first operation within the infinite loop, the first call can be omitted. True, you can do this if the state conditions are the same under all conditions (initial entry, first return, second return and so on), but there are times when this condition isn't met. Strictly speaking we have different state conditions, and the STDs should reflect this. Unfortunately, this can result in complex and unmanageable diagrams. Therefore the simpler – if somewhat incorrect solution – is chosen. In such cases be *very* careful in the organization of the structure chart.

8.2.4 The Activator prompt

Now for the last type of prompt, the Activator. Experience has shown that, for some people, Activators can be a difficult topic to assimilate. So the explanation here is taken at a gentle (if apparently long-winded) pace.

To demonstrate its use, let us look at a small (hypothetical) monitoring and control system. The DFD for this system – the 'Lube Pump' – is that of Figure 8.25.

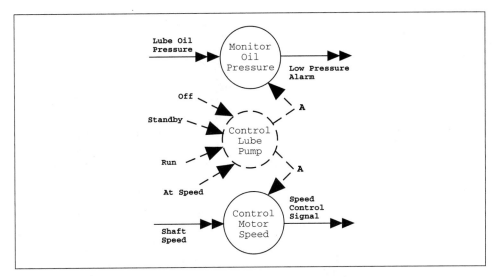

Figure 8.25   Review of the Activator prompt.

Its corresponding STD is shown in Figure 8.26.

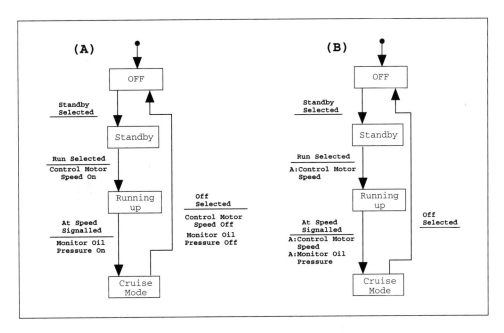

Figure 8.26   Activators and STDs.

This, as you can see, is drawn twice. Figure 8.26(a) defines the desired behaviour of the system, and really has no connection with the DFD. Diagram Figure 8.26(b) says exactly the same thing as (a), but *is* directly related to its parent CT Control Lube Pump. In the following description of system behaviour, refer to Figure 8.26(a).

The computer system is designed to control motor speed and to monitor oil pressure. From (a) we can see that the initial state is OFF. It remains there until Standby is selected, whereupon it enters the Standby mode (for simplicity assume that the event doesn't generate a response). When Run is selected the motor is run-up, its speed being put under automatic control. At a preset speed value the command At Speed is signalled. The system now enters Cruise mode, running under automatic speed control. However, it is now continuously monitored to detect and warn of low lube oil pressure. This state of affairs continues until Off is selected, where a transition to the OFF mode is made. The Off command (event) evokes two responses: automatic speed control is turned off and oil pressure monitoring is suspended.

Assume that we decide on the functional structure depicted in the DFD of Figure 8.25. Two DTs are used, both controlled by a single CT, Control Lube Pump. Activators are used as the controlling prompts. The behaviour of the CT is defined in the STD of Figure 8.26(b), which is fairly clear-cut. Data transformations are turned on by the activation action; they go off automatically when a state change occurs. Note that the DT Control Motor Speed is activated twice. The first time is on transition to the Running up state, the second on entry to the Cruise Mode. This second activation is needed because the DT goes off automatically when the Running up mode is left.

Thus an activator can be thought of as an 'enable' on entering a state and the corresponding 'disable' on leaving it.

From this information the structure chart of Figure 8.27 is derived, the corresponding code being given in Figure 8.28.

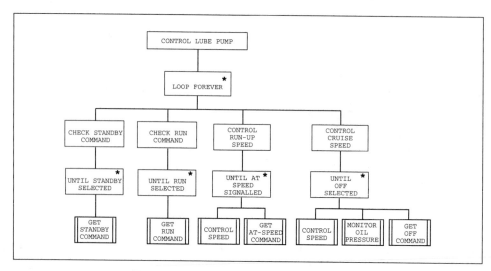

Figure 8.27 Structuring the Activator prompt.

```
                    (* Run Control Lube Pump Program Forever *)
                    LOOP

                        (* Check for Standby command *)
                        REPEAT
                            GetCommand (Standby);
                        UNTIL Standby;

                        (* Check for Run command *)
                        REPEAT
                            GetCommand (Run);
                        UNTIL Run;

                        (* Control Run-up speed *)
                        REPEAT
                            ControlSpeed;
                            GetCommand (AtSpeed);
                        UNTIL AtSpeed;

                        (* Control Cruise speed *)
                        REPEAT
                            ControlSpeed;
                            MonitorOilPressure;
                            GetCommand (Off);
                        UNTIL Off;

                    END LOOP;
```

Figure 8.28   Code implementation for Figure 8.27.

You may feel that the Activator is not really needed; after all, you could achieve the same ends using the E/D prompts. Yes, you could. But the benefits of using the Activator will only become clear with practice and experience. The advantages are:

- You can tell instantly from your STD which DTs are active within specific states. With the E/D prompt you have to search carefully for the activations and de-activations.
- You are forced to define explicitly, on a state by state basis, the active DTs.
- These two factors make it easier to generate the structure chart.
- You are likely to make fewer mistakes when producing the structure chart.
- This approach is much better when using a decentralized control approach.
- It is easier to trace the design progress through the various diagrams down to the source code level.
- The generation of the SC (certainly at the higher levels) can be fairly easily automated.

8.2.5   Prompts – a last comment

It is important to be consistent in how you use prompts. In that way fewer mistakes are made, and your designs are easier to review. One cannot be dogmatic here, but the following rules appear to work well:

(a)   Use the Enable/Disable prompts to control concurrent tasks.
(b)   If a transformation is required to run once only on *each* activation, use a trigger prompt. This applies whether the DT is prompted once, twice or many times during execution of the complete program.

(c)   If your hardware has inbuilt memory (latches), then it can be set up with a single write operation. In that case, control the DT as a triggered operation.

(d)   Otherwise control DTs using activators.

8.3   Control transformations and levelled diagrams

8.3.1   Defining dynamics within a child DT

Up to this point only single-level DFDs have been implemented (a very unlikely real situation). Where individual DTs are levelled – but we *do not* need to define dynamics at the lower levels – no further CTs exist. This could be the case for the top-level DFD of Figure 8.29.

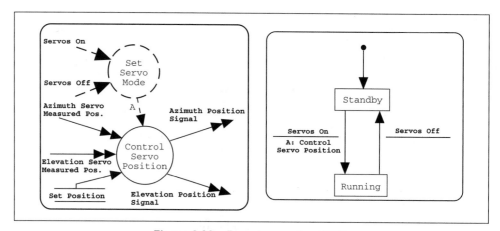

Figure 8.29   Example – top-level DFD.

The DFD/STD diagrams describe the statics and dynamics of a two-loop servo position control system. When Servos On is selected, the DT is activated, positioning both Azimuth and Elevation servos. This operation continues until the command Servos Off arrives. Figure 8.30 gives the corresponding structure chart and source code.

Suppose now the system specification is amended. Because of power supply limitations, only one servo motor can be run at a time. Therefore it is decided to position the Azimuth servo first, followed by the Elevation servo. The question is: how and where is this information shown? The answer? On the levelled DFD for the DT Control Servo Position (Figure 8.31).

Here we have two DTs, Position Azimuth Servo and Position Elevation Servo. A single CT Control Servo Drives is used to provide activating prompts for the DTs. Each DT transmits a signal to the CT, indicating that positioning has been completed. The STD shows that the initial state is Azimuth Mode, in which the Azimuth servo is positioned. The event (signal) Azimuth Servo Positioned leads

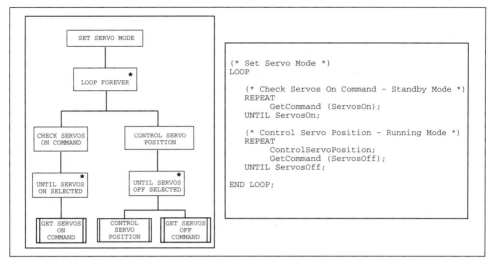

Figure 8.30 Structuring and implementing the DFD of Figure 8.29.

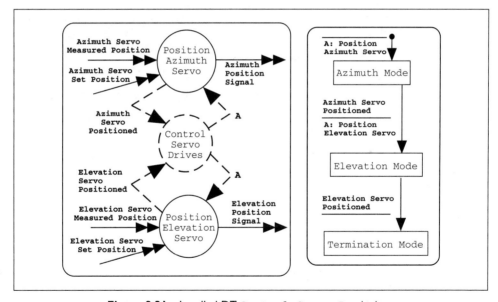

Figure 8.31 Levelled DT `Control Servo Position`.

to a state change to the Elevation Mode; the corresponding response is to activate positioning of the Elevation servo. When position correspondence is attained, the signal `Elevation Servo Positioned` is generated. This causes a state change to the Termination Mode. Translation of this information into structure chart form is shown in Figure 8.32.

The corresponding code implementation is also given in this diagram.

Now let us carefully review these diagrams, together with the final source code. It

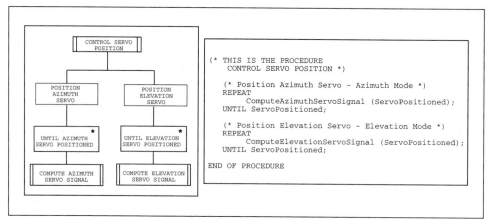

Figure 8.32 Structuring and implementing the DFD of Figure 8.31.

is *vital* that our understanding of the picture semantics is correct (or, at the very least, their meaning is interpreted in a consistent and agreed manner). We are, remember, mainly interested in behavioural aspects. Figure 8.29 DFD tells us that the DT Control Servo Position is activated by the CT Set Servo Mode. The behaviour of the CT is defined using the STD of Figure 8.29. This shows that:

- The system normally runs as a two-state infinite loop.
- the DT is active as long as the system is in the Running mode.

Inspection of Figure 8.30 reveals that this information has first been translated correctly into SC form, then into source code. It is *explicit* that activation and deactivation of the DT is the responsibility of the CT Set Servo Mode. Please re-read the last sentence; this is a most important point. What it means is that the CT not only turns the DT on; it *must* be able to turn it off as well. We do not delegate this action to any lower level within the DFD structure.

Control Servo Position is implemented as a procedure. For simplicity, parameters have been omitted. Repetitive execution of the procedure is controlled by the Boolean signal Servos Off. The levelled DFD of the DT (Figure 8.31) defines the statics and dynamics of the DT itself. But remember: the child only has meaning when the DT is activated (in our case, when the procedure is invoked). When this occurs it can be seen that:

- Two DTs are executed.
- The first is Position Azimuth Servo. This is performed until the signal Azimuth Servo Positioned is received by the controlling CT Control Servo Drives.
- Translation to Elevation Mode takes place, and the DT Position Elevation Servo is activated. This ceases on receipt of the control signal Elevation Servo Positioned.
- Termination mode is entered. This corresponds to completion of the procedure.

You might argue that the final state Termination Mode is somewhat redundant. After all, you wouldn't finish the procedure Position Elevation Servo until the servo is positioned. While this is true, it does have an important implication. That is, to interpret the diagram, you *have* to know what happens in the system. In other words, you must carry implicit information with you. But, by showing the termination state, we define explicitly:

- precisely what state the system ends up in when the DT has finished executing
- how and why we get into that state

The SC of Figure 8.32 defines the structure of the DFD program, together with its associated source code. There is, of course, no concept of trying to define a termination state on these; it is the natural termination of the procedure. It is good practice at this stage to re-check that the system behaviour (as stated in the STD) is correctly implemented. What Figure 8.31 says is that:

- When the DT Control Servo Position is activated, the first operation is to run the child DT Position Azimuth Servo.
- On completion of azimuth positioning, this DT is deactivated. Position Elevation Servo is now activated.
- When elevation positioning is achieved, this last DT is deactivated, and the STD is terminated.

Thus, each time the parent DT is activated, the same sequence of events takes place. The parent is activated by invoking Control Servo Position; the code within this defines the levelled DFD behaviour.

8.3.2 *Control flows that cross DT boundaries*

In the example of Figure 8.31, the two flows Servo Positioned came out of DTs. That is, they were generated within the DTs, crossing the DT boundaries on their way to the CT. You can see (Figure 8.32) that this process was handled using parameter passing methods. Experience has shown that this concept, and its implementation, are readily assimilated. However, the reverse case – flows entering a DT – seems to be a much more difficult one to grasp. To demonstrate this issue, consider a modified version of the servo controller (Figure 8.33).

Here new input and output control signals have been added: Pause, Resume and Servo Paused. These are connected directly to the DT Control Servo Position. Furthermore, it can be seen that they are concerned with the behaviour of the CT Control Servo Drives. These controls have been added so that operators can stop the servos using local control switching.

What Figure 8.33 tells us is that:

- Control signals Pause and Resume are used *within* the DT Control Servo Position.
- Control signal Servo Paused is generated inside the DT, being used in the outside world.

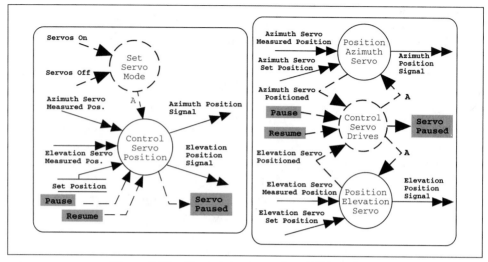

Figure 8.33   Control signals crossing a DT boundary.

- All these signals are linked in with the dynamic behaviour of the DT. This is specified by the STD associated with CT `Control Servo Drives`.
- If the DT `Control Servo Position` is inactive, these signals have no meaning. That is, the inputs `Pause` and `Resume` cannot affect the behaviour of the system. Likewise, no meaning can be attached to the output `Servo Paused`.

The STD of Figure 8.34 defines the dynamics of the system.

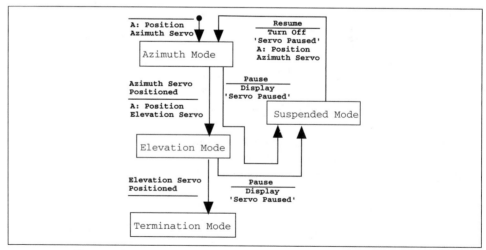

Figure 8.34   STD for CT `Control Servo Drives` of Figure 8.33.

Read through this carefully to make sure that you understand how the system is meant to work (why we should want it to behave like this is not open to discussion). The corresponding SC is shown in Figure 8.35.

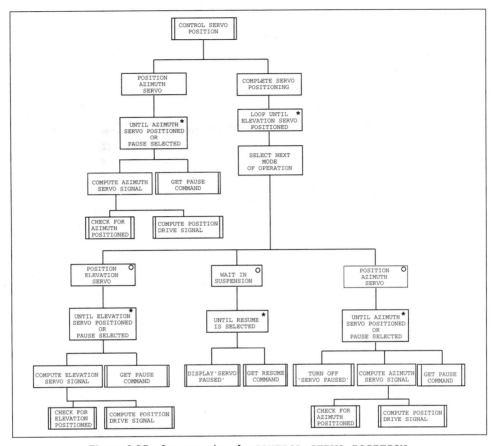

Figure 8.35 Structure chart for CONTROL SERVO POSITION.

This is one example where a structure chart could, with a small change to the STD, be greatly simplified. All that is needed is to make *all* entry conditions to the Azimuth Mode state identical. This would allow us to remove the first sequence item Position Azimuth Servo (and its complete tree structure) from the SC.

Listing 8.2 gives a part emulation of the DT Control Servo Position (a more complete version of this is in Listing 8.3, given at the end of this chapter).

Normally we would package the software of Listing 8.2 within a subprogram, and invoke it as described in Figure 8.30.

You can see that the original higher level design aspects are still valid. The servos only run when Servos On is commanded, being switched off by the Servos Off signal. Note how we have been able to keep the top-level operations unchanged. Modifications have been done only to the lower-level activities. This approach is strongly recommended because it:

- Keeps related items close together. We don't end up with a wide separation (in program terms) between stimulus and response. For instance, the system only

```
BEGIN
(*CONTROL SERVO POSITION *)
   (* Position Azimuth Servo *)
   LOOP (* Position Azimuth Servo *)
      CheckForAzimuthPositioned (AzimuthPositioned);
      IF AzimuthPositioned THEN NextMode := Elevation; EXIT
      END;
      ComputeAzimuthPositionDriveSignal;
      GetPauseCommand (Pause);
      IF Pause THEN NextMode := Suspended; EXIT
      END;
   END; (* of loop Position Azimuth Servo *)

   (* Complete Servo Positioning *)
   REPEAT (* Until Elevation Servo Positioned *)
   (* Select Next Mode of Operation *)
      IF NextMode = Elevation THEN
         (* Position Elevation Servo *)
         LOOP (* Position Elevation Servo *)
            CheckForElevationPositioned (ElevationPositioned);
            IF ElevationPositioned THEN EXIT
            END;
            ComputeElevationPositionDriveSignal;
            GetPauseCommand (Pause);
            IF Pause THEN
               NextMode := Suspended; EXIT
            END;
         END; (* loop Position Elevation Servo *)

      ELSIF NextMode = Suspended THEN
         (* Wait in Suspension *)
         LOOP (* Wait in Suspension *)
            DisplayServoPaused;
            GetResumeCommand (Resume);
            IF Resume THEN
               NextMode := Azimuth; EXIT
            END;
         END; (* loop Wait in Suspension *)

      ELSIF NextMode = Azimuth THEN
         (* Position Elevation Servo *)
         LOOP (* Position Azimuth Servo *)
            TurnOffServoPaused;
            CheckForAzimuthPositioned (AzimuthPositioned);
            IF AzimuthPositioned THEN
               NextMode := Elevation; EXIT
            END;
            ComputeAzimuthPositionDriveSignal;
            GetPauseCommand (Pause);
            IF Pause THEN
               NextMode := Suspended; EXIT
            END;
         END; (* loop Position Azimuth Servo *)

      ELSE
         WriteString ('ERROR'); WriteLn;
      END; (* if NextMode = Elevation *)
   UNTIL ElevationPositioned;
END Listing82.
```

Listing 8.2.

responds to the signals `Pause` and `Resume` when `Control Servo Position` runs. Likewise, the output `Servo Paused` can only be generated by this subprogram.

- Allows us to focus on system behaviour within very specific scenarios (and not get confused with or side-tracked into more global issues).
- Results in designs which have high stability.
- Makes it much easier to implement and test out modifications.

8.4 Connecting to the outside world

You may not have noticed, but one very important point has so far had minimal discussion: exactly how control signals are interfaced to the outside world. The examples used here have, so far, been carefully chosen to lull you into complacency. Unfortunately, as soon as you begin to do real design work, you will find many and varied pitfalls. So, why do we have problems, and how can we overcome them?

Within the computer system there is no difficulty in distinguishing between control (event) flows and data flows. Both items are needed to describe the design fully. However, our difficulties come when we look beyond the computer, to the external devices. The cause of our difficulties comes (in my view) from the definition of what an 'event' is. In their book *Structured Development for Real-Time Systems*, Ward and Mellor define an event as ' ... simply signals that indicate that something has happened or give a command'. While this may be fine for analysing systems, it doesn't work quite so well when designing them. This issue is further clouded by defining events as time-discrete actions. So, given this information, how would you categorize the items listed in Table 8.1?

Table 8.1.

Source/destination	Signal characteristics
Push-button	0 V, 24 V d.c.
On/off selector switch	On $\Rightarrow$ 5 V d.c.
Pressure sensor	0–10 V d.c., analogue signal, continuous signal
Sonar echo	Pulse signal, range 0–100 µV, 1 pulse per second, 100 kHz carrier
Digital tachometer	0–1000 pps, TTL compatible
Serial communications line	SDLC protocol, RS422 line signals
Single-phase induction motor	0 V, 115 V a.c.
Induction motor speed controller	TTL level serial line, 0–1 kHz clock
Stepper motor	Four-phase drive, 12 V, 0–6000 steps per second

The push-button is the one which meets all the criteria of the event. No signal is present until the button is pressed (assume press to close the contacts), and it arrives at a discrete point in time. Number 2, the on/off switch, certainly produces signals at specific instants. However, the electrical signals may, or may not, be always present – it depends on the design. With the sonar echo signal, the issue is once more clear-cut. It is a classical case of a discrete data item. Or is it? In some circumstances we may be interested only in the presence (or absence) of an echo. Is this an event? After you've assessed all items in this table, I'm sure that either:

- you'll be quite confused, or
- you will have eventually arrived at a decision, but then find that other designers disagree with your conclusions

As stated earlier, the root cause is taking an analyst's description over to the design phase.

Therefore, at the design stage, to avoid philosophical confusion and brain damage:

(a) Use the overall *system* diagram as the basis for the context diagram.
(b) Categorize all input/output flows as *data*.
(c) Route these to data transformations.
(d) For inputs that are used as signals, generate these signals in the DTs. Route the signals as controls (events) to appropriate CTs.
(e) For outputs which are used to control items, use a CT to prompt their generation.
(f) Use the electrical/physical characteristics of signals to classify them as time-continuous or time-discrete.
(g) Do not bother to distinguish amplitude-discrete from amplitude-continuous signals.

In structured design terms this may be a form of heresy. Fortunately, it does have the advantage of being simple, clear-cut and consistent. To support this technique, four simple DFD icons are required (Figure 8.36).

In Figure 8.36(a), a DT takes in a discrete data flow, and generates a control (event) signal. We have a similar situation in Figure 8.36(b), except that the input is a continuous data value. In Figure 8.36(c), a control signal into a DT causes a discrete data signal to be generated. The final case, Figure 8.36(d), is where the output data signal is a continuous valued item.

To see how these can be applied, take the DFD of Figure 8.37.

Here we have a small system: a motor switching control unit. It takes in the time-discrete commands Start and Stop, and outputs the signals Motor On and Motor Off (also time-discrete). To acquire the input commands, the Start and Stop signals are interrogated until a state change is seen. On the output side, it is assumed that the hardware has inbuilt memory; hence only a single write is required to set either output line. Thus the input DTs' Get Commands are controlled by the CT using Activators. Triggers are used to prompt the two Switch Motor output DTs. System dynamics are defined in Figure 8.38.

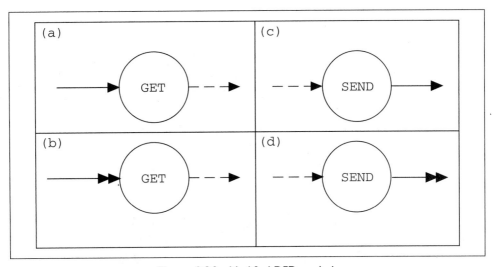

Figure 8.36 Modified DFD symbols.

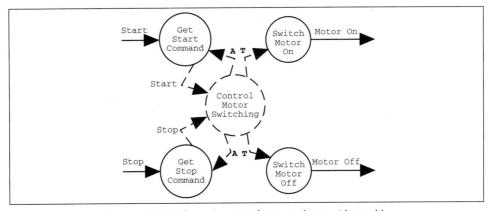

Figure 8.37 Example – interfacing to the outside world.

The combined DFD and STD information is the basis for the design of the structure chart of Figure 8.39.

To simplify this design the initial response (Get Start Command) has been assimilated into the continuous loop.

Compare this design with that of Figures 8.1 and 8.6. You can see that they are describing exactly the same system. In fact, the structure charts are – apart from naming aspects – identical. Thus this method of dealing with external signals has not in any way distorted the eventual implementation. What it has done, though, is to make all interfacing to the outside world clear, explicit and well defined. Further, the technique is one which is totally consistent, in that (put very simply):

- DTs 'do' things.
- CTs 'control' things.

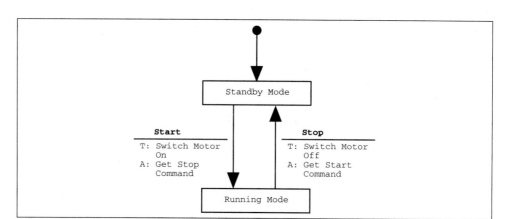

Figure 8.38   STD for Figure 8.37.

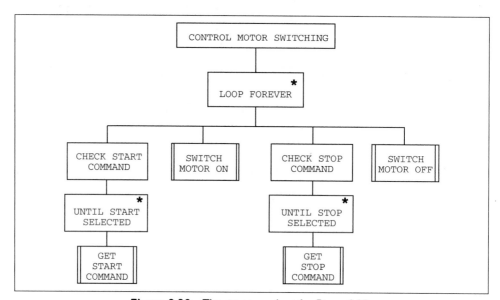

Figure 8.39   The structure chart for Figure 8.37.

8.5   The common module issue

The final point to be covered in this chapter is that called the 'common module' issue. An example of this occurred earlier, but discussion of it was deliberately left until now.

To see how and why we get common modules, first consider the DFD of Figure 8.40.

This is the description of a system which includes keyboard, screen and serial communication devices. Its behaviour is given in Figure 8.41.

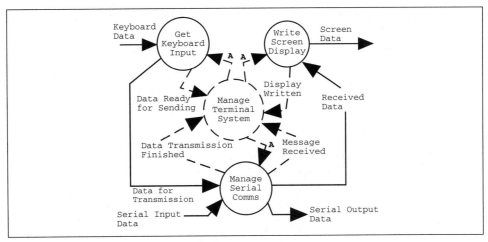

Figure 8.40 Example DFD to show the common module issue.

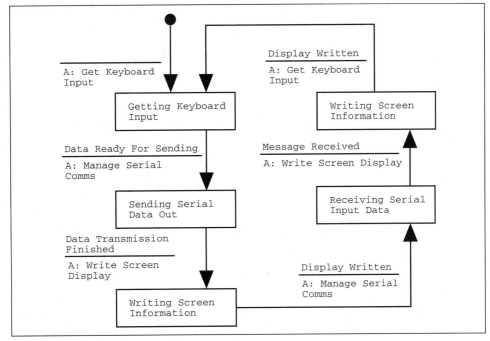

Figure 8.41 STD for CT Manage Terminal System.

On power-up, the keyboard is polled to get a message which is then transmitted over the communication network. The Data Ready for Sending event indicates that the message is complete and can be transmitted. After data is sent a confirmation message is written to the screen. The system now enters a network listening mode, looking for incoming data. When a message is received from the network it is displayed on the screen. Polling of the keyboard is once more resumed, and the whole cycle repeated.

The structure chart design for this is given in Figure 8.42.

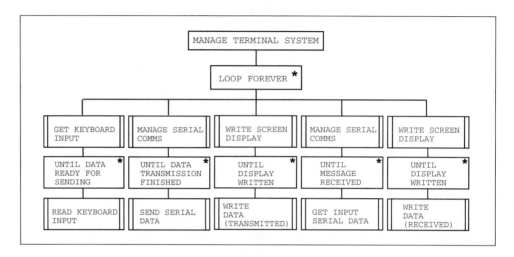

Figure 8.42   Structure chart for DFD Manage Terminal System.

This, only the top-level solution, is simple and straightforward. But note well that the DT Manage Serial Comms is used in *two* distinct places. Thus two separate points in the program are coupled together by the one software machine – the *common module*. The same is true of Write Screen Display. What does this mean? It is that the structure chart is not a pure tree; in reality it has degenerated into a mesh. If the SC had been drawn as a Yourdon diagram, this would have been shown explicitly. Unfortunately, Jackson diagram semantics do not allow this. Every time we use a module we have to enter it on the diagram.

There is an important (and, on first meeting, a subtle) difference between Manage Serial Comms and Write Screen Display. For serial data handling, two different sub-modules, Send Serial Data and Get Input Serial Data, are used. Both are packaged within the subprogram Manage Serial Comms. On invoking this subprogram we can define – using control flags – which sub-module is to be used. Therefore, by careful design, the common coupling produced by the serial comms machine can be minimized. Unfortunately, the screen display module always does the same thing; only the data to be written changes. This design solution will cause very tight coupling between all users of such common modules.

Is common coupling dangerous? Should we avoid it at the application level? The obvious answer is yes. But, in practice, *can* we avoid it? Very unlikely – without producing a complex, awkward and unnatural solution, that is. What you *must* realize is that the coupling results from decisions made when designing the DFD. So, if you end up with common coupling, what should you do? Distorting a perfectly good design to eliminate such coupling seems likely to create, not solve, problems. The best advice is to:

- Identify all common modules.
- Define, within each common module, its list of clients (remember, this is at the application, not service, level).
- If possible, package separate operations (within the common module) in distinct subprograms. Select these using control couples.
- Make sure that all common data items are highlighted.
- Ensure that all pre- and post-conditions are defined.

It may be worth amending the structure chart notation to mark up such common modules.

Review

As a result of studying this chapter, you should now:

- understand the steps involved in going from the real-time DFD to source code via the structure chart
- fully appreciate the use of control transformations to control and interact with data transformations
- know how to implement (in code) control transformations, using both centralized and distributed techniques
- understand the pros and cons of the two implementation methods
- have a full, clear understanding of Enable, Disable, Trigger and Activator prompts
- see why these are applicable to different situations, and know how to implement them at the code level
- know how to define dynamics at the various levels within a data flow diagram
- understand why control flows cross DT boundaries, and know how to implement such flows
- see why there are advantages in treating all input/output signals as data flows
- appreciate what a common module is, what its inherent dangers are, and how these can be mitigated

Exercises

Repeat the Exercises of Chapter 7, but with all input/output handled by data transformations. Produce a full set of design diagrams (context, DFDs, STDs and SCs) together with the corresponding source code.

```
MODULE Fig835;
FROM InOut IMPORT Write, WriteLn, WriteString,
                  Read, ReadLn, ReadInt;

TYPE
   MODE = (Azimuth, Elevation, Suspended);

CONST
   On  = TRUE;
   Off = FALSE;
   Yes = TRUE;
   No  = FALSE;

VAR
   AzimuthPositioned   : BOOLEAN;
   ElevationPositioned : BOOLEAN;
   Pause               : BOOLEAN;
   Resume              : BOOLEAN;
   Answer              : CHAR;
   NextMode            : MODE;

PROCEDURE TurnOffServoPaused;
BEGIN
   WriteString ('Turning off Servo Paused indication ');
   WriteLn; WriteLn;
END TurnOffServoPaused;

PROCEDURE DisplayServoPaused;
BEGIN
   WriteString ('Displaying Servo Paused indication ');
   WriteLn; WriteLn;
END DisplayServoPaused;

PROCEDURE CheckForAzimuthPositioned
                       (VAR AzimuthPositioned : BOOLEAN);
BEGIN
   WriteString ('Is Azimuth Positioned?   Y or N '); WriteLn;
   Read (Answer); WriteLn;
   Answer := CAP (Answer); Write (Answer); WriteLn;
   IF Answer = 'Y'
      THEN AzimuthPositioned := Yes
      ELSE AzimuthPositioned := No
   END;
END CheckForAzimuthPositioned;

PROCEDURE CheckForElevationPositioned
                       (VAR ElevationPositioned : BOOLEAN);
BEGIN
   WriteString ('Is Elevation Positioned?   Y or N '); WriteLn;
   Read (Answer); WriteLn;
   Answer := CAP (Answer); Write (Answer); WriteLn;
   IF Answer = 'Y'
      THEN ElevationPositioned := Yes
      ELSE ElevationPositioned := No
   END;
END CheckForElevationPositioned;
```

Listing 8.3. *(continued)*

Listing 8.3   219

8.3. *Continued*

```
PROCEDURE GetPauseCommand (VAR Signal : BOOLEAN);
BEGIN
   WriteString ('Is Pause selected?   Y or N '); WriteLn;
   Read (Answer);
   Answer := CAP (Answer); Write (Answer); WriteLn; WriteLn;
   IF Answer = 'Y'
      THEN Signal := On
      ELSE Signal := Off
   END;
END GetPauseCommand;

PROCEDURE GetResumeCommand (VAR Signal : BOOLEAN);
BEGIN
   WriteString ('Is Resume selected?   Y or N '); WriteLn;
   Read (Answer);
   Answer := CAP (Answer); Write (Answer); WriteLn; WriteLn;
   IF Answer = 'Y'
      THEN Signal := On
      ELSE Signal := Off
   END;
END GetResumeCommand;

PROCEDURE ComputeElevationPositionDriveSignal;
BEGIN
   WriteString ('Computing Elevation Drive Signal'); WriteLn;
END ComputeElevationPositionDriveSignal;

PROCEDURE ComputeAzimuthPositionDriveSignal;
BEGIN
   WriteString ('Computing Azimuth Drive Signal'); WriteLn;
END ComputeAzimuthPositionDriveSignal;




BEGIN
   ElevationPositioned := No;
   AzimuthPositioned   := No;
   Pause := Off;

   WriteString ('Start of programme - In Azimuth Mode'); WriteLn;
   LOOP (* Position Azimuth Servo *)
      CheckForAzimuthPositioned (AzimuthPositioned);
      IF AzimuthPositioned THEN NextMode := Elevation; EXIT
      END;
      ComputeAzimuthPositionDriveSignal;
      GetPauseCommand (Pause);
      IF Pause THEN NextMode := Suspended; EXIT
      END;
   END; (* of loop Position Azimuth Servo *)

   WriteString ('Start of Complete Servo Positioning');
   WriteLn; WriteLn;
   REPEAT (* Until Elevation Servo Positioned *)
```

Listing 8.3.   *(continued)*

8.3. *Continued*

```
        IF NextMode = Elevation THEN
            WriteString ('In Elevation Mode'); WriteLn;
            LOOP (* Position Elevation Servo *)
              CheckForElevationPositioned (ElevationPositioned);
              IF ElevationPositioned THEN EXIT
              END;
              ComputeElevationPositionDriveSignal;
              GetPauseCommand (Pause);
              IF Pause THEN NextMode := Suspended; EXIT
              END;
            END; (* loop Position Elevation Servo *)

        ELSIF NextMode = Suspended THEN
            WriteString ('In Suspended Mode'); WriteLn;
            LOOP (* Wait in Suspension *)
              DisplayServoPaused;
              GetResumeCommand (Resume);
              IF Resume THEN NextMode := Azimuth; EXIT
              END;
            END; (* loop Wait in Suspension *)

        ELSIF NextMode = Azimuth THEN
            WriteString ('In Azimuth Mode'); WriteLn;
            LOOP (* Position Azimuth Servo *)
              TurnOffServoPaused;
              CheckForAzimuthPositioned (AzimuthPositioned);
              IF AzimuthPositioned THEN NextMode := Elevation; EXIT
              END;
              ComputeAzimuthPositionDriveSignal;
              GetPauseCommand (Pause);
              IF Pause THEN NextMode := Suspended; EXIT
              END;
            END; (* loop Position Azimuth Servo *)

        ELSE
            WriteString ('ERROR'); WriteLn;
        END; (* of IF NextMode = Elevation *)

    UNTIL ElevationPositioned;

    WriteString ('Now terminating'); WriteLn;

END Fig835.
```

Listing 8.3.

9
Concurrent systems:
The task model of software

We come now to the highest level of software design for single-processor systems — the task level. Our basic objective here is to structure the design as a set of cooperating software processes which execute concurrently. More correctly, we should say quasi-concurrently (or, for brevity, multitasking). Clearly, only one software process can execute at any one time in a single processor design. Moreover, it isn't sufficient just to design the application software in this way. It is also necessary to supply mechanisms which enable tasks to execute in a multitasking fashion.

This topic is a relatively specialized and advanced one. Therefore only the basic issues are covered. However, this chapter should provide a solid foundation for further work, covering aspects such as:

- what concurrency and quasi-concurrency are
- why software is designed and implemented based on a tasking model
- design via the tasking diagram
- independent and interdependent tasks
- multitasking and time-sharing techniques
- task priorities, responsiveness and latency
- scheduling aspects
- tasking using interrupts
- mutual exclusion mechanisms and the semaphore
- task intercommunication requirements and techniques

9.1 Concurrency in computer systems

Suppose that a computer system is required to deal with the situation shown in Figure 9.1.

This is part of a building management, monitoring and control system. The computer system is required to perform two tasks. One is the monitoring of all alarm sensors in the building, providing a continuous display of system status on the security guard's terminal. The other is control of the building's heating and ventilation system. Assume that these tasks are independent of each other; that is, there is

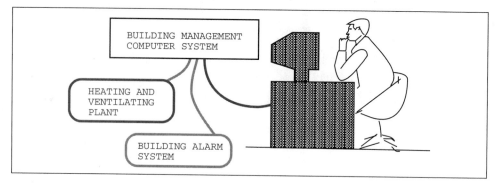

Figure 9.1 Multiple computer-based tasks.

no task interaction. The question is, what is a sensible approach to the design and build of the system software?

Here there is a need to run both tasks simultaneously, or *concurrently*. It also happens that, in this particular case, both must run continuously. The ideal solution to this requirement is to dedicate a processor to each task; that is, to provide a multi-processor design. But suppose that, for whatever reason, a single processor only may be used. As a result, both tasks must be hosted on the same machine. Clearly, only one task at a time can be executed. Thus some form of processor time-sharing must be implemented. This is here called *multitasking* or, more correctly, *quasi-concurrency*. Designing software for use in a multitasking environment requires skill, rigour and professionalism. The rest of this chapter is devoted to this important topic.

The starting point in multitasking design is the *tasking structure diagram* (Figure 9.2) or, for short, the tasking diagram.

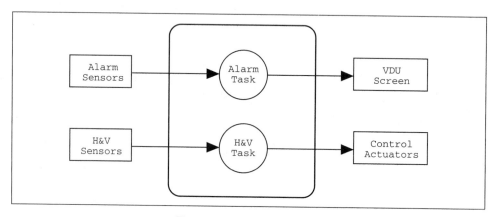

Figure 9.2 Tasking diagram.

Its purpose is to show:

- the number of tasks in the system

- the external connections to the tasks
- any interconnection between tasks (none shown here)

Note that there is no generally agreed name for this diagram.

It can be seen from Figure 9.2 that it is similar in appearance to a top-level DFD. However, it is emphatically *not* the same as the DFD, as each task bubble represents a (quasi-) concurrent software unit.

When designing multitasking software, the highest level design diagram is, as before, a context diagram. Levelling this gives the tasking diagram, as, for instance, Figure 9.2. This example is very simple, consisting only of two independent tasks, Alarm and H&V. Each task levels to a top-level DFD, being implemented as a sequential software program. At this stage it is assumed that you are competent to design such sequential software. Therefore we shall concentrate almost entirely on design at the tasking level.

The tasking diagram, although relatively simple, is a crucial aspect of the design method. Using this as the starting point of the design affects *all* subsequent decisions and developments. The advantages of doing this are that the software is easier to:

- design
- build
- test
- integrate

Unfortunately, there are also some disadvantages:

- To make it work, some form of run-time support mechanism (software and/or hardware) must be provided.
- The support facilities use CPU time, thus reducing the amount of processing time available for the application software. That is, CPU utilization is reduced.
- Debugging of the total software system can, in some circumstances, be quite difficult.
- In poorly designed systems task interaction can lead to quite unexpected – and sometimes disastrous – behaviour (this is why multitasking is forbidden in highly safety-critical systems).

You will appreciate these points only after having worked through a full design example.

9.2 Concurrency with independent tasks

9.2.1 Simple time-sharing methods

In the example of Figure 9.2, the tasks are independent of each other. That is, when the Alarm task runs, it produces no effect on the behaviour of the H&V task (and vice versa). However, they need to cooperate with each other when using shared items – either computer resources or external devices (the most obvious example of a shared item is the CPU itself). Thus the software needs to be structured to prevent tasks clashing when accessing such items.

The simplest way of tackling this issue is the method outlined in Figure 9.3.

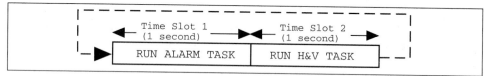

Figure 9.3   Sequential task operation.

Each task is implemented as say a subprogram; the two are then bolted together and run as a continuous loop. Thus we have two periodic tasks, each having a period of 2 seconds.

The pros of this approach are that:

- The design uses well-established methods.
- Implementation is relatively straightforward.
- No support mechanism is needed as, to the processor, this looks just like a single sequential program. There is no concept of task switching on the processor itself.
- The resulting programs are (if properly designed) well controlled and predictable in operation.
- Debugging is no more difficult than that required for single-task implementations.

For slow embedded systems this method might well be the best solution. If it is, then use it. However, we may run into the following two problems when using this technique:

- time responsiveness
- failure to run tasks

Time responsiveness

Suppose that each task takes 1 s to execute. Thus the alarm system can be updated only once every 2 s. Further, no alarm handling at all can be performed for the duration of the H&V task. Likewise, the H&V system is uncontrolled while the Alarm task is running. This might not cause difficulties; a 2 s response could be acceptable. But now suppose that we build a 10-task system, each task having a 1 s run time (Figure 9.4).

Now the alarms are checked only on a 10 s basis; the H&V system is uncontrolled for a 9 s duration. Is this performance adequate? Most unlikely. And, of course, as more tasks are added, performance further deteriorates.

We could try to improve performance by:

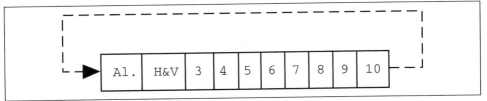

Figure 9.4 Sequential task operation – 10-task system.

- identifying the more important tasks
- giving them greater use of the CPU

This is demonstrated in Figure 9.5.

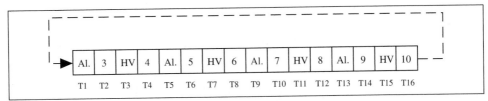

Figure 9.5 Revised task sequence.

Here the Alarm and H&V tasks are activated on a 4 s basis, a significant improvement. However, the program organization has become more complex, even for this simple scenario.

There is yet another aspect to task responsiveness which arises when task times – execution and period – are quite different. To show this, let us revert to the two-task scenario.

Suppose that the Alarm task requirements call for alarm checking at least every 0.5 s (but may be faster if so desired). Suppose also that we rewrite the code so that the task takes 100 ms to execute. Given that the H&V task takes 1 s to run, a significant change must be made to the software. One possible way to meet the revised specification is shown in Figure 9.6.

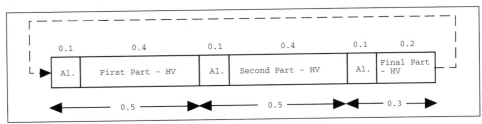

Figure 9.6 Interleaved task execution.

This is actually much more difficult to implement than it seems. How, for instance, can we identify the insertion points for the code of the Alarm task? Code execution time is notoriously hard to come by in the first place. And even if timing values *can* be obtained, it only needs a change of clock speed to invalidate them (never mind a change of processor type). Now try to extend this approach to a 10-task system with varying timing requirements – a daunting problem, at the very least.

Failure to run tasks

Let us move on to the second issue, failure to run tasks. Assume that the tasking arrangement is that of Figure 9.4. The program runs in a continuous loop, beginning with the execution of the Alarm task. But what would occur if, for instance, it entered an infinite loop in task 3? In this case all tasks would cease to work; no special precautions have been taken. For embedded systems we should always use a watchdog timer to detect situations like this. Should the program malfunction the watchdog times out, normally forcing a program restart. In our case the result is that the Alarm task once more begins execution, then the H&V task, then task 3 ... and again the program hits an infinite loop. The net result is that tasks 3 to 10 never get executed – all because of a problem in just one task.

Given this task structuring then, for embedded applications, such (exceptional) situations cannot be allowed to persist. How exceptions are dealt with depends very much on individual applications. In general it is likely that a controlled shutdown would be initiated. Unfortunately, the result is a computer system which has only two modes of operation – fully functional or totally non-functional. Yet there are many applications where fail-soft, graceful degradation performance would be preferred. If task 3 could be bypassed, for instance, then the rest of the system would carry on working. But with the simple tasking scheme used here it isn't possible to achieve this. Major improvements are needed.

This section has highlighted a number of drawbacks inherent in the 'single program' implementation of tasking. We can now go on to look at various ways of overcoming them. And note that the techniques discussed later are not necessarily mutually exclusive – combinations can be used to good effect.

9.2.2 Time slicing of tasks

We can begin to improve on the single sequential format by:

- structuring each task as an independent unit
- running each task for a period of time, then swapping to the other task

The basic idea is illustrated in Figure 9.7.

Organizing tasks to run in a particular fashion, and at specific times, is called *scheduling*.

Unfortunately, in its current form, this makes little impact on the timing performance issues. But if the tasks are run 'a bit at a time' in time-sliced fashion (Figure 9.8), major benefits ensue.

This scheduling mode forms the basis of *round robin* operation.

Provided that each time slice is relatively short (typical figures for embedded systems lie in the range 1–100 ms) both tasks will appear to run simultaneously. Tasks are inactive only for very short periods, and the blocking effect of long tasks

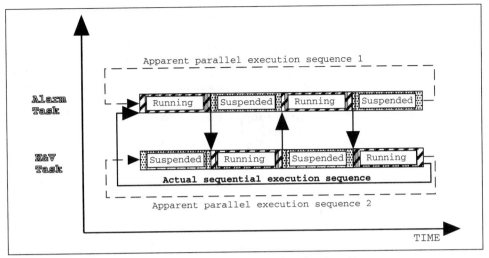

Figure 9.7 Essentials of time-shared multitasking.

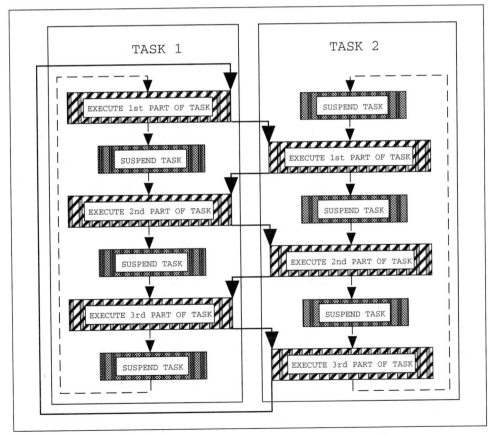

Figure 9.8 Time slicing of tasks (round robin operation).

disappears. Further, should a new task be added to the system, it will start executing relatively quickly. However, don't lose sight of the fact that the time taken to execute all tasks is unchanged (in fact it actually increases somewhat, for reasons which will be explained later). The question now, though, is how do we make such scheduling work?

9.2.3   Multitasking – application and support level software

The tasking diagram can be visualized as consisting of two parts: an application section and a support section (Figure 9.9).

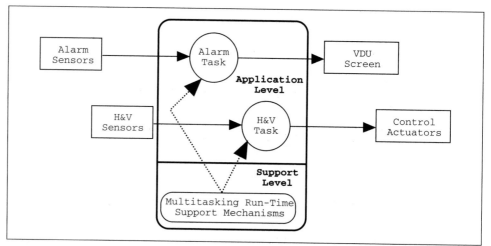

Figure 9.9   Tasking diagram – application and support levels.

The application level in this diagram is the same as the tasking diagram of Figure 9.2. Sitting 'below' this are the run-time support mechanisms, the things which actually make multitasking work. The basic functions of the support level (Figure 9.10) are the:

- creation of tasks in the first place (that is, defining a complete section of sequential code to be a task; it is not the writing of the code itself)
- activation of tasks; it should take a positive action to make tasks runnable ('live')
- management of live tasks, including their deletion from the system (terminated or 'killed')

After tasks have been created, they can exist in a number of states, as shown in Figure 9.11.

Executing is self-explanatory. And, because this is a single-processor system, one task, and only one task, can be in this state. *Ready* (or *waiting*) denotes a task which would like to run, but which has to wait its turn. *Suspended* tasks are those which are waiting for something to make them ready again. This might, for instance, be an external signal or an internal time delay. *Terminated* tasks are those which have been killed off; they are never going to be executed again.

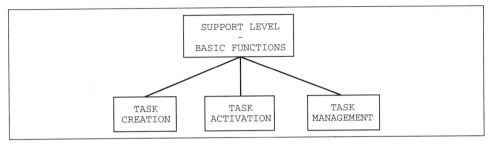

Figure 9.10 Basic requirements of the support level.

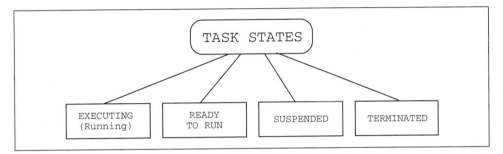

Figure 9.11 Possible task states.

There is a simple reason for providing a support mechanism. It enables the designer of the application software to concentrate on the application itself. In an ideal world, no attention would have to be given to the multitasking aspects. For embedded systems, the nearest we come to this is to implement tasking using a real-time executive (RTEX). The application engineer uses its facilities via a set of software 'hooks' into the RTEX. However, a detailed review of real-time executives and operating systems is beyond the scope of this text. We shall therefore limit ourselves to the basics of the subject.

9.2.4 *Tasking via coroutines*

Some computer languages – Ada, for example – have fully fledged tasking facilities. As such, the tasking model is language-dependent (as are the implementation aspects). For that reason no more will be said on language-dependent tasking mechanisms. However, a simpler mechanism is that of the coroutine. Although their use and syntax are language-related, they are all built on the same basic ideas. A coroutine is similar to a subroutine in that it:

- is a sequential program unit
- has its own code and data
- has to be expressly activated

However, there are important differences between the two (Figure 9.12).

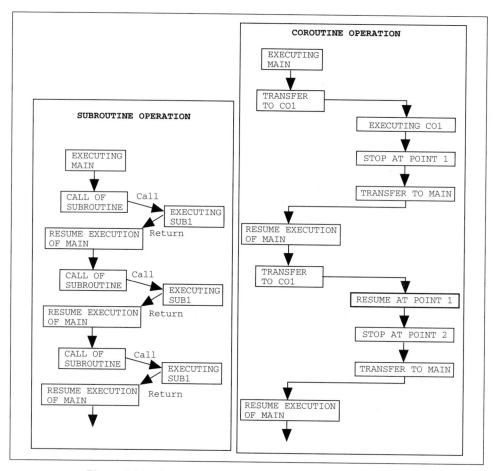

Figure 9.12   Subroutines vs. coroutines – conceptual differences.

Assume first that we have a conventional code implementation consisting of a foreground (main) program and a single subroutine (Sub1). At some point the foreground program calls Sub1, which then begins executing. On completion, control returns to the main program, restarting at the code statement which follows the call. Each time Sub1 is called, this process is repeated; the same code is executed. Thus the relationship between the two is a master–slave one.

Now consider where the software is structured as a main program and a single coroutine (Co1). Here there is no concept of a master and a slave – both have equal standing (in fact we can view the main program as just another coroutine). Assume that the main coroutine is running, and reaches a point where it transfers control to Co1. main ceases to execute, being replaced by Co1. This runs until it meets a statement which tells it to transfer control to main. It suspends execution, transfers to main, which then restarts at the statement following the original transfer command. It (main) runs until a second transfer command is reached. As a result, control is handed over to Co1, which begins executing *at the point where it previously stopped.*

This runs until it meets the next transfer to main command, suspends execution, transfers to main ... and so on. This behaviour, that of two independent but co-operating tasks, is illustrated in Figure 9.13.

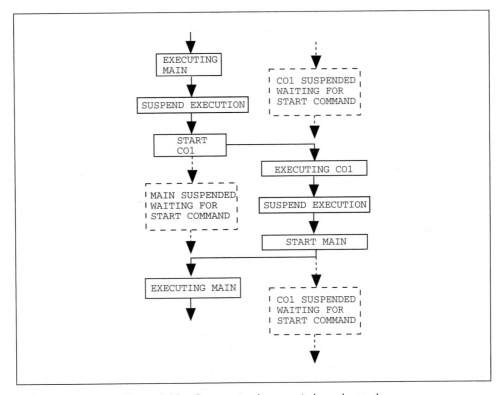

Figure 9.13 Cooperation between independent tasks.

A simple program example which uses coroutines is given in Listing 9.1.
The major points to note here are that:

- The coroutine facility is provided as part of the programming language.
- Each coroutine behaves like an individual program, having its own code and data space. However, it can access items which are globally available, such as common data stores, I/O devices and the like.
- The development/compiler/language package must include a run-time coroutine support mechanism.
- Transfer decisions are made within each coroutine, not by an external software unit. Thus each coroutine voluntarily relinquishes its hold on the processor.
- There is no theoretical limit to the number of coroutines in a system. In the end, practical considerations determine how many can be sensibly used in any particular application.
- Syntax details are language specific.

```
MODULE Protest1;
(*******************************************************)
(*  This is an example of the coroutine construct  *)
(*                  Listing 9.1                     *)
(*******************************************************)

FROM SYSTEM IMPORT ADDRESS, NEWPROCESS, TRANSFER,
                WORD, ADR, SIZE;
FROM InOut IMPORT WriteString, WriteLn;
VAR
    FirstProcessExample, OpeningProcess : ADDRESS;
    ProgramArea : ARRAY [0..255] OF WORD;

(* Here is the code of the process *)
PROCEDURE DemoProcess;
BEGIN
    (* We arrive into the process at this point *)
    WriteString ('Now in the Demo Process'); WriteLn;
    TRANSFER (FirstProcessExample, OpeningProcess);
    (* We leave the process now, returning to
        OpeningProcess *)
END DemoProcess;

BEGIN (* ProcessTest1 *)
    NEWPROCESS (DemoProcess, ADR(ProgramArea),
                SIZE(ProgramArea), FirstProcessExample);
    TRANSFER (OpeningProcess, FirstProcessExample);
    (* We leave the main program at this point.  On
        return the statement below is executed *)
    WriteString ('Back in the opening process now');
END Protest1.
```

Listing 9.1   An example of the coroutine construct.

The coroutine can be a very effective design method for slow/soft systems. However, for fast (and, in particular, hard) applications, they are probably best used in conjunction with other methods.

9.2.5   A centralized scheduler

Coroutine operation is analogous to an orchestra playing without a conductor. To achieve a quality performance there must be effective cooperation between its individual sections. But this cooperation is, in a sense, self-imposed by the players (as dictated by the score, of course). Contrast this with the results obtained when the conductor runs things. Naturally this assumes that the conductor is, at the very least, competent.

We can extend this idea to multitasking operation, by replacing the decentralized control of coroutines with a centralized unit (Figure 9.14).

The two tasks, Alarm and H&V, are run under the control of a task scheduler. It, the scheduler, decides when and why the tasks are made active. It does *not*, however, decide what processing is performed by the tasks. That is defined by the task design and implementation.

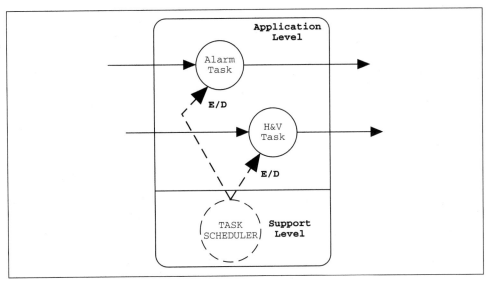

Figure 9.14 Centralizing the control – the scheduler.

The result is that much greater control can be exerted over system behaviour. Further, scheduling design is easier to implement and timings become more predictable.

In Figure 9.14 the task scheduler icon is identical to a control transformation. Likewise, task control signals have been denoted as prompts. There are two reasons for using this notation. First, the action involved is, at heart, the same as that performed by a CT. Second, few CASE tools provide icons specifically for task level diagrams. And only the more expensive ones can be extended to include user-defined symbols.

Assuming that Figure 9.14 represents our task level design, how would we go about implementing the scheduler? First consider the simplest scheduling policy, round robin (Figure 9.15).

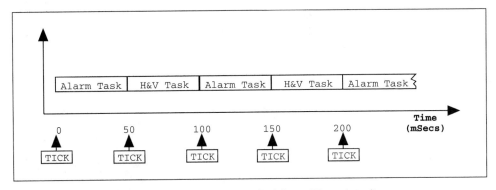

Figure 9.15 Round robin scheduling – 50 ms time slice.

Here there is a requirement to execute tasks using time slices of 100 ms. The basic idea is simple, but it relies on maintaining accurate timing. The most common and dependable way to do this is to use a hardware timer – the 'tick' timer (Figure 9.16).

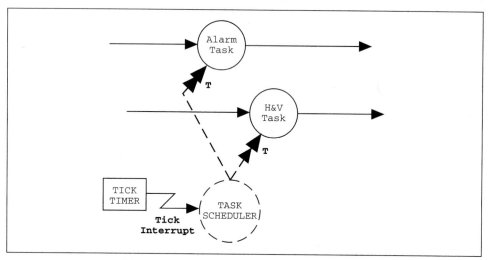

Figure 9.16   Implementing time slicing – the tick.

This is not to be confused with a calendar clock (although it may well be used as part of the calendar system). The tick is produced at predefined intervals to generate a processor interrupt. This invokes an interrupt service routine (ISR) to perform the task scheduling function. Consider once again the application of Figure 9.15. Here scheduling is very simple indeed. The scheduler, when activated, merely decides which task should run in the next time slot. It installs this (say the Alarm task) on the processor, sets it running, and then effectively goes to sleep. On receipt of the next tick interrupt, the running task is suspended and the scheduler activated. It repeats the rescheduling process, but now installing the H&V task. This activity is repeated at each tick time.

Trigger prompts are used, in this sense, to establish a conceptual point. The interpretation is that when a trigger prompts a task it runs for its designated time slot. Control is then returned to the scheduler. Of course we may well have cases where a task completes before the time allocation has expired. What happens then? With simple scheduling, program execution stops – things recommence with the next tick. More flexible designs allow the scheduler to regain control immediately.

Figure 9.15 is, in one sense, misleading: it doesn't show the time given over to task scheduling and switching activities. Precisely what happens at run time depends on individual designs. However, in general we would expect to find behaviour similar to that defined in Figure 9.17.

Here, the operation of the system is depicted using a state transition diagram. On start-up the initial state – the loading of the processor registers with scheduler task data – is entered. Scheduling decisions are made, then the register data is saved. The application task data is installed in the processor registers, and the application

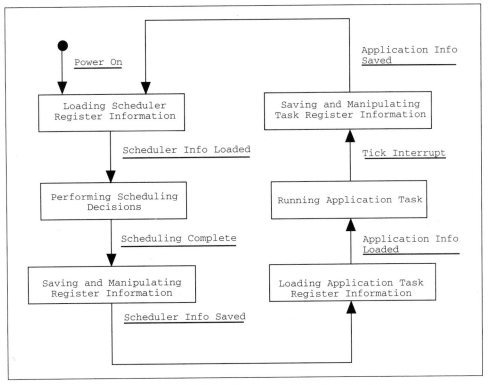

Figure 9.17 Task switching operation and overheads.

begins to execute. This continues until the tick interrupt arrives (for simplicity, tick timer handling has been omitted). The tick ISR is activated, and immediately begins saving the application task data. It then loads the scheduler task data (which had earlier been stored away) and once more performs the scheduling task. The whole action is then repeated as long as the system is powered up.

Now, only the application task actually carries out useful work. All the rest is an overhead just to make multitasking work. How significant is this overhead? This is a very difficult question to answer; so much depends on scheduling policies, processor types and clock speeds. But rough and ready figures can be produced. Assuming:

(a) simple round robin scheduling
(b) that all activities are software driven (no special hardware devices provided)

then the time taken to swap two tasks is likely to be in the range 20–300 μs. This is insignificant with a tick time of 100 ms. Given the worst case value (300 μs) the processor utilization is 99.7%. However, if the tick time is set to 1 ms, this drops to 70%, a significant reduction. Thus, from a point of view of utilization, long tick intervals are desirable. But, to provide good responsiveness, short periods are required. Getting it 'right' is somewhat of a balancing act.

The reason for highlighting this issue is to make *you*, the designer, consider task structuring most carefully. For any given system, increasing the number of tasks increases the amount of task switching. This leads to a decrease in processor utilization. However, if you try to correct for this by extending the tick period, system responsiveness suffers. This is why one of the golden rules of multitasking design is to minimize the number of tasks.

9.2.6 Recognizing and handling task importance – priorities

Up to this point nothing has been said about task importance. The assumption, implicit, is that all tasks have equal standing. Now let us see why, in some situations, a task priority order must be defined. First, though, some definitions:

- Synchronous or periodic tasks: ones that repeat at regular intervals or periods. Typical of these are control loop functions which execute at fixed sample times.
- Asynchronous or aperiodic tasks: ones that execute when commanded to do so, and then revert to a suspended state. Such commands occur at random times.
- Background task: a task which runs continuously while power is on, being structured as a loop. Generally any functions within it are not time-critical.
- Task deadline (T_d): the time by which task computations must have finished.
- Response time (T_r): the time between readying a task and having the task completed.

Note: T_d = (Actual Time Service Demanded + T_r)

Assume that we have a two-task system. One, task 1, is the background task. The other, task 2, is aperiodic (Figure 9.18).

When activated it must complete within 1 s (its response time). Its actual computation time (execution time) is 800 ms. The system uses round robin scheduling, having a tick time of 100 ms. Scenario 1 of Figure 9.18 shows system operation when only the background task is active – task 2 is inactive.

Now suppose that task 2 is readied and activated (scenario 2), beginning executing at t = 100 ms. Thus its deadline falls at t = 1100 ms. It runs in 100 ms chunks, taking 800 ms of computer time to complete. However, because of the time-slicing arrangement with the background task, 1500 ms elapses before it finishes. This is 500 ms beyond its specified deadline. Thus it is clear that simple round robin scheduling is not up to handling situations like this. Changes are necessary.

Suppose we give task 2 precedence over (higher priority than) task 1, and re-run the operations (scenario 3; Figure 9.19).

The situation is as described earlier, task 2 being readied and set running at t = 100 ms. After this, however, things are somewhat different. At each tick reschedule, task 2 is reinstalled on the processor; it, remember, has highest priority. The result is that it finishes executing at t = 900 ms, beating its deadline by 200 ms.

You can see that task 1 cannot run during this period of time. As this is the background task there isn't likely to be a problem. But what about dealing with timing issues when a system contains multiple tasks? Clearly this topic requires much thought and attention. Such aspects are beyond the scope of this text, but hopefully this simple example has given an insight into the complexity of the problem.

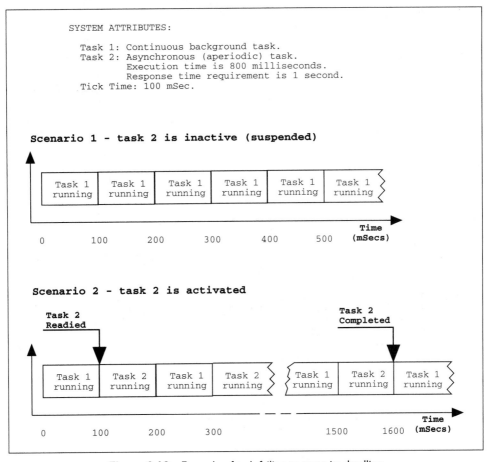

Figure 9.18   Example of task failing to meet its deadline.

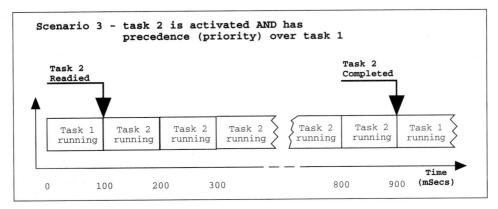

Figure 9.19   The use of task precedence – 'the right to precede'.

9.2.7 *Responsiveness and task latency*

In general terms, task latency is the time which elapses between readying a task and starting its execution. Here, to cover all possible situations, the definition is modified somewhat: task latency is 'the time between demanding the service provided by a task and the actual start of task execution'. In this context, *demanding service* and *readying a task* are synonymous.

Let us now see how latency and responsiveness interact (Figure 9.20).

Once more our system consists of two tasks. One (task 1) operates continuously in the background; the other (task 2) is aperiodic. The aperiodic task execution time

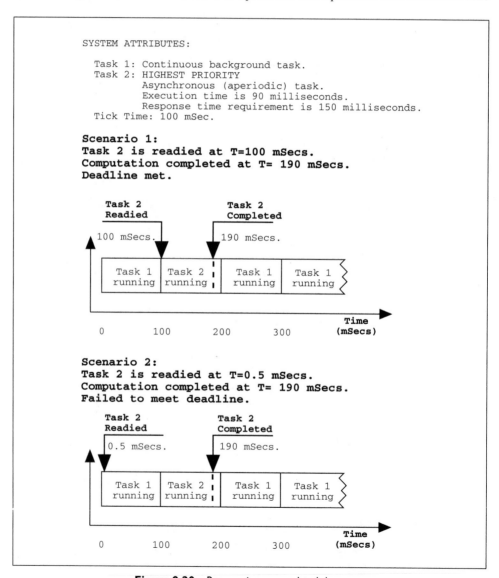

Figure 9.20 Responsiveness and task latency.

is 90 ms, its required response time being 150 ms. It has the higher priority. Round robin scheduling is used, using a tick time of 100 ms.

In scenario 1, task 2 is readied just before a tick arrives (t = 100 ms). As a result, it is set running straight away; there is negligible latency. It completes execution at t = 190 ms, beating its response requirement by 60 ms.

Now take scenario 2. Here task 2 is readied at t = 0.5 ms, but doesn't start running until t = 100 ms. The task latency is 99.5 ms. As a result, it fails to complete until t = 190 ms, a response time overshoot of 39.5 ms.

How can this failure be corrected? One solution would be to reduce the tick time; reschedule more frequently. But the associated drawbacks (discussed earlier) may be unacceptable. What then? The answer lies in realizing that the problem is due to system latency. If such delays can be eliminated, the task will meet its deadline. By servicing the request instantly (or, at the very least, with minimal delay) latency becomes insignificant. But this means overriding the scheduler, which, remember, is happily marching to the tick drumbeat. Thus it is necessary to use interrupts with urgent tasks, as shown in Figure 9.21.

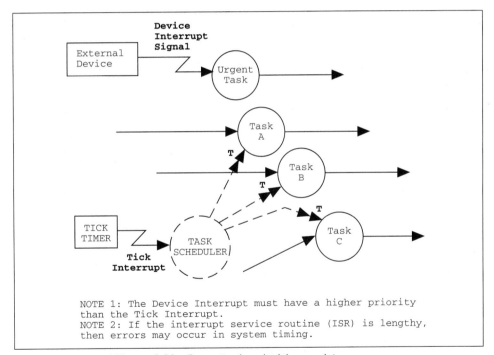

Figure 9.21 Bypassing the scheduler – task interrupts.

Here tasks A, B and C run under scheduler control. Separate from these is the interrupt-driven 'Urgent Task'. As shown, the interrupting source is an external device, a very common feature of embedded systems. When the device produces an interrupt signal it activates the corresponding ISR, which executes the Urgent Task. The device interrupt, of course, must have higher priority than the tick in order to block out the scheduler.

This design approach solves one problem. Unfortunately, it may introduce others. Such blocking can unwittingly lead to timing problems in the other tasks. Hence careful performance analysis must always be done on multitasking designs.

Note that it is also perfectly acceptable to use software interrupts for this function.

9.2.8   Embedded systems – an effective scheduling strategy

When a system uses a task scheduler, we would normally bypass it only in extreme circumstances. Otherwise quite erratic time responses may be obtained. Round robin scheduling, as you have seen, gives controllable and reasonably predictable performance. Unfortunately it can also produce unacceptable delays in task execution. As such it isn't, by itself, suitable for hard fast systems. Improvements are needed.

Over the years many scheduling policies have been devised. Of these, those most commonly used in embedded systems are expounded in Figure 9.22.

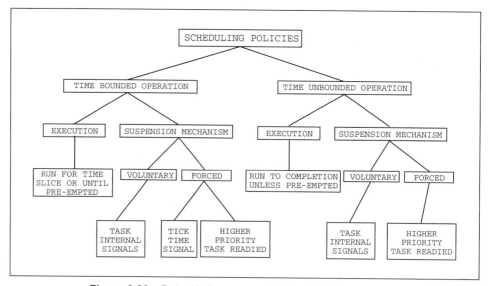

Figure 9.22   Embedded systems – effective scheduling strategies.

First, all tasks are given a priority value or number. The *least* important ones may be allocated the same number, and formed into the 'time-bounded' group. All other tasks are grouped together as the 'time-unbounded' ones.

The scheduling rules for time-unbounded operation are that:

(a) Only ready tasks can be set running.
(b) The ready task having highest priority is the one selected.
(c) An executing task will, wherever possible, run to completion without a break. There is no time slicing.
(d) Any running task can be replaced at any time if circumstances warrant it (this is called pre-emption).

(e) A running task can only be pre-empted by a task which:
- is ready *and*
- has a higher priority

(f) A pre-empted task is returned to the ready state. It is reinstalled at the earliest possible time.

(g) An executing task voluntarily gives up use of the processor when it reaches completion. However, it may also release the processor *before* it finishes. This normally happens when, for some reason, it cannot proceed with program execution.

(h) Voluntary suspension is initiated by internal signals produced within the task program. The result is that the task is put into a suspended state. It is subsequently awoken when conditions make it possible for execution to recommence.

These behavioural aspects are defined in the state transition diagram of Figure 9.23.

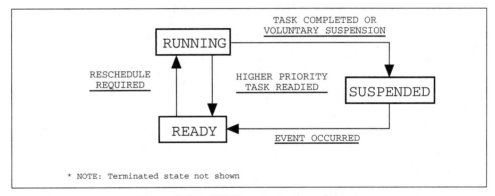

Figure 9.23 STD for a time-unbounded task.

Time-bounded tasks are executed in time-sliced round robin fashion. We can afford to use this scheduling method, as such tasks are the slower softer ones. In general, task suspension and pre-emption are similar to those of the time-unbounded group. However, task switching (pre-emption) now also takes place at regular intervals, the tick time.

As described here, round robin scheduling is used only at the lowest priority level. It is possible, however, to apply this technique at any level in the priority structure. That is, we might have a group of tasks at, say, level 2 priority, and another group at level 6. Within each grouping all tasks execute in time-sliced mode. However, they retain their priority setting with respect to other groups. Forced suspension is implemented using the priority pre-emption mechanism.

9.2.9 *Tasking via interrupts*

It is a basic tenet of this chapter that designing software using a task-based method has many advantages. There are times, though, when using a task scheduler may cause difficulties. For instance, in a small microcontroller, there might only be a limited amount of RAM store (say 128 bytes). This will almost certainly preclude conventional multitasking where (typically) a minimum of 256 bytes is allocated per task. Problems may also arise in very fast systems, where task switching overheads become unacceptable. And, of course, the scheduler software adds to the code size of the system. It is impossible to have a multitasking design without incurring store and time overheads. Fortunately, for many small embedded applications, a compromise solution is acceptable. This provides tasking via interrupts (the 'poor man's scheduler'; Figure 9.24).

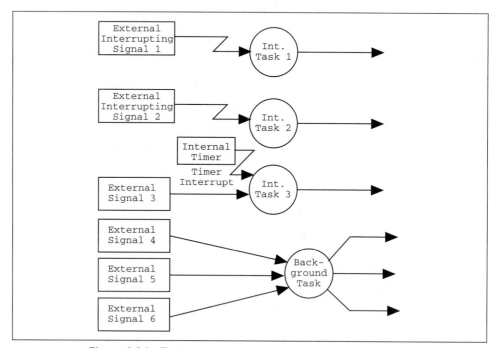

Figure 9.24   Tasking via interrupts – simplistic but fast scheduling.

In this example the software system consists of four tasks. Three are interrupt-driven; the other is the background task. Tasks 1 and 2 are activated by external signals, and task 3 by an internal timer. As discussed earlier, the background task is written as a single sequential program, operating in a continuous loop. Here, for instance, one of its functions would be to perform polling of the external signals 4, 5 and 6.

With this method there is no scheduler, no time slicing and no individual task data stores. The interrupt mechanism provides fast, prioritized task responsiveness (task priorities are determined by the corresponding interrupt priorities). Yet at the same time the software can still be designed as a set of individual cooperating processes. There is no doubt that the resulting implementation can be made small and fast. In fact, tasking via interrupts was indeed the earliest form of 'multitasking'. Unfortunately, it does have disadvantages, some significant, the main ones being that:

(a) We are constrained to have only interrupt-driven tasks and a single background task. For small systems (say a few kilobytes of code) this is manageable; in larger systems the background task becomes quite unwieldy. In effect, we find ourselves packing a number of tasks into its single sequential task.
(b) The designer/programmer must have very good understanding of interrupt organization and mode of behaviour. It may also be necessary to be proficient in assembly language programming.
(c) Likewise, a detailed knowledge of the hardware system (interfacing subsystems, timers, programmable devices and so on) is needed.

Nevertheless, if:

- your system is a small one and
- you are very proficient in both hardware and software areas

then this can be a most effective design and implementation technique.

9.3   Safe sharing of system resources

9.3.1   The need for mutual exclusion

Sharing of system resources is a topic sufficiently important to warrant a section of its own. Unfortunately, the basic ideas, although straightforward, are often presented in a confusing way. Here, to avoid clutter and get to the heart of the matter, a simple scenario is considered (Figure 9.25).

The example computer system consists of two items: a processor board and an interface board. There are two I/O subsystems on the interface board. One is for analogue signal handling, the other for switch monitoring and control. These are controlled by the processor via a programmable interface device. The interface

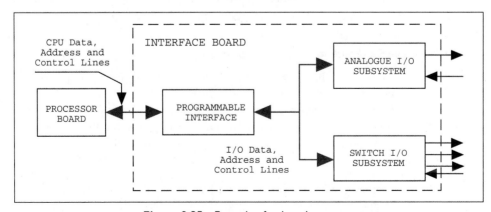

Figure 9.25   Example of a shared resource.

device deals with all address, control and data signals on the interface board. To access the I/O subsystems, the processor has to carry out four distinct operations:

- Configure the programmable interface.
- Set up address information.
- Set up data handling operations.
- Generate the appropriate set of control signals.

Let us assume that the software consists of two independent tasks. One performs analogue signal handling, the other handles switch interfacing. Thus, even though the tasks are independent, they share the use of a common resource: the interface device. As a result there is always a chance that:

- task A is in the process of accessing an I/O subsystem *and*
- a task switch takes place under scheduler control *and*
- task B begins executing, and at a later stage begins to access the I/O subsystem *and*
- a task switch takes place back to task A

The question is: when task A resumes execution, will the interface configuration be the same as that at task suspension time? Frankly, we have no idea. But, if it isn't, this is where our problems start.

Remember, task suspension and resumption are transparent to individual tasks. That is, they are unaware of task switches, carrying on as though nothing has happened. So, when task A resumes, it continues executing a defined set of operations on the interface – which, unfortunately, may now be in a very different state. An apparently valid write to the analogue output could, for instance, produce total chaos in the switch subsystem.

It is obvious then that where tasks share resources, some form of access control mechanism is needed. At any one time, one, and only one, task can be allowed to access the resource (and in a safe and controlled manner). That is, when any task uses a shared resource, it must exclude all others – a *mutual exclusion* mechanism. We talk about such shared resources as *critical* items or – in code terms – critical areas.

9.3.2   The single flag method

It might seem that there is a simple solution to this problem: protect the critical areas using some form of access indicator or *flag* (Figure 9.26).

Here, critical items are placed within a protected area. A single flag is used to denote the state of the critical area. Flag up indicates that the resource is free and may be used by any task. Flag down shows that a task is currently using the resource. Thus, if a task wishes to use the resource, it first checks the flag. Assume in this case that it is free. The task sets it to `resource in use`, and proceeds into the critical area. Now suppose that a task switch take place. Task 1 is put into the ready state and task 2 begins executing. At some later point, task 2 wishes to use the shared resource. It checks the flag and finds the resource in use. As a result it suspends itself,

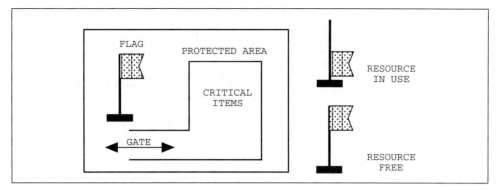

Figure 9.26 Concept of the single flag method.

usually informing the scheduler of the situation. Task 1 is reactivated, finishes with the resource, and exits the critical area. As it does so it raises the flag to show that the resource is free. When task 2 is next readied it can safely proceed to enter the critical area.

The single flag method appears to provide direct and effective mutual exclusion. In microprocessor systems the flag would normally be implemented as a single variable (or even a single bit). Let us use a single byte, called `Peripheral_Interface_Flag`. Resource free is indicated by it having the value 00(H). When the resource is in use it is set to 01(H). Thus when a task wishes to access the resource, it first checks the flag status. Providing it is free, the task sets the flag to 01(H), and proceeds to use the critical item. We would expect to see the operations shown in Listing 9.2 taking place at the code level.

```
1.  READ IN Peripheral_Interface_Flag
2.  COMPARE WITH 00(H)
3.  IF True THEN
        WRITE OUT 01(H) to Peripheral_Interface_Flag
    ELSE
        Jump to suspension routine
4.  Use the shared resource as required (execute critical section)
5.  WRITE OUT 00(H) to Peripheral_Interface_Flag
```

Listing 9.2

There are no problems here, or so it seems. Unfortunately not; there is one great lurking danger. Imagine that the running task (A) has read in the flag value, and finds that it is free. But between obtaining the flag and later writing out the new value, a task switch takes place. It then turns out that the new task (B) also wishes to use the shared resource. A check of the flag shows that all is clear. So B sets the flag to resource in use and proceeds into the critical area. However, when task A is restored, it continues under the impression that only *it* has access to the resource. The protection mechanism has been well and truly breached.

As you can see, the fault arises because reading and setting the flag are separate actions. Two solutions to this are to:

- use only a single processor instruction to carry out both actions or
- prevent task switching during the read and set operations

Many modern microprocessors provide a single test and set assembly-level instruction. Use this if it is available and suitable for the application. However, if this isn't possible, the code needs to be modified along the lines of Listing 9.3.

```
1. DISABLE task switching (usually by disabling interrupts)
2. READ IN Peripheral_Interface_Flag
3. COMPARE WITH 00(H)
4. IF True THEN
       WRITE OUT FF(H) to Peripheral_Interface_Flag
   ELSE
       Jump to suspension routine
5. ENABLE task switching
6. Use the shared resource as required (execute critical section)
7. WRITE OUT 00(H) to Peripheral_Interface_Flag
```

Listing 9.3

The solution offered here as a way of providing mutual exclusion is only one among many, but it is simple, effective and easy to implement. As a result it is a widely used technique. Yet its current structure can lead to performance problems by producing task priority inversion.

9.3.3   The priority inversion problem – task blocking

With the design given above, a task (A) may be in its critical section when the scheduler decides to do a task swap. Suppose that the new task (B) wishes to use the resource held by A. On checking the flag, it will find the resource unavailable, and will thus suspend itself. The mutual exclusion mechanism is working as planned. But what if B actually has a higher priority than A? This makes no difference to the protection method; B still gets blocked out. So what we have is a task A blocking one which has higher priority; B cannot proceed until A allows it to. The system behaves as if the priorities have reversed: a *priority inversion*.

In a two-task system the performance deterioration is unlikely to be a great problem. But look at the situation shown in Figure 9.27.

Suppose we have a five-task system, comprised (in order of priority) of tasks A, B, C, D and E. Task E is executing and has grabbed a resource that it shares with A. All other tasks are suspended, waiting for a wake-up call (Figure 9.27(a)). Suddenly, and simultaneously, A, B, C and D are readied (Figure 9.27(b)). A, having highest priority, pre-empts E, which is then placed at the end of the ready queue of tasks (Figure 9.27(c)). At some point, A tries to use the shared resource, finds itself locked out, and then self-suspends (Figure 9.27(d)). It is replaced by B, which runs to completion, and then suspends. This is repeated for C and for D; then E is set executing once more. Only when it releases the mutual exclusion lock can A replace it. We gave A highest priority because it is an important task. Yet it has been forced to wait for all other tasks to execute because of the mutual exclusion locks. Clearly this sort

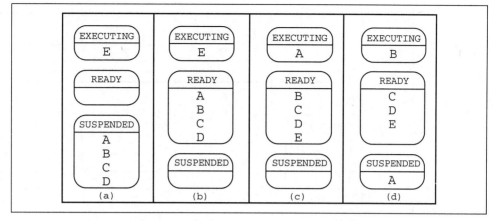

Figure 9.27 The priority inversion problem.

of performance cannot be accepted.

This issue has been researched to death by academics. Numerous solutions have been proposed, many bringing complexity and performance problems with them. The method advocated here may not be the most elegant, but it is safe, secure, simple and visible. What we do is to modify the earlier approach, as shown in Listing 9.4.

```
1. DISABLE task switching (usually by disabling interrupts)
2. READ IN Peripheral_Interface_Flag
3. COMPARE WITH 00(H)
4. IF True THEN
       WRITE OUT FF(H) to Peripheral_Interface_Flag
   ELSE
       Jump to suspension routine
5. Use the shared resource as required (execute critical section -
                                 Keep short as possible)
6. WRITE OUT 00(H) to Peripheral_Interface_Flag
7. ENABLE task switching
```

Listing 9.4

First, task switching is forbidden while a task is in its critical area. Second, the critical code is kept as short as possible. Hence, re-running the earlier scenario, we end up with the sequence depicted in Figure 9.28.

Observe that task E still blocks out A, but only when it is in the critical area. Once it exits from this it is pre-empted. The delay to A is – with good design – minimal.

You could argue that the above method could, for a single-processor system, be simplified. There is no need to have an access flag if interrupts and task switching can be disabled. A task, if it wishes to use a shared resource, first disables these functions. From this point on no other task can run. Therefore it is impossible for a clash to take place. Nevertheless, it is recommended in general that the flag method should be used. This allows us to:

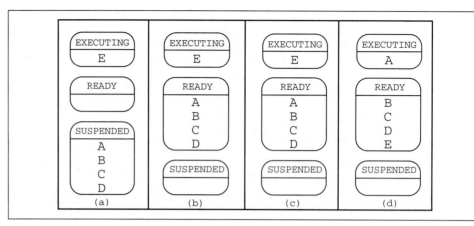

Figure 9.28   Solving the priority inversion problem.

- Use a consistent design approach in both single and multiprocessor systems.
- Be selective in the level of task blocking. With the current method all interrupts are disabled, even if they make no use of the shared resources. This may cause problems in the handling of fast interrupt-driven tasks.
- Perform check conditions on flag status without necessarily using protected resources.

There is one significant weakness with these mutual exclusion techniques. Setting the flag to in use and then later clearing it to free are two quite separate actions. There is always a possibility that the programmer may forget to clear the flag – mistakes do happen. Thus it is strongly recommended, when using a shared resource, to encapsulate all operations in a single subprogram. In that way safe and secure behaviour is ensured.

9.3.4   The semaphore – an introduction

One well-known and widely used access control mechanism consists of:

- A protected variable called a *semaphore* and
- Two access and control operations for use with the semaphore. Here they are named Wait and Signal (conventionally they are defined as P and V, from the Dutch *Passeren* – to pass – and *Vrygeven* – to release).

Each shared resource is protected by a specific (individually named) semaphore, based on the concepts illustrated in Figure 9.29.

Here the shared resource can only be accessed through a single entry point protected by an electronic sign – the semaphore.

Before operations commence, the sign is set to show GO (equivalent to initializing the semaphore).

Now let us examine what happens in a number of scenarios.

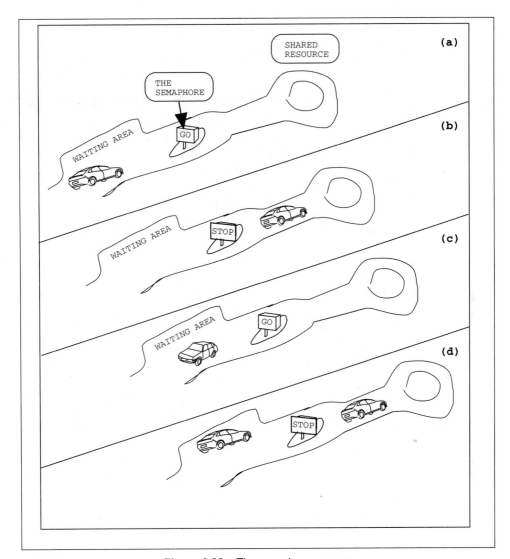

Figure 9.29   The semaphore concept.

First user arrives

After initialization, a user (task) who wishes to access the shared resource approaches the entry point (Figure 9.29(a)). He first checks the status of the electronic sign, and finds it at GO. This indicates that it is safe to enter the critical area; it also automatically sets the sign to STOP. The user may now proceed (Figure 9.29(b)). What happens within the critical area is of no concern to the semaphore; you may do what you like. However, on leaving, the user must reset the sign to GO (Figure 9.29(c)).

We are now back to where we started from. The whole process repeats itself when another user arrives wanting to enter the critical area.

Second user arrives while the resource is being used

The user checks the sign status and finds it at STOP (Figure 9.29(d)). As a result she moves to the waiting area, waiting for the resource to become free. In effect the task 'goes to sleep'. Unless special actions are taken – such as putting on a time limit – the user will wait forever (suspended). Note that any such special features are regarded as exception actions, and are not part of the semaphore itself.

At some point the user within the critical area finishes with the shared items. It is at this point that things are different. On leaving, he doesn't change the sign to GO. Instead it is left at STOP. However, the emerging user gives authority to the waiting task to enter the critical area (which it now proceeds to do).

Resource in use, one task waiting, another user arrives

When a third user arrives, access checks are made in the same way. Because the sign is at STOP, this user also joins the waiting queue, behind user two. Thus users are queued first-in, first-out (FIFO) (other queuing rules may also be used if so desired).

Checking the sign and setting it to STOP (or else suspending the task) is carried out by the `Wait` operation. Setting the sign back to GO or waking up a waiting user is the function of the `Signal` operation.

The semaphore comes in two versions, the binary and the counting types. They differ only in the detail of their operation. Let us first consider the binary type.

9.3.5 The binary semaphore

`WaitForAccess` and `SignalResourceFree` are general procedures, having the form shown in Listing 9.5.

```
(* Part of WaitForAccess   *)
   IF Semaphore = GO THEN
      SetSemaphoreTo STOP
   ELSE
      SetTaskTo Waiting
```

```
(*Part of SignalResourceFree*)
   IF Task = Waiting THEN
      WakeupTask
   ELSE
      SetSemaphoreTo GO
```

Listing 9.5

You can see that a semaphore can only have one of two values, hence the name binary. Each semaphore, of course, is unique.

It is imperative that both `Wait` and `Signal` are indivisible operations. That is, once invoked, the sequence of instructions cannot be stopped (otherwise we would be back to the problems of the simple single flag exclusion mechanism). One way to achieve this is to build procedures as shown in Listing 9.6.

These would be used within a program in the way shown in Listing 9.7 (assume that the semaphore is called `TuningValues`).

```
PROCEDURE WaitForAccess              PROCEDURE SignalResourceFree
         (S :Semaphore);                      (S :Semaphore);
BEGIN                                BEGIN
   DisableInterrupts;                   DisableInterrupts;
   IF S = NotBusy THEN                  IF TaskWaiting THEN
      S := Busy;                           WakeUpTask;
   ELSE                                 ELSE
      SuspendTask;                         S := NotBusy;
   END; (* of IF *)                     END; (* of IF *)
   EnableInterrupts;                    EnableInterrupts;
END WaitForAccess;                   END SignalResourceFree;
```

Listing 9.6

```
BEGIN
   ProgramCode;
   WaitForAccess (TuningValues);
   UseSharedItems;
   SignalResourceFree (TuningValues);
   MoreProgramCode;
END.
```

Listing 9.7

The semaphore concept, unfortunately, does not enforce the pairing of
WaitForAccess and SignalResourceFree. Hence it is recommended that the programmer should implement this matching wherever it is feasible to do so. Thus, by
using procedurization, the code above may be modified as shown in Listing 9.8.

```
BEGIN
   ProgramCode;
   AccessTuningValues;
   MoreProgramCode;
END.
```

Listing 9.8

Just a small implementation point. Here, AccessTuningValues is very specific; it
can be used only with the shared resource TuningValues. The program design
could be made more general, as for example:

AccessSharedResource (SemaphoreName, Resource);

Up to this time each task which invokes WaitForAccess also calls
SignalResourceFree. But it doesn't have to be like this. They – wait and signal –
can be activated by any task of our choosing. This feature is an essential part of the
counting semaphore.

9.3.6   The counting semaphore

The counting or *general* semaphore is used where it is required to protect a set of resources. It is a fundamental point that all items in each set are identical. For example, one set might consist of a set of data items, say bytes. Another might be a collection of hardware devices, say a quad UART (universal asynchronous receiver–transmitter) communications subsystem. Here it is only necessary to bar access to the protected region (suspend tasks) when *all* items are in use. This is where the counting function comes in; it allows us to keep track of the current situation. Let us see how it may be applied, using the quad UART example in an embedded communications network. This consists of four identical serial data channels, each driven by a UART. Any software task may use any channel. The set of resources (the UARTs) are protected by a counting semaphore called UARTsemaphore. It differs from the binary semaphore in the following way:

- It has a range of values, in this case 0 to 4.
- This value shows the number of free devices. Zero means that all UARTs are being used.
- On initialization, all devices are assumed to be free. The value is set to 4.
- When a task wishes to use a UART, it first checks the semaphore value. A non-zero number shows that it is free.
- Once access is granted, the task reduces the value by 1. It then proceeds to use the UART.
- On completion, the task first increments the semaphore value by 1, then exits the shared resource.

The original access control operations now become those shown in Listing 9.9.

```
PROCEDURE WaitForUart                    PROCEDURE SignalUartFree
  BEGIN                                    BEGIN
    DisableInterrupts;                       DisableInterrupts;
    IF UartS > 0 THEN                        IF TaskWaiting THEN
      Decrement(UartS);                        WakeUpTask;
    ELSE                                     ELSE
      SuspendTask;                             Increment(UartS);
    END; (* of IF *)                         END; (* of IF *)
    EnableInterrupts;                        EnableInterrupts;
END WaitForUart;                           END SignalUartFree;
```

Listing 9.9

UartS is the counting semaphore. Note that its value is *never* allowed to go negative.

Important memory jog: semaphores must *always* be initialized before use.

9.4 Interdependent tasks – synchronization and communication

9.4.1 Background aspects

Suppose the aim here is to design the software for a small stability augmentation control system. The starting point is, as usual, the context diagram (Figure 9.30).

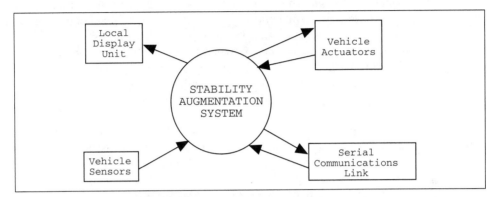

Figure 9.30 Example system context diagram.

A decision is made to use a multitasking solution. Hence the first quest is to create a good tasking structure. The result of this exercise is the tasking diagram of Figure 9.31.

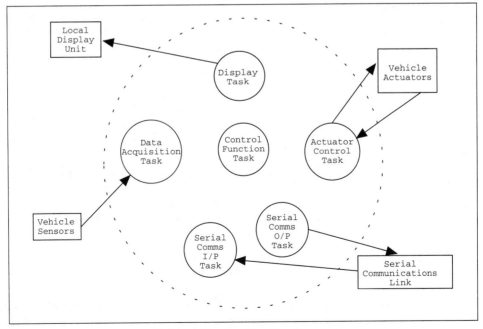

Figure 9.31 Partial tasking diagram.

At this stage, only the tasks themselves have been identified. What is missing is information concerning task intercommunication. Therefore it is necessary to establish what interactions might take place. The starting point for this is to look at the overall system operation.

First, suppose that the task `Serial Comms O/P` holds data messages for transmission by the UART. However, data is sent only when a polling command is received from the network. This arrives, of course, via the `Serial Comms I/P` task. Hence the input task must signal the output task to start transmitting its information. Note, though, that there is no transfer of data between the tasks, only signalling. Thus the operation of the output task is synchronized with that of the input one.

The input task, after setting the signal, may do one of two things. First, it could continue with further processing, quite independent of output task functions. Second, it might wait until the output task has responded to the signal; only then will it proceed.

Now to look at a second type of task interaction. The operator requires a display of the plant state, as produced by the various sensors. Sensor information is gathered by the `Data Acquisition` task. However, display information is put out by the `Display Task`. Thus there is a need to transfer data between the two tasks. However, it may not be necessary to synchronize their activities.

The third type of task interaction occurs in the control loop of the system. This function is performed by the `Data Acquisition`, `Control Function` and `Actuator Control` tasks. The output from the first forms the input to the second. In turn, its output is the input to the third task. This clearly is a data transfer requirement. However, it is essential that all tasks work in a carefully coordinated manner – a task synchronization requirement. Thus here we have both data transfer and task synchronization.

Figure 9.32 defines the general set of task intercommunication requirements.

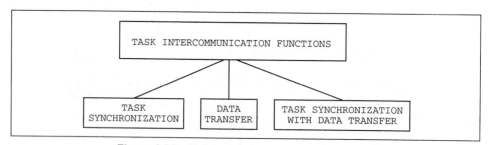

Figure 9.32   Task intercommunication requirements.

Various mechanisms have been developed to implement these features. The following sections describe them in more detail.

Note: the word 'intercommunication' has been chosen in preference to 'communication'. In the context of multitasking, 'communication' is often taken to mean 'communication of data'.

9.4.2   *Task synchronization only*

The dictionary definition of synchronize is 'to cause to operate simultaneously'. Here 'synchronization' is used in a slightly looser form; it relaxes the requirement for simultaneous operation. Thus task synchronization is taken to mean 'to provide task coordination'.

The basic reason for synchronizing tasks is to ensure that operations are performed:

- in the correct order, and/or
- at the correct time

Here tasks are event- not data-dependent. Events may come from the outside world (for example, Handwheel Engaged, Weight Switch Closed, Start Button Pressed). Alternatively, they may be internal to the computer (Transmit Message, Time Delay Expired, Hold Pitch). Two components are used to cater for event-driven situations: event flags and task signals (Figure 9.33).

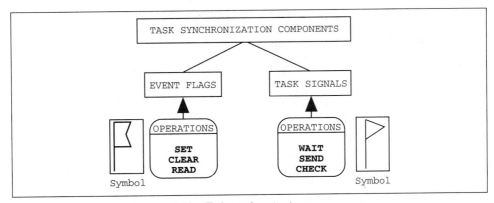

Figure 9.33   Task synchronization components.

Event flags

Flags would normally be used where task synchronization is required *without* the need for tasks to operate simultaneously. The operations used with flags are Set, Clear and Read. A flag may be a word, byte or (especially at assembly language level) a single bit. When using flags, the need for mutual exclusion of operations should always be assessed.

A powerful feature of this method is that a single word (or byte) can represent a group flag. Here each bit is controlled by a specific event; thus logical ANDing and ORing can be performed on the bitset. This is significantly faster than performing logical operations on sets of words or bytes.

Signals

Where there is a need to lock tasks together at some particular point, signals are used. Three operations can be applied to the signal (Figure 9.34): Send, Wait and Check (other terms are often used to describe these actions).

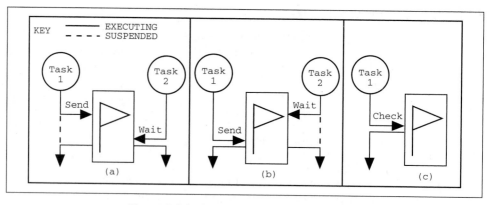

Figure 9.34   Synchronizing tasks using signals.

As shown here, Task 1 uses SendSignal to invoke synchronization, with Task 2 using WaitForSignal. Consider first where Task 1 reaches the synchronization (or rendezvous) point before Task 2 (Figure 9.34(a)). It performs a Send operation (*sends a signal*), but finds that Task 2 isn't ready to synchronize. As a result it suspends itself. At some later time Task 2 invokes a Wait operation (*waits for a signal*). It finds that Task 1 is waiting at the rendezvous point. Consequently it:

- awakens Task 1 and
- carries on executing

The next example (Figure 9.34(b)) shows where Task 2 has reached the synchronization point first. Here *it* suspends until Task 1 sends a signal. When this happens, Task 1 finds that Task 2 is waiting for it. It responds by:

- awakening Task 2 and
- carrying on executing

In some circumstances we may wish to check for synchronization but make suspension an option. This is particularly useful where a receiver task has a number of synchronizing signals. The check operation returns the status of the signal but doesn't halt execution. Such decisions are made by the checking task.

Note that with a multitasking (single-processor) system it isn't possible for both tasks to arrive simultaneously at the synchronization point.

A closer look at signal operation reveals that the signal itself must consist of two separate components (Figure 9.35).

This is due to:

- the two-way nature of information transfer and
- the fact that we can't specify the rendezvous order

These components, identified as Sender Status and Receiver Status, are binary-valued. Their two values are AtSyncPoint and NotAtSyncPoint.

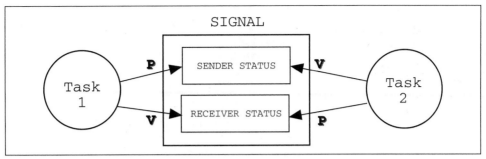

Figure 9.35   Signal structure.

From what has gone before, it should be clear that mutual exclusion must be applied to the signal. The basic approach then is outlined in Listing 9.10; this should be self-explanatory.

```
IN SENDER TASK                          IN RECEIVER TASK

PROCEDURE SendSignal (Receiver,         PROCEDURE WaitForSignal (Receiver,
            Sender : BOOLEAN);                      Sender : BOOLEAN);
BEGIN                                   BEGIN
 DisableInterrupts;                      DisableInterrupts;
 IF Receiver = AtSyncPoint THEN          IF Sender = AtSyncPoint THEN
    Receiver := NotAtSyncPoint;             Sender := NotAtSyncPoint;
    WakeUpReceiverTask;                     WakeUpSenderTask;
 ELSE                                    ELSE
    Sender := AtSyncPoint;                  Receiver := AtSyncPoint;
    SuspendSenderTask;                      SuspendReceiverTask;
 END (* of IF *)                         END (* IF *)
 EnableInterrupts;                       EnableInterrupts;
END SendSignal;                         END WaitForSignal;
```

Listing 9.10

(Note: the construct IF Receiver = AtSyncPoint THEN could, of course, be written as IF Receiver THEN. The style of Listing 9.10 is used for reasons of clarity).

From a program design point of view it is much clearer to use named signals. One approach to this is given in Listing 9.11.

9.4.3   Data transfer only

A common operation in multitasking systems is to transfer data between tasks without any need for task synchronization. Such data movements can be unidirectional or bidirectional, selective or non-selective. These requirements have led to the widespread use of two particular data transfer methods (Figure 9.36):

- pools – for non-selective data transfer
- channels (also called pipes or buffers) – for selective data transfer

```
TYPE
    Signal = RECORD
                  Receiver : BOOLEAN;
                  Sender   : BOOLEAN;
               END;
CONST
    AtSyncPoint      = TRUE;
    NotAtSyncPoint = FALSE;
VAR
    InterlocksClear : Signal;

PROCEDURE SendSignal (SigName : Signal);
BEGIN
    .
    IF Signame.Receiver = AtSyncPoint THEN
    .
    .
END SendSignal;
```

```
(* SENDER TASK *)                    (* RECEIVER TASK *)
Task 1 Code;                         Task 2 Code;
SendSignal(InterlocksClear);         WaitForSignal(InterlocksClear);
More Task 1 Code;                    More Task 2 Code;
```

Listing 9.11

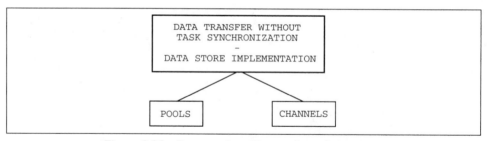

Figure 9.36 Data transfer without task synchronization.

The pool

The pool (Figure 9.37) is a data storage area which can be written to and/or read from by any task – and at any time.

It is an effective means of sharing data between a number of tasks, not merely a select pair. Senders deposit (write) information into the store; receivers extract (read) such stored information. Thus writers and readers need have no knowledge of each other; only the pool itself is of interest. As shown here, Task 1 is a reader and Tasks 2 and 3 are writers.

Normally pools are implemented in RAM. Hence reading has no effect on the stored data; that is, it is a non-destructive operation. However, writing to a RAM

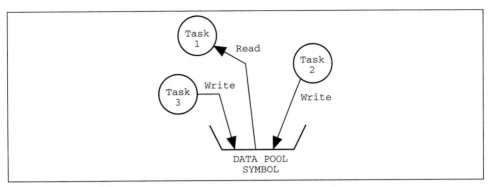

Figure 9.37   The pool.

store causes the old data to be replaced (overwritten) by the new values. Thus sending information to a pool *does* overwrite the old data.

Data security can be enhanced by using a number of pools, each dedicated to specific data groups. This limits potential users of the data and eliminates global data problems, yet supports very fast data transfer. The read and write operations can be built in many different ways. Where possible it is best to use procedurization to buffer the application designer from machine detail. Hence something like:

ReadFromPoolName (Data); and WriteToPoolName (Data);

would be suitable. However, pool usage is a random affair; we can't predict in advance when tasks will access the data. So it is necessary to put mutual exclusion on top of the basic read/write operations. Normally the binary semaphore would be employed, as shown in Listing 9.12.

```
Wait (SemaphoreName);
ReadFromPoolName (Data);
Signal (SemaphoreName);

Wait (SemaphoreName);
WriteToPoolName (Data);
Signal (SemaphoreName);
```

Listing 9.12

The Wait and Signal pairing needs to be enforced. Therefore it makes sense to encapsulate the protected read/write operations into single procedures (as described earlier in the section on semaphores).

The channel
A channel forms a pipe to carry data between tasks (Figure 9.38).

Here Task 1 sends data to Task 2 via the channel, a classical producer–consumer relationship. The channel itself provides temporary storage of the data. Normally the channel would be made large enough to carry a number of data words, not just one. A single data unit at a time is inserted into the channel by the sender. Likewise, the

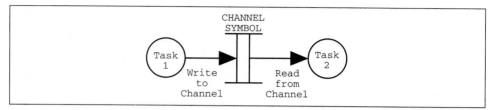

Figure 9.38 The channel.

reader extracts data in the same way. The first item sent is the first to be read, a first-in, first-out (FIFO) operation. Thus insertion and extraction are asynchronous processes.

An important question is why a multi-word channel might be needed in the first place. To answer this, consider the following situation. Suppose that as soon as Task 1 produces (writes out) a data word Task 2 reads it – before Task 1 has time to over-write it. Is channel storage required here? Clearly not. But what if Task 2 isn't ready to read the data as it is being produced? Or what if Task 2 *is* ready, but cannot match the speed of Task 1? In both cases temporary storage of data is required to prevent the loss of information.

Channels are usually constructed from RAM. Small data items (such as bytes) are sent directly via the pipe. Transporting large items, such as arrays or lists, could be done in the same way. However, this is likely to be a time-consuming process, causing significant delays in the processor system. To overcome this problem, pointers to the data, not the data itself, are sent down the pipe.

How large should channels be? Well, there are good practical reasons for limiting their size. First, in any real system, there is a finite amount of RAM. This is especially true of small microcontrollers. Second, long queues can lead to long delays between depositing and extracting data items (a transport delay). Thus we always aim to minimize channel size, bottom limits being dictated by the:

- amount of data to be transferred
- sending (producing) rate
- reading (consuming) rate

Inserting and removing data are basically simple write and read functions. However, it is also necessary to make sure that:

- When writing data, there truly is space for it in the channel.
- When reading data, there actually is data in the channel.

One widely used method for building channels in embedded systems is the circular queue or ring buffer (Figure 9.39).

The example here can store 10 data items. Before use it must always be initialized to the empty state (Figure 9.40).

The start and end addresses of the data area, which define channel size, are fixed. However, two movable pointers, Front and Rear, are used to keep track of the

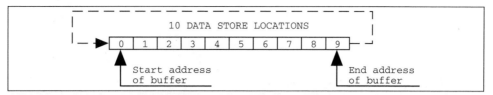

Figure 9.39 Channel structure – the circular buffer.

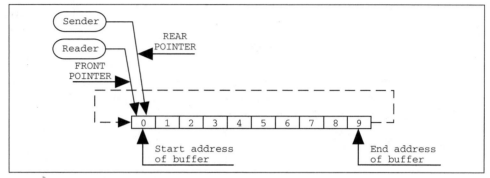

Figure 9.40 Circular buffer – initial state.

channel state. `Front` is associated with the reading activity and `Rear` with writing. The effect produced by inserting four data items is shown in Figure 9.41.

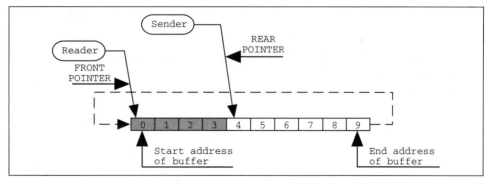

Figure 9.41 Circular buffer – four data items inserted.

This involves four data writes and one change to the `Rear` pointer value. Now removing one data item from the channel results in the situation shown in Figure 9.42.

A single read is performed, followed by a change of the `Front` pointer value. Note, most importantly, that the stored data itself has not moved. Instead of shifting data as reads are performed, we merely redefine the front point of the queue.

These two pointers also provide a simple means of checking on the channel state. If the two pointers become equal as writes are made, then the channel must be full.

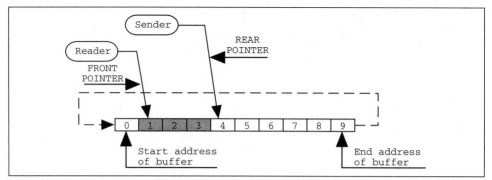

Figure 9.42 Circular buffer – one data item removed.

Conversely, if this happens as reads are made, the channel must be empty.

Many programming approaches can be used in the building of channels. The basis for one method is given in Listing 9.13.

```
                          BASIC ITEMS

CONST
   ItemStore=Array[0..9] (* 10 elements *)
TYPE
   Channel = RECORD
                DataStore : ItemStore;
                Front     : [0..9];
                Rear      : [0..9];
            END; (* of record *)
VAR
   Channel1 : Channel;
```

```
(* BASIC INSERT OPERATION *)        (* BASIC REMOVE OPERATION *)
IF Rear = ((Front+1) MOD 10) THEN   IF Front = Rear THEN
   SuspendSendingTask                  SuspendReceivingTask
ELSE                                ELSE
   Channel1.DataStore[Rear]:= Data;    Data := Channel1.DataStore[Rear];
   Rear = (Rear + 1) MOD 10;           Front = (Front + 1) MOD 10;
END; (* of IF *)                    END; (* of IF *)
```

Listing 9.13

To make it easier to distinguish between the full and empty states, one store location is sacrificed. The channel empty condition is as shown in Figure 9.40. However, channel full is detected when the front pointer is set to one location behind the rear pointer. Unfortunately, we cannot use the simple check:

```
IF Rear = (Front + 1) THEN
```

This is unable to deal with the case where Front is pointing to location 9 and Rear at 0. Instead, the following must be applied:

$$\text{IF Rear} = ((\text{Front} + 1) \text{ MOD } 10) \text{ THEN}$$

Note: both pointers are initialized to zero.

Using this approach eliminates the possibility of overwriting existing data if the channel is full. Likewise, when the channel is empty, reading is suspended. Unfortunately, there is still more to be done to make this a secure communications method. It is essential to implement access control (mutual exclusion) for the two tasks. Thus the complete insert and remove operations become, in general terms, those shown in Listing 9.14.

INSERT OPERATION	REMOVE OPERATION
`Wait(NotFull);`	`Wait(NotEmpty);`
`Wait(ChannelFree);`	`Wait(ChannelFree);`
`WriteDataToChannel;`	`ReadDataFromChannel;`
`Signal(ChannelFree);`	`Signal(ChannelFree);`
`Signal(NotEmpty);`	`Signal(NotFull);`

Listing 9.14

It is essential that a sending task checks that there is free space in the channel before grabbing it. Likewise, a receiving task needs to know that the channel contains data before acquiring it. If the order of the first two `Waits` is reversed, deadlock can occur (work it out for yourself).

Note also that `Wait(NotFull)` and `Signal(NotFull)` are in different tasks. The same is true for `Wait(NotEmpty)` and `Signal(NotEmpty)`. Forgetting to do one of these signals will lead to major problems. Therefore it is good practice to devise standard insert and remove procedures to encapsulate these functions.

One final point: it is possible to have many senders and many readers using a single channel. This should be avoided where possible; it brings a new set of (potential) problems with it.

9.4.4 Task synchronization with data transfer

Now for the final intercommunication mechanism: synchronization together with data transfer. The two aspects to be handled here are event signalling and the movement of data. You can see from the example above that the channel can be adapted to perform this function. However, we shall only (and always) use the channel for non-synchronized data transfer. Thus there is never any confusion in the semantics of the tasking diagram. Instead, the unit used here is the *mailbox* (Figure 9.43).

This is a data store area together with associated synchronization mechanisms consisting of event signals, `Post`, `Pend` and `Check`.

Data to be transferred between the tasks is sent via the mailbox. The sending task deposits data into (*posts to*) the mailbox as a write operation. Similarly the acceptor task extracts data from (*pends on*) the store by reading from it. In practice, data pointers – not the data itself – are sent through the mailbox. This speeds up operations, sometimes significantly.

Synchronization is attained by suspending tasks at the rendezvous point (Figure 9.44).

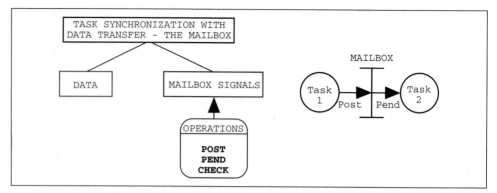

Figure 9.43 The mailbox – task synchronization with data transfer.

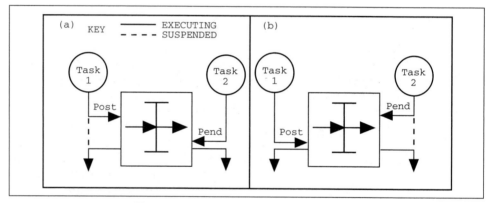

Figure 9.44 Post and pend synchronization.

Strictly speaking, the first arrival is suspended. In Figure 9.44(a), for instance, Task 1 (the sender) posts to the mailbox before the acceptor task is ready to receive. As a result it suspends until Task 2 pends on the mailbox. At this point it resumes execution. Conversely, if Task 2 pends first, *it* gets suspended until Task 1 posts. What this implies is that the task that first accesses the mailbox self-suspends. It is later awoken by the other task (for the two-task relationship shown here).

This example involves only a one-to-one task link. It is also possible to design mailboxes for many-to-one, one-to-many and many-to-many communication. However, one-to-one is a safe and secure method, and should be used wherever possible.

Mailboxes are one of the most commonly used components in modern operating systems. They come in many and varied structures; applications are also quite varied. In extreme cases systems have used the mailbox to implement all intertask communication and synchronization functions. Semaphores, flags, queues, ring buffers, the mailbox proper – these are just some items built using the basic mailbox structure. We though shall restrict it to the handling of data transfer with task synchronization in a one-to-one relationship.

The amount of data sent via the mailbox does not have to be of fixed size. Remember, the actual information posted into the mailbox is usually a pointer to the data – not the data itself. However, we expect the receiving task to accept the full amount of data at synchronization time. Therefore, conceptually the data transferred between tasks is a single unit.

If we apply mutual exclusion to post and pend, the basic mailbox operations become those shown in Listing 9.15.

SEND TO MAILBOX Wait(MailboxFree); PostToMailbox; Signal(MailboxFree);	GET FROM MAILBOX Wait(MailboxFree); PendOnMailbox; Signal(MailboxFree);

Listing 9.15

9.4.5   A last comment

To round this section off, let us see how the various components might be used. Take, for instance, the incomplete tasking diagram of Figure 9.31. Adding synchronization and communication features to this results in the final version given in Figure 9.45.

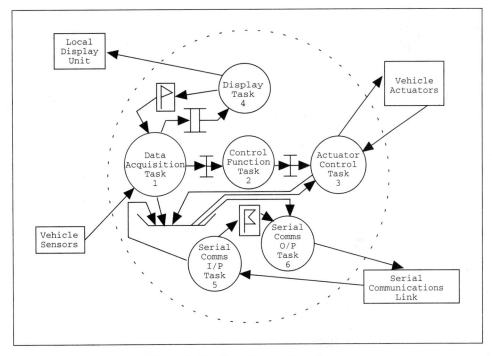

Figure 9.45   Completed tasking diagram.

The following components are shown:

(a) Mailboxes – for synchronization and data transfer between Tasks 1, 2 and 3. These would certainly be required if the tasks operated at different sampling rates (for instance where multi-rate sampling is used).

(b) Event flag – for synchronization of Tasks 5 and 6, the serial communication functions.

(c) Task signal – between Tasks 4 and 1. This could be used, for instance, for Task 4 to inform Task 1 that it requires an update of display data.

(d) Channel – from Task 1 to Task 4, to carry the display data between the two tasks.

(e) Pool – shared by Tasks 1, 2, 3, 5 and 6. Here:

- Task 1 writes current sensor data to the pool.
- Task 5 writes in control information (obtained from the serial input line) for use by Tasks 2 and 3.
- Task 3 writes in actuator status (for Task 6).
- Task 3 reads actuator loop control settings.
- Task 2 reads control algorithm tuning information.
- Task 6 reads data for onward transmission to the serial output line.

In order to show message passing between tasks, a message sequence diagram may be used (Figure 9.46).

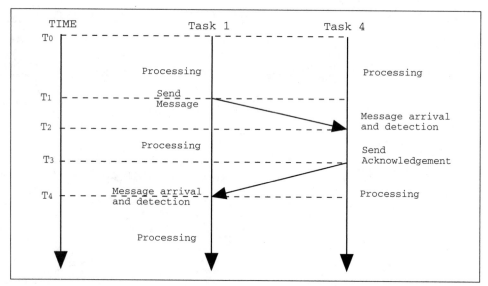

Figure 9.46 Message sequence diagram.

Each task has its own time line or *trace*, where time runs from top to bottom of the diagram. When Task 1 sends a message to Task 2, an arrowed line is drawn from 1 to 2. Here, for instance, Task 1 sends a message to Task 2 at time T_1. This is detected by Task 2 at time T_2. In turn, Task 2 sends a message at time T_3 to Task 1, which is detected at time T_4. Note that there is little reason to include task communication components on this diagram – *unless their use is critical to the transaction scenario.*

The complete system behaviour is defined using a combination of state machine (STD) and message sequence diagrams (Figure 9.47).

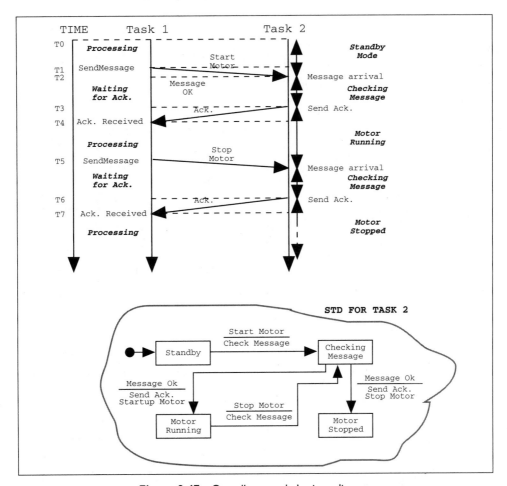

Figure 9.47 Overall system behaviour diagram.

One way of looking at this is that the sequence diagram gives an outside or overall level view of system behaviour. In contrast, each STD defines the behaviour of each task, an inside viewpoint.

Clearly the two sets of diagrams must be consistent, But to be able to achieve this, it is first important that you clearly understand the difference between a *message* and an *event*. An event is a 'signal' which produces a state change. On the sequence diagram, a message may or may not be an event. However, an event is always a message. For example, a message from Task 1 to Task 2 might contain updating information for a control algorithm of Task 2. In this case there is no change in the dynamic behaviour of Task 2. However, if the message is 'start machine', then clearly the state of Task 2 must change. By definition, the message is an event as far as the state machine of Task 2 is concerned. Therefore it is strongly recommended that when showing behaviour, a subset of the sequence chart (one which contains events only) is used.

9.5   Reducing processor loading – forming rate groups

Let us briefly look at a technique that can be used in some circumstances to reduce processor loading so that:

- All periodic tasks are executed at their correct periods and run to completion at each activation.
- Processor loading is spread evenly over time. This generally gives best performance in the presence of aperiodic tasks.

Suppose that an existing multitasking design consists of both aperiodic and periodic tasks. Details of the (three) periodic tasks are given in Table 9.1.

Table 9.1.

Task no.	Period (ms)	Run time (ms)
1	10	4
2	19	4
3	41	2

In order to meet this requirement the tick timer must have a resolution of 1 ms; that is, it must interrupt at a 1 ms rate. Clearly, the resulting processor overhead is considerable, and may significantly degrade system performance. One way to improve the situation is to reduce the tick interrupt rate. Consider the effect of changing task periods so that their timing relationship is a simple one, as shown in Table 9.2.

Table 9.2.

Task no.	Period (ms)	Run time (ms)
1	10	4
2	20	4
3	40	2

Task 2 now has a period which is twice as long as that of Task 1. For Task 3, the ratio is four. With this arrangement the tick resolution can be changed to 10 ms.

What has been done is to organize processor execution as a series of *minor cycle* time slots. Each one has the same duration: that of the shortest period (in this case

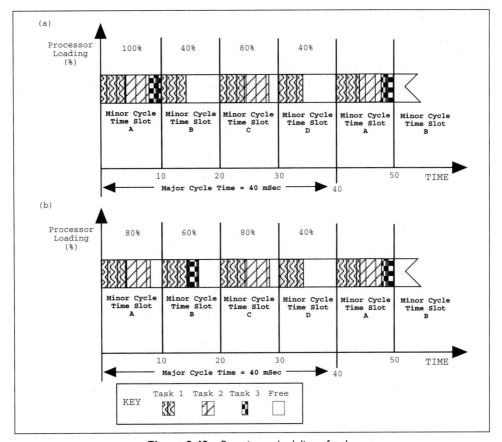

Figure 9.48   Run-time scheduling of tasks.

10 ms). Tasks are allocated to specific time slots, resulting in the run-time scheduling of Figure 9.48(a).

The point at which the allocation pattern repeats defines the duration of the *major cycle* time, here being 40 ms. You can see that a group of tasks are *launched* into execution within each time slot (leading to the expression *rate groups*). With this arrangement the code for all tasks is collected into one module, organized as a sequential program. At each tick time the scheduler control software merely decides which section of the code to execute (this will be demonstrated in Chapter 10).

One potential weakness with the schedule of Figure 9.48(a) is that the processor loading is very uneven (ranging from 40% to 100%). As a result there could be problems if an aperiodic task goes active during a heavily loaded period. It may produce considerable disturbance, causing a number of tasks to go late. One way to alleviate this is to 'spread' the periodic tasks so as to even out loading variations (Figure 9.48(b)). Of course, the effectiveness of the schedule depends very much on the nature of the aperiodic tasks. Unfortunately these, by their very nature, are not deterministic; they must be described in statistical terms. Such modelling is beyond the scope of this text, but you should be aware of the issue.

Review

In this chapter you have seen that designing software based on a tasking model is a powerful technique. Getting it right at this stage sets the scene for a sound system. Getting it wrong – or failing to adopt a sound design method – can be catastrophic: witness the Therac-25 radiation machine which, through poor multitasking design, killed at least six people. If you have taken the lessons of this chapter on board, you now:

- understand the role of multiprocessing and multitasking in software systems
- see the benefits of using a task-based design approach
- recognize the performance penalties incurred with multitasking
- appreciate that performance modelling is an essential feature of real-time systems design
- know the format, content and use of the tasking diagram
- see how it relates to the various other software design diagrams
- understand how to implement simple tasking structures using interrupts
- realize why a number of scheduling policies may be applied to embedded applications
- appreciate that mutual exclusion mechanisms are an essential part of multitasking design
- know how to use the binary and counting semaphores
- understand the role, structure and use of task intercommunication components – flags, signals, pools, channels and mailboxes
- know how to reduce processor loading by forming tasks into rate groups

Exercises

9.1 A small embedded system is designed to control the positioning of a mechanical handling device. The desired position is set by an operator, using a joystick unit. Also, it is required to accurately, quickly and smoothly follow the operator commands. The software is a multitasking design, consisting of four tasks:

Task	Execution time (ms)
Cyclic scheduler	1 (include context switch)
Control algorithm	50
Identification algorithm	600
I/O handling	10

Explain why the use of a simple cyclic scheduler is likely to lead to performance problems (supported by first-order calculations). How would round robin scheduling alleviate the problems, and what are the consequences of using such a policy?

9.2 An automated manufacturing unit is used for the processing of machined parts. Specifically it carries out precision drilling on machine blanks under robot control. It consists of:

- an operator's I/O panel
- a parts-handling robot (the 'handler')
- a drilling robot (the 'driller')
- a single microprocessor-based controller

The I/O panel contains a floppy disc, load, start and stop control switches, and status indicators for the robots. All handling and drill information is loaded into the system, from the floppy disc, when 'load' is selected. When this has been accepted by the controller, starting is permitted. Once the start switch has been pressed, the system begins the processing of the parts. In normal circumstances this continues until stop is selected.

The two robots work independently but cooperatively. They interact only during the drilling operation itself. This consists of:

- the handler bringing a part to the machining position
- the driller drilling the required number of holes
- the handler removing the part on completion of drilling

Each robot also performs a set of individual pre- and post-drilling operations.

Produce a tasking diagram for this system, including all appropriate communication components. Show task interactions using a message sequence diagram, and produce state diagrams for each task.

9.3 For the system of Exercise 9.2, identify potential error conditions. Suggest suitable exception handling strategies for the various errors. Show how you would modify your existing diagrams to take exception handling into account.

9.4 A processor contains the following sets of periodic tasks:

Task no.	Period (ms)	Run time (ms)
1	15	1.9
2	11	0.4
3	5	1.0
4	19	2.1
5	31	1.5

Form a set of rate groups so as to minimize the required tick interrupt rate. Define the minor and major cycle times. Further, distribute tasks so that processor loading in each time slot is relatively even (calculate and show this value). Assume that the total rescheduling time is 0.5 ms. Calculate the overall processor utilization.

10

Design example – chilled water controller:

A structured design solution

We are now in a position to tackle a more complex design example. Specifically it concerns the software design and implementation for the Chilled Water (CW) system detailed in Appendix A. The objectives of this chapter are, using structured design techniques, to:

- take the reader through the complete design process, starting with a specification and finishing with source code
- identify the major stages in this process
- define the aims of, and the methods used in, these different stages
- show how concurrency, timing and interfacing aspects significantly influence the design
- outline a general approach for the packaging and organization of the source code

10.1 Initial design

Let us begin by assuming that the system and hardware designs are finalized; no changes will be made. In reality, of course, these may well be affected by later software developments. But for the purposes of this example it simplifies things if such aspects are fixed.

Using the information given in Appendix A, the first design step is to develop the system context diagram. The result for the CW system is given in Figure 10.1.

Note that all design diagrams in this chapter have been produced using the SELECT Yourdon CASE tool.

As discussed in Chapter 8, all external I/O signals are considered to be data. Furthermore, a simple rule is used to distinguish continuous from discrete signals. A discrete signal is one whose value can change in discrete steps at specific points in

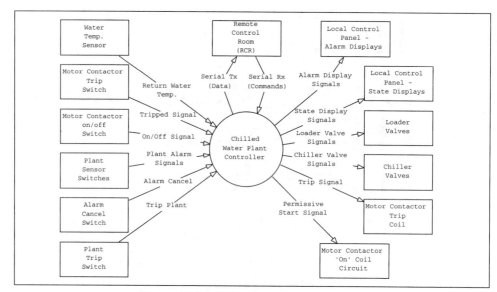

Figure 10.1 CW system – context diagram.

time. Otherwise, the signal is a continuous one (not entirely a satisfactory definition, but one which can be supported by the CASE tool notation).

Entries will have been made automatically in the data dictionary for these signals (courtesy of the CASE tool). Now is the time to begin building up the information in the DD. There are two good reasons to do so. First, it reduces the workload later in the project (when, all experienced designers will tell you, it becomes much more intense). Second – and more importantly – it forces the software designer to examine, in depth, many system and hardware features. Through this exercise most (ideally all) errors, ambiguities and omissions can be identified and eliminated.

10.2 Timing and tasking issues

10.2.1 Timing aspects

The following section is taken from Appendix A.

Preliminary studies indicate that the following timings should be complied with:

- Control loop: 1 s sample rate required.
- Alarm and protection subsystem: 0.5 s updating required.
- Displays: 0.5 s updating required.
- Loading/unloading time, 25% to 100% and vice versa: 1 min minimum.
- Starting up: low oil pressure alarm to be inhibited for 20 s. No. 2 chiller valve to be energized for the first 20 s.
- Remote control room information update: 1 s intervals.
- Response to remote control room commands: 1 s.
- Detection of failure of the serial data link to RCR: within 10 s.

A study of the serial communications hardware design has raised another timing issue. The maximum storage for incoming message bytes is limited. As a result, when a continuous byte stream is sent, data overwrite occurs at $(t+50)$ μs.

It is also decided that switch inputs will not be polled. Instead, interrupts are to be used.

10.2.2 Tasking aspects

The two major task categories met in embedded systems (see Chapter 9) are:

- synchronous (periodic)
- asynchronous (aperiodic)

Two further minor categories are also encountered:

- untimed continuous (background)
- single run (one shot)

(Note: sporadic tasks are here viewed as a special case of the periodic task.)
An analysis of the system reveals the following information:

(a) synchronous or periodic operations

- alarm monitoring: 0.5 s period
- protection function: 0.5 s period
- display updating: 0.5 s period
- temperature control of the CW water: 1 s period
- sending data to the remote control room (RCR): 1 s period

(b) asynchronous or aperiodic events

- switch signal inputs
- receipt of data from the RCR

(c) untimed background task: nothing specified

(d) one shot

No task specified, but one will be required for initializing the computer system.

10.3 Concurrency – developing the tasking model

10.3.1 Defining the task set

It can be seen from the preceding section that the overall tasking model must support:

- five periodic operations
- a very fast, hard aperiodic event handler (serial comms data input)
- a number of slower hard response aperiodic tasks (dealing with switch input signals)
- a one-shot initialization task
- two time-delay functions

In general, we wish to attain good responsiveness and make efficient use of processor time (for example, to minimize operations concerned with software management). To achieve this, task numbers should be kept to a minimum, resulting in the following design decisions:

- All periodic operations are to be grouped into a single composite periodic task, the Main Control Task (MCT).
- All switch inputs are to be dealt with by one Switch Handling Task.
- Time delay operations are to be handled within the periodic task.
- Serial input data is to be managed by a single Serial Comms I/P Task.

However, it is decided to provide a separate task for the transmission of serial comms data – Serial Comms O/P Task. Its function is to control data transmission operations only; organization and formatting of data is not within its brief. This decision is made with a view to software flexibility and potential for future expansion.

The result is a tasking structure which consists of five separate tasks (Figure 10.2).

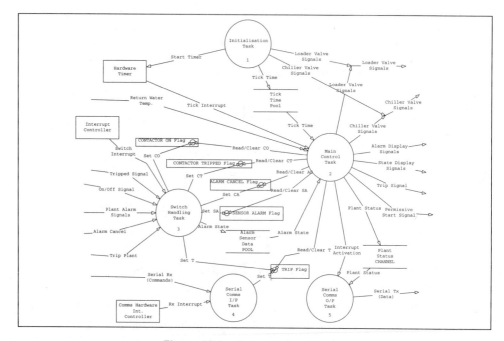

Figure 10.2   Task structure diagram.

10.3.2 *Establishing inter-task communication*

Good multitasking designs ensure that tasks speak to each other via sets of communication components (flags, channels, pools). Note though that *actual* task intercommunication arrangements depend on system requirements, system design and task structuring. Also it is important – at this level of design – to identify all mutual exclusion requirements.

Based on work carried out so far, the task intercommunication structure of Table 10.1 is envisaged.

Table 10.1 Task intercommunication structure.

Sender task	Information	Receiver task	Communications component
Switch Handling	Contractor On	MCT	Flag
	Contractor Tripped	MCT	Flag
	Trip Plant	MCT	Flag
	Sensor Alarm	MCT	Flag plus Pool
	Cancel Alarm	MCT	Flag
Serial Comms In	Trip Plant	MCT	Flag
MCT	Plant Status	Serial Comms Out	Interrupt plus Channel

The individual components – five flags, one channel, one pool and one interrupt signal – are shown in Figure 10.2. Note also that there is an additional item, Tick Time Pool, linking Initialization with MCT. A design decision was made that time delays and rate change calculations would be made within MCT. To facilitate this, the tick time value is provided to MCT.

Observe also the addition of two devices external to the software: Hardware Timer and Comms Hardware Int. Controller. These could have been shown on the context diagram. However, the advantages of introducing them here are three-fold. First, the complexity of the context diagram is reduced. Second, their role within the system is highlighted. Third, these specific hardware/software interactions – quite crucial ones at that – are emphasized.

A final point to note is the use of an interrupt to activate the Serial Comms O/P Task. Again, this is a design decision, based on the aim of highly decoupling this task from the others.

We are now in a position to begin the design of individual tasks. Normally before doing so a scenario diagram defining inter-task messaging would be produced. Here, however, there is little need for this as all communication goes to, or emanates from, the MCT. Further, most periodic tasking is performed under the control of the MCT.

From here onward the design example centres on the Main Control Task.

10.4 Sequential modelling of periodic tasks

Levelling the task structure diagram leads to the DFD for the main control task (Figure 10.3).

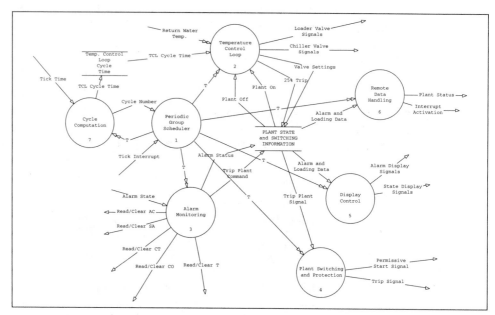

Figure 10.3 Main control task DFD.

Each data transformation (DT) corresponds to one of the periodic tasks listed earlier, together with one additional process, `Cycle Computation`. Its function will be explained shortly.

The next design step is to arrange the periodic tasks into rate groups (see Chapter 9). The result, taking into account the timing requirements of the system, is that:

- Two groups of tasks are formed, A and B.
- Group A consists of the periodic tasks `Temperature Control Loop`, `Alarm Monitoring`, `Plant Switching and Protection` and `Display Control`.
- Group B consists of `Alarm Monitoring`, `Plant Switching and Protection`, `Display Control` and `Remote Data Handling`.
- The minor cycle time is 0.5 s.
- The major cycle time is 1 s.

These points are shown in Figure 10.4.

Now to return to the additional DT `Cycle Computation`. The DT is concerned with two aspects of rate group operations: cycle time and cycle number. This data is required for use within the main control task. The advantage of the chosen arrangement is that it decouples cycle timing from tick timing; that is, changes in tick time

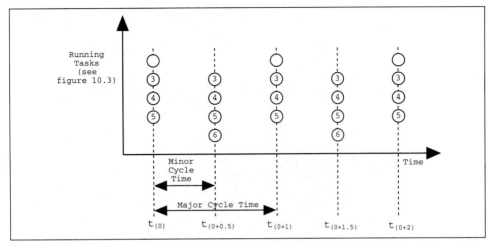

Figure 10.4 Rate groups for periodic tasks.

do not lead to changes in cycle time or numbering. Moreover, it keeps rate group calculations local to the MCT task (their natural home).

Figure 10.3 shows that central to the main control task is the control transformation `Periodic Group Scheduler`. Entering this CT is the `Tick Interrupt`, the activating signal for scheduler operation. Note that the CT dynamics are defined in the STD of Figure 10.5.

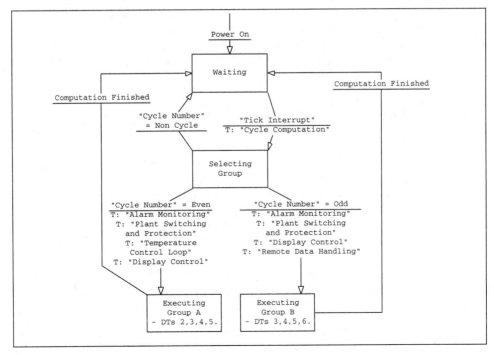

Figure 10.5 STD for `Periodic Group Scheduler`.

It can be seen that, on power-on, the scheduler enters a waiting state. Setting up and activating the tick timer and interrupt are functions of the background task; thus they do not show in the scheduler STD. Once interrupts are enabled – and a tick interrupt arrives – the scheduler moves to the Selecting Group state. This is exited when the cycle computations are finished. An even cycle number leads to the execution of Group A DTs, odd values causing Group B to be activated. A 'non-cycle' number takes the system back to the waiting state (only when the tick rate is greater than the cycle rate will this occur).

In each group, the DTs are run one after the other, using normal sequential programming. On completion of a run, the system reverts to the waiting state, ready to go on the next interrupt. Note that care must be taken to ensure that the DTs are sequenced correctly. If ordering *must* be adhered to then, in general, a more complex CT must be used to enforce it. The example here is a borderline case. Ordering is *important*, though not *essential*. Further, as the design is fairly simple, it isn't too difficult to keep track of the execution order.

You will see that all data is transferred between DTs via the data store Plant State and Switching Information. The reason for this is basically one of design simplicity. A consequential effect, however, is that all information becomes global, being accessible to *all* DTs. Fortunately, in practice this is unlikely to be a problem; the scope of the data can be restricted to a single program module.

One small point is worthy of mention: the naming of DTs. In earlier chapters the importance of good naming has been stressed many times. For data transformations the use of active verbs was recommended. Yet in Figure 10.3 noun clauses are used. This is somewhat contradictory, you may feel. There is, in fact, logic at work here. The answer lies with what the figure represents – a collection of *tasks*. And tasks are usually best identified using names.

We can now start designing individual periodic tasks, the topic of the next section.

10.5   Detailed DFD development – the temperature control loop

Levelling DT 2 (Temperature Control Loop) of Figure 10.3 leads to the DFD of Figure 10.6.

Here all activities are carried out under the control of the CT Temp. Loop Control, as defined in the STD of Figure 10.7.

The two, taken together, fully define the operation of the temperature control loop. It can be seen that when the DT Temperature Control Loop is turned on it enters the Checking Plant State. As a result, on the first activation of MCT, a transition will be made into the Plant Off state (on system power-up the plant *must* be off). At the same time, DTs Set Valves and Drive Valves are triggered. Each succeeding activation of the temperature control loop produces the same result until Plant On is signalled. The resulting response is that:

(a) DT Compute Loading Step is executed. The permissible step change (per period) in valve loading setting is calculated and stored.

(b) Get Water Temp. is activated to acquire the temperature of the return water.

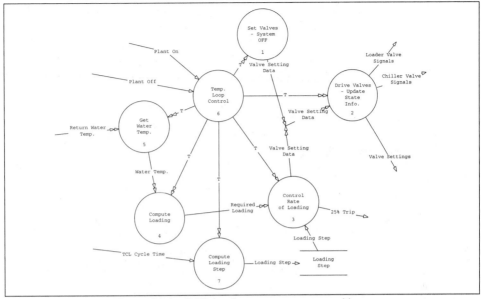

Figure 10.6   DFD for the temperature control loop.

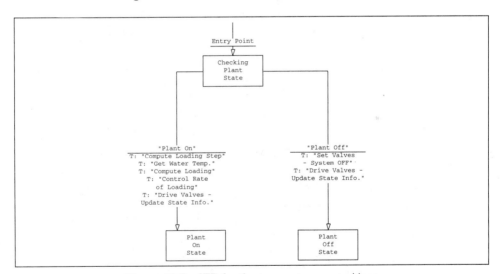

Figure 10.7   STD for the temperature control loop.

The input data is filtered and scaled as required, the conditioned value being output as Water Temp.

(c) Compute Loading now runs, calculating the required loading of the system.

(d) The required loading is translated into valve setting data by the DT Control Rate of Loading. Taken into account here is the permitted step change of loading.

(e) Finally, the valves themselves are set to the required state by Drive Valves. At the same time, the valve setting data is updated.

If, during the `Plant On State`, the required loading falls below 25%, then the `25% Trip` signal is generated.

You will see from Figures 10.6 and 10.7 that the DTs are turned on using trigger prompts. The interpretation, of course, is that each DT is executed only once per activation of the parent DT `Temperature Control Loop`. This is quite consistent with the overall design.

10.6 Design at the SC level

10.6.1 The main control task

The objective now is to translate the information from Figures 10.3 (a DFD) and 10.5 (its associated STD) into structure chart form. Remember, though, that when dynamics are present, SC design is driven mainly by the STD, not the DFD. Thus Figure 10.5 provides the essential information for building the structure chart of Figure 10.8.

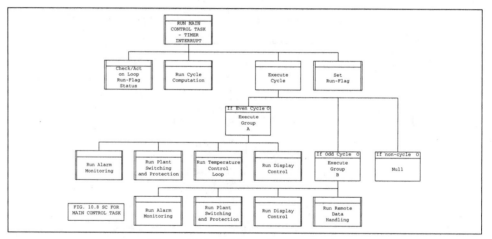

Figure 10.8   SC for main control task.

Here only two features need an explanation: the first and final SC boxes. Otherwise the diagram is self-explanatory.

New operations have been added at the SC design level, to do with a loop run flag. As pointed out much earlier, this is quite acceptable provided diagram (and thus design) consistency is maintained. It also enables us to keep DFD levelling to a sensible, comprehensible amount. Further, we are dealing here with activities very closely related to program operation.

The main control task is designed to be activated by the tick interrupt. Thus task activation is guaranteed provided the timer interrupts continue to function correctly. Unfortunately there isn't a similar guarantee that the code will execute correctly. For instance, a program error could result in `Run Alarm Monitoring` entering a continuous loop. And, in the original design, this would go undetected – the system would be out of control and unprotected. Run flags can be used to detect such exception conditions. Here, for instance, the loop run flag is checked and set to 'run' at the start of a run. On finishing the run the flag is set to 'run completed'. Thus, on starting the next cycle, a check can be made to see that the previous run was completed. Exception detection and response mechanisms are invoked within the procedure `Check/Act on Flag Status` (note: this also has to identify the first run of the main control task).

10.6.2   The temperature control loop

The temperature control loop SC is derived from the design information of Figures 10.6 (DFD) and 10.7 (associated STD). As before, the SC design (Figure 10.9) is dictated largely by the STD.

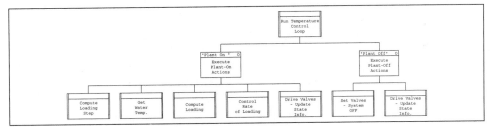

Figure 10.9   SC for temperature control loop.

This is quite a straightforward diagram.

10.7   Program development

How software is implemented in a target system depends significantly on:

- hardware structure
- programming language
- compiler features (including libraries)
- the processor itself
- operating system support (and if used, the type)

As a result, detailed implementation aspects are very parochial. Moreover, they are likely to be of limited interest to the reader. Therefore no attempt is made to produce a functionally complete design. Instead, the more important features of the overall process are highlighted. The aim is to demonstrate general design aspects using one specific programming approach.

There are two distinct aspects to the coding of the design. The first is the development of the multitasking software. Second comes the production of individual tasks using sequential program constructs. However, it is a mistake to think of them as isolated activities. In reality they interact to a high degree, design progressing in an iterative fashion.

Implementing the multitasking aspect is the smaller, but more difficult, phase. The design driver for such work is the task structure diagram, in this case Figure 10.2. Observe that this has five tasks. It has already been decided that simple 'multi-tasking' – interrupt-activated tasks – is sufficient for our needs. But there is no need for interrupt activation of the initialization task. As it is a one-shot operation, it can simply be called during program start-up. The remaining four tasks, however, *are* interrupt-driven.

Listing 10.1 – the module Tasker – gives the core aspects of the top-level code.

```
MODULE Tasker;
(*******************************************************)
(* This is the task level module.  As implemented here *)
(* it tests out interrupt activation of the individual *)
(* tasks.  The test interrupts are software-generated. *)
(*                    LISTING 10.1                      *)
(*******************************************************)

FROM SYSTEM    IMPORT ADDRESS, ADR, INT, REGISTERS,
                      ENABLE, DISABLE;
FROM InOut     IMPORT WriteString, WriteLn;
FROM IntVects  IMPORT PlantVector247, PlantVector248,
                      PlantVector249, PlantVector250;
FROM Initial   IMPORT InitializationTask;
FROM Switchin  IMPORT SwitchHandlingTask;
FROM CommsIn   IMPORT SerialCommsInTask;
FROM CommsOut  IMPORT SerialCommsOutTask;
FROM MainCT    IMPORT MainControlTask;

VAR
    Regs : REGISTERS;
    Done : BOOLEAN;

BEGIN
    DISABLE;
    PlantVector247 (ADR(SerialCommsInTask));
    PlantVector248 (ADR(SerialCommsOutTask));
    PlantVector249 (ADR(SwitchHandlingTask));
    PlantVector250 (ADR(MainControlTask));

    InitializationTask ;
    ENABLE;

    (* Test of the interrupt-driven tasks *)
    INT (247, Regs);
    INT (248, Regs);
    INT (249, Regs);
    INT (250, Regs);

END Tasker.
```

Listing 10.1   The task level module.

The executable code opens by linking tasks with interrupt vectors ('planting' the vectors). Following this the initialization task is called. These actions are performed while interrupts are disabled. The final section activates the four tasks using software interrupt commands. Normally specific hardware interrupts would trigger the tasks; what is given here is a preliminary test routine to check out interrupt operation. Observe that interrupts are planted using procedures imported from a service module IntVects. Details of the module are shown in Listing 10.2.

```
IMPLEMENTATION MODULE IntVects;
FROM SYSTEM IMPORT ADDRESS;
TYPE
    InterruptVector = RECORD
                          Offset : CARDINAL;
                              Segment : CARDINAL;
                          END;
VAR
    Int246 [0H:03D8H] : InterruptVector;
    Int247 [0H:03DCH] : InterruptVector;
    Int248 [0H:03E0H] : InterruptVector;
    Int249 [0H:03E4H] : InterruptVector;
    Int250 [0H:03E8H] : InterruptVector;

PROCEDURE PlantVector247 (ISR : ADDRESS);
BEGIN
    Int247.Offset := ISR.OFFSET;
    Int247.Segment := ISR.SEGMENT;
END PlantVector247;

PROCEDURE PlantVector248 (ISR : ADDRESS);
BEGIN
    Int248.Offset := ISR.OFFSET;
    Int248.Segment := ISR.SEGMENT;
END PlantVector248;

PROCEDURE PlantVector249 (ISR : ADDRESS);
BEGIN
    Int249.Offset := ISR.OFFSET;
    Int249.Segment := ISR.SEGMENT;
END PlantVector249;


PROCEDURE PlantVector250 (ISR : ADDRESS);
BEGIN
    Int250.Offset := ISR.OFFSET;
    Int250.Segment := ISR.SEGMENT;
END PlantVector250;


BEGIN
END IntVects.
```

Listing 10.2

```
DEFINITION MODULE AbsAdd;
VAR
   AlarmCancelFlag [8400H:0H]        : BOOLEAN;
   ContactorOnFlag [8400H:2H]        : BOOLEAN;
   ContactorTrippedFlag [8400H:4H]   : BOOLEAN;
   SensorAlarmFlag [8400H:6H]        : BOOLEAN;
   TripFlag [8400H:8H]               : BOOLEAN;
   TickTimePool [8401H:0H]           : REAL;
END AbsAdd.
```

Listing 10.3

```
IMPLEMENTATION MODULE CommComp;
FROM SYSTEM IMPORT DISABLE, ENABLE;
FROM InOut IMPORT WriteLn, WriteString;

PROCEDURE SetFlag (VAR Flag : BOOLEAN);
BEGIN
   DISABLE;
   Flag := Set;
   ENABLE;
END SetFlag;

PROCEDURE ReadFlag (VAR Flag : BOOLEAN) : BOOLEAN;
BEGIN
   DISABLE;
   RETURN Flag;
   ENABLE;
END ReadFlag;

PROCEDURE ClearFlag (VAR Flag : BOOLEAN);
BEGIN
   DISABLE;
   Flag := FALSE;
   ENABLE;
END ClearFlag;

PROCEDURE PutInPool (PoolName : CARDINAL;
                     VAR Data : INTEGER);
BEGIN
   WriteString ('PutInPool not yet implemented');
   WriteLn;
END PutInPool;

PROCEDURE GetFromPool (PoolName : CARDINAL;
                       VAR Data : INTEGER);
BEGIN
   WriteString ('GetFromPool not yet implemented');
   WriteLn;
END GetFromPool;

BEGIN
END CommComp.
```

Listing 10.4

You will also note that there is no reference to the communication components in Listing 10.1. That is because access to these is made from within the individual tasks.

Listing 10.3 contains a module called AbsAdd. Its function is to act as a place-holder for all absolute addresses (except the interrupt vectors) used in the software. There are two advantages in centralizing address information. First, it is easier to keep track of the location and use of such items. Second, address conflicts and inconsistencies – potential problems when the information is scattered throughout the code – are minimized. The example shows that the communication flags have been allocated absolute addresses. There is one major advantage in locating program items at specified locations: target debugging is immensely simplified. This is a personal approach – it works for me – but you may choose to tackle it differently.

The third program item Listing 10.4, module CommComp, is included for a number of reasons. First, it demonstrates the implementation of the service module concept. In this case the service is support for inter-task communication. Second, the flag procedures Set and Clear show how to provide a simple but effective mutual exclusion (access protection) mechanism. It relies on the use of the interrupt DISABLE and ENABLE statements. Conceptually this raises the priority of the procedures to the highest level – one form of priority inversion. The final reason for including the code is to enable the reader to make sense of Listings 10.5 and 10.6.

The STDs of Figures 10.5 and 10.7, together with the SC of Figure 10.8, provide the basis for Listing 10.5.

```
IMPLEMENTATION MODULE MainCT;
FROM CommComp IMPORT Set, Clear, ReadFlag, ClearFlag, GetFromPool;
FROM AbsAdd IMPORT  AlarmCancelFlag,  ContactorOnFlag,
                    ContactorTrippedFlag, SensorAlarmFlag,
                TripFlag, TickTimePool, DataValues;
FROM Periodic IMPORT  RunAlarmMonitoring,RunRemoteDataHandling,
                      RunTempControlLoop, RunDisplayControl,
                      RunPlantSwitchingProtection,
                      RunCycleComputation;
TYPE
    CycleRange = [-1 .. 1];
CONST
    NonCycle  = -1;
    EvenCycle =  0;
    OddCycle  =  1;
VAR
    CycleNumber : CycleRange;
    Cycle : INTEGER;
    TCLcycleTime : REAL;
    ValveSettings : DataValues;
    AlarmLoadingData : DataValues;
    AlarmStatus : DataValues;
    TripPlantCommand : BOOLEAN;
```

Listing 10.5

(continued)

Listing 10.5 *Continued*

```
    TripPlantSignal : BOOLEAN;
    PlantOn  : BOOLEAN;
    PlantOff : BOOLEAN;
    Trip25   : BOOLEAN;
    RunFlag  : BOOLEAN;

PROCEDURE CheckLoopRunFlag (VAR Flag : BOOLEAN);
BEGIN
END CheckLoopRunFlag;

PROCEDURE MainControlTask() [INTERRUPT];
BEGIN
    CheckLoopRunFlag (RunFlag);
    (* Note: in the event of an error, an exception will be raised
       using an interrupt.  There will be an unconditional transfer
       of control to the exception handler.  This procedure also
       deals with the watchdog timer                           *)
    RunCycleComputation (Cycle, TCLcycleTime);
    CycleNumber := Cycle;

    IF CycleNumber = EvenCycle THEN
       RunAlarmMonitoring (AlarmStatus, TripPlantCommand);
       RunPlantSwitchingProtection (TripPlantSignal);
       RunTempControlLoop (TCLcycleTime, ValveSettings,
                            PlantOn, PlantOff, Trip25);
       RunRemoteDataHandling (AlarmLoadingData);
    ELSIF CycleNumber = OddCycle THEN
       RunAlarmMonitoring (AlarmStatus, TripPlantCommand);
       RunPlantSwitchingProtection (TripPlantSignal);
       RunDisplayControl (AlarmLoadingData);
       RunRemoteDataHandling (AlarmLoadingData);
    ELSIF CycleNumber = NonCycle THEN
    END; (* of IF statements *)
    RunFlag := Set;
END MainControlTask;

BEGIN
END MainCT.
```

Listing 10.5

Listing 10.6 – only part complete – is included to demonstrate use of the inter-task flags.

```
IMPLEMENTATION MODULE Initial;
FROM InOut IMPORT WriteLn, WriteString;
FROM AbsAdd IMPORT  AlarmCancelFlag,  ContactorOnFlag,
                    ContactorTrippedFlag, SensorAlarmFlag,
            TripFlag;
FROM CommComp IMPORT  SetFlag, ClearFlag, Set, Clear;
FROM Timers IMPORT RunTimer1;

CONST
    HalfSecond = 0.5;

PROCEDURE InitializationTask;
BEGIN
    ClearFlag(AlarmCancelFlag);
    ClearFlag(ContactorOnFlag);
    ClearFlag(ContactorTrippedFlag);
    ClearFlag(SensorAlarmFlag);
    ClearFlag(TripFlag);
    RunTimer1(HalfSecond);
END InitializationTask;

BEGIN
END Initial.
```

Listing 10.6

Review

In this chapter you have learnt about:

- the use of a multi-stage design process – essentially a separation of concerns between initial design, concurrent (task) level work, development of individual tasks and code implementation
- the purposes of, and activities within, each stage
- the interrelationship between the stages
- the need to establish timing and tasking aspects early in the design cycle
- the importance of the task level design, and the influence of timing issues on the resulting structure
- the use and implementation of task intercommunication components
- the application of interrupt techniques to achieve simple concurrency
- how to organize periodic tasks into rate groups for implementation as sequential code
- how to apply an ordered, traceable approach to a design

Part 2:
Object-oriented design

11

Object-oriented design concepts

Object-oriented (OO) techniques are not new. The early ideas surfaced in the mid-1960s in Norway, being very much associated with the programming language SIMULA. This was followed in the early 1970s by Smalltalk, which brought with it a whole new philosophy of programming. However, it wasn't until the late 1980s that object orientation began to make a major impact on mainstream programming. At the present time the language scene is quite stable, the leader (by a large margin) being C++ (but it is now being challenged by Jarrow). However, the development of design techniques lagged somewhat behind the languages. The result is that there is no single accepted OO design method. Therefore, in this text, it is more important to concentrate on fundamentals rather than any specific method.

The purpose of this chapter is to introduce the concepts of object-oriented design (OOD). To a lesser extent it also demonstrates, in a conceptual way, some basic ideas of object-oriented programming (OOP). It includes the following:

- how systems can be described in terms of a set of collaborating objects
- the fundamental aspects of systems and objects
- a detailed view of objects and their attributes
- introduction to classes
- issues in modern software design: templates, encapsulation, interfacing, information hiding and inheritance
- object relationships, communication and control
- the three basic models of object-oriented design

This introduction can be seen as a condensed version of later chapters. Consequently there is some repetition of this material in those chapters.

11.1   Introduction to object-oriented design

Object orientation has one simple, central feature. It is that designs may be structured as sets of interconnected, collaborating objects. There are, of course, many associated and important aspects of object-oriented design; these will be discussed shortly. However, it is essential to any further study that you truly understand this key issue of OOD. In general, the concepts involved can be explained in non-software terms. To demonstrate these, consider a small example system – a fuel valve actuator (Figure 11.1(a)).

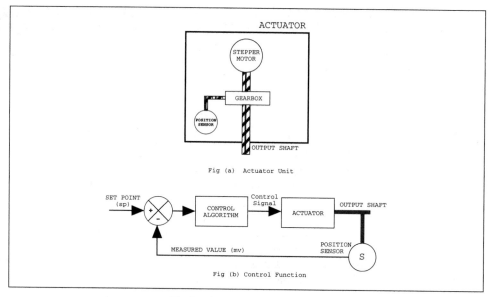

Fig (a) Actuator Unit

Fig (b) Control Function

Figure 11.1   Example system.

The design requirement is to develop an automatic controller for the actuator, performing the control function given in Figure 11.1(b). It is also required to carry out some form of manual (human) control of the unit.

Using our knowledge and experience, we decide that a suitable solution is that of Figure 11.2.

The result is a system which consists of three separate physical items or 'objects': controller, actuator and local control panel. These form a set of interacting machines which communicate by signalling to each other. For instance, the control panel sends the demanded position value to the controller. In turn, the controller sets the actuator position by sending control signals to the actuator.

There are two quite different ways to view such object-based designs (Figure 11.3).

First there is the external – system-oriented – view. Then there is the internal or object level view. Each view consists of three distinct aspects: structure, behaviour/communication, and function. The external view emphasizes:

- the overall system function
- the role of objects within a system
- the relationship of objects
- the interaction of objects
- the communication *between* objects

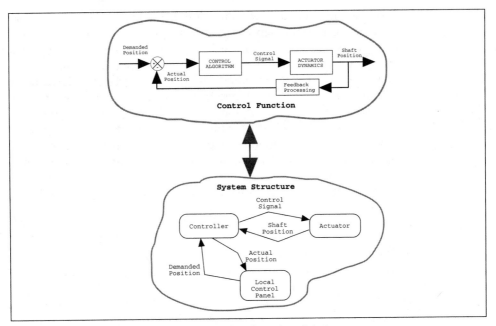

Figure 11.2   An object-based design.

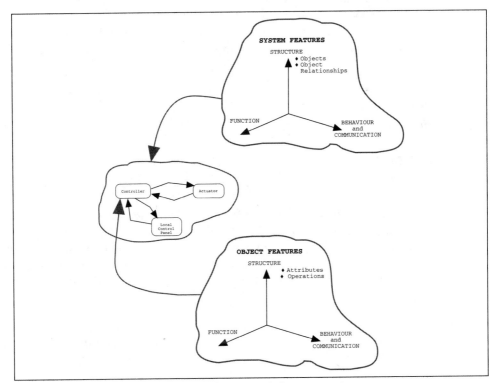

Figure 11.3   System and object viewpoints.

In contrast, the internal view focuses on the qualities of individual objects.

Consider first the design of the system. All three aspects have to be taken into account when carrying out the design. However, always remember that the resulting system is required to perform some desired function (in this example, to control actuator position and provide human–machine interfacing). Thus the driving force in the design process is that of system functionality (implicit in this is performance). The *collective* behaviour of the set of objects must provide this functionality. Moreover, the objects need to communicate with each other in order to collaborate. At this level of design, there is one primary objective: to strike a balance between structure, behaviour and communication while meeting system functional requirements.

Now take the design of individual objects. Each one is required to carry out some particular function; to do this it must:

- be correctly structured
- behave in a predefined manner
- provide communication interfaces

For the moment we shall ignore how the functional specification is deduced. It does, in essence, depend on the application area of the system; this topic is covered in detail in Chapter 12.

As with all designs, there is no uniquely correct solution. There are usually a few good ones – and many poor ones. What criteria can we use to gauge the quality of the result (we assume, of course, that it meets its specification)? Even in the cutting edge of OO technology, the old, established measures of coupling and cohesion can yield good results.

11.2 The object in more detail

11.2.1 Qualities of objects

In OO work, objects can have many forms. Take, for example, those shown in Figure 11.4.

The first, an aircraft, is a physical one. The dog is also physical, but here we have a real live item, as opposed to the inanimate aircraft. The third object, the electronic diary, can be viewed in two ways. First, we could think of it in physical terms. Alternatively, it can be viewed as a conceptual item: a store of information. But, no matter how we choose to categorize objects, all can be described in terms of their:

- attributes
- operations
- dynamic aspects (states and transitions between states)
- function

In simple informal terms, an object is an entity ('a thing with distinct existence')

Figure 11.4   Example of objects.

which behaves in a particular way. It is essential to recognize that each object in a system is unique and has its own identity. Consider, for example, a tray-load of oranges which appear to be identical in colour, shape and size. Even so, this is still a collection of distinct objects.

Attributes

These are 'qualities' which enable us to describe, or relate to, an object. Examples of these are given in Table 11.1.

Table 11.1   Attributes of objects.

Aircraft	Dog	Diary
Weight	Breed	Title
Range	Colour	Publisher
Payload	Age	Year

Operations

Operations are actions carried out by, or performed on, objects; see Table 11.2.

Table 11.2   Operations.

Aircraft	Dog	Diary
Arm	Feed	Update entry
Launch missile	Bath	Generate prompt
Roll	Exercise	Change address

An important point: from here on we will use 'operation' in a more restricted way. Operations are actions carried out by an object in response to some external stimulus.

Dynamic aspects

Most real-time objects have different modes of behaviour, these being time and/or event dependent (Table 11.3).

Table 11.3 Dynamic aspects.

Aircraft	Dog	Diary
Cruising	Sleeping	Data entry mode
Landing	Eating	Prompt generation
Climbing	Running	Message generation

It has already been shown (Chapter 6) how dynamic behaviour can be modelled with finite state machines. Such machines can be expressed using state transition diagrams (STDs). Not surprisingly, STDs (also called *state diagrams*) are widely used in OO design. Detailed coverage of the topic is given in Chapter 13.

Function

This is not such a clear-cut issue; it depends on what aspect of the object is under consideration. We might, for instance, be concerned with functional behaviour at a very high level (Table 11.4).

Table 11.4 General functional view.

Aircraft	Dog	Diary
To provide close air support to ground forces	To guard home	To record daily activities

But we may be also be interested in detailed functional activities. For example, in particular modes of operation, specific functions may have to be performed (Table 11.5).

Table 11.5 Specific functional view.

Aircraft	Dog	Diary
Missile launch phase	Feeding mode	Update
1. Arm missile	1. Find food bag	1. Open diary
2. Acquire target	2. Rip bag open	2. Select day
3. Fire missile	3. Eat food	3. Make entry

The use of data flow diagrams to define functional behaviour has already been covered (Chapter 4). DFDs are also used in some OO design methods, though the topic is somewhat contentious. Detailed aspects are discussed in Chapter 14.

11.2.2   Objects from the outside

Another key aspect of OO design is how objects are 'seen' by other objects – the outside view (Figure 11.5).

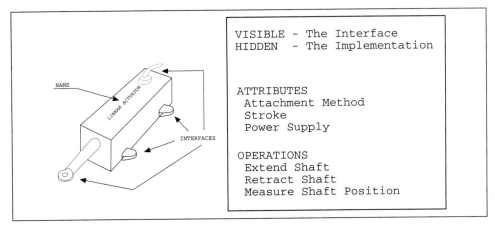

Figure 11.5   The object from the outside.

The visible items are the object attributes, operations and interfaces. In this example, the actuator object has the attributes of weight, size, stroke and motor type. Its defined operations are Extend Shaft, Retract Shaft and Measure Shaft Position. Finally, it has a set of electrical and mechanical interfaces, allowing it to interact with the outside world. The inside, however, is hidden; no information is given concerning the implementation.

This example also illustrates other important features of object-oriented design: encapsulation, interfacing and information hiding. An alternative view of the actuator (Figure 11.6) emphasizes these points.

The actuator interfaces provide the 'hooks' between the object and its external world. They should always be visible and explicit (especially important when dealing with software). As a result, this object can be replaced by any object which has identical interfaces – without disturbing the rest of the system structure. Clear, sound interfaces also simplify the task of testing the object and verifying its performance.

Using this approach, it is possible to replace an object with one which has:

- identical functionality and behaviour
- modified functionality and/or behaviour

The first case is frequently met when dealing with physical devices. For example, consider the task of replacing your car's exhaust system. It is a straightforward

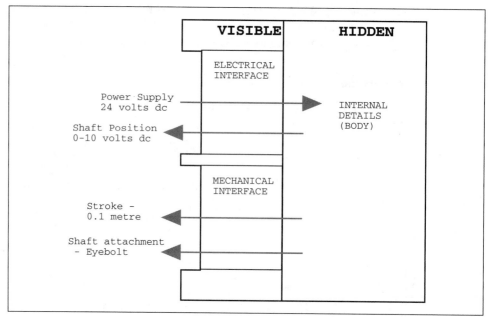

Figure 11.6 Encapsulation, interfacing and information hiding.

operation to remove the old item and fit the new one. In software systems there are similar considerations (even though software doesn't wear out). We may wish to replace an object by one which has improved performance – speed, storage, accuracy – yet retain functionality and behaviour. Such targets are frequently attained merely by using improved algorithms.

Important as this is, the second factor is, for software, likely to be the most important. An unfortunate – but widespread – view of software is that it is an easy item to change. The result of this thinking? In many projects the software *is* constantly in a state of flux. There are good reasons for this: correcting mistakes, upgrading performance, introducing new functionality, to name but a few. Such an approach may not be desirable; it is, though, the way that software is developed in the real world. To ignore this and seek an 'ideal' design method is, at best, a fruitless task. Object-based techniques, with their concept of 'plug-replacement' software, can significantly ease the software development process.

Summarizing, from an external point of view, an object:

- is seen as a single unit
- has a well-defined function or purpose (*what* it does)
- encapsulates all resources required to achieve that purpose (*how* it does it)
- has distinct separation of 'what' from 'how'
- hides implementation aspects from the outside world
- has a well-defined, clean interface which acts as the 'access window' of the object. Only this is visible to the outside world

It is also important that the object should not produce side-effects (which would negate many of the benefits of OO design). To achieve this, there should be no bypassing of the interface.

11.3 OOD – key design and build issues

11.3.1 Introduction

The points raised above may seem to be familiar. They are, in fact, identical to those used in Chapter 3 to describe the qualities of modules. So, are objects and modules the same? In terms of the issues covered so far, the answer is yes. Therefore it is possible (and sensible) to produce object-based designs using the module concept. The object, however, takes the concept of the module much further, bringing in some very new ideas. These, it is claimed, can make a major impact on software productivity and reusability. In fact, many developers consider that the *raison d'être* for OO techniques is precisely these objectives. In software terms, these represent the step from object-based design to object-oriented programming (OOP); more of this later. First, let us, by looking at manufacturing methods, get to the heart of the matter.

Contrast the use of medieval handcrafting with modern production methods (Figure 11.7).

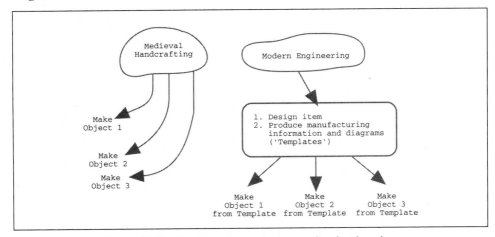

Figure 11.7 Manufacturing methods – medieval and modern.

With the handcrafting approach, each item produced is truly individual. Plans might (or more likely, might not) exist. But the end product depends much on the talent, technique and whims of the craftsman. Modern production methods run counter to this. They are based on the idea of making items from plans, using defined, controlled and consistent manufacturing methods. This approach enables high-quality low-cost goods to be produced – with a less skilled workforce. Essential to this process is good design with full, correct design and manufacturing documentation.

What has this got to do with software? You may have already observed that, currently, much software is produced in medieval fashion. Design is subordinated to manufacture (coding). The 'craftsman' (aka programmer) reigns supreme. Many programmers consider the development of software to be an individual, creative exercise. In such circumstances it is no surprise that, in general, productivity is low and quality quite variable.

These have now become extremely important issues as software moves out of the handcrafting phase. Object orientation offers a number of ways to improve the situation. Two particular ideas are of special importance here: design templates (*classes*) and design extensibility (*inheritance*).

11.3.2   The class

The class is equivalent to a template or plan. This defines *what* the attributes of objects are, together with object operations (Figure 11.8).

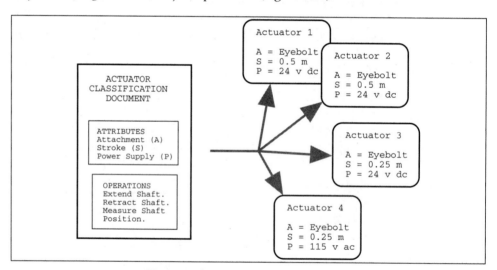

Figure 11.8   Concept – class and object.

In the example here, the attributes for the actuator class are:

- Attachment
- Stroke
- Power Supply

The class operations are:

- Extend Shaft
- Retract Shaft
- Measure Shaft Position

Using this template, individual objects are constructed. That is, we *instantiate* the class.

Observe that the class document does not specify *values* for these items. We supply value information in order to build specific actuators (objects). Thus every object manufactured from this template has the same attributes. However, the individual attribute *values* may or may not be the same, as shown in Figure 11.8. Here, Actuators 1 and 2 are identical, but are still individual, distinct objects. Actuator 3 has a different stroke from 1 and 2, while 4 requires a different power supply.

It is important that you clearly understand the class concept; it is a key feature of much OOP work. *The* essential point is that we work from an adaptable template; manufacture is a 'turn the handle' type of operation.

11.3.3   *Design extensibility and inheritance*

Let us assume that we have reached a stage where the use of the class is an accepted technique. Thus the class forms the primary template for the manufacture of objects; individual objects are 'customized' by setting attribute values. Then, as stated earlier, *all* objects have the same set of attributes (and, note, operations). How, in this situation, should we respond to a requirement to produce a new design – one which is almost, but not quite, the same as the original? This is illustrated in Figure 11.9.

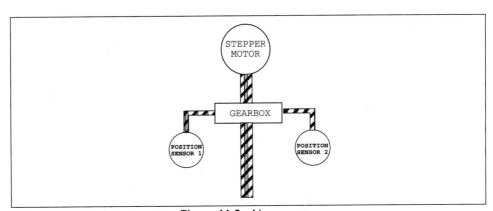

Figure 11.9   New actuator.

Here there is a requirement to produce an actuator which differs in only one respect from the earlier version: it has an additional position sensor. One quite practical way to deal with this is by a process of adaptation. That is, take the original design, copy it, then modify it to meet the new function. However, there is another way to tackle this problem (Figure 11.10).

The idea here is to take the basic unit (Figure 11.10(a)), and extend it by adding the new piece (Figure 11.10(b)) to it. The result is shown in Figure 11.10(c). This process is called *inheritance*.

With adaptation we end up with two quite distinct designs. With inheritance, we have the original design plus an extension. There are pros and cons in these two

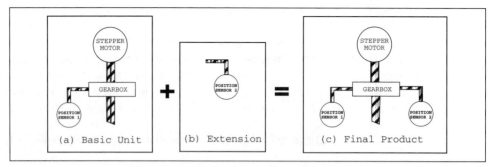

Figure 11.10 Extending a design by inheritance.

approaches. More will be said on this subject when software inheritance is covered in some detail (Chapter 12).

11.4 Object relationships, communication and control

11.4.1 Background

In the previous section, emphasis was placed on the individual object. However, this is only one part of the design jigsaw. To understand system operation fully we must also take into account:

- how objects relate to each other
- how objects communicate
- any form of control ('command') structure in the object system

You will find in practice that relationships, communication and control are often interdependent.

Diagrams are one of the clearest ways of showing these points. Unfortunately, there is no agreed, standard diagramming method. Some techniques have separate diagrams for each design aspect. Others, as you will see later, use a single diagram to illustrate a number of properties. And, just to add confusion, each technique has its own set of symbols (icons). The diagrams used here are not based on any specific method, but, where possible, follow OMT notation.

11.4.2 Object relationships

An OO design consists of a set of objects which collectively perform some desired function. An important aspect of the design work is to establish precisely how the objects relate to each other (Figure 11.11).

As shown here, the following relationships exist:

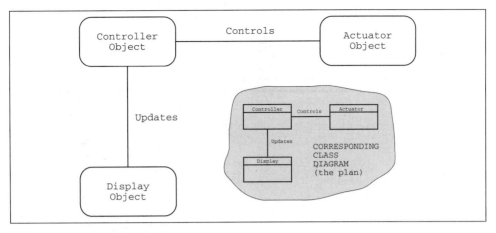

Figure 11.11   Showing object relationships – the 'object diagram'.

- The controller object controls the actuator object.
- The actuator object is controlled by the controller object.
- The controller object updates the display object.
- The display object is updated by the controller object.

By putting this information down on a diagram, the designer is forced to make relationships visible. As a result, design review and assessment is more readily carried out. Simple but penetrating questions such as 'does it make sense?' are more easily devised. Note also that such diagrams highlight inter-object coupling (and hence connection complexity).

Included in Figure 11.11 is the template or class diagram from which the object diagram is derived. Shown on this is the relationship between the classes, called a class *association*.

Classes and class structures are an important aspect of OOD, and are covered in depth in Chapter 12. For the moment, however, only a general appreciation of the roles of classes and objects is needed.

It is important to realize that an object can have one of three roles. It may (Figure 11.12):

- use other objects: the `Local Control Panel` object (a client – must have a required interface)
- be used by other objects: the `Actuator` object (a server – must have a provided interface)
- both use and be used by other objects: the `Controller` object (an agent – the most general case)

All required and provided facilities should be handled via the object interfaces. Some design methods (HOOD, for example) require that such facilities are explicitly listed as part of the object definition. In others (OMT, for example), provided facilities are shown explicitly, but not the required ones.

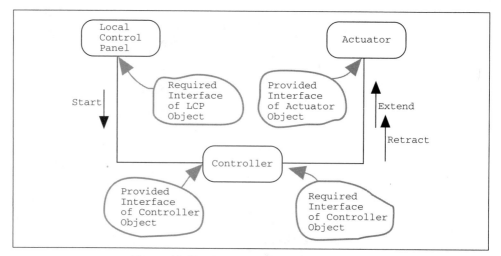

Figure 11.12   Required and provided interfaces.

Frequently objects are themselves made up from a set of smaller objects (Figure 11.13).

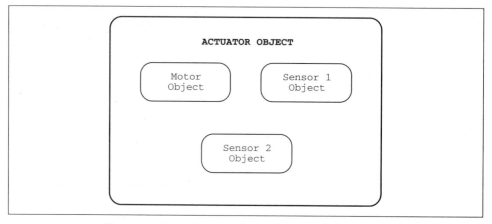

Figure 11.13   Objects made up of objects – 'aggregation'.

This presents an alternative view of the actuator object of Figure 11.9. It shows that this 'parent' object has three 'child' objects: Motor, Sensor 1 and Sensor 2. We say that the parent is the aggregate of its children; the process is termed *aggregation.*

You need to be careful and consistent when dealing with aggregation. There are two ways of looking at it. In the first, the parent does not exist as an entity in its own right. Only when all the children are assembled together does it come into being. Alternatively, the parent is seen as a distinct object which *contains* a set of child objects. More will be said about this later.

Inheritance, of course, sets up particular class relationships. If *all* classes are instantiated, there is a true object relationship – a hierarchical one. More of this later.

11.4.3   Object communication

The design stage outlined above establishes the broad relationship between objects. What follows are activities which firm up on this by specifying, in detail, inter-object communication. Such communication, remember, is implemented by passing messages between the objects (Figure 11.14).

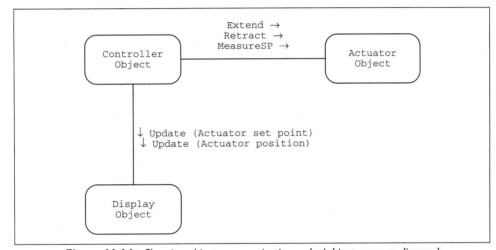

Figure 11.14   Showing object communication – the 'object message diagram'.

These are listed on the object message diagram, the general format being:

MessageName {DirectionArrow}

as in

Extend →

Be aware that some OO methods include object communication diagrams which are quite different – in content and presentation – from Figure 11.14. Moreover, some techniques combine the communication diagram with the object diagram – and call the result an object diagram; most confusing.

Make sure that you understand the difference between object relationships and object communication. Review Figures 11.11 and 11.12. From this you can see that the controller *controls* the actuator (the relationship). It does this by *passing messages* extend, retract and measure to the actuator (the communication).

Objects, from a communication point of view, come in two flavours: passive and active. In Figure 11.15, objects A and B are passive ones.

Assume that object A demands a service from B. What it does is to send a message to B, transferring control to it. Object B then actions the request. On completion of the demanded action control is returned to A, the calling object.

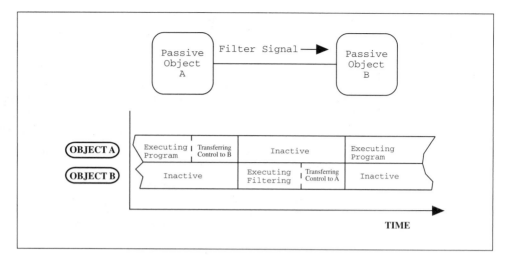

Figure 11.15   Passive object behaviour.

By contrast, active objects can execute simultaneously. Consider a scenario similar to the previous case, but where both objects are active ones (Figure 11.16(a)).

Object A sends a message to B. However, control is not transferred; both objects continue to execute in parallel. The behaviour in such a case is best shown using a *message trace* diagram (Figure 11.16(b)).

Whether objects are active or passive, the important points are (Figure 11.17) that:

- Any object has an associated set of operations.
- The implementation of an operation is called a *method*.
- Operations are activated (invoked) by sending a *message* to the object.

Thus each message must have an associated method.

The subject is covered in more detail in Chapter 15.

11.4.4   Exerting control – an object hierarchy

We may choose to design our system using a hierarchical object structuring; that is, where objects control the activities of other objects (Figure 11.18).

As shown here, the controller object directs the activities of the display and actuator objects (a master–slave relationship). It is easy to jump to the conclusion that the slave objects are passive types. This is not necessarily the case; all three might, in fact, be active ones. For instance, the controller object could be a scheduler in a multiprocessing system, executing on a scheduler processor. Associated with this are two other processors, one for display and the other for actuator control. However, hierarchical structuring is most frequently met when building systems using passive objects.

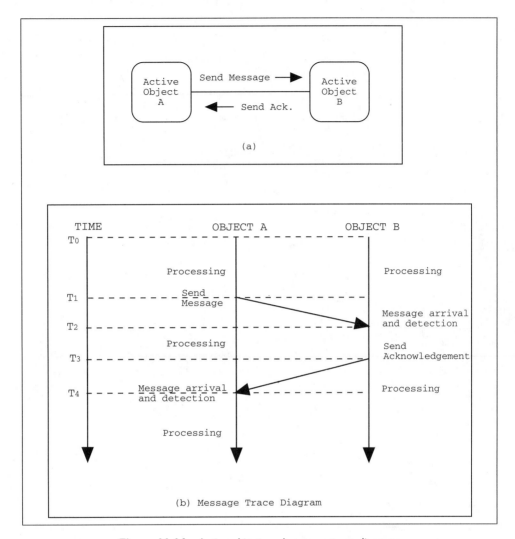

Figure 11.16   Active objects and message trace diagrams.

11.5   The models of OO design

To recap: we define an object-oriented design as one that consists of a set of communicating, collaborating objects. An object is a machine which has a number of defined operational states and a defined means to change these states. Put another way, an OO design is made up of specific objects which perform particular functions in a dynamic manner.

There are many different OO design methods. They frequently approach the subject in different ways, using different notation and diagramming methods.

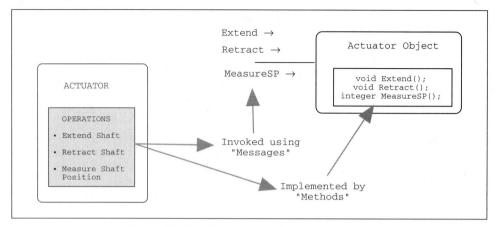

Figure 11.17 Concept – methods and messages.

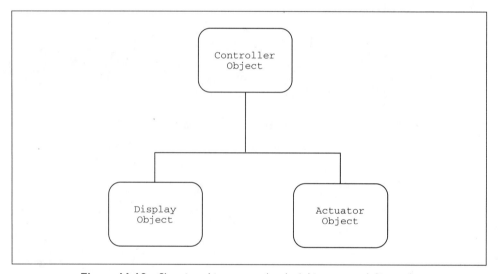

Figure 11.18 Showing object control – the 'object control diagram'.

Nevertheless, three fundamental models predominate in all techniques (Figure 11.19):

• object model (what an object is)
• dynamic model (object communication and behaviour)
• functional model (what it does and how it does it)

These models are the subject of the next three chapters.

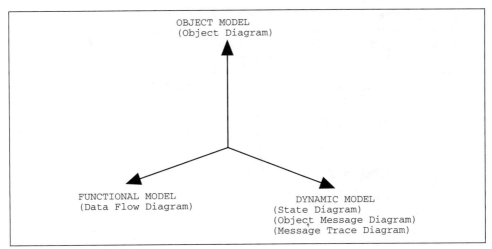

Figure 11.19   The three models used in OO design.

Review

You should now:

- understand the concept of modelling a system as a set of cooperating objects
- appreciate that both systems and objects can be described in terms of their structure, dynamics and function
- know what is meant by class, association, instantiation, attribute, message and method
- realize the importance of encapsulation, interfacing and information hiding
- see why it is useful to define the provided and required interfaces of objects
- know what server, client, agent, passive and active objects are
- understand what inheritance and aggregation are
- perceive how objects can be controlled using hierarchical structures
- grasp the role of the three models of OO design
- recognize the types of diagram shown in Table 11.6

Exercises

11.1   Categorize the following as classes or objects:
Einstein
Painter
Spacecraft

Table 11.6 Diagram – type and purpose.

Diagram type	Purpose
Class diagram	To show the classes in a system, together with their associations
Object diagram	To show the objects in a system, together with their relationships
Message trace diagram	To show interactions between objects as time progresses
Object message diagram	To show the messages which flow between objects
State diagram	To define the dynamic behaviour of objects
Data flow diagram	To define the processing carried out within the system or by specific objects

Cruise liner
Apollo 13
Titanic
Scientist
Van Gogh

11.2 Sort the following list into classes and their attributes.
Sail size
No. of vehicles
Hire costs
Coach company
Length
Drivers' names
Cruising yacht
No. of berths

11.3 Form an inheritance hierarchy for the following data items monitored by an aircraft flight recorder (the 'black box' recorder):
Recorder data
Engine JPT
Track
Roll rate
Heading
Navigation data
Vehicle motion
Engine speed
Yaw rate
Engine data
Autopilot data
Pitch rate

11.4 Give one example of an embedded system where:

(a) the number of objects is fixed for the life of the program
(b) the number of objects changes during program execution

11.5 Suppose that in our design there is an object, Filter say. One, and only one, Filter object is required for this application. Also, it is unlikely to be reused – without major change – in other designs. How important, in these circumstances, is the class construct?

11.6 Why is the class structure an important feature in the design of graphical user interfaces (GUIs)?

11.7 For the system described below, produce the:

- object diagram
- object message diagram
- message trace diagram

A machine control system consists of four major subsystems:

- configuration and management subsystem (CMS)
- machine coordinator (MCS)
- lubrication (LS)
- drive dynamics (DDS)

The run-time operation begins when CMS is activated by the operator. It sends a message to all other subsystems (a broadcast), requesting them to perform software self-tests. CMS waits until a reply indicating success is received from all subsystems before proceeding further. Assuming success (fault modes are defined later), it then issues a 'ready' broadcast command. MCS responds with a reload request, causing CMS to download the control program to MCS. MCS acknowledges this. As a result a 'system configured' broadcast is made by CMS.

A short time later MCS sends an initialize command to LS and DDS. It then sends a start command to LS. LS begins its start sequence, and, on completion, signals 'OK' to MCS. MCS now sends a start command to DDS. When DDS has reached its normal running speed, it sends the signal 'at speed' to MCS.

On completion of the manufacturing run, MCS sends a 'standby' command to LS and DDS.

12
The object model

Chapter 11 ended by identifying the fundamental models used in object-oriented design: object, dynamic and functional. In this chapter we concentrate on the concepts and implementation of the object model. Its role is to describe real-world systems in terms of objects, their characteristics and their relationships. As such it shows a static view – provides a 'snapshot' – of such systems; that is *what* they do. But a more important question is *why* do we produce this model in the first place? The reasons are twofold. First, in order to develop it, we are forced to investigate, in depth, the real-world system. Thus we are more likely to produce designs that actually meet client requirements. Second, it acts as a driving force for the design of the code-level model.

The objectives of this chapter are to:

- revisit the basic aspects of the object diagram
- introduce two approaches to object modelling: data-driven (information modelling) and responsibility-driven
- review traditional information modelling techniques and show how these relate to modern object-oriented methods
- revisit the class and object, introducing association, generalization (inheritance), specialization and aggregation
- describe the concept and use of responsibility-driven modelling using class–responsibility–collaboration (CRC) methods

12.1   Introduction and recapitulation

This is a short but important section which aims to show concisely the role of the object model. Let us illustrate this by example. Suppose that we wish to develop a processor-based controller for the temperature control system of Figure 12.1(a).

Its purpose is to maintain the temperature in an aircraft cockpit at a value set by the flight crew. This value is input using the control panel man–machine interface (MMI). The actual temperature (derived from a sensor) is compared with the desired value by the controller. Any differences cause the computer to send corrective signals to a mixer valve actuator. The result is that the hot/cold air ratio mix is changed

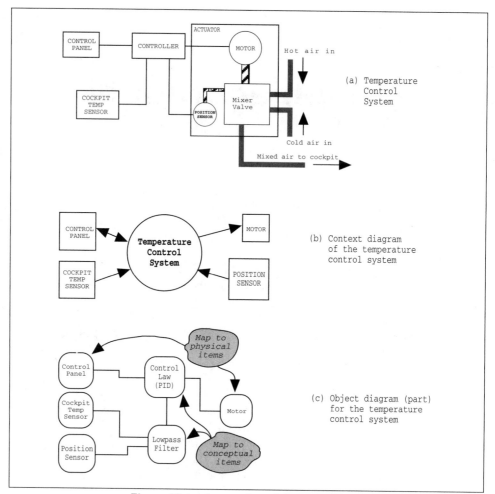

Figure 12.1   An overview of object modelling.

to produce the desired air temperature. The controller also makes use of the valve position information to improve system control dynamics.

The primary design responsibility for a system like this lies with the environmental engineers – not the controller designer. Only later are computer specialists introduced to the job. In many cases such specialists (particularly software engineers) have little or no previous experience in the application domain. Thus the development of the computer system depends heavily on input from system experts – in this case the environmental engineers. In the early stages of the design the object diagram acts as a valuable communication tool. However, before launching into object modelling, it is strongly recommended that you produce a system context diagram (Figure 12.1(b)) (even if your preferred OO design method doesn't include such a diagram). This is a valuable way of identifying and defining all items and signals external to the software. It also keeps your thoughts focused on the problem, not its solution.

Following this we set out to build the object model. This, in simple terms, defines the structure of the computer-based system as a set of interrelated objects. It consists of objects based on both external and internal features. Some of the objects map to physical items, others to conceptual ones. These points, for our example system, are illustrated in Figure 12.1(c).

Note that external objects are sometimes known as actors and sometimes as agents (it depends on the design methodology).

At this stage the design is unfinished; much information concerning object qualities and operations is missing. However, in *overall* structural terms, the object model is complete. We could now proceed to elaborate and refine the model, proceeding to detailed design and coding. Unfortunately, there is one great problem with the description given here: it gives absolutely no indication how to go from system design level to the object model. Just how does one arrive at a particular solution? The rest of this chapter is devoted to answering that question, describing the use of two particular modelling techniques.

The first is based on information modelling – a data-driven approach. The other depends to a large extent on assigning responsibilities to objects – a responsibility-driven method. Later, in Chapter 14, a third procedure – one based on structured methods and data flow diagrams – is described. It has been left until later as it fits in more naturally with that chapter. Also, it is much less widely used than the approaches described here (although all can be combined, to good effect).

Remember, though, that whichever method you choose, the important qualities of an object are that it:

- is seen as a single unit
- has a well-defined function or purpose (*what* it does)
- encapsulates all resources required to achieve that purpose (*how* it does it)
- has distinct separation of 'what' from 'how'
- hides implementation aspects from the outside world
- has a well-defined, clean interface which acts as the 'access window' of the object. Only this is visible to the outside world

12.2   Information modelling – traditional methods

The OO data-driven approach is heavily based on traditional information modelling methods (old wine in new bottles?). Here, to set the groundwork for later work, a review of these older concepts is given. The object model makes much more sense once these ideas have been grasped.

Figure 12.2 shows the relationship between the:

- real world (reality)
- information model of reality, and
- software (or code) model – the implementation of the information model

Here we express our view of reality as a visual (pictorial) information model. The

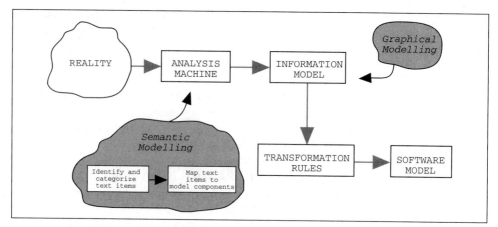

Figure 12.2 Generating the information and software models.

model is derived using an 'analysis machine' involving semantic modelling (in other words, defining what we *have* and what it *means*). It must also be understood that this technique has its roots in database design. Thus it is not surprising that the identification and categorization of data (information) is a primary operation.

Central to the modelling process is the concept of an *entity*. Chen defines this to be a 'thing' which can be distinctly identified. Thus any complete system consists of a set of individual things or entities. From that point of view, the actuator of Figure 12.1 is an entity. Likewise, the control panel, cockpit temperature sensor and controller are also entities. Be clear on one point: we are talking about specific items. Entities, however, do not have to be physical in nature. The object FILTER, for instance, is an example of a *software* entity.

The starting point for information modelling is to list all (relevant) entities within the system being modelled. Having defined an entity, we then need to describe exactly what it is. This we do by listing its qualities or properties. Thus a particular actuator – fuel cock, say – could be described as having a weight of 1 kg and a length of 200 mm (Figure 12.3).

These properties – perhaps more precisely *property values* – are said to belong to the entity. Using this information, a defining *property set* can be formed. One of these properties is, in fact, the name of the entity. Therefore, in this case the set consists of Name, Weight and Length. Note that in the context of data modelling, the word *attribute* is synonymous with *property*.

Individual entities which share the same property set can be grouped together to form an entity set: LINEAR ACTUATORS, for instance. Thus all actuator entities which have the properties of Name, Weight and Length belong to the same set. It is also possible to approach this process from another direction. That is, first define the entity set, and, from that, form the property set. This second method is often the most natural way of working with real, physical things. But when dealing with abstract or conceptual things, it may be easier to go the

entity → property value → property set → entity set

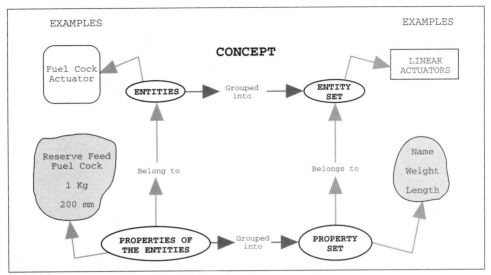

Figure 12.3   Entities and properties.

route. Frequently it is necessary to go around this loop a number of times to reach a satisfactory result.

For the moment let us leave it at that. We will, nevertheless, return to the topic shortly in the context of object identification. First, though, a brief theoretical digression which leads into methods for defining relationships. To illustrate this, take the situation in which a software company employs designers to work on projects. Thus we have entity sets `Designers` and `Projects` (Figure 12.4).

This is shown using set – Venn diagram – notation. Initially no designers are allocated to projects; thus the sets do not overlap (Figure 12.4(a)). At some point, certain designers are assigned to specific projects, leading to set overlap (Figure 12.4(b)). The diagram shows that both sets are related, although it isn't clear exactly what the relationship is. This can be specified in tabular form, as shown in Table 12.1.

It shows that designer Shap (an entity) works on two projects (two distinct entities), while Birch works on one project only. The 'X' denotes 'project worker', this forming the relationship between the project and the designer.

The general (set) relationship may also be given in diagram form (Figure 12.4(c)): the Entity Relationship Diagram (ERD). Here, entity sets are represented as rectangles. Relationships are shown by drawing connecting lines between sets via relationship sets (the diamond symbol). Attribute sets are attached to the entity sets to which they belong.

Now for a most important conceptual point. The relationship tells us *how* designers and projects are related or *associated*. It does not, however, specify *what* a designer does to a project. Or, for that matter, what is done *to* a project by a designer (such information may, of course, be implicit in the relationship diagram). Be clear on this point, as associations are an important feature of data-oriented systems. In simple terms, if entities 1 and 2 are associated, then:

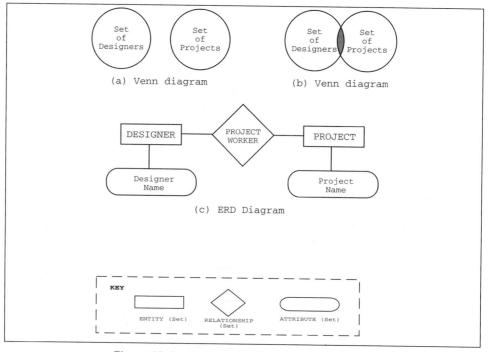

Figure 12.4 System entities and their relationships.

Table 12.1.

Project	Designer	
	K. Shap	**J. Birch**
Tigerfish	X	X
Swordfish	X	—

- entity 1 may house data of use to entity 2 or
- entity 2 may house data of use to entity 1 or
- entity 1 may house data of use to entity 2 *and* entity 2 may house data of use to entity 1

We are now in a position to produce an ERD for the temperature control system of Figure 12.1. The result is that of Figure 12.5.

You will see that part of the diagram uses dotted, not solid, lines. Here, this represents optional information (note: it is not standard ERD notation). This demonstrates that the ERD is not unique; it depends on the relevance of the information. For instance, a system designer will be concerned mainly with overall operation. The full diagram is appropriate here. However, a software designer has less need for such information; the optional aspects can safely be omitted.

Designers involved in developing embedded systems such as the temperature controller often find that ERDs:

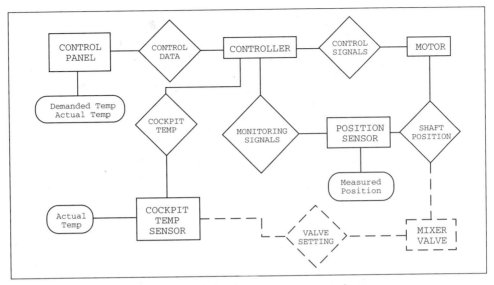

Figure 12.5 ERD for the temperature control system.

- tell them little that isn't already documented elsewhere
- are not all that useful as a software design aid

Hence it isn't surprising to find that ERD modelling has played only a small role in embedded systems design. In contrast, it is central to the development of information-based systems such as databases.

12.3 Deriving the object model – a data-driven approach

12.3.1 Information modelling – object-oriented methods

Modern object-oriented methods of information modelling are based on ER techniques. However, they both refine and extend these earlier ideas, expressing the constructs via an object model. Figure 12.6 illustrates a simple version of this model when applied to the temperature control system.

This consists of a group of associated (related) object classes where, in simple terms:

Object class is equivalent to **(Entity Set + Attribute Set)**

Note 1: From here on, *object class* will be called *class*.
Note 2: Just a recap: an *association* specifies a relationship between classes.

This definition is, in fact, incomplete; the class also includes operations performed by or on the class. Thus:

Class = (Entity Set + Attribute Set + Operation Set)

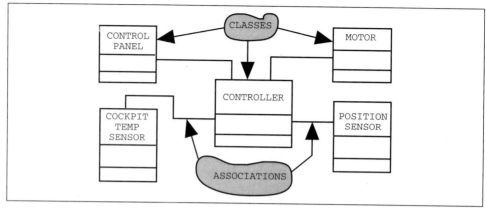

Figure 12.6 Basic object model – temperature control system.

An object is equivalent to a *particular* entity, the complete definition being:

Object = (Entity + Attributes + Operations)

Both the class and the entity set act as templates: the object and the entity are 'things' built from such templates.

A major problem with OO terminology is the lack of standardization. For simplicity and consistency, we shall use the following terms when dealing with the object model:

- *Class diagram*: a diagram which shows the classes of a system together with their associations.
- *Object diagram*: a diagram which shows the set of objects present in a system, together with their relationships.

Thus the model can be expressed in both class and object forms.

12.3.2 *Data modelling – top-down and bottom-up methods*

Returning to the design of the object model, the primary aim here is to develop the class diagram. To do this we need to identify the:

- classes
- attributes of classes
- operations by and on classes
- relationships between classes

This presents us with a problem similar to that found when developing the ERD. Do we start with a specific item (the object) and then generalize into a class – or do it the other way round? For information-based systems, the first technique is advocated – although in practice the process is an iterative one.

This is fine as far as it goes, but how does one actually find the objects? One practical starting point is shown in Figure 12.7.

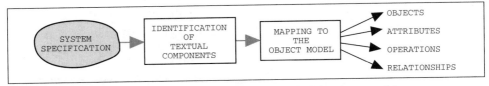

Figure 12.7 Identifying the components of the object model.

The input to the process is the text of the system specification. Specific words and/or phrases are picked out and mapped across to components of the object model. A *rough* guide to this is as follows:

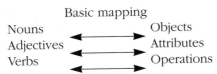

In some situations there is relatively little difficulty in identifying objects. This happens when the design involves:

- physical devices (actuator, controller, sensor)
- conceptual items (filter algorithm, signal correlator, control law)
- people, expressed as their roles (maintainer, controller, operator)

Defining objects in this way is called a top-down identification process. Unfortunately there are situations – most often met in information management systems and the like – where it is not all that obvious what the objects are. For these situations we use the *attributes* as the driving force in defining the objects. This is called a bottom-up method of object identification.

First, consider the top-down approach. The opening stage is to identify and list the *objects* in the system. Then, for each object, list its attributes. To illustrate this, take the temperature control system. Its specification (in part) reads:

The system contains a 1 kg 200 mm stroke linear actuator. The controller signals this Air Mixer actuator to cause it to extend or to retract its shaft.

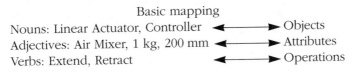

These are now grouped on an object by object basis, as for instance:

Object	Attributes	Operations
Linear Actuator	Air mixer, 1 kg, 200 mm	Extend, Retract

The specification makes it clear how the objects relate (or are connected) to each other. This connection is defined to be a *link* between the objects.

The next stage, identifying potential classes from the object collection, can frequently be a difficult one (especially in data-driven systems). For simplicity, let us take an easy case. Suppose the system specification also contains the statement:

The ramjet scoop is actuated by a 2 kg 300 mm stroke linear actuator.

From this it is clear that it would be logical to form a LINEAR ACTUATOR class (Figure 12.8).

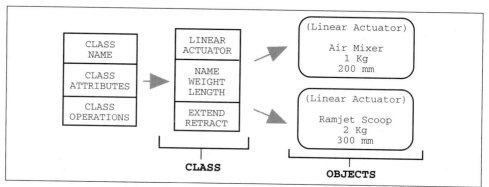

Figure 12.8 Class and object notation (OMT).

The notation used here is that of OMT. Observe that the class attributes are *named* items, object attributes being actual *values*. Operations are not shown in the object diagram.

Now let us turn to identifying objects using the bottom-up technique. As this is more likely to be used in information systems, a different example scenario is used. Assume the following is part of a staff information document for a charter holiday company:

Credit card telephone bookings may be accepted. When doing so, first note and verify the name on the card, the card number and the card's expiry date. Once a suitable holiday has been agreed (resort, accommodation, duration), make the flight booking. Obtain the flight number, departure airport, destination airport, times of departure and arrival, and special meal requirements.

The following attributes can be extracted from the specification:

name, number, expiry date, resort, accommodation class, duration, flight number, departure airport, destination airport, departure time (out), arrival time (out), departure time (return), arrival time (return), special meals

Next, try to establish natural groupings (note that there may well be overlap between the groups). Give each group a name.

card name, number, expiry date → **Credit Card**

name → **Customer**

resort, date, duration, accommodation → **Holiday**

flight number, departure airport, destination airport, departure time, arrival time → **Flight**

flight number, date, customer name, special meals → **Flight Booking**

Each group is a potential class, in this case giving those of Figure 12.9.

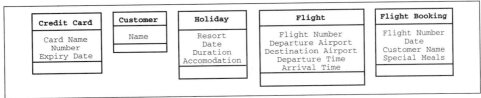

Credit Card	Customer	Holiday	Flight	Flight Booking
Card Name Number Expiry Date	Name	Resort Date Duration Accomodation	Flight Number Departure Airport Destination Airport Departure Time Arrival Time	Flight Number Date Customer Name Special Meals

Figure 12.9 Example bottom-up class identification.

This is a first-cut solution. Almost certainly it will need refining, if not substantial modification. Moreover, even this simple example has no unique solution. Much depends on how we view the problem and how we intend to use the information.

Before closing this section, one more aspect of class/object correspondence must be revisited – *associations*.

12.3.3 Associations revisited

In OMT notation, the relationship between classes is defined to be an *association*; relationships between objects are called *links*. Thus an association acts as a template for a link; a link is an instantiation of an association. The question now is: given one association on a class diagram, how many links will we find on the object diagram? This, in fact, is related to the topic of *multiplicity*; that is, how many instances of one class relate to instances of another class. This is defined using the notation of Figure 12.10(a).

An example class diagram is given in Figure 12.10(b). Following this are various possible instantiations of the class structure – the object diagram.

Figure 12.10(c) shows one-to-one multiplicity. In Figure 12.10(d) the multiplicity is one-to-two (a particular implementation of the one-to-many relationship), and so on for Figures 12.10(e) and (f). Note that defining multiplicity is important in the design of data-handling structures.

A quick recap of the subject matter discussed so far is given in Figure 12.11.

In all designs, we should start with a diagram(s) which defines the structure and operation of the system itself. The next step (from a software point of view) is to develop the class diagram for this system. This is used as the template for specific implementations; that is, producing the objects (the class instantiation).

Now that you have (or should have) a clear understanding of the class construct, it is easier to answer one key question. Why are classes such a central part of OO design? The reasons are threefold. A well-organized class should be:

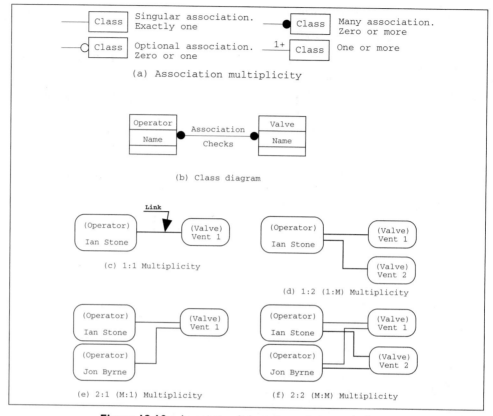

Figure 12.10 Association, links and association multiplicity.

- easy to reuse
- easy to maintain
- readily extensible (as will be shown shortly)

Unfortunately, deriving such classes is not easy (many published papers comment on this point). It takes time, experience and perseverance.

12.3.4 Extensibility – generalization, inheritance and specialization

Product extensibility is something we meet in all walks of life. For instance, car manufacturers usually produce a basic version of each model. But you can, if you so choose, have many features added to this (such as electric windows, traction control and air conditioning). This is a simple example of *generalization* (the basic model) and *specialization* (basic plus extras). Figure 12.12 illustrates this point.

Here the general item (or class) is Actuator; an extended, specialized, version is the Actuator with Position Sensor. Various alternative names are used to define generalization and specialization, as shown in Table 12.2.

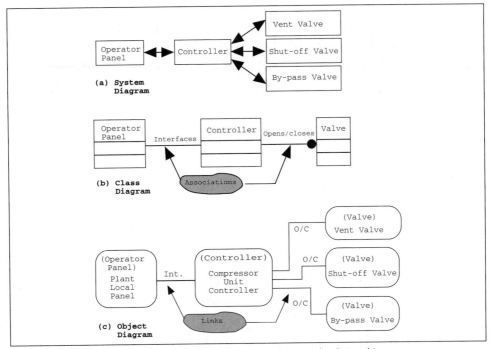

Figure 12.11 Class and object (instance) relationship.

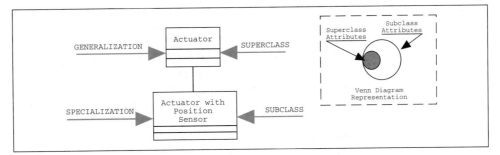

Figure 12.12 Class generalization and specialization.

Table 12.2.

Concept	Alternative names		
Generalization	Superclass	Base class	
Specialization	Subclass	Extended class	Derived class

The relationship between the subclass and the superclass may also be shown in Venn diagram form. This shows most clearly that a subclass contains (or *inherits*) the attributes of the superclass. It also contains additional features specific to that subclass. In other words, specialization occurs when something is added to the general model.

As shown in Figure 12.12, there is only one subclass. There is no reason, though, why there cannot be many extended classes of any superclass. Figure 12.13(a), for instance, shows inheritance where there are two subclasses.

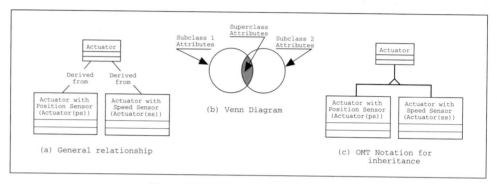

Figure 12.13 Emphasizing inheritance.

Each subclass inherits the properties of the superclass but extends them in different ways. This point is well illustrated in Venn diagram form (Figure 12.13(b)). Figures 12.13(a) and (c) bring out the hierarchical nature of the relationship (note the layout and format of the OMT diagram). In particular, the OMT diagram emphasizes the *is-a* aspect of this. Every Actuator(ps) is also categorized as an Actuator. This is also true for every Actuator(ss). However, not every Actuator is an Actuator(ps); it could be an Actuator(ss).

Each subclass may itself be treated as a superclass for the development of further subclasses. This leads to a general, straightforward hierarchical inheritance model. Unfortunately, this nice clean structure can, in practice, be warped beyond recognition. In particular, where a class is derived from two (or more) superclasses – *multiple inheritance* – structures can become quite complex. We, however, will keep things as simple as possible.

12.3.5 Composite objects – aggregation

Up to now we have seen the object or class as a single entity. It is possible, though, for an object to consist of various parts. The concept is shown in Figure 12.14(a).

This, from a high-level view, contains one object only: the Generating Set. In fact the generating set consists of two major components, a Power Unit and a Generating Unit. Each of these in turn is made up of further components. Thus the generating set is said to be an *aggregate* object; it is a combination of its parts. Using OMT notation, the aggregation relationship is shown in Figure 12.14(b). Here the top-level object Generating Set is defined to be a *parent*. The contained objects Power Unit and Generating Unit are *children* of this parent. They in turn act as parents to their child objects.

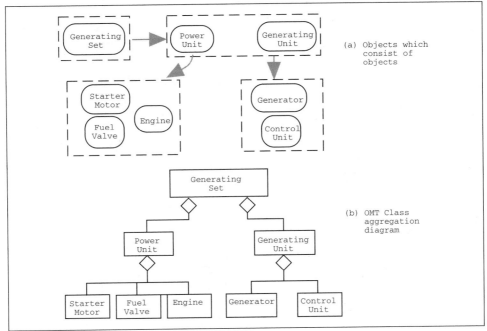

Figure 12.14 Object aggregation.

Unfortunately, the model is an ambivalent one. Consider aggregation as presented using HOOD notation in Figure 12.15(a).

This shows that the object `Valve Actuator` is composed of three components. The interface structure makes it clear that all operations are actually performed by the child objects. Thus the parent object is fundamentally a *container* for its children. Now look at Figure 12.15(b), the same information in OMT form. One could interpret this to mean that the design is made up of four objects. That is, `Valve Actuator` is an *object* in its own right which also contains three other objects. Thus there are (at least) two ways of viewing aggregation.

This doesn't make a great deal of difference at the conceptual level of design. However, it *is* important at the implementation stage. The first (container) model implies that all the executable code is in the child objects. However, in the second model, the parent object has an existence independent of its children – it can have executable code which is entirely its own. Nevertheless, in either case, aggregation defines a *has-a* relationship (for instance, a `Valve Actuator` has a `Motor` and a `Position Sensor` and a `Velocity Sensor`).

12.4 Deriving the object model – a responsibility-driven approach

12.4.1 General concepts

Those with a background in information systems (databases and the like) find it easy to apply data-driven methods to OO design. In contrast, many designers of

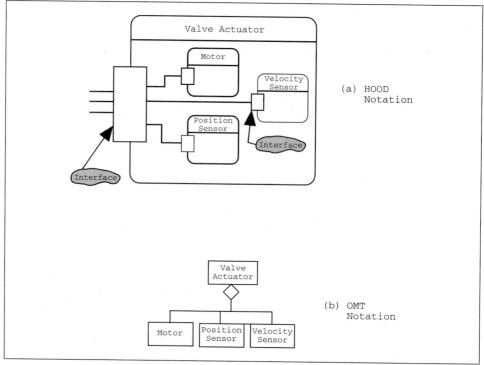

Figure 12.15   Another view of aggregation – object decomposition.

real-time systems find it difficult to come to terms with this approach. This is especially true where they have worked with systems having significant dynamic behaviour. Their (natural) tendency is to concentrate on:

- what a system does
- how it does it
- why it does it
- when it does it

Data is secondary, and rightly so. In systems like these, the data may *affect* behaviour; generally it does not *dictate* what happens. Thus the information-based design
techniques do not fit in well with the reality of such systems.

Naïve suggestions have been made that the problem should be adjusted to suit
the design method (but that's another story). Clearly what is needed is a method
which fits in naturally with our view of systems. One such technique is called a
responsibility-driven approach. This hinges on two facts. First, in an OO system, it is
the objects that cause things to happen. Second, in any practical design the objects
have to work together – they collaborate. The basics of the technique can be outlined using a simple, non-computer example (Figure 12.16(a)).

Here we have our dragon boat racing team, consisting of rowers, a drummer and
a helmsman (the objects). Each object has its own particular job to perform.

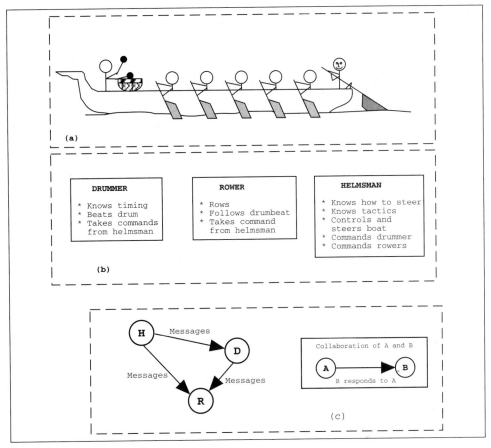

Figure 12.16 Collaborating objects.

However, all need to work together in a defined way in order to be successful (win races). Suppose we had to write out a simple job specification for the team members. The result might be something like that in Figure 12.16(b). The resulting collaboration structure is given in Figure 12.16(c).

Let us now analyse the job specification, taking the helmsman (object) as example. It can be seen that there are three aspects to this. The specification defines:

- what the object knows – information or *knowledge* (steering techniques, tactics)
- what the object does – *service* (steers and controls boat)
- who the object works with – *collaboration* (the drummer and the rowers)

Note that objects collaborate by sending messages to each other. This may also be viewed as a client–server model, where any object can be a client, a server, or both.

Knowledge and service will, from now, be grouped together as *responsibilities*. Thus the total system can be described in terms of classes, responsibilities and collaboration – CRC.

12.4.2 More on the CRC method

The CRC method was invented by Beck and Cunningham originally as a teaching aid for object-oriented design. From this modest beginning, it has been successfully used in the development of real systems. It is primarily a front-end technique, used in the early stages of software design. Following the rules of the method, we:

    (a) Identify potential classes using system information.
    (b) For each class, define its responsibility. Remember, this is the knowledge held by the class and the service that it provides.
    (c) For each class, define its collaborators. These are defined to be *other* classes having information and/or services needed by the class under design.
    (d) Repeat until satisfied.

There is, though, much more to it than this. It is based very much on:

- gaining a good understanding of the problem to be solved
- emphasizing what the objects are responsible for and what information they share
- de-emphasizing what they have (their attributes)

From a practical point of view, CRC design involves:

- driving towards a solution by executing *operational scenarios*
- developing the classes and objects via *group activities*
- using a single *physical card* to represent each class or object
- *recording* all relevant information on the cards
- *positioning* the cards to emphasize relationships
- developing the design in an *incremental* fashion

How information is laid out on a CRC card is up to the individual. That used by the original developers is given in Figure 12.17(a).

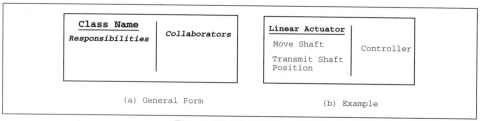

Figure 12.17 CRC card.

    As stated, a single card carries the information for a class. It is identified with the class name. On it is listed the responsibilities of the class, together with the collaborators of that class. A simple example is given in Figure 12.17(b).
    The suggested approach to developing the object model is to first pick out the most obvious classes, then identify likely behavioural scenarios, and play through

these (using 'what-if' questions extensively). As responsibilities and collaborators emerge from this role playing, note these on the relevant cards. During this period it is possible that new responsibilities are discovered. These can either be allocated to the current classes or else new classes can be created to handle them. During the exercise, if a class becomes complex, consider splitting it into two (or more) classes.

The process described above is repeated until a satisfactory solution is obtained. For the simple temperature control system the result might be that shown in Figure 12.18.

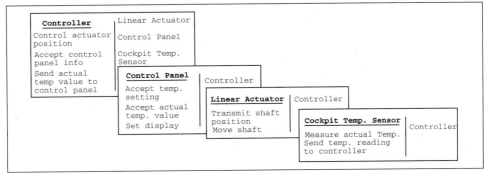

Figure 12.18   CRC cards for the temperature control system.

The use of CRC cards will be returned to in the design example of Chapter 16.

12.5   Diagram to code

This section demonstrates how the various object diagram constructs are translated into source code. Four aspects are covered: class, inheritance, aggregation and association (Figure 12.19).

These code examples have been kept extremely simple to bring out the essentials of the topic. In many cases the operations performed are mere emulations of practical ones. Aspects such as efficiency and 'elegance' (whatever that means) are subordinated to visibility. But please remember, this is not a programming text.

The class – Figure 12.19(a)

Figure 12.19(a) is an OMT class diagram for a class called PPI. This represents a processor–peripheral interface device which has a single data port. All we can do with the device is to send data to its data port. We define the class to have a single attribute Port Data and a single method Send Data To Port. Listing 12.1 shows how this class may be declared. Observe that the actual object which we work with is Bus_Interface. If desired, more objects of class PPI could have been produced; each would be a separate, distinct instantiation.

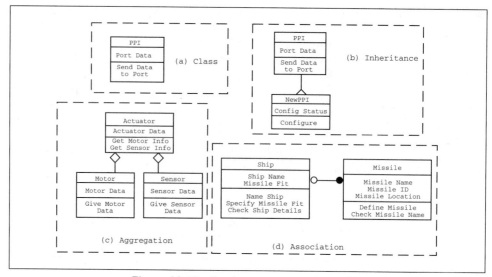

Figure 12.19 Specimen constructs for coding.

Inheritance – Figure 12.19(b)

Let us assume that we intend to use a new type of PPI, identified as PPI8255. This houses a single data port and a single configuration register. Data can, as in the previous case, be sent to the port. The device itself can be configured as active or standby.

A new, separate class could be produced for this item. However, by using inheritance (Figure 12.19(b)), the new class (PPI8255) builds on the features of the base class (PPI). We therefore define the class to have a second attribute, Configuration Status, together with a new method, Configure. Listing 12.2 illustrates this.

Note that in the main program, objects of both the base and superclass are used.

Aggregation – Figure 12.19(c)

In (c), the Actuator object consists of (is an aggregate of) objects Motor and Sensor. Thus the parent object is Actuator, the others being its children. Data items have been omitted to keep the example small and simple. Thus its implementation (Listing 12.3) has no class data members. You will also see that, at the main level, the child objects are hidden within the parent (Hotwell). External interactions take place with Hotwell, yet the operations are actually performed by the children. This, of course, is just one way to implement aggregation.

Association – Figure 12.19(d)

Association, to the embedded systems designer, is generally less important than the other topics of OO design. However, it is also probably the least well understood aspect of the object model. To clarify the situation, a reasonable amount of detail needs to be presented.

Figure 12.19(d) shows two classes, Ship and Missile, which are associated with

```
#include <iostream.h>

// ──── HERE IS THE CLASS DECLARATION ───────// 
class PPI
     {
     int
        PortA;   /* CLASS MEMBER - In this example happens
                              to be private */

     public:

          /* A CLASS MEMBER FUNCTION */
              void Send_Data_To_Port (int Port_Data)
          {
                  PortA = Port_Data;
             cout << "Port A has been loaded with "
                << Port_Data;
          } /* end SendDataToRegister */

     };  /* end of class PPI */
// ──── END OF THE CLASS DECLARATION ───────// 


void main()
{
// INSTANTIATING THE CLASS - OBJECT is Bus_Interface
PPI
   Bus_Interface;

   cout << "Listing 12.1 \n\n";
   // USING THE OBJECT
   Bus_Interface.Send_Data_To_Port (255);
   cout << "\nProgram finished";
}
```

Listing 12.1 An introduction to the class.

each other. The association is via the data contained in the classes. It can be seen that Ship holds data concerning the missile fit on the vessel (Missile Name). Looking at Missile, we can see that *it* specifies which vessel the missile is fitted to (Missile Location). Thus the two classes are related by the content of the data. To translate Figure 12.19(d) into code, the approach given in Listing 12.4 could be used.

Here there are two distinct classes, each with its own operation set. The example shows how to manipulate the various objects, such as the ship Nottingham and the missile M1. Unfortunately, with this solution, the association is entirely in the mind of the designer – there is no automatic link between the classes. How then can we ensure consistency of the data? With the existing design, we can't. What is needed is a mechanism to provide the missing automatic link. This is done in Listing 12.5, using pointer operations.

```cpp
#include <iostream.h>

class PPI
    {
    int
         PortData;
    public:
              void Send_Data_To_Port (int Port_Data)
              {
                   PortA = Port_Data;
                   cout << "Port A has been loaded with "
                        << Port_Data << "\n";
         } /* end SendDataToRegister */
      };/* end of class PPI */


class PPI_8255 : public PPI
    {
    int
         Config_Register;
     public:
              void Configure (int Config_Data)
              {
                   Config_Register = Config_Data;
                   cout << "The configuration register has been loaded with
"
                             << Config_Data<< "\n";
              } /* end Configure   */
         };/* end of class PPI_8255 */



void main()
{
/* INSTANTIATING THE CLASS PPI - OBJECT is BusA */
PPI
    BusA;
/* INSTANTIATING THE CLASS PPI_8255 - OBJECT is BusB */
PPI_8255
    BusB;

const int
     Output_Mode = 127;

   cout << "Listing 12.2 \n\n";
   /* USING THE BASE CLASS OBJECT */
   cout << "Sending data to port A of Bus A \n";
   BusA.Send_Data_To_Port (255);

   /* USING THE SUPERCLASS OBJECT */
   cout << "Configuring Bus B \n";
   BusB.Configure (Output_Mode);
   cout << "Sending data to port A of Bus B \n";
   BusB.Send_Data_To_Port (32);

   cout << "\nProgram finished";
}
```

Listing 12.2   An introduction to inheritance.

```
#include <iostream.h>

//——————————— THE PARENT CLASS - ACTUATOR ——————————————//
class Actuator
{
   //=========== THE CHILD CLASS - MOTOR =====================//
   class Motor
   {
      public:
      //- CHILD METHOD -//
      void GiveMotorData()
      {

        cout << "\nThe motor type is a Slosyn stepper " <<  "\n";
      };/* end GiveMotorData */

   };/* end class Motor   */
   //=========== END CHILD CLASS MOTOR =====================//

   //=========== THE CHILD CLASS - SENSOR =====================//
   class Sensor
   {
      public:
      //- CHILD METHOD -//
      void GiveSensorData()
      {
        cout << "\nThe sensor is a Linvar rotary type " << "\n";
      };/* end GiveSensorData */

   };/* end class Sensor   */
   //=========== END CHILD CLASS SENSOR =====================//

   public:
   /* Creating a motor object */
   Motor ServoMotor;
   /* Creating a sensor object */
   Sensor PositionSensor;

   //——- PARENT METHODS ——//
   void GetMotorInfo ()
   {
      ServoMotor.GiveMotorData();
   }; /* end GetMotorInfo */

   void GetSensorInfo ()
   {
      PositionSensor.GiveSensorData();
   };  /* end GetSensorInfo */

};/* end class Actuator   */

//——————————- END PARENT CLASS ——————————//

void main()
{
/* CREATING AN ACTUATOR OBJECT */
Actuator Hotwell;

   cout << "Listing 12.3 \n\n";

   /* ACCESSING THE CHILD OBJECT - CLASS MOTOR */
   cout << "\nGetting data on the motor \n";
   Hotwell.GetMotorInfo();

   /* ACCESSING THE CHILD OBJECT - CLASS SENSOR */
   cout << "\nNow getting data on the sensor \n";
   Hotwell.GetSensorInfo();

   cout << "\nProgram finished";
} /* end main */
```

Listing 12.3 Demonstration of aggregation.

```
#include <iostream.h>
#include <string.h>

//——————— THE CLASS SHIP ——————//
class Ship{
char ShipName[20];
char MissileFit[30];
public:
   void NameShip (char Name[]){
      strcpy (ShipName, Name);
   } /* end NameShip */
    void SpecifyMissileFit (char Fit[]){
      strcpy (MissileFit, Fit);
   } /* end SpecifyMissileFit */

   void CheckShipDetails(){
      cout << "\n\nThe name of this ship is " << ShipName;
      cout << "\nThe missile fit is " << MissileFit;
   } /* end CheckShipDetails */

};
//——————— END CLASS SHIP ——————//

//——————— THE CLASS MISSILE ——————//
class Missile{
char MissileName[20];
char MissileID[30];
char MissileLocation[30];

public:
   void DefineMissile (char Name[], char ID[], char Place[]){
      strcpy (MissileName, Name);
      strcpy (MissileID, ID);
      strcpy (MissileLocation, Place);
   } /* end NameMissile */
   void CheckMissileName(){
      cout << "\n\nThe name of this missile is " << MissileName;
      cout << "\nThe ID of this missile is " << MissileID;
      cout << "\nThe location of this missile is " << MissileLocation;

   } /* end CheckMissileName */
};
//——————— END CLASS MISSILE ——————//

void main()
{
 Ship Nottingham, Broadsword;
 Missile M1, M2;

   cout << "Listing 12.4 \n\n";

   Nottingham.NameShip ("Nottingham");
   Nottingham.SpecifyMissileFit ("Seadart Ser. no. GWS/SD/1970");
   Nottingham.CheckShipDetails ();

   Broadsword.NameShip ("Broadsword");
   Broadsword.SpecifyMissileFit ("Seawolf Serial no GWS/SW/1980 ");
   Broadsword.CheckShipDetails ();

   M1.DefineMissile ("Seadart", "Ser. no. GWS/SD/1970", "Nottingham");
   M1.CheckMissileName ();

   M2.DefineMissile ("Seawolf", "Serial no GWS/SW/1980 ", "Broadsword");
   M2.CheckMissileName ();

   } /* end main */
```

Listing 12.4 Setting up relationships between classes.

```
# include <iostream.h>
# include <string.h>
class Missile;

class Ship {
private:
    char ShipName[50];
public:
    Ship(char* setname);
    void PrintShipName();
    void MissileTransaction(Missile* newMissile);
};
class Missile {
private:
    char MissileName[100];
public:
    Missile (char* missileName);
    void PrintMissileName();
    void MissileTransaction(Ship* newShip);
};

void main(){
Ship Ship1("Coventry");
Ship Ship2("Broadsword");
Missile Missile1 ("Seadart, Ser.No. GWS/SD/1970");
Missile Missile2 ("Ikara, Ser.No. GWS/IK/1980");

    Missile1.MissileTransaction(&Ship1);
    Missile1.MissileTransaction(&Ship2);
    Ship1.MissileTransaction(&Missile1);
    Ship1.MissileTransaction(&Missile2);

}// end of main
/////////////////////////////////////////////////
Ship::Ship(char* setname){
    strcpy (ShipName, setname);
}
void Ship::PrintShipName(){
    cout << "\n The Ship is " << ShipName;
}
void Ship::MissileTransaction (Missile* newMissile){
    cout << "\n\n Updating Ship entry";
    PrintShipName();
    newMissile->PrintMissileName();
}

Missile::Missile (char* missileName){
    strcpy(MissileName, missileName);
}
void Missile::PrintMissileName(){
    cout << "\n The Missile is " << MissileName;
}
void Missile::MissileTransaction (Ship* newShip){
    cout << "\n\n Updating Missile entry";
    PrintMissileName();
    newShip->PrintShipName();
}
```

Listing 12.5   Setting up associations – basic aspects.

Only the outline of the approach is given here. A full solution would need additional methods, in particular ones to provide secure access to the class data.

Generally there is a trade-off between strength of encapsulation and efficiency of operation. It may also make sense in some applications to devise a new (in this case, third) class to handle the association. This is equivalent to a link-type record in database design. In C++ it would most likely be implemented as a container class.

Summary and review

Newcomers to OO design frequently find that developing the object model is not an easy task. It usually takes a number of passes through the design to get a good solution. The process isn't helped by the fact that some design methods generate confusion, not clarity. Problem areas include:

- the use of inheritance
- the distinction between aggregation and inheritance
- the relationship with the dynamic and functional models
- the non-rigorous (sometimes vague) techniques for classifying objects
- confusion of terminology (such as class, class instance, object)

The use of class and object diagrams is also a clouded issue. It is recommended that you should produce diagrams to meet the needs of the problem – not slavishly follow a prescriptive design method. In general, both class and object diagrams should be produced. However – as pointed out elsewhere in this text – this may not be essential. For example, take the two extremes of embedded designs. First we have the case where:

- many items are produced
- all use identical software
- the end application isn't specifically known

Examples of these are microwave controllers, engine management systems and security alarms. For these we could probably work successfully with the class diagrams only.

Then there is the other end of the product spectrum, where:

- few items (sometimes only one) are produced
- much of the high-level software may be specially tailored for the application
- applications themselves tend to be quite individual (oil platform systems, experimental aircraft and so on)

Here there is a close link between the software and the application itself. In this case we are likely to think much more in terms of specific objects rather than classes. Moreover, reusability *per se* is *not* a primary aim in such designs – thus reducing the importance of the class construct.

In conclusion, you should now:

- understand the role, content and structure of the object model
- appreciate the difference between data-driven and responsibility-driven modelling methods
- see that the data-driven approach has its roots in traditional information modelling techniques
- grasp the difference between bottom-up and top-down data-driven object modelling
- know what an ERD is
- know, in general terms, what entities, relationships and attributes are
- understand the concepts and code implementation of class, object, link, association, superclass, subclass (and inheritance) and aggregation
- appreciate the rationale for, and use of, CRC cards
- feel that you would be able to run a design session using the CRC card technique

Exercises

12.1 Categorize the following as classes or objects:
Vehicle brake lights
Unmanned space vehicle
The Vatican fax machine
Elevator emergency button
Mobile telephone
HMS *Trafalgar*
Credit card reader
Type 23 frigate

12.2 Sort the following list into classes and their attributes. Sketch the resulting class diagrams.
Wingspan
No. of aircraft
Airspeed
Aircraft carrier
Displacement
Length of flight deck
Boeing 777
Model
Altitude

Would a change of aircraft type – from a 777 to a carrier-based F18 – influence your decisions?

12.3 Sort the following list into classes, their attributes and their methods. Sketch the resulting class diagrams.

Size
VCR
Fast Forward
Shaft Speed
Start
Record
Stop
Output Voltage
Motor–Generator
Set
Weight
Pause
Frequency

12.4 Sketch six possible instantiations of the class diagram of Figure 12.20.

Figure 12.20.

What requirement does this lead to in your chosen programming language (hint: see `constructors` and `destructors`).

12.5 Produce a class diagram from the object diagram of Figure 12.21.

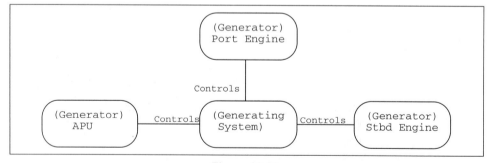

Figure 12.21.

12.6 Using the information given below, produce a class diagram which incorporates inheritance showing the base class and the derived classes. Suggest attributes and methods for each class.

Classes:

Sensor, Gyro Compass, Altimeter, Pressure Sensor, Cabin Pressure Sensor, Ambient Air Pressure Sensor, Magnetic Compass

12.7 Produce object diagrams for the class diagrams of Figure 12.22.

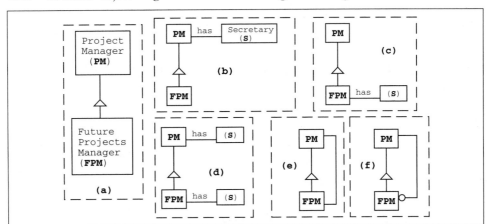

Figure 12.22.

12.8 What are the correct meanings of Figures 12.23(a) and (b)? Produce sets of object diagrams (instantiations) for the class diagrams.

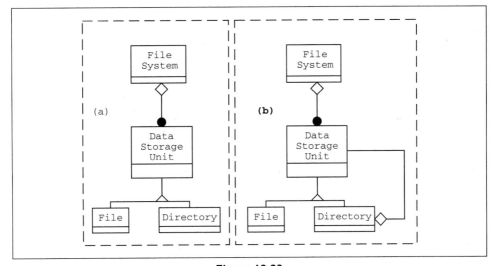

Figure 12.23.

12.9 When – and why – is the responsibility-driven approach to deriving the object model likely to produce better results than the data-driven techniques?

12.10 Nancy Wilkinson suggests that the optimal group size for a CRC card session is five or six people. Can you think of reasons to support this recommendation?

12.11 You are responsible for organizing and running a CRC card session. Who would you select to take part in this?

13
The dynamic model:
Object communication and behaviour

Let us begin with a brief recapitulation. First, any practical OO system consists of a collection of objects. Second, the overall operation of a system depends on the behaviour of its objects. To be more precise, it depends on both individual *and* collective actions. Objects, to achieve desired system level goals, need to interact – that is, to communicate and collaborate. Third, in virtually all situations, behaviour is dynamic, not static. Changes may be prompted by the passage of time, internal (software) events or events generated externally.

From this it is clear that any realistic dynamic model of an OO design is a two-level one. That is, it must represent both system level *and* object level operation.

The purpose of this chapter is to:

- review the basic ideas of class (object) relationships, and relate these to the need for inter-class messaging
- establish the need to show both collective and individual object behaviour
- define the roles and features of the state model and the event scenario model
- review and compare the Mealy and Moore finite state machines
- introduce statecharts as a means of modelling state behaviour
- introduce the OMT dynamic model

The fundamentals of this topic – defining system dynamic behaviour – are discussed in Chapter 6. It is essential that you study this before progressing further.

13.1 Basic aspects

There is some overlap between the issues discussed here and aspects of development using CRC techniques. Just to avoid confusion, let us assume that we started the design using an information-based approach. Such data-driven methods emphasize the development of the object model; other factors are subordinated. The result is a class diagram, together with a corresponding object diagram (Figure 13.1).

Here, at the object model stage, we have identified the classes and objects in the

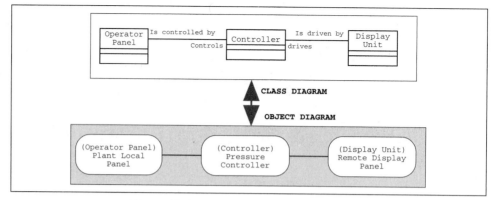

Figure 13.1 Example class and object diagram.

system. Each object has its associated attributes and operations. The associations between the classes and the links between objects have also been defined. Note that in this particular example, each association has been written out twice (for example, *is driven by* and *drives*). It is more usual to show only a single name, the association direction being implied.

The design at this point is still quite incomplete, for four reasons. First, relationships tend to be expressed in general terms. A typical description might be 'Controller *drives* Display Unit'. This gives little clue to the specific mechanisms needed to support object interaction. Second, no information is given as to when and why objects communicate. Third, it cannot be seen what effects are generated by such communication. Finally, we cannot see how the objects behave over their lifetimes. Clearly, what is needed is a model which shows the full dynamics of OO designs.

The model used here sets out to present both system-level *and* object-level detail. Its underlying concepts are defined in Figure 13.2.

The purpose of the system-level view (Figure 13.2(a)) is to highlight the *external* aspects of object-based designs, namely:

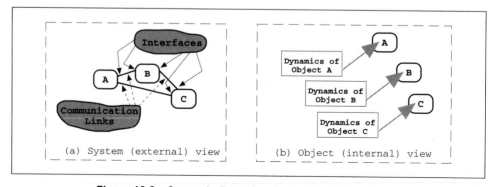

Figure 13.2 System (collective) and object (individual) views.

- what information flows between the objects (communication)
- what function(s) the individual objects perform
- what interfaces they present to other objects
- when and why objects interact (behaviour)

In contrast, the object level view emphasizes the *internal* features of individual objects, specifically their:

- data
- operations
- behaviour over time

This chapter is concerned with communication and behavioural aspects – loosely, and for simplicity, *dynamics* (Figure 13.3).

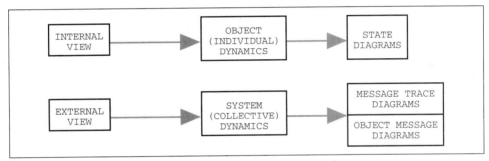

Figure 13.3   Describing dynamics – the two complementary views.

This figure emphasizes a number of points. One: there are two distinct, but complementary, ways of viewing system dynamics. Two: different techniques and diagrams are used to illustrate the two views. Three (implicit): the views must be consistent.

A number of diagrams are required to illustrate system dynamics. The *state* diagram is used to define the dynamics of *individual* objects. To show *collective* behaviour the *message trace* and *object message* diagrams are employed.

Where should one start when developing the dynamic models? Unfortunately, there is no consensus on this in the OO world; it varies from method to method. One practical approach is first to concentrate on producing an overall design and then consider the details of individual objects. But, as with all approaches, this is an iterative one – the two aspects will almost certainly affect each other.

13.2   The dynamic models

13.2.1   *The external model – showing object interactions*

Let us start the dynamic modelling by producing a diagram which shows object interaction (we assume that a preliminary class diagram has already been produced).

In OO design, an object (the *sender*) invokes a response from another object (the *receiver*) using messages (Figure 13.4).

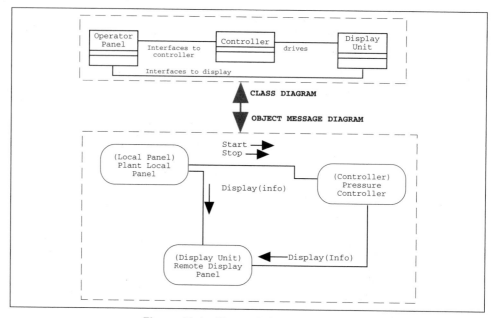

Figure 13.4 Class and object interaction.

The upper part of the figure is the class diagram; the lower part is a corresponding object message diagram. The example system consists of three objects: Plant Local Panel, Pressure Controller and Remote Display Panel. A message specifies what the receiver should do. Precisely how it does it is up to the receiver, defined by its operation(s). Therefore, in considering the collective behaviour of objects, both messages and operations have to be taken into account. The key to identifying these is to establish clearly:

• what interactions take place between objects
• why they occur
• when they take place
• what effects they generate within objects

Interactions take place for specific reasons and (usually) generate specific responses. A particular set of such interactions is called a *scenario*. Each scenario may be shown using a message trace diagram (Figure 13.5).

This relates to the object diagram of Figure 13.4. Here each object has its own 'column' or *time line*, where time runs from top to bottom. Thus event sequencing also runs in the same direction. The scenario given here is quite a simple one, but does illustrate the points listed above.

(a) What interactions take place?

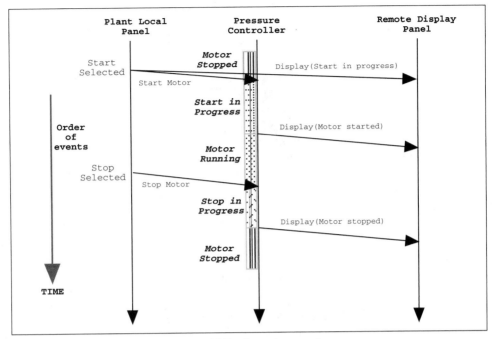

Figure 13.5 Example scenario.

   (i) The local panel sends the message `Start Motor` to the pressure controller.
        It also sends `Display Start in Progress` to the display panel. Later it
        sends `Stop Motor` to the pressure controller.
   (ii) The pressure controller sends two messages to the display panel: `Display`
        `Motor Started` and `Display Motor Stopped`.

(b) Why are the messages sent?
   (i) `Start Motor` and `Display Start in Progress` are sent because/when
        `Start Selected` occurs at the local panel.
   (ii) `Stop Motor` is sent when `Stop Selected` takes place.
   (iii) `Display Motor Started` is sent by the pressure controller to indicate that
        the motor has started.
   (iv) `Display Motor Stopped` is sent to show that the motor has stopped.

(c) When are messages sent?

   This information is derived from operational scenarios. Such information is specified in, or elicited from, the system requirements documents. What the scenario diagram shows is the sequence in which events occur. Time is generally
   relative, not absolute. Further, in many cases, we are interested only in the
   sequencing itself, not time values.

(d) What effects are generated within objects?

   As shown here, the message `Start Motor` causes the pressure controller to change *state* from `Motor Stopped` to `Start in Progress`. Similarly, `Stop Motor` changes the state from `Motor Running` to `Stop in Progress`.

When `Start Motor` arrives at the pressure controller, the motor begins its start-up operation. This can be deduced from the state information `Start in Progress`. Such information *could* be made explicit by showing object operations on the trace diagrams. However, operations are considered to be internal to the object, and are best shown elsewhere. Thus an incoming message affects a state (as shown on the message diagram), not a *specific* operation.

To keep the diagram simple, all other states have been omitted in this example.

Observe that in Figure 13.5 *all* messages are events (and thus *directly* invoke state changes). What we have here is a *subset* of the message trace diagram, the *event trace* diagram. Here each individual object treats an incoming message as an event which leads to a state change within the object. Thus it must appear as an event in the object state diagram (see later).

13.2.2 The internal model – showing object dynamics

During design, the state model for each object is derived (in part if not in full) from the event scenario model. Such models can be expressed using finite state machines, such as the state transition (or merely state) diagram. One form, the *Mealy* machine, has already been covered extensively (Chapter 6). Using this notation we can express the dynamics of the object `Pressure Controller` of Figure 13.5 as shown in Figure 13.6.

However, other forms of finite state machine are often used in OO design, in particular the *Moore* machine. The fundamental difference between the two is illustrated in Figure 13.7.

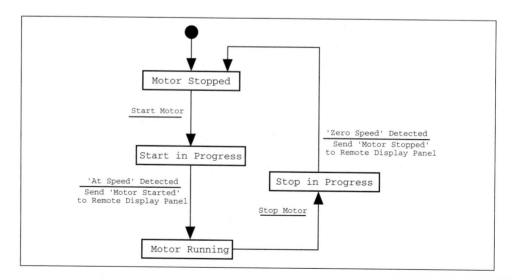

Figure 13.6 State diagram for object `Pressure Controller`.

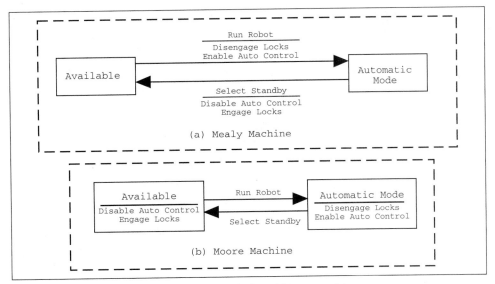

Figure 13.7 The Mealy and Moore machines.

Both machines describe the same dynamic operation of a very simple two-state robot. State 1 is Available and state 2 is Automatic Mode. Transition from Available to Automatic Mode takes place in response to the event Run Robot. Similarly, the event Select Standby causes a transition from Automatic Mode to Available. Thus, in terms of state and event information, both diagrams are much the same. The essential difference is to do with the *actions*. In the Mealy machine, actions are associated with events. For the Moore machine, actions are linked to states. Take, for instance, Figure 13.7(a). Assume that the robot is currently in the Available state. When the event Run Robot arrives, this causes a state change to take place. It also generates two actions: Disengage Locks and Enable Auto Control. Now consider Figure 13.7(b). When the same state transition takes place, the same actions are generated. However, these are connected with the *state*, not the *event*. Hence when the system is in Available mode (Figure 13.7(b)), the actions Disable Auto Control and Engage Locks are performed.

Thus both diagrams show the same information (they are, after all, describing the dynamics of the same system). However, the presentation of information – and its interpretation – differs. How significant are these differences? One major point emerges when changes are made to the operation of an existing system. Assume that the robot system is, at a later stage, modified to include a manual control feature. Hence a new mode – Manual – is added to the STD. The revised specification reads:

When the system is in automatic mode, it can be switched into manual control. This disables the automatic function, and enables manual control of the robot. The reverse process can be performed by switching from manual to auto. It is also possible to go into available from the manual mode of operation.

First, consider the modifications needed to show this on the Mealy machine diagram (Figure 13.8(a)).

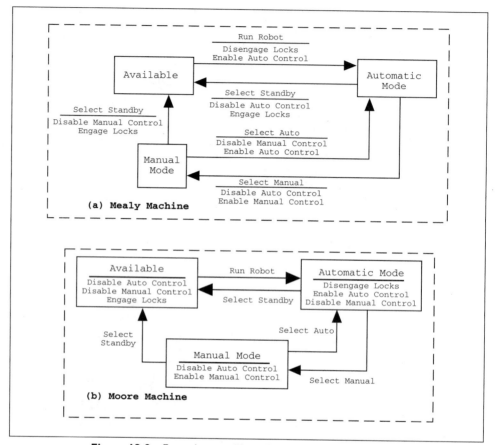

Figure 13.8 Example – modifying the state transition diagrams.

Read through the diagram; its meaning should be quite clear. But what isn't obvious at first viewing is the issue of consistency of states. When the system enters Available, it can do so from either Automatic Mode or Manual Mode. Now, in state modelling, a state should be uniquely defined. To guarantee this for the Available state, the actions corresponding to event Select Standby depend on the *current* state. That is, when the system is in automatic mode, Select Standby generates actions Engage Locks and Disable Auto Control. However, when in manual mode, the same event generates Engage Locks and Disable Manual Control. From this it can be seen that actions must be checked out thoroughly to ensure state consistency. In complex state diagrams this requires great care and attention.

Now let us turn to the Moore machine (Figure 13.8(b)). Each state, remember, has a defined, related set of actions. Introducing new states may or may not affect the existing design. Here, for example, the action Disable Manual Control has been added to `Available`. But the central point is that we concentrate mainly on what happens within the state and less on where we've come from or where we're going to. The result is that Moore diagrams tend to be easier to modify than Mealy types.

Each machine has its pros and cons. Modification, after all, is only one aspect to be considered. Presentation and extraction of information are also important. One strength of the Mealy machine is that action/event relationships are emphasized, and for many embedded systems designers, these are primary considerations. The Mealy machine is widely used in structured design, by Ward–Mellor and Hatley–Pirbhai. In contrast, the Shlaer–Mellor OO analysis method employs the Moore machine. It may, in fact, be possible to get the best of both worlds by combining the two machines. This approach is taken in OMT modelling.

Before closing this section, one minor point needs addressing: class versus object state diagrams. It is important to understand that there is a single STD for a class; this represents *potential* behaviour. However, each object has its own STD, used to describe its *actual* behaviour. This is shown in Figure 13.9.

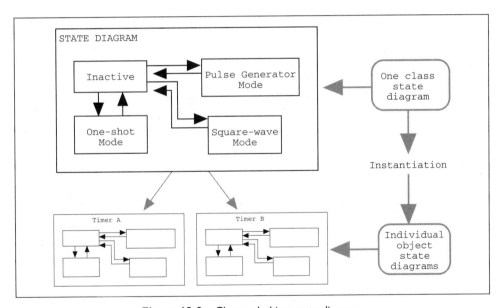

Figure 13.9 Class and object state diagrams.

Assume that we are modelling the state system of a programmable timer integrated circuit. This class of IC has a four-state mode of operation: inactive, one-shot, pulse and square-wave. Each individual IC of this type (an instantiation of the class) has its own STD which is identical to the class one.

13.2.3 Linking the external and internal models

At this point we have seen how to represent both the external and internal dynamic models of object-based systems. An essential (though so far implicit) point is that these views must be consistent with each other. However, such consistency can only be attained by using well-defined techniques. The approach used here for developing and linking the two models is demonstrated using the example system of Figure 13.10.

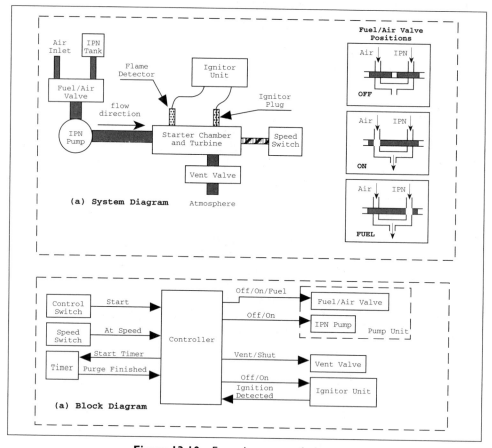

Figure 13.10   Example system – fuel starter.

This is a block diagram of a liquid fuel starter system, showing all major components. Here, the central item is the controller. From the diagram, it can be seen that it controls the:

- pump unit (which consists of a valve and pump)
- vent valve
- ignitor unit
- timer

Input signals are sent to the controller by the:

- control switch
- speed switch

- timer
- ignitor unit

Each item in the diagram may be considered to be an object (in OO terms, that is). The next operation is to generate the dynamic models, following the route defined in Figure 13.11.

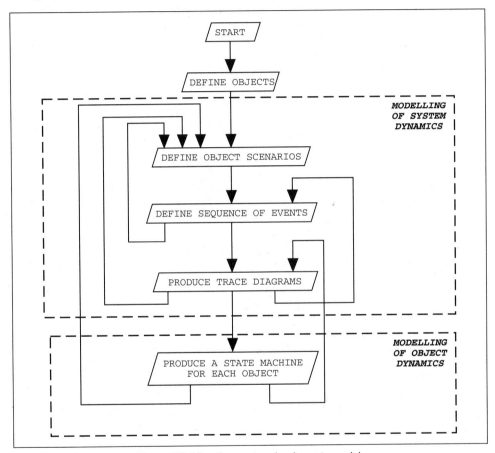

Figure 13.11   Generating the dynamic models.

This illustrates the stages (and their relationships) involved in producing the system and object dynamic models. First, the various operational scenarios are defined. These fall into two categories: normal and abnormal (fault) behaviours. Generally, it is easiest to first produce the normal scenarios and then consider the effects of faults. In this example, normal operations consist of a number of scenarios: start-up sequence, normal running and shutdown, for instance. For each one an individual trace diagram is produced. The designer may choose to keep these entirely separate. Alternatively, it may be helpful to combine some (or indeed all) in one diagram.

Frequently, this first effort exposes problems with the system specification. This in turn may lead to a re-evaluation of the scenarios, possibly resulting in a revised set. Each changed version needs to have its event sequence redefined and its event scenario diagram revised. Note also that there are many local loops in this process. Such iterations and revisions are a normal and natural part of any real design activity.

The process is repeated until the designer is satisfied with the model of system behaviour. After this, work can begin on modelling the behaviour of individual objects in terms of state machines. The outcome of this may (unsurprisingly) directly affect the external model. If major problems are discovered, it might be necessary to go back and redefine the scenarios (for *software* objects, this could mean revising the object model itself).

One specimen scenario for the fuel starter system – the start-up phase – is given in Figure 13.12.

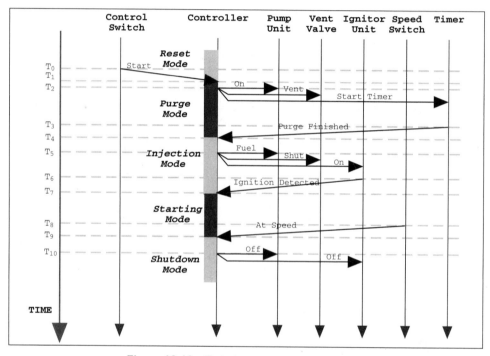

Figure 13.12 Typical scenario – start-up phase.

This shows the set of events which take place during the start-up phase of operation. Sequencing is as follows:

Initial condition: CONTROLLER IN RESET MODE.

T_0: Control Switch object sends Start command to Controller.
T_1: Controller receives Start command.
END OF RESET MODE

START OF CONTROLLER PURGE MODE.

After a short time interval (during which some computation is performed), time T_2

is reached.

T$_2$: Controller sends:
On signal to Pump Unit.
Vent signal to Vent Valve.
Start signal to Timer

T$_3$: Timer sends Purge Finished to Controller.
T$_4$: Controller receives Purge Finished signal.
END OF CONTROLLER PURGE MODE

START OF CONTROLLER INJECTION MODE
T$_5$: Controller sends:
Fuel signal to Pump Unit.
Shut signal to Vent Valve.
On signal to Ignitor Unit.

T$_6$: Ignitor Unit sends Ignition Detected to Controller.
T$_7$: Ignition Detected received by Controller.
END OF CONTROLLER INJECTION MODE

START OF STARTING MODE
T$_8$: Speed Switch sends At Speed signal to Controller.
T$_9$: At Speed received by Controller.
END OF STARTING MODE

START OF SHUTDOWN MODE
T$_{10}$: Controller sends:
Off signal to Pump Unit.
Off signal to Ignitor Unit.

At the same time we build the object message diagram (OMD). This, remember, is based on the object diagram, but also carries object message information. The information contained on the trace diagram defines the messages to be shown on the OMD (Figure 13.13).

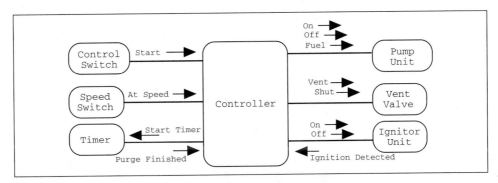

Figure 13.13 Preliminary object message diagram.

Note that in this particular case we *could* have obtained the message information from the system diagram. However, for many applications (databases, for example), it is doubtful whether such an approach would work. Here the trace diagram (or its equivalent) becomes essential.

The OMD and the scenario diagram form a matching pair. Always cross-check to ensure they are consistent. If the check is satisfactory, proceed to develop the STD for each object. This process is illustrated for the controller object of Figure 13.12. As shown, its event/time line is divided into discrete sections or modes (for mode read state). Each mode of the Controller then becomes one of the states in its STD (Figure 13.14).

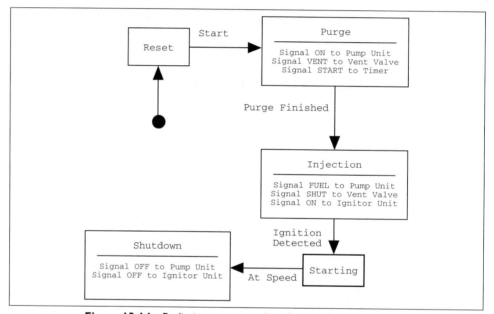

Figure 13.14   Preliminary state machine for the Controller object.

Here a choice has been made to use a Moore machine. Observe that, in this example, each input signal to the Controller maps to an event on the STD. Similarly, each outgoing signal maps to an action or response.

The states of Figure 13.14 have been derived from just one scenario. To build the full state model, however, all scenarios must be worked through. Only then can the STD be considered to be complete.

13.3   Introduction to statecharts

Statecharts, devised by David Harel, are state transition diagrams. These are based on, but substantially extend, the Mealy machine. More importantly (from the point of view of this text), the dynamic model of OMT stems from the statechart model.

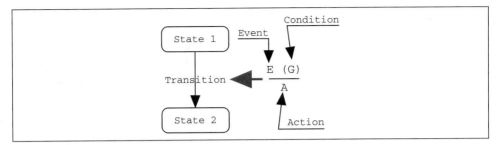

Figure 13.15   Statechart – basic notation.

Moreover, the diagramming notations are very similar. Therefore it is desirable to understand statechart concepts and notation.

Figure 13.15 illustrates the basic notation of the diagram.

Shown here is a two-state machine with a single transition from state 1 to state 2. The notation used for events and actions is similar to that of the Mealy machine. However, an additional factor is introduced – the idea of a condition or guard (G) on the transition. The reading of the diagram is that 'if event E occurs, then the system will transfer to State 2 provided condition G is true'.

What is given here is a one-level or *flat* state diagram. A major difficulty with such diagrams (discussed earlier) is that they can rapidly become cluttered and complex. Statecharts tackle these drawbacks by providing both refinement and depth, using substates (Figure 13.16).

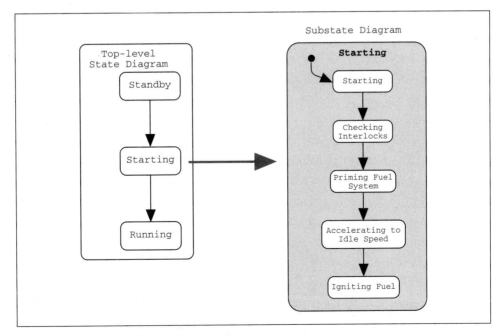

Figure 13.16   Refinement (depth) and substates.

Here the top-level diagram is a three-state one: Standby, Starting and Running. Analysis of Starting shows that this actually consists of a number of localized states – the *substates*. Including this information on the top-level diagram would transform it from a three-state to a six-state description (which shows how quickly flat state diagrams can 'explode' as more detail is added). Refining the state information into a separate child diagram allows detail to be hidden and yet remain accessible (shades of structured design). Thus refinement is a top-down concept, each top-level state encapsulating a set of substates. Note that a high-level state is really an abstraction of the substates. Consider, for example, when the system is in Starting mode. It must actually be in one of the designated substates. To be more precise, in one and *only* one substate.

When developing the state model, the designer may easily end up with an overly cluttered diagram. The problem then is how to simplify it and yet retain all the state information. This can be done by building a hierarchical state structure from the bottom up – clustering substates to form a superstate(s). Thus for the Starting state of Figure 13.16, we might first identify the substates. The next move would be to cluster these together and so form the superstate Starting. Such combining leads to simpler diagrams which are more easily understood.

Further simplification is possible, as demonstrated in Figure 13.17.

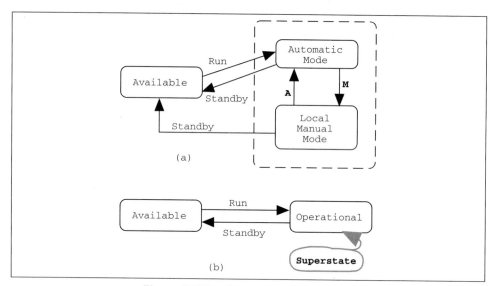

Figure 13.17   Clustering and superstates.

Here Figure 13.17(a) shows a three-state machine, where Automatic and Local Manual are defined to be 'operational modes'. It can be seen that when in any operational mode, selecting Standby puts the machine into Available. In Figure 13.17(b) the two substates Automatic and Local Manual have been clustered to form a single superstate, Operational. Note, though, that only a *single* Standby arc is shown. This notation is useful for defining state changes under fault (exception) conditions.

Having built a hierarchical structure, some means of navigating through it is necessary. In statecharts this is done by zooming-in and zooming-out of diagrams (Figure 13.18).

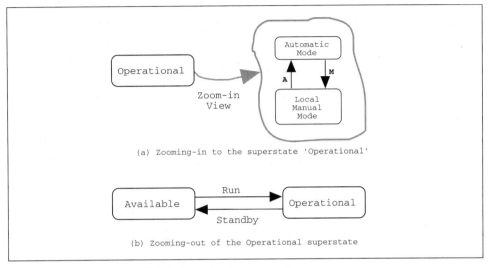

(a) Zooming-in to the superstate 'Operational'

(b) Zooming-out of the Operational superstate

Figure 13.18 Zooming-in and zooming-out in statecharts.

Zooming-in takes us inside a superstate to show the substate diagrams (in this case into `Operational`). Zooming-out takes us from a substate diagram to the next higher-level state view.

All state diagrams need to identify the initial or default state. Figure 13.19 shows how this is done in statecharts.

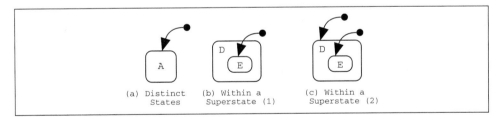

(a) Distinct States
(b) Within a Superstate (1)
(c) Within a Superstate (2)

Figure 13.19 Notation for default (initial) state.

Figure 13.19(a) applies to a distinct, single-level state. It is similar to that used earlier (Chapter 6), and should be familiar. However, when superstates are involved, a small modification is made to the basic notation (Figure 13.19(b)). The default arc is used to define the *substate* that becomes active on entry to the state machine. An alternative form (Figure 13.19(c)) is more helpful when zooming operations are performed.

This section would be incomplete without looking at the ability of statecharts to portray concurrent behaviour. First, let us return to the object message diagram (OMD) of Figure 13.13, reproduced in part in Figure 13.20.

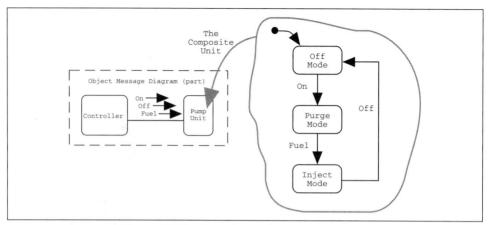

Figure 13.20 State diagram for a composite unit.

The pump unit was originally treated as a single unit, its behaviour being described using a single state diagram (Figure 13.20). However, as shown in Figure 13.10, the unit is actually a composite item. It consists of a fuel–air valve and an IPN pump – two separate, concurrently operating components. Thus each has its own mode of behaviour, given in Figure 13.21.

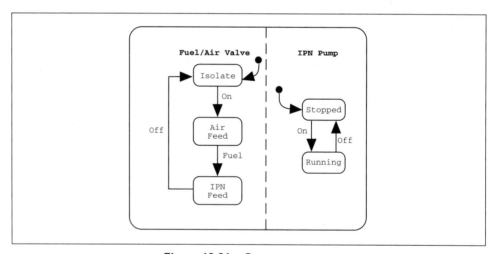

Figure 13.21 Concurrent states.

It is possible to produce combined states for composite units, as illustrated in Figure 13.22.

This is a useful diagram for reviewing the operation of concurrent units. Unfortunately, for large systems, combined state diagrams may become complex and difficult to use. In such applications their benefits are doubtful. Moreover, combining state diagrams is not a trivial matter.

In closing, observe that Figure 13.21 provides information relating to:

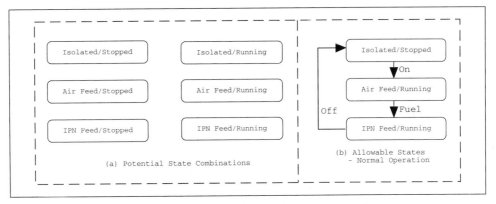

Figure 13.22   Combined states for concurrent units.

- independence of component states
- synchronization between component states

Here Fuel changes the state of the fuel–air valve only. It has no effect on the IPN pump – *independence* of behaviour. In contrast Off and On cause a simultaneous state change in both components – *synchronization*.

13.4   OMT notation – a brief review

As mentioned earlier, the OMT dynamic model is based on that of the statechart. It also extends and provides variations on its predecessor. Some of these are useful, others of doubtful value. Figure 13.23 contains those which are most likely to be used in practice.

Figure 13.23(a)(i) shows the fundamental state/event/guard/action notation of the OMT state diagram. On a small but important point, OMT defines actions as being *instantaneous operations*.

Initial states are illustrated in Figure 13.23(a)(ii), while final states are defined in Figure 13.23(a)(iii). Figure 13.23(b) shows how attributes of events can be added to state diagrams. Here an object has two states, Ready to Weigh and Computing Cost. A state change takes place when the event Load on Bridge occurs. Associated with this event is the attribute Weight.

Up to this point, the notation is essentially that of a Mealy machine. OMT, how-ever, also brings in aspects of the Moore machine, by associating operations with states. Such state-related operations are grouped into four categories; operations per-formed:

- on entry to a state
- within the state
- on exit from the state
- during a self-transition (a transition back to the original state)

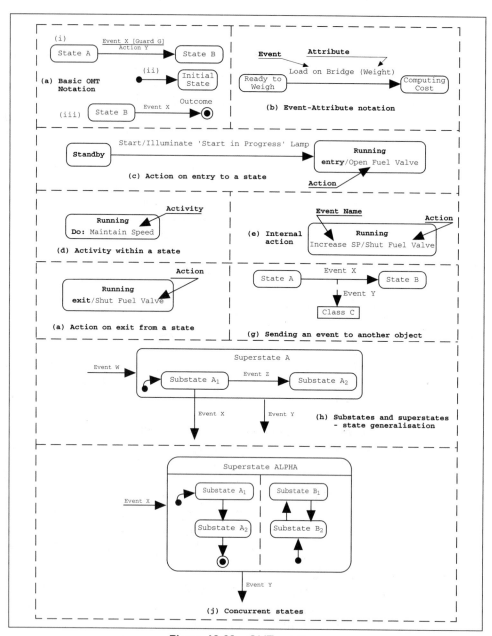

Figure 13.23 OMT notation.

Entry to a state is shown in Figure 13.23(c). Here, when event Start arrives, the action Illuminate 'start-in-progress' Lamp is performed. The system now enters the Running state. On entry the **action** Open Fuel Valve is conducted (note well; this is defined to be an action). The identifier **entry/** is used to denote such actions.

Once the entry action(s) has (have) been executed, the system proceeds into what might be called a steady state condition. It remains in the state, performing a required set of operations called *activities*. An activity is defined to be an operation that takes time to complete. Figure 13.23(d) indicates that the operation Maintain Speed is an activity by the keyword **do:**. While in a state, events may arrive which – although they generate actions – do not cause a state change. Figure 13.23(e) illustrates the notation used, which is of the form **Event Name/Action Generated**.

When a state is exited, exit operations are effected. These are identified using **exit/** (Figure 13.23(f)).

The self-transition is slightly unusual. When an event arrives it produces an action, but there is no resulting state change. More strictly, we consider that a transition is made out of a state and then back into the same state. This might perhaps seem a pedantic point. Not with OMT though; here it is an extremely important aspect because, when a self-transition occurs, all exit and entry actions are performed. Note this well.

Entry and exit actions are *always* completed. This, however, is not necessarily true of activities. For instance, an event which generates a state change may arrive during the execution of an activity. The result is that the activity is terminated and then the exit actions performed.

The notation of Figure 13.23(g) is used to show the sending of events to other objects.

Substates and superstates (Figure 13.23(h)) are illustrated much like the statechart method. Here a transition is made into superstate A when event W occurs. What actually happens is that substate A_1 becomes active. Should event Z arrive, the system moves into substate A_2. But, if event X is generated instead, the system will transit out of substate A_1 (and thus out of the superstate). Event Y causes an immediate transition out of the superstate, irrespective of the substate conditions.

Finally, concurrent states are identified using the notation of Figure 13.23(j). Here a superstate ALPHA consists of two concurrent substates, A and B. The superstate is activated by event X: this causes the system to enter substates A_1 and B_2. As shown, substate A could reach a termination condition while the superstate is active. Substate B denotes cyclic operation. Irrespective of the actual situation, transition out of ALPHA takes place when event Y arrives.

OMT diagrams will be met again in the design example of Chapter 16.

13.5 Diagram to code

In this concluding section some example diagram-to-code constructs are illustrated. Three major points are covered:

- translating state transition information to program form (Figure 13.24)
- using messaging to implement inter-object communication (Figure 13.25)
- showing object communication and interaction, incorporating both external and internal models (Figure 13.26)

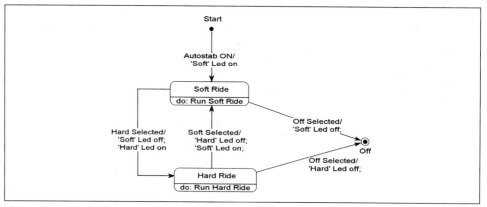

Figure 13.24   Example implementation of state diagram.

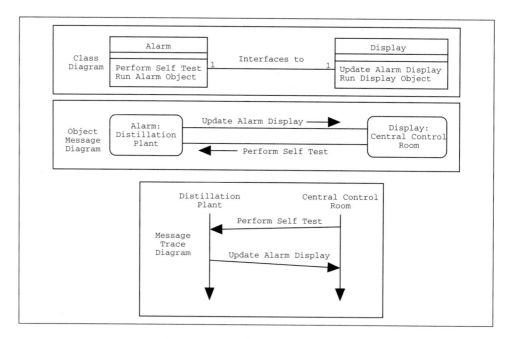

Figure 13.25   Example implementation of object communication.

The examples, as before, are deliberately kept very simple. More detail will be met in the design example in Chapter 16.

The state transition diagram – Figure 13.24

Figure 13.24 is an OMT state transition diagram for a class (AutoStab) which has two modes of operation – Soft Ride and Hard Ride. When the AutoStab is selected ON, the system enters the Soft Ride mode. At the same time an LED – Soft – is put on to indicate the mode of operation. In this mode the system continuously performs an activity designated as Run Soft Ride.

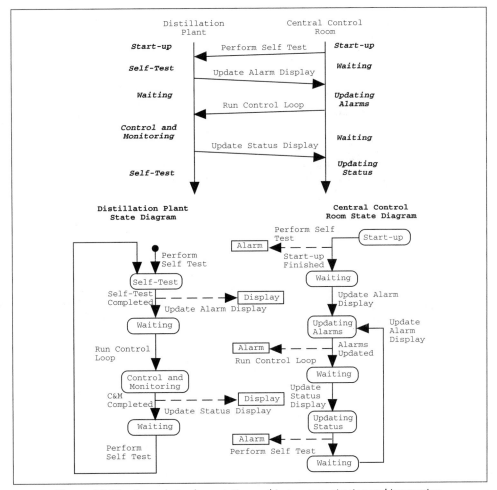

Figure 13.26 Example implementation – object communication and interaction.

Study the rest of the diagram until you are sure you understand it. Now turn to Listing 13.1.

There are two major sections. First there is the class AutoStab. Next there is main. This is used here (for demonstration only) to mimic the action of a class which interacts with AutoStab. Within this is the creation and use of an instantiation of class AutoStab – the object EFA. When the program is run, the function call EFA.PutAutoStabOn() is executed. This starts up the process depicted in Figure 13.24. Subsequent actions depend on the keyboard selections H, S or O (note that in order to concentrate on essentials, defensive programming is omitted).

You can see there are no entry, exit or internal actions in this example. In fact, unless there are exceptional circumstances, a restricted dynamic model will be used in this text. Entry and exit actions will normally be incorporated as actions on transitions. Internal events are replaced by self-transitions. This simplifies the design and makes it easier to maintain diagram-to-code consistency (a personal opinion).

```
#include <iostream.h>
#include <string.h>

enum RideMode {Soft, Hard, Off};
//------------- THE CLASS AutoStab --------------//
class AutoStab {
private:
    char RideSelection;

public:
    void GetRideSelection (char &Selection);
    void ManageSoftRideMode (RideMode &NextState);
    void ManageHardRideMode (RideMode &NextState);
    void PutAutostabOn();
};
//------------- END CLASS AutoStab --------------//

//**************************************************//

void main()
{
AutoStab EFA;
    cout << "\n Listing 13.1";
    EFA.PutAutostabOn();
    cout << "\n Autostab is OFF";

} /* end main */
//**************************************************//


void AutoStab::GetRideSelection (char &Selection)
    {
    cout << "\n Make Ride Selection"
         << " -  H(ard) or S(soft) or O(ff)\n";
    cin >> Selection;
    cout << "\n The selection is " << Selection << "\n";
    }

void AutoStab::ManageSoftRideMode (RideMode &NextState)
{
    do {
        cout << "\n\n In Manage Soft Ride Mode";
        GetRideSelection (RideSelection);
        }
    while (RideSelection == 'S');

    if (RideSelection == 'H'){
        cout << "\n Soft Led off" << "\n Hard Led on";
        NextState = Hard;
    }
    if (RideSelection == 'O'){
        cout << "\n Soft Led off";
        NextState = Off;
    }
}
```

Listing 13.1   STD example – Autostab dynamics.   (continued)

Listing 13.1 (continued)

```
void AutoStab::ManageHardRideMode (RideMode &NextState)
{
    do {
        cout << "\n\n In Manage Hard Ride Mode";
        GetRideSelection (RideSelection);
        }
    while (RideSelection == 'H');
    if (RideSelection == 'S'){
        cout << "\n Hard Led off" << "\n Soft Led on";
        NextState = Soft;
    }
    if (RideSelection == 'O'){
        cout << "\n Hard Led off";
        NextState = Off;
    }
}

void AutoStab::PutAutostabOn() {
RideMode NextMode = Soft;

    cout << "\nAutostab is on";
    cout << " \nSoft Led on \n";

    do {
        switch (NextMode){
            case Soft : ManageSoftRideMode (NextMode); break;
            case Hard : ManageHardRideMode (NextMode); break;
        } // end switch
    }
    while (NextMode != Off);

}
```

Using messaging to implement inter-object communication – Figure 13.25

Figure 13.25 illustrates the class, object message and message trace diagrams for an example object communication scenario. Listing 13.2 is the corresponding code implementation.

In embedded system design, a most important use of this construct is at the application level. At this level there is (with few exceptions) only a single instantiation of a class. Thus the approach used in Listing 13.2 is to define the collaborating objects explicitly, as in Table 13.1, for instance.

Table 13.1.

Class	Object	Collaborating object	Collaboration
Alarm	Distillation Plant	Central Control Room	Update Alarm Display
Display	Central Control Room	Distillation Plant	Perform Self Test

```
/************************************************/
/*      This demonstrates inter-object messaging    */
/*                Listing 13.2 - V2.0               */
/************************************************/
# include <iostream.h>

class Display;
/////////////////////////////////////////////////////////////////////////
class Alarm {
public:
        void RunAlarm(Display &DisplayAdd);
        void PerformSelfTest();
};
/////////////////////////////////////////////////////////////////////////
class Display {
public:
        void RunDisplay(Alarm &AlarmAdd);
        void UpdateAlarmDisplay();
};
/////////////////////////////////////////////////////////////////////////
void main() {
Alarm DistillationPlant;
Display CentralControlRoom;

        cout << "Listing 13.3 ";
        CentralControlRoom.RunDisplay(DistillationPlant);
        DistillationPlant.RunAlarm(CentralControlRoom);
}
/////////////////////////////////////////////////////////////////////////

        void Alarm::PerformSelfTest() {
            cout << "\n Distillation Plant doing self test";
        }
        void Display::UpdateAlarmDisplay() {
            cout << "\n Control room updating alarm displays";
        }
        void Alarm::RunAlarm(Display &DisplayAdd) {
            cout << "\n\n Alarm object is boss";
            DisplayAdd.UpdateAlarmDisplay();
        }
        void Display::RunDisplay(Alarm &AlarmAdd) {
            cout << "\n\n Display object is boss";
            AlarmAdd.PerformSelfTest();
        }
```

Listing 13.2   Demonstration of inter-object messaging.

You can see from the code that two actions are carried out by main:

- start-up of objects (for example, *DistillationPlant.RunAlarm*).
- Designation of collaborators (for example *DistillationPlant   ...* *(CentralControlRoom)*)

Collaboration information is passed into the objects using address – not pointer – techniques (once again, a personal preference). The rest of the code should be self-explanatory.

Showing object communication and interaction, incorporating both external and internal models (Figure 13.26)

Here the scenario of Figure 13.25 has been elaborated, each object now having its dynamic behaviour defined using a state diagram. Compare the trace diagram and state diagrams with the resulting code implementation (Listing 13.3).

```
# include <iostream.h>

class Display;

class Alarm{
private:
    enum State {SelfTest, Control};
    State NextState;
public:
    Alarm();
    void PerformSelfTest();
    void RunControlLoop();
    void RunAlarm(Display &DisPlayAdd);
};

class Display{
private:
    enum State {StartUp, UpdatingAlarms, UpdatingStatus};
    State NextState;
public:
    Display();
    void UpdateAlarmDisplay();
    void UpdateStatusDisplay();
    void RunDisplay(Alarm &AlarmAdd);
};

void main(){
int Loops;
Display CentralControlRoom;
Alarm DistillationPlant;
//Using fixed loop for demo purposes only
    for (Loops = 1; Loops <= 4; Loops++){
        CentralControlRoom.RunDisplay (DistillationPlant);
        DistillationPlant.RunAlarm(CentralControlRoom);
        }
}

Alarm::Alarm(){
    NextState = SelfTest;
```

Listing 13.3 Demonstration of object communication and interaction.   *(continued)*

Listing 13.3 *(continued)*

```
}
Display::Display(){
    NextState = StartUp;
}
void Display::RunDisplay(Alarm &AlarmAdd){
    switch (NextState)
    {case StartUp: cout << "\n\n Display Object Starting";
                AlarmAdd.PerformSelfTest();
                break;
    case UpdatingAlarms: cout << "\n\n Display is Updating";
                AlarmAdd.RunControlLoop();
                break;
    case UpdatingStatus: cout << "\n\n Status is Updating";
                AlarmAdd.PerformSelfTest();
                break;
    }
  }

void Alarm::RunAlarm(Display &DisplayAdd){
    switch (NextState)
    {case SelfTest: cout << "\n\n Alarms are Self Testing";
                DisplayAdd.UpdateAlarmDisplay();
                break;
     case Control:  cout << "\n\n Now Running Control Loop";
                DisplayAdd.UpdateStatusDisplay();
                break;
    }
}

void Display::UpdateAlarmDisplay(){
    cout << "\n Sending 'Update Alarm Displays'";
    NextState = UpdatingAlarms;
}
void Display::UpdateStatusDisplay(){
    cout << "\n Sending 'Update Status Displays'";
    NextState = UpdatingStatus;
}

void Alarm::RunControlLoop(){
    cout << "\n Sending 'Run Control Loop' ";
    NextState = Control;
}

void Alarm::PerformSelfTest(){
    cout << "\n Sending 'Self Test'";
    NextState = SelfTest;
}
```

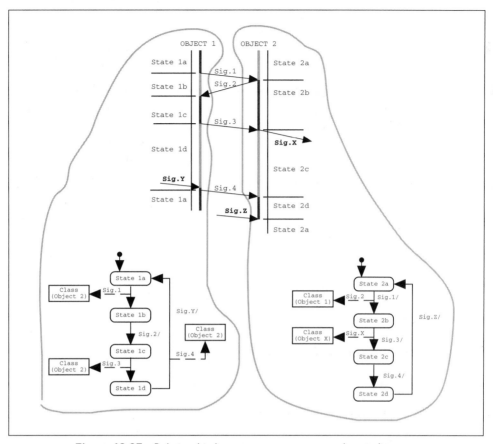

Figure 13.27   Relationship between message trace and state diagrams.

Summary and review

To summarize: each object has its own event/time line on the message trace diagram (Figure 13.27).

These lines run from top to bottom. If an object (1) sends a message to another object (2), then an arrowed line is drawn from 1 to 2. An incoming message is usually (but not always) seen as an event by the receiving object. An outgoing one is an action performed by the transmitting object. Where the diagram contains events only, it is called an event trace diagram.

All operational scenarios need to be identified, together with their associated dynamic behaviour. For each object, its states are defined by splitting the event/time line into distinct sections. Here, for example, object 1 is shown to have states 1a, 1b, 1c and 1d. Precisely how these various states are derived is a design decision. Do not fall into the trap of automatically linking incoming messages with state changes.

At the end of this work, each object will have one complete state diagram. Balance checks – on actions, events and states – should be carried out between the trace diagram(s) and the state diagrams.

By now you should:

- understand why models are needed to show object behaviour (both collective and individual)
- know what scenarios are, what they describe, and how they are used as part of the design process
- appreciate the use of message trace, event trace and state diagrams
- see how the three diagrams relate to each other
- know how to use these diagrams during the design process
- see how object messages translate to events and actions on the state diagrams
- understand what Mealy and Moore state machines are
- appreciate the pros and cons of the two machines
- perceive how statecharts extend the basic Mealy machine through hierarchical structuring, refinement of state machines (substates, superstates) and concurrency of operation
- see how the OMT dynamic model relates to statecharts
- recognize that the OMT model combines features of the Mealy and Moore machines
- understand the difference between actions and activities
- appreciate that actions are generated in response to events, to entries to states and to exits from states

Exercises

13.1 Produce a state diagram to describe the dynamic operation of a VCR. Limit yourself to the following actions: Play, Stop, Fast Forward and Rewind. Assume that the default condition is Stop. Assume also that the unit always has to stop when going between modes of operation. To achieve this, Stop must be selected. Assume that all selections are push-button types.

13.2 Repeat Exercise 13.1 where mode changes can be made without Stop being selected (for example, when running in FF, Rewind might be selected).

13.3 Produce the object message and message trace diagrams for the following scenario.

A communications system consists of two objects, a primary station (PS) and a secondary station (SS). There are two modes of transmission: PS to SS and SS to PS. Transmission is always initiated by the primary:

(a) Obtaining SS data: PS sends a POLL message to SS.
  (i) If no data is available SS replies with a NACK message. This is the end of the transaction. PS terminates the session.
  (ii) If SS data *is* available, then SS sends the full data stream. When all data has been received PS sends ACK to SS to finish the session.
(b) PS sending data to SS: PS sends a SEL message to SS. SS responds with ACK. PS sends data. When all data has been received by SS it sends ACK. PS terminates the session.

13.4 Describe the dynamics of the following system using a single state diagram.

A microprocessor is fitted to control the operation of an aircraft undercarriage (u/c) system which has the following modes of operation:

(a) Power is switched on – hydraulic valves set to closed. Assume that the u/c is locked down. The three u/c Down switches are closed, and the cockpit display shows three greens.

(b) Nose wheel centralized AND u/c weight switches operated AND airspeed switch operated THEN selection of UP is permitted.

(c) UP selected. Up hydraulic valve is opened, u/c retracts. As soon as the u/c moves the Down switches open, causing the display to show three reds.

(d) Undercarriage fully retracted. This operates (closes) the three u/c Up switches. As a result the Up hydraulic valve is closed and the cockpit display goes off.

(e) Down selection made. The Down hydraulic valve is opened. As a result the u/c begins to move, opening the u/c Up switches. This causes the cockpit display to show three reds.

(f) Undercarriage fully down. This closes the u/c Down switches. As a result the Down hydraulic valve is closed and the cockpit display shows three greens.

Now ready for repeat operation.

13.5 For the following system, produce trace, object message and state diagrams.

A manufacturing unit consist of three objects: Operators Panel (OP), Handler Robot (HR) and Driller Robot (DR). The overall function of the unit is to drill sets of holes in a metal casting automatically. The purpose of HR is to pick up a blank casting, position it for drilling, and then stack it after drilling. The function of DR is to perform the actual drilling. A simplified operational description is given below.

(a) HR operations

From reset position:

(i)   Rotate to input stack of blank castings.

(ii) Pick up casting.

(iii) Move to drill position (only if DR is retracted).

After drilling, when DR is back in retracted position:

(iv) Rotate to finished stack.

(v) Stack the casting.

(vi) Move to reset position.

(b) DR operations.

From reset position:

(i)   Fit correct drill bit.

(ii) When blank casting in position, advance to drill position (only when HR has positioned casting for drilling).

(iii) Carry out drilling operation.

(iv) Move back from drill position (retract).

(v) Remove drill bit.

14

Functional modelling of objects

Functional modelling is a way to describe what a system does, or what should happen within a system. Unfortunately, this is a somewhat contentious subject in OO; there is much disagreement on its value. Many designers consider that the model is irrelevant and should be omitted altogether. The situation is muddied further by the different ways in which functionality can be modelled.

Be that as it may, a study of object-oriented design would be incomplete without covering the topic. The purpose of this chapter is to show how models are used to define object functional behaviour. It:

- first gives an brief overview of three particular techniques: the Rumbaugh OMT DFD, the Shlaer–Mellor Action DFD and the traditional DFD
- illustrates, for each case, the relationship between the object model and the functional model
- describes in more detail the features of the OMT and traditional DFD approaches

You will find it an advantage to study Chapter 4 before going any further.

14.1 Setting the scene

14.1.1 Introducing the OMT DFD (Rumbaugh approach)

This has its roots in the work of Rumbaugh and fellow workers, to describe, in their words 'computations within a system'. Figure 14.1 illustrates the basic ideas of this method.

Starting from a system specification, the object model is produced. This consists of a set of classes (objects). The purpose of the functional model is to specify *what* happens to these objects. As shown here, this is modelled as a single-level DFD containing external devices (D), software processes (P) and connecting data flows.

For each class of the object model a set of operations is identified (Figure 14.2).

Each operation has a corresponding process in the functional model. For instance,

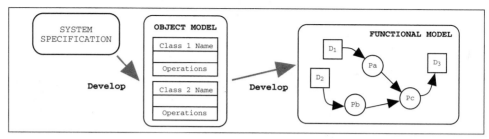

Figure 14.1 Basic concept of the OMT DFD.

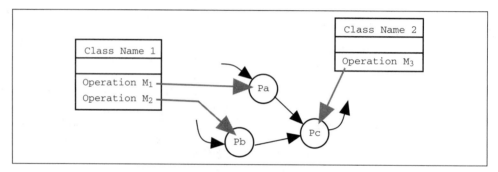

Figure 14.2 DFD process – class operation relationship.

operation M_1 of ClassName 1 maps to the process P_A, M_2 to P_B. Likewise, operation M_3 of ClassName 2 maps to P_C. Observe that one cannot deduce the relationship of the various operations merely by looking at the class diagram. Note that, at the code level, each process is implemented as a class method.

14.1.2 Introducing the action DFD (Shlaer–Mellor approach)

The approach to functional modelling devised by Sally Shlaer and Tony Mellor is quite different. Their aim is to show what processing is performed by (on) an object when it is in a particular state (Figure 14.3).

Here, once the object model has been derived, a dynamic model is produced for *each* object. This specifies the behaviour of the object in terms of a state model. Associated with each state is a set of actions. The functionality of these actions is defined using a data flow diagram (hence the name 'action' DFD (ADFD)). As shown in Figure 14.3, the dynamic model consists of two states, 1 and 2. This model, in the Shlaer–Mellor method, is a Moore machine. Here, remember, actions are associated with states, not transitions. Listed on the diagram are the actions executed in each state. The processing performed by these actions is expressed using a DFD, one DFD per set of actions. Thus here the complete functional model consists of two individual data flow diagrams. One represents the processing carried out in state 1, the other that of state 2.

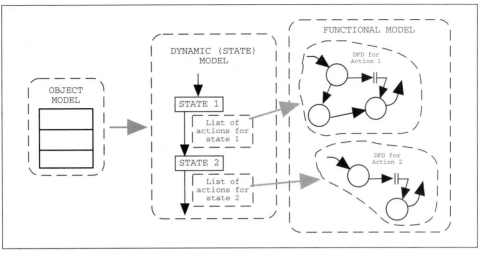

Figure 14.3 Defining class (object) actions using DFDs.

14.1.3 Revisiting the traditional DFD

Traditional DFDs were first developed as part of structured design techniques. Their concepts, notation and uses are described comprehensively in Chapter 4. Fundamentally, these perform the same role as OMT DFDs. In fact, there is no reason why a design specified using both techniques shouldn't yield identical results. However, the development of the functional models is done in quite a different way. With the OMT method, emphasis is placed on first defining the object model. Only later is the functional model produced. In contrast, the traditional technique is to produce a functional model – based on the system specification – at the outset of design work. This functionality, together with other (system-related) factors, leads to the production of the object model (Figure 14.4).

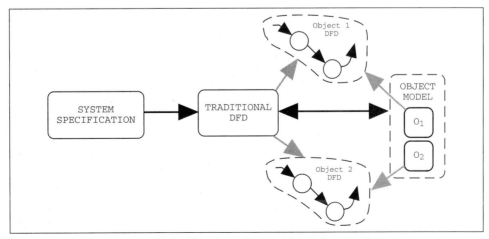

Figure 14.4 Identifying objects and their functionality.

What is done is first to collect sets of processes together to form logical groupings and then to map each group to an object.

14.2 The OMT DFD in more detail

14.2.1 Basics

The intention of this section is to give a general view and better appreciation of the OMT DFD. It is *not* a detailed design document. The important point is that you should become familiar and comfortable with OMT functional diagrams.

First, we need to look at the notation used and the meaning of the symbols. The basic symbols used in OMT DFDs are shown in Figure 14.5.

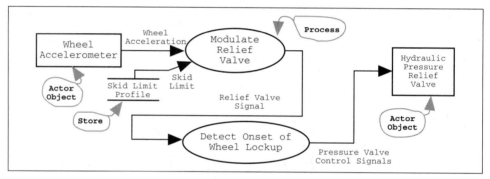

Figure 14.5 Basic symbols – OMT DFD.

If you have studied Chapter 4, these will be familiar. Four aspects are given here: processes, data flows, stores and external devices. Processes, represented by ellipses, transform input data to output data in some predefined manner. Data flows are the 'pipes' along which data moves through the model. Stores – depicted using parallel lines – are just that: passive stores of data. External devices (external to this part of the software system, that is) are sources or sinks of data. In OMT terminology these are *Actor Objects*, being shown as rectangles.

The example of Figure 14.5 shows a data flow Wheel Acceleration being generated by the actor object Wheel Accelerometer. This is input to the process Detect Onset of Wheel Lockup. Also input to the process is the stored data value Skid Limit Profile. Using these inputs, the process computes the output data value, Relief Valve Signal. This is then transformed by the process Modulate Relief Valve to produce the Pressure Valve Control Signals – the output to the actor object Hydraulic Pressure Relief Valve.

14.2.2 More on flows and stores

Frequently there is a need to copy and/or split data flows (Figure 14.6).

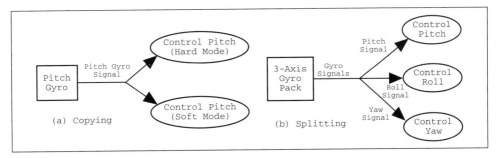

Figure 14.6   Data flows – copying and splitting.

In Figure 14.6(a), the input data flow Pitch Gyro Signal is used by two different processes. Thus the same data value is sent ('copied') to both Control Pitch (Hard Mode) and Control Pitch (Soft Mode). The flows leaving the fork aren't labelled, as they are the same as the inflow. By contrast, the output flows in Figure 14.6(b) *are* labelled. What is shown here is an input flow which consists of three components: Pitch Signal, Roll Signal, Yaw Signal. This may be viewed as an aggregation of data. The individual parts are then split out and sent on to the appropriate destination.

Data stores are considered to be passive objects in OMT. Their roles and access mechanisms are shown in Figure 14.7.

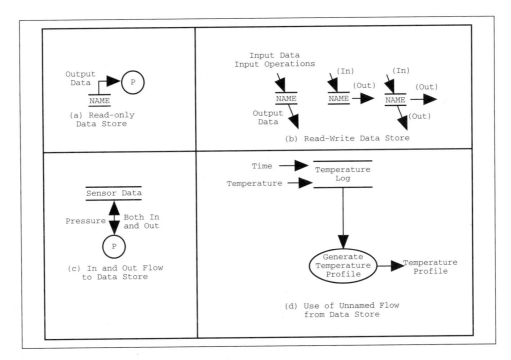

Figure 14.7   Data stores.

Figure 14.7(a) represents an output or read-only operation, used typically for lookup operations (such as algorithm coefficients or alarm limits). The name of the store is given on the diagram, together with that of the output data.

In and out operations are shown in Figure 14.7(b). On this there are separate readers and writers of the data stores. As defined in the original version of OMT, output arrows indicate data obtained from the store. Input arrows, however, represent two factors:

- data input to the store, or
- operations which modify the stored data (such as adding or deleting elements)

Figure 14.7(c) illustrates in–out operation. Here we have a single process reading from and writing to a data store Sensor Data. This is indicated by using two arrows on one data flow line. Clearly the data item Pressure must be the subject of both operations.

There are times when we can use unnamed data flows (Figure 14.7(d)). On this appears a store Temperature Log in which sets of measurements are stored (*logged*). Observe that there is an output flow from the store that has no label. The notation implies that the entire log is read in by the process Generate Temperature Profile.

Note that each store must have a unique name.

One construct which is unique to OMT is that of object creation. With this feature a data flow can generate an object for use by another process (Figure 14.8).

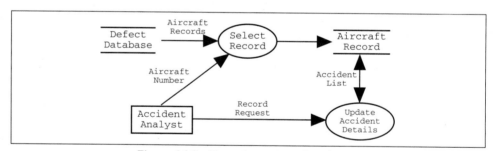

Figure 14.8   Dynamic creation of an object.

Here the Accident Analyst enters an Aircraft Number into the system. This causes the process Select Record to extract the record for that aircraft from a defect database. In effect, it dynamically creates a store object, Aircraft Record, this being accessed later by Update Accident Details.

The DFD shows what processing can be carried out by the system. It does not, though, show what happens in a particular scenario (such as which processes are performed, and in what order they are executed). Such information must be derived from the dynamic model. However, it can often be easier to grasp the overall behaviour of a system using the DFD. Thus to aid comprehension, dynamic aspects are integrated with functional aspects through the use of control flows (Figure 14.9).

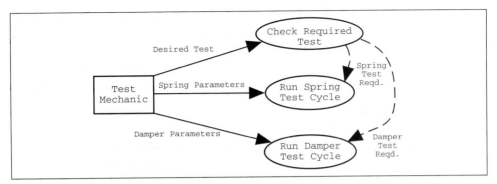

Figure 14.9   Control flows.

Control flows – denoted by dotted flow lines – are used to show the presence of decision-making. Here there are two such flows, Spring Test Required and Damper Test Required. These are considered to be Boolean values that 'switch' processes on. They are generated by decision-making data transformations, that in Figure 14.9 being Check Required Test. In this scenario, the Test Mechanic enters data for components to be tested: springs and dampers. Following this, a selection, Desired Test, is made. The process Check Required Test evaluates the input data, and then switches on – selects – either Run Spring Test Cycle or Run Damper Test Cycle.

14.2.3   Relating the functional and object models

How do the object and functional models relate to each other? The original work on OMT is slightly ambivalent, but a reasonable interpretation is given in Figure 14.10.

Remember, the functional model shows the complete set of operations of the system. However, when tying this in with the object model, we find that three basic relationships exist.

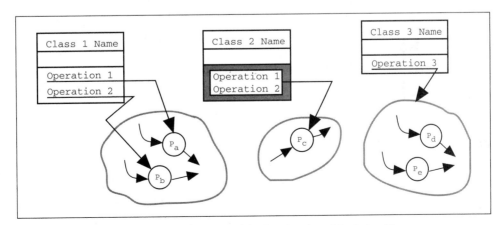

Figure 14.10   Object model – functional model relationship.

(a) Each operation may have a corresponding process on the DFD. Here object 1 (more precisely, class 1) contains two operations. As shown here, Operation 1 maps to Process P_a of the functional model, while operation 2 maps to P_b.

(b) A number of operations may be defined using a single process. A single high-level process in the functional model (P_c) is actually implemented by two operations in the object model.

(c) A single operation may relate to a number of processes. Here, for example, operation 3 is split across processes P_d and P_e. Such a situation can occur where the object model is itself decomposed. For instance, Object 3 may represent an aggregation of objects; the processes then correspond to operations of the individual component objects.

The situation, unfortunately, is made less clear by later changes to the OMT method which 'de-emphasizes' the functional model.

To conclude this section, a very simple example is given in Figure 14.11.

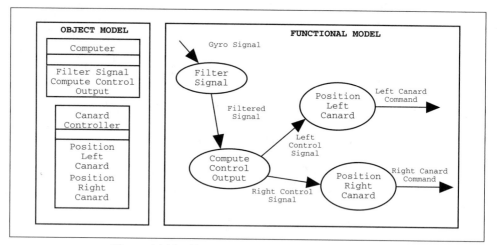

Figure 14.11   Example of function–object relationship.

Here the system contains two objects, `Computer` and `Canard Controller`. The operations of the `Computer` object are `Filter Signal` and `Compute Control Output`. Those for the `Canard Controller` are `Position Left Canard` and `Position Right Canard`. The function carried out is reasonably self-explanatory. Observe that the exercise shows a one-to-one operation/process relationship. It should be noted that if more detail is needed the processes may be decomposed (levelled).

14.3   Using the traditional data flow diagram

Traditional DFDs have been covered extensively in Chapter 4 and onwards as part of structured design. In this technique, system analysis and design begins with the production of a context diagram. The diagram is then elaborated (levelled) to produce a first-level data flow diagram. Further levelling is carried out until the designer reaches a satisfactory conclusion. Here we have a well-established process, one which has been used extensively in real-time designs. The question here though is 'does it have a role to play in object-oriented design?'. Much blood (metaphorically speaking) has been spilt over this issue. In fact, a DFD can be put to good use, because it:

- gives an overall view of the *system*
- allows us to concentrate on the signals/commands flowing between external items and the software of the system
- defines the functional operation of the overall system
- provides a mechanism to identify potential objects

These points are demonstrated in the simple example system of Figure 14.12.

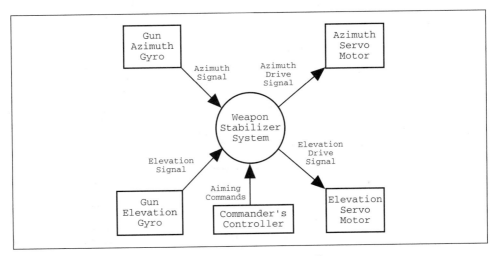

Figure 14.12 Traditional context diagram – small weapon servo system.

You can see immediately how it highlights the essentials of the system. Further, it forces us to think of the software as:

- one component within a complete system
- a black box unit at this level of design

The first-level DFD is given in Figure 14.13.

This, if you have studied Chapter 4, is a simple revision exercise. Bear in mind, however, that the DFD is not derived in an arbitrary manner. It is devised using our knowledge of the functional and operational requirements of the system. Implicit in the design (analysis?) technique are the following aims:

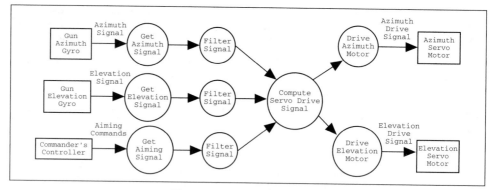

Figure 14.13 First-level DFD.

- to clearly identify the separate functions of the system
- to form logical groups of functions having good cohesion and low coupling

The first-level DFD should reflect this approach, with a process corresponding to a group. Thus each group – or a combination of groups – is a candidate object. It is at this point that we diverge from the structured design route. The next operation is to identify sensible grouping of processes, allocating each group to an object (Figure 14.14).

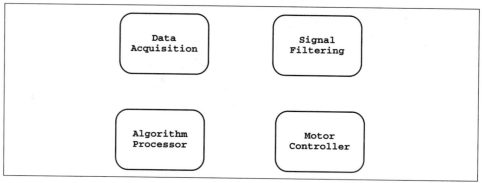

Figure 14.14 Candidate objects (classes).

Further object development may be carried out as desired; OMT, CRC or any other method can be employed.

The strength of this approach is that it drives the design from the perspective of the system, not the software. More will be said on this in Chapter 15.

14.4 Diagram to code

To demonstrate use of the functional model, consider the system described by the class diagram of Figure 14.15.

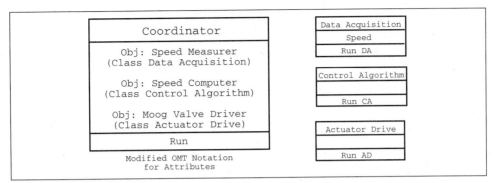

Figure 14.15 System class diagram.

Here the class `Coordinator` uses objects of classes `Data Acquisition`, `Control Algorithm` and `Actuator Drive`. What we have then is a master/slave relationship (the layout has been chosen to suggest this might be the case). The function of `Coordinator` is a very simple one; to organize the execution sequence of the slave objects. Note that these objects are listed as attributes of the `Coordinator` class (Listing 14.1).

The processing performed by each of the slave objects is shown in the data flow diagrams of Figure 14.16. Study this carefully.

For brevity, only `DataAcquisition` is fully implemented (and even so, it is really only demonstration code). The other classes are implemented as dummy stubs.

Turning to class `DataAcquisition` in Listing 14.1, you will see that each data transformation has a corresponding function (these being listed as operations in the class diagram). These are orchestrated by the function (operation) `RunDA`. One attribute only is declared at the class level – `ValidSpeedSignal`.

The coordinator object `CruiseControl` (see `main`) is set running by calling on its operation `Run`. This first sets `SpeedMeasurer` executing by the call `SpeedMeasurer.RunDA`. This in turn starts the execution of the individual functions of `SpeedMeasurer`. Once these have finished, `SpeedComputer` is called, the sequence completing with `MoogValveDriver`.

Comment and review

Each of the methods described in detail has pros and cons. Of the two, the weaker is OMT (which is probably why it has been de-emphasized). The semantics are open to misinterpretation (although some would say that the basic definitions are somewhat woolly). The effectiveness of traditional DFDs to perform functional modelling – within the context of OO design – depends to a large extent on how they are used. Many consider that they are totally incompatible with OO concepts and thinking. Others manage to apply them without appearing to suffer any great angst.

At this stage, you should now:

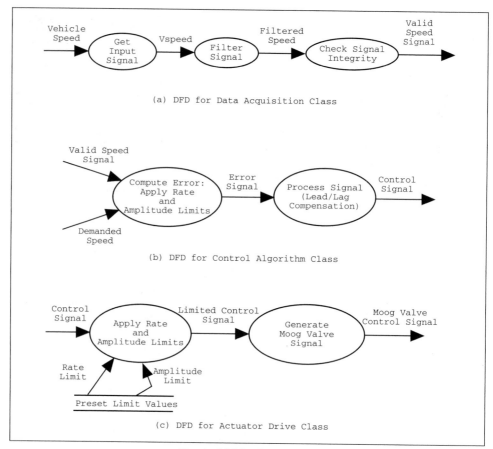

(a) DFD for Data Acquisition Class

(b) DFD for Control Algorithm Class

(c) DFD for Actuator Drive Class

Figure 14.16 Class DFDs.

- appreciate that there is no uniquely correct way of specifying system functionality
- understand the fundamentals of two particular techniques: OMT and traditional DFDs
- see how, for each approach, the object and functional models relate to each other
- have an understanding of the basic syntax and semantics of the methods
- realize that there is a great deal of commonality between the techniques
- appreciate the importance of showing control information in the functional model

Exercises

14.1 An electromechanical valve is driven by a stepper motor, its position being measured by a rotary potentiometer. Closed-loop position control is provided

```
# include <iostream.h>
/********************************************************/
class DataAcquisition {
public:
      void RunDA();
private:
      float ValidSpeedSignal;
      void GetInputSignal(int &Vspeed1);
      void FilterSignal (int Vspeed1, float &FilteredSpeed1);
      void CheckSigIntegrity (float FilteredSpeed1,
                              float &ValidSpeed1);
};
/********************************************************/
/********************************************************/
class ControlAlgorithm {
public:
      void RunCA();
private:
};
/********************************************************/
/********************************************************/
class ActuatorDrive {
public:
      void RunAD();
private:
};
/********************************************************/

class Coordinator {
public:
      void Run();
private:
      DataAcquisition   SpeedMeasurer;
      ControlAlgorithm SpeedComputer;
      ActuatorDrive     MoogValveDriver;
};
/********************************************************/
void main()
{
Coordinator CruiseControl;

      cout << "\n Cruise Control";
      CruiseControl.Run();
      cout << "\nEnd of demo " ;
}
/********************************************************/


void DataAcquisition::GetInputSignal(int &Vspeed1)
{
      cout << "\n\nEnter Speed value\n";
      cin >> Vspeed1;
}
```

Listing 14.1 Functional modelling example.   (continued)

Listing 14.1 (*continued*)

```
void DataAcquisition::FilterSignal (int Vspeed1, float &FilteredSpeed1)
{
    FilteredSpeed1 = (0.5 * float(Vspeed1));
    cout << "\n\nThe filtered speed value is  " << FilteredSpeed1;
}

void DataAcquisition::CheckSigIntegrity (float FilteredSpeed1,
            float &ValidSpeed1)
{
    if (FilteredSpeed1 < 100)
    {
        ValidSpeed1 = FilteredSpeed1;
        cout << "\n\nSignal is valid - value is -->" << ValidSpeed1;
    }
    else
    {
        ValidSpeed1 = 100;
        cout << "\n\nSignal is invalid - value used is -->" <<
ValidSpeed1;
    }
}

void DataAcquisition::RunDA()
{
int   Vspeed;
float FilteredSpeed;

    GetInputSignal(Vspeed);
    FilterSignal (Vspeed, FilteredSpeed);
    CheckSigIntegrity (FilteredSpeed, ValidSpeedSignal);
}


void ControlAlgorithm::RunCA()
{
    cout << "\n\nControl algorithm executed";
}

void ActuatorDrive::RunAD()
{
    cout << "\n\nActuator signal generated";
}

void Coordinator::Run()
{
    SpeedMeasurer.RunDA();
    SpeedComputer.RunCA();
    MoogValveDriver.RunAD();
}
```

for the valve using a dedicated microcontroller. Part of the function of the controller is given below. Produce a data flow diagram which expresses this function.

The motor is driven in on–off mode, and is bidirectional. To set the valve position, the controller first compares the actual position with the desired position. The result of the comparison is the position error. When this error exceeds a preset value (the upper threshold), the motor is switched on. The direction of travel is such that it reduces the error. When the error falls below a lower threshold value, the motor is switched off. At all times the valve position is to be updated for use by the display process.

In the remote mode of operation the desired position is provided by a software process 'remote comms'. However, it is also possible for an operator to override the remote system. This is done by switching to 'local control'. In local mode the valve position is set by the operator using open and close push-buttons.

14.2 The following is a description of one function of a microcomputer-based attitude sensing system (a *dipmeter*) for use in oil well exploration.

The unit measures the output of three orthogonal accelerometers. Using this it computes slant angle (SA) and slant angle bearing (SAB). This data is to be sent to a serial comms handler for onward transmission to the surface.
The input signals from the accelerometers are defined as V_x, V_y and V_z.

Calculations are performed as follows:

(a)   Correction for axis static misalignment.

$$E_1 = V_x - V_y D_{xz} + V_z D_{xy}$$

$$E_2 = V_x D_{yz} + V_y - V_z D_{yx}$$

$$E_3 = -V_x D_{zy} + V_y D_{zx} + V_z$$

The *D* values are stored in memory.

(b)   Compute SA and SAB.

$$SA = \arctan [(E_1^2 + E_2^2)^{1/2}/E_3]$$

$$SAB = \arctan (E_1/E_2)$$

Produce a data flow diagram which represents this function.

14.3 Produce a DFD to show how the following battery monitoring system functions.

In computing the battery state of charge, the monitoring unit measures battery voltage, current and temperature at regular intervals. At each interval, after making the measurements, it computes the incremental charge (the change in battery charge) for that period. Then, using this value, it updates the state-of-charge indicator.

In computing incremental charge, it must first determine whether the change is positive (a charging current) or negative (discharge current). If the change is positive, a simple ampere-hour calculation is made of the incremental charge value. However, if the change is negative, the following calculations are made:

(a)   The actual current value (I_a) is modified as a function of the measured discharge rate (I_{c1}).

(b)   The resulting output of the calculation is then adjusted to take into account battery temperature (I_{c2}).

(c)   Using I_{c2}, the charge change is calculated (in ampere hours).

15

Object structuring, communication and control:

A systems-driven approach

The last few chapters have dealt with individual topics of OO design. What these show is that there is no single, agreed way of developing software; the designer has a choice of techniques. Some of these tend to concentrate on one aspect to the detriment of others (for example, over-emphasizing the object model). This results in a fragmented – and perhaps abstract – design, often isolated from implementation issues.

There are many driving forces behind the choice of technique: company policy, CASE tool support, personal prejudices and commercial hype, to name but a few. However, when making decisions, bear in mind one guiding rule. Whichever method is used, the steps through design and implementation must be clear, logical and simple. Otherwise be prepared for many trials and tribulations.

This chapter has one primary objective: to define a clear and workable design framework for the development of the software system. The key to this is first to identify the processors required in a system (multiprocessor/multicomputer structuring). Following this, the task structure of each processor is defined: the multitasking design stage. Finally, a design is produced for each task, one which may be implemented as sequential code. However, to follow the rationale expounded here, it is first necessary:

- to consolidate and extend understanding of object attributes and behaviour
- to show that system-related factors are major driving forces in the development of the object model
- to explain the importance of taking a concurrency-first design approach

Note: the emphasis here is on the *object*, not the class.

15.1   Qualities of objects

15.1.1   Overview

Much of the information contained here is essentially review and consolidation of earlier work. What it does, though, is pull together various aspects of object features to form an integrated view.

There are four major factors to be considered when structuring object-based systems (Figure 15.1):

- object type
- interfacing relationships between objects
- grouping of objects – hierarchy and decomposition
- object control mechanisms

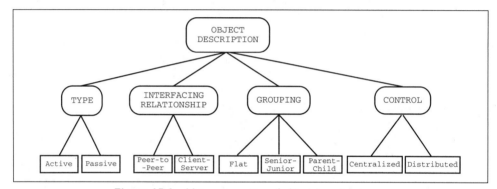

Figure 15.1   Major properties of object-based systems.

It should be clear that these aspects are, in many cases, interdependent. Let us consider each in turn, beginning with types.

15.1.2   Object type

There are basically two object types, concurrent (*active*) and sequential (here called *passive*) (Figure 15.2).

Active objects (Figure 15.2(a)) execute simultaneously (concurrently). Inter-object communication is usually achieved via message passing which, in many cases, is bidirectional. Also, when an object sends a message to a second object, it may or may not wait for a reply. That is, communication may be non-blocking or blocking, examples being given in Figure 15.2(a).

In practical systems there are two forms of concurrency: real and apparent. Real (true) concurrency can only be achieved by using hardware. This occurs in multiprocessor and in multicomputer systems. Here there is a natural mapping of processors to objects. True concurrency also arises where dedicated hardware is used to implement specific functions within a processor design (for example, using an application-specific integrated circuit (ASIC) to perform a fast Fourier transform of a digi-

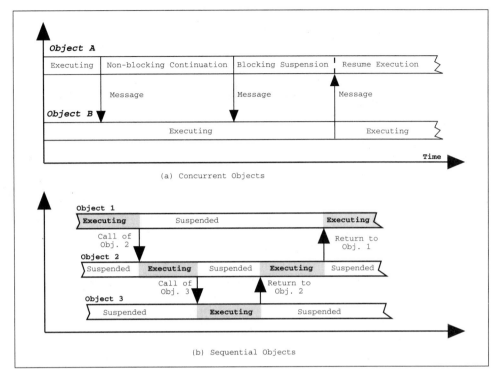

Figure 15.2   Concurrent vs. sequential objects.

tal signal). In this case the ASIC itself can be treated as a concurrently executing object.

Apparent concurrency takes place in multitasking and/or interrupt-driven designs. Hence, *within* a processor, a task maps simply and logically onto an object. Note that for multitasking designs, the application software must generally be supported by a real-time executive (RTEX).

Contrast this with a system which consists of passive objects (Figure 15.2(b)). Here, one, and only one, object ever executes at any one time. That is, if an object calls on a second object, the first one suspends while the second executes. Thus the object model can be implemented using standard sequential code constructs.

There is an important message for the designer here: design and implementation are inextricably linked. If, for instance, a design requires that objects *must* execute in parallel – but the actual hardware cannot support this – then great grief will result. Or take, for example, designing for implementation on a single processor which is equipped with an RTEX. The designer isn't constrained in the number, structuring and communication aspects of the objects. Yet the run-time performance is profoundly affected by such factors. Finally, object orientation encourages the designer to think in terms of parallel activities. But where the design is implemented using passive objects the result may be complex interactive sequential software.

15.1.3 Interfacing relationships

Let us now move on and look at object interfacing relationships (Figure 15.3).

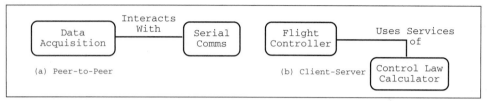

Figure 15.3 Interfacing relationships – peer-to-peer and client–server.

In a peer-to-peer relationship (Figure 15.3(a)), any object can call on any other object. Here, as an example, a data acquisition object interacts with a serial comms object. Information is passed in both directions (generally true of peer-to-peer dealings). As a result, object 1 must have details of the interface of object 2. Likewise, object 2 must understand the features of the object 1 interface.

Figure 15.3(b) shows an example of a client–server relationship. Here the client, a flight controller object (object 1), makes use of the control law server, object 2. To do this, object 1 must know how to access (use) object 2. However, there is no need for object 2 to understand anything about object 1.

Note that interfacing aspects say nothing about the use of passive or active objects. But it will become clear during design that these *do* affect the choice of object type. For instance, a peer-to-peer relationship is best implemented using active objects. By contrast, client–server operation is not so clear-cut. In some applications this is most easily supported using passive objects. In others – a distributed system for example – it may be essential to use active objects.

15.1.4 Grouping objects – hierarchy and decomposition

Object grouping (Figure 15.4) is closely related to, but not quite the same as, relationships.

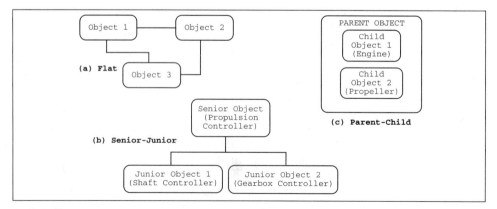

Figure 15.4 Object grouping.

Note that the notation used here is an *ad hoc* one.

In the simplest case (Figure 15.4(a)), the organization is a 'flat' one; that is, it contains no hierarchy, nor is there any object decomposition. The relationships could be peer-to-peer or client–server (or if you *do* want to confuse people, a mixture); it isn't possible to tell this from the diagram. Such structures are most often met in small designs.

With larger and/or complex systems, it may be very useful to organize objects in a hierarchical manner (Figure 15.4(b)). This is called a senior–junior structure. With this, a senior object uses the operations provided by its juniors to achieve its ends (a form of manager–worker collaboration). For instance, a propulsion controller (the senior object) may call on both shaft and gearbox controllers (the juniors) in order to fulfil its function.

It might seem that the senior–junior grouping is the same as a client–server relationship. Not so (although in practice a particular implementation may turn out in this way). To clarify this, take the example of Figure 15.4(b). Here the shaft controller not only responds to commands from the propulsion controller; it may also generate requests for actions to be carried out by other objects. All such actions, though, are directed to, and controlled by, the senior object. However, the primary issue here is not control *per se*. Rather, it is how the objects are *organized* to perform the desired system function.

The hierarchy can be extended to as many levels as desired. It is sensible, though, to keep these to a minimum; wherever possible start off by aiming for a flat structure.

Figure 15.4(c) illustrates the basics of a parent–child arrangement. This also indicates a form of hierarchy, but is really quite different from the previous case. Here the child objects, taken together, implement the function defined by the parent. As an example, the shaft controller may in fact consist of both an engine unit and a propeller unit; taken together they provide the shaft control facility. This can be viewed as aggregation.

In essence, the senior–junior hierarchy is similar to that of the module structure chart (Chapter 3); for *module* read *object*. The parent–child decomposition can be seen to be like that of the program structure chart (Chapter 2). In Figure 15.4(c), the parent object is equivalent to the top level of the chart; the child objects are the same as leaf items.

It is important to realize that the objects in Figures 15.4(a) and (b) may, if desired, be decomposed into child objects.

No mention has been made here of inheritance. The reason is simple, although it may well be disputed by other designers. In this chapter, design is concerned almost entirely with application – not service – software (application and service software are discussed in Chapter 3), and, at the application level, most objects are singular. That is, each class has only one instantiation. Moreover, personal practical experience indicates that there is limited scope for reuse of application software. Thus, in these circumstances, inheritance offers few benefits yet introduces extra complexity.

15.1.5 Control aspects

We come now to the question of how control is exercised in our design. The two extremes are fully centralized and fully distributed (Figure 15.5).

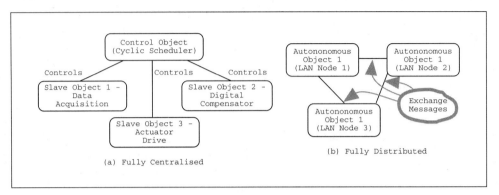

Figure 15.5 Centralized vs. distributed control.

With fully centralized control (Figure 15.5(a)), all decision-making is housed in one object (the control object). At the other extreme – fully distributed (Figure 15.5(b)) – control functions are distributed among the set of system objects.

In a fully centralized system, the control object treats all others as slaves. It dictates what, when and why actions should be taken. The slaves respond to commands in a predefined manner. The example here is that of a simple cyclic scheduler. Here, for example, scheduling control is performed by the control object: the scheduler itself. This has three slave objects, each performing a particular task. The scheduler activates first the data acquisition object, to gather and condition data. On completion of this work, the digital compensator is instructed to process the acquired data. Finally, the actuator drive object is instructed to send out appropriate control signals.

With a fully distributed system, decision-making is distributed across the system. This approach, for instance, is used in the access control mechanism of Ethernet networks. Here each network node is autonomous, all access decisions being made locally. However, they are made in conjunction with other nodes (objects) by sending messages out onto the network. In essence we have a set of federalized, collaborative and cooperating objects.

Object grouping and object control are certainly interrelated. However, do not confuse the two. One deals with structuring, the other with control. To clarify this, compare Figure 15.4(b) with Figure 15.5(a). In the first, the propulsion controller object has a clearly defined task. In order to carry this out it calls on the resources of its juniors. In the second, the cyclic scheduler has no knowledge of the work performed by its slaves. It merely carries out a set of predefined operations: start task, run for set time, stop task.

15.2 Tackling concurrency – identifying the processors

15.2.1 Background

The first rule of embedded systems design? System requirements should drive the software, not the other way round. You don't have to do it like that, of course. And let me assure you that you will find software designers who disagree with this rule. So why not take the opposite approach? This may, after all, produce an optimal software design. True; unfortunately, there is no guarantee whatsoever that the resulting *system* is optimal. And do remember what our basic objectives are: to meet a set of system requirements.

By taking this as a starting point, it is found that the earliest design decisions relate to processor organization. A number of factors drive us down this road, important ones being:

- physical organization (for example, public utilities, factory (manufacturing) applications, vehicle systems)
- computer performance (for example, simulation, array processing, weapon systems)
- safety (for example, fly-by-wire systems, reactor control, medical treatment)

These cover a very large range of applications and, of course, are not mutually exclusive. So it is worth looking into them in a little more detail, starting with physical layouts.

The utilities (gas, electricity, water) have systems which are large, complex and geographically dispersed. Modern systems rely heavily on distributed computerized structures, for reasons of reliability, performance and flexibility (software problems are the penalties to be paid for such improvements). The number and siting of processors are determined mainly by such factors, *not* software issues.

Where performance (response time, throughput and so on) is of concern, a single processor may just not be powerful enough; a number have to be used. This is especially true for fast signal processing functions (to put this in perspective, one air-to-air missile system currently in development uses five PC601 microprocessors). In an ideal world, a full assessment of the processing requirements would be made; then the processor configuration defined. Reality tends to be different. In order to meet project time-scales, hardware and software design are usually carried out in parallel, which means that decisions regarding processor structure *have* to be made at a very early stage of a project.

For safety-critical systems, redundant components are essential. This applies to all items – sensors, actuators, displays and so on – not only to computers. Triple-redundancy is commonplace, while for highly critical systems, full quad-redundancy is used. Such requirements, although they predate the digital computer, raise a special issue in processor-based systems: the prevention of common-mode software failures. Thus not only is there a need to use redundant computers; a mix of processor types, programming languages and software development groups is also called for.

It is important to point out that quite a different approach would probably be used for developing data-intensive systems (such as management information systems, distributed databases and financial planning services). Modern systems rely heavily on the use of distributed client–server structures. As a result there is considerable flexibility in choosing the distribution of both hardware and software. Such problems are not considered here.

15.2.2   An overview of the design process

To illustrate the concurrency-first approach, take an example of a mainstream application: a distributed networked system (Figure 15.6).

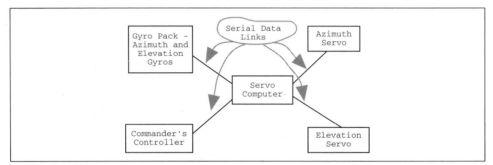

Figure 15.6   Example – distributed networked control system.

Here we have a distributed version of the weapon servo system of Figure 14.12. It consists of five separate units: a gyro pack, commander's controller, two servos and a servo computer. The gyro pack contains two gyros, azimuth and elevation. Communication, at the electrical level, is implemented using serial data links. This arrangement has been devised in order to simplify and minimize vehicle cabling (compared with hardwired systems). Here there is true concurrency, which has a profound effect on the object model.

Figure 15.5 gives only one view of the system. It is also necessary to define its function, as for instance in Figure 15.7.

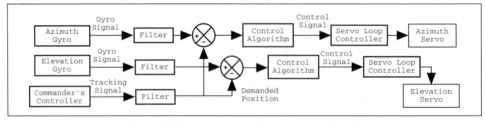

Figure 15.7   Control system functional diagram.

Observe that this diagram gives a good overall view of system operation *and* the interrelation of its subsystems.

At this stage there is no great need to delve into the details of such functions. What we have to do, however, is decide how to map the functions onto objects. This process must also take into account the physical aspects of the system. Here the set of major objects tends to be closely related to the overall system design. Thus, in developing the object model, two factors must first be addressed (Figure 15.8):

- physical organization
- functional operation

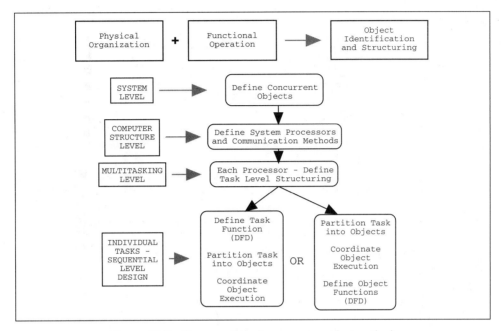

Figure 15.8 The essentials of a concurrency-first method.

This approach may seem simplistic. However, in practice it is natural and straight-forward (and works well). To reiterate: the overall structure is dictated very much by the system components, their functionality and their physical location. For this example, the result is the object diagram of Figure 15.9.

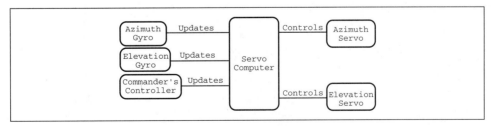

Figure 15.9 Control system object diagram.

Other system-related factors also influence design decisions. For example, it may be essential to ensure that both the azimuth and elevation controls are tightly synchronized. Stringent timing specifications may have to be met. Also, the gyro and servo components may have quite limited computing power. The result (for this design) is a decision to include a servo computer within the overall system.

By definition, system-related factors are system-specific. Thus it is hard to generalize about such issues; they must be evaluated on a case-by-case basis.

It is a simple step from the object diagram of Figure 15.9 to the object message diagram (Figure 15.10).

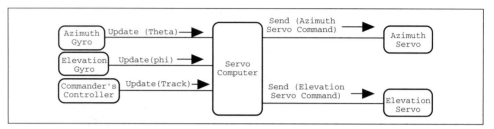

Figure 15.10 Object message diagram.

These are identical apart from the attached text information. Note, however, its function: to detail clearly and explicitly the interactions which take place between the objects. It is also appropriate to consider the grouping and control aspects of objects during these early stages.

At this point we have defined:

- all the concurrent objects
- the general functionality of each object
- the interaction between objects
- object grouping and control

Two points should be noted:

- When designing the application software, it is much more natural to talk about specific objects, not classes.
- At the application level there tends to be a one-to-one class/object relationship.

What the object message diagram gives is essentially a static view of the system – a snapshot of the messaging between objects. What is also needed is information on how the objects interact *dynamically*. To do this a set of scenarios are analysed with the aid of event trace diagrams (Figure 15.11).

In the first instance, normal modes of operation are identified. For example, at sample update time t_0, the gyro pack sends θ and ϕ values to the servo computer. On receipt of the information, the servo command signals are computed (which takes a finite amount of time). At the end of the computation time, t_1, the commands are transmitted to the two servo units. Each unit now responds by positioning its servo, completing at time t_2. This sequence of actions forms one complete scenario; others can be extracted from the event trace diagram.

When this task is complete, all normal operational scenarios will have been defined. The next task – a most important one – is to check that all system timing

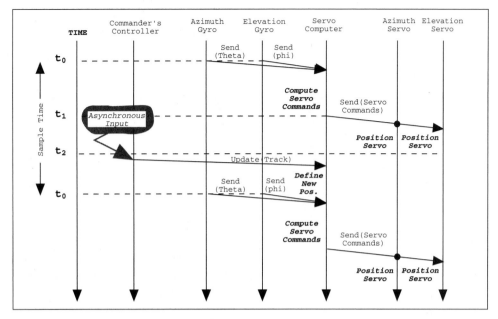

Figure 15.11   Event trace diagram.

(performance) requirements are met. To do this, performance modelling must be carried out. How such modelling is done will depend on individual circumstances. Facilities may, if you are fortunate, be provided within a CASE tool suite. Other options include the use of simulation tools, modelling tools or predictive calculations. This last method works well for totally deterministic situations – somewhat of a limitation, unfortunately. We run into difficulties when statistical variations have to be taken into account. However, if worst-case values are used, the results can be treated with some confidence.

At this stage the basic system error modes can be investigated. From such scenarios a preliminary exception-handling strategy can be prescribed.

What has been done so far is to generate a 'first-cut' design. Yet almost without exception you will need to retread your steps. Why? Because these individual stages are not isolated 'islands'; decisions made in one area may well produce significant effects in others. Thus, in general, the design process is continued iteratively (Figure 15.12).

It ends when the designer is satisfied with the software structure at the multiprocessor level. In practice, of course, there is rarely a clear-cut finishing point; real design is a constant ongoing activity.

15.3   Multitasking issues

The next step is to look into each processor in turn. Assume that we choose to implement the design using a multitasking solution. Consequently the software

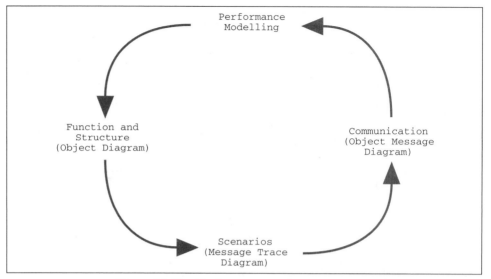

Figure 15.12   The basic iterative design procedure.

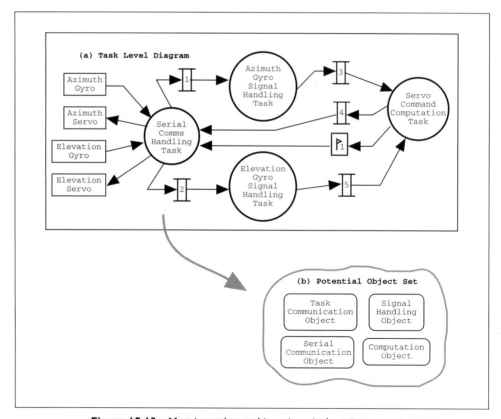

Figure 15.13   Mapping tasks to objects in a single-processor unit.

consists of a set of concurrent tasks and related task intercommunication components. To represent this, a task-level diagram is used. Such a diagram is that of Figure 15.13(a), produced for the servo computer object of Figure 15.9.

Information is sent around the system using messages, while coordination is attained via synchronization components. The notation used here – although not any specific type – will be familiar to designers of multitasking systems. Observe that the gyros and servos are shown as *devices* external to the computer software. This is a conceptual view of the problem; in physical terms the computer deals with a set of serial communications signals. Also hidden from view is the driving engine of the multitasking design: the executive or operating system.

It can be seen that there is a natural mapping of tasks and communication components to objects. In Figure 15.13 for instance, the task model (Figure 15.13(a)) maps to the object model of Figure 15.13(b). This initial object model is then iteratively refined and elaborated, following the route given in Figure 15.12. When a satisfactory result is attained, work can proceed into the next stage: the design of individual tasks.

15.4 Task design

For the moment we will ignore how tasks are managed in the processor system. Our purpose now is to devise the object structure of each task *in such a way that it can actually be built*. In doing so one fact must be kept in mind: a task is implemented as sequential code.

A powerful way to get at the object structure is to produce a DFD for the task object – defined here as the Object DFD (ODFD). Let us apply this to the Azimuth Gyro Signal Handling Task (or object) of Figure 15.13. The result is shown in Figure 15.14.

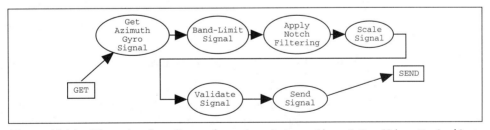

Figure 15.14 Object data flow diagram for Azimuth Gyro Signal Handling Task **object.**

Here the gyro signal is obtained (from a task communication channel) by the Get process. It is band-limited, notch-filtered and then scaled. Following this a signal validation check is performed. If the test is successful, the signal is sent out to another task communication channel.

Assuming the solution is acceptable, the next move is to group the individual processes together to form objects. In this example four groups have been identified (Figure 15.15):

- getting the signal (Reader)
- signal processing (Signal Processor)
- signal validation (Validation) and
- sending on the processed signal (Sender)

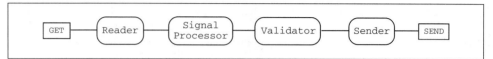

Figure 15.15   Object partitioning of the object DFD of Figure 15.14.

It seems reasonable to implement the Gyro Signal Handling object using a parent–child structure. But what is the most appropriate control structure? Let us show how system requirements affect such decisions. It is specified that the gyro signals be sampled every 5 ms. Hence a design decision is made to include an interrupt-driven child object, Signal Handler Manager, in the design (Figure 15.16).

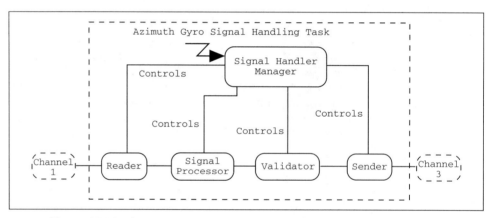

Figure 15.16   Object diagram for Azimuth Gyro Signal Handling object.

This acts as the overall manager of the child objects. When an interrupt occurs, it first invokes Reader. Following this, the Signal Processor is used, then Validator, and finally Sender.

Each individual object may now be constructed using, in the simplest form, procedures.

You might argue that a single class, Gyro Signal Handler, should be constructed. Then both the azimuth and elevation signal handlers would be derived using inheritance. This is a valid comment, but frankly, is it worth the bother of dealing with inheritance for just two objects?

Further discussion *vis-à-vis* design will be deferred to the design example of Chapter 16.

15.5 Multitasking design – diagram to code

In earlier chapters we covered the majority of code constructs used in OO design. The one topic not examined so far in detail is that of concurrency (more specifically quasi-concurrency or multitasking). To implement larger multitasking designs, it is recommended that standard commercial real-time executives be used. These are many and varied, needing specialized knowledge to apply them. For that reason they are not dealt with in this text. Here we shall limit ourselves to simpler designs, where concurrency is achieved using interrupt-driven code.

There is a major problem in demonstrating, via code examples, the basics of interrupt operations. That is, such techniques depend on the:

- processor type
- hardware configuration
- compiler

The aim here is to produce code that can be executed for learning purposes. Thus all examples are devised to run on a standard PC when compiled by the Borland C++ compiler (Version 4.5). These programs show how the basic set of multitasking design structures (Figure 15.17) may be implemented.

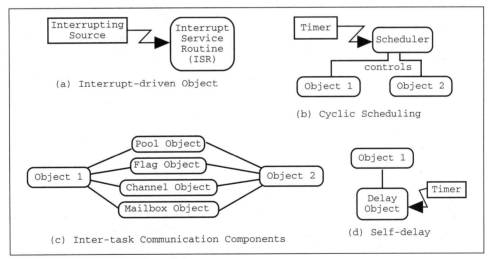

Figure 15.17 Basic structures in multitasking design.

Central to these is the interrupt-driven object (Figure 15.7(a)), identified as ISR (Interrupt Service Routine). The complete construct comprises the interrupt and the ISR. A zig-zag line or 'lightning flash' is used to denote the interrupt (a notation very widely used in the embedded-systems world).

When the interrupt occurs, the code of object ISR is executed. However, to get this to actually work, several actions have to be carried out behind the scenes. To see why, some knowledge of interrupt operations is required.

Any particular processor system can support a fixed number of interrupts (typically ranging from 2 to 256). Each individual interrupt (if used) must be connected to a specific ISR. This ensures that when an interrupt is activated, the correct service routine is executed. Various methods are used to achieve this automatic routing or 'vectoring'. In PC systems:

- Each interrupt has a defined location in RAM.
- All interrupts are grouped together in one area of memory (the *interrupt vector table*).
- Each location is used to hold the address of its related ISR.
- Each location is 'hard-wired' to a specific interrupt number.
- When an interrupt is activated, the vector table is accessed automatically. The information stored there then vectors the processor to the correct ISR.
- On completion of the routine, the program which was interrupted is restored to its original state (that which pertained when the interrupt occurred).

By using standard compiler-supplied routines, saving and restoring of processor information is done 'automatically'. There is no need for the programmer to get involved in such highly detailed operations.

The first program (Listing 15.1) merely introduces some basic operations associated with interrupts. To demonstrate this, a software-generated interrupt, number 255, is used (for more information, consult your compiler manual).

Here the core aspect is the interrupt service routine itself. This is implemented as a function (`SetValue`), the code of the ISR being encapsulated within the function. Its declaration format explicitly defines that it is an interrupt routine. Within the ISR, the first action is to disable all interrupts (and so prevent the routine itself from being interrupted). It then sets `Count` to 50. The final action is to re-enable the processor interrupts. Note that only in some cases is it necessary to disable interrupts while running the ISR.

You will also see that a second interrupt routine is declared. This, `OldValue`, is a pointer to – address of – an interrupt function. It is used in this program only as a temporary storage location.

In `main`, we first save the information stored at vector location 255 (so that it can be restored later). Next the new ISR is installed or 'planted', using the Borland `_dos_setvect` function. The result is that function `SetValue` is associated with vector 255. Following this a software interrupt is generated by the call `geninterrupt`, resulting in the execution of `SetValue`. Return to the calling program is automatically carried out on completion of the ISR. At this point the original ISR is restored by the call `_dos_setvect`.

A note in passing. Interrupts under DOS are not re-entrant. Therefore, do not use any operations within the ISR which call on processor interrupts (`cout` and `cin`, for example). Unfortunately, this severely limits the code functions which can be used for demonstration.

Moving on, Listing 15.2 shows how interrupts can be triggered by hardware.

Here the on-board PC timer is used to activate the interrupt `LoopTimer`. Each time the interrupt runs (approximately every 55 ms), the variable `ElapsedTime` is incre-

```
#include <iostream.h>
#include <dos.h>

void interrupt SetValue(...);
void interrupt (*OldValue)(...);

int Count =0;

void main()
{
    cout << "\nProgram IntDemo3.cpp";
    cout << "\nThe value of Count is  " << Count;

    /* Saving the original interrupt, Int255  */
    OldValue = _dos_getvect(255);

    /*    Install the new ISR    */
    _dos_setvect (255, SetValue);

    /* Software call of interrupt 255 */
    geninterrupt(255);

    /* Replace the original ISR */
    _dos_setvect (255, OldValue);

    cout << "\nThe new value of Count is  " << Count;

}

void interrupt SetValue(...){
    disable();
    Count = 255;
    enable();
}
```

Listing 15.1 Introduction to interrupts, showing full interrupt operation.
(Note: DOS is not re-entrant; hence the interrupt routine is very simple.)

mented. This item is used within the main or 'background' program. The second (final) action is to call the DOS timer interrupt routine. Its purpose is to ensure that a further interrupt is generated.

In main, the ISR is planted at vector address 8. This location is, by design, connected to the hardware timer. Following this the program enters a loop which is terminated when a key on the keyboard is pressed. The loop puts out a message to the screen every 1.1 s (approximately).

Listing 15.3 shows how the technique can be used to implement cyclic scheduling (Figure 15.17(b)).

Here the two objects to be scheduled are RobotLoop and RobotDisplay.

For simplicity the scheduler object is built from the code of main. RobotLoop is designed to run every 1.1 s, RobotDisplay every 2.75 s.

Next for consideration is the issue of inter-task communication. As discussed

```
#include <conio.h>
#include <iostream.h>
#include <dos.h>

void interrupt LoopTimer(...);
void interrupt (*DosTimer)(...);

int Period = 20;
int ElapsedTime =0;

void main()
{
    cout << "\nProgram Cyc_1obj.cpp";

    DosTimer = _dos_getvect(8);
    _dos_setvect (8, LoopTimer);
    while (! kbhit()) {
        if (ElapsedTime >= Period) {
            cout << "\nLoop Running";
            ElapsedTime = 0;
        }//end if
    } // end while
    _dos_setvect (8,DosTimer );
}//end main

void interrupt LoopTimer(...){
    ElapsedTime++;
    DosTimer();
}
```

Listing 15.2 Simple cyclic scheduling of a single object, using timing provided by the standard DOS timer to give a periodic time of 1.1 s.

earlier, each task maps to an object (which may well be a composite one). And, of course, these objects interact with each other. The question is: how should such interactions be handled in OO design? In this text the following approach is taken:

- All inter-task communication is shown explicitly.
- Such communication is done by message passing.
- All information is transmitted via communication components (flags, pools, channels, mailboxes; see Chapter 9).
- Specific components are used in specific applications.
- Each component is implemented as an object.

Figure 15.17(c) illustrates two objects communicating via (amongst others) a pool object. This action is demonstrated by the code of Listing 15.4.

Here the two objects are RobotLoop (object 1) and RobotDisplay (object 2). RobotLoop is an interrupt-driven object (see the ISR), while RobotDisplay is activated by main. When the timer interrupt awakens the RobotLoop, it (the object)

```
#include <conio.h>
#include <iostream.h>
#include <dos.h>


class Control {
public:
    void Run() {
        cout << "\nControl Loop Running";
    }
};//end class Control

class Display {
public:
    void Run() {
        cout << "\nDisplay Running";
    }
};//end class Display

//Global information for time management
void interrupt LoopTimer(...);
void interrupt (*DosTimer)(...);
volatile int RobotTime = 0;
volatile int DisplayTime = 0;

void main()
{
int RobotPeriod = 20;
int DisplayPeriod = 50;
Control RobotLoop;
Display RobotDisplay;

    cout << "\nProgram Listing 15.3 - Sched1.cpp";
    DosTimer = _dos_getvect(8);
    _dos_setvect (8, LoopTimer);
    while (! kbhit()) {
        if (RobotTime >= RobotPeriod) {
            RobotLoop.Run();
            RobotTime = 0;
        }//end if RobotTime
        if (DisplayTime >= DisplayPeriod) {
            RobotDisplay.Run();
            DisplayTime = 0;
        }//end if DisplayTime
    } // end while !kbhit
    _dos_setvect (8,DosTimer );
}//end main

void interrupt LoopTimer(...){
    RobotTime++;
    DisplayTime++;
    DosTimer();
}
```

Listing 15.3   Simple cyclic scheduling of two objects, using timing provided by the standard DOS timer to give a periodic time of 1.1 s.

```
/*******************************************/
/* This shows interobject (task) communication using */
/* a pool object                                      */
/*******************************************/
#include <conio.h>
#include <iostream.h>
#include <dos.h>
enum Status {Off, On};
enum Slot {One, Two};
class Pool;

class Display {
public:
        void Run();
        void GetStatus();
        void DefinePoolObject (Pool &PoolObject);
        void AddOfPoolObject();
private:
        Pool *pPool1;
};//end class Display

class Pool {
        Status PoolStatus;
public:
        void SetStatusOn() {
                PoolStatus = On;
        }//
        void SetStatusOff() {
                PoolStatus = Off;
        }//
        Status GetStatus() {
                return PoolStatus;
        }//
};//end class Pool

//Global items
Display RobotDisplay;  //The display object
Pool RobotDataPool;    //The pool object
//Global information for time management
void interrupt RobotLoop(...);
void interrupt (*DosTimer)(...);
volatile int RobotTime = 0;
volatile  Slot TimeSlot = One;

void main()
{
int Num;

        cout << "\nProgram Listing 15.4 - Comm1.cpp";
        RobotDisplay.DefinePoolObject(RobotDataPool);
        cin >> Num;
        DosTimer = _dos_getvect(8);
        _dos_setvect (8, RobotLoop);
        RobotDataPool.SetStatusOn();

                RobotDisplay.Run();

        _dos_setvect (8,DosTimer );
}//end main
```

Listing 15.4   Inter-object (task) communication using a pool object.   (continued)

Listing 15.4 (*continued*)

```
/////////////////////////////////////
void interrupt RobotLoop(...){
const int RobotPeriod = 20;

        disable();
        RobotTime++;
        if (RobotTime >= RobotPeriod) {
                if (TimeSlot == One) {
                        RobotDataPool.SetStatusOn();
                        RobotTime = 0;
                        TimeSlot = Two;
          }
           else {
                        RobotDataPool.SetStatusOff();
                        RobotTime = 0;
                        TimeSlot = One;
                }//end if else
        }//end if RobotTime
        enable();
        DosTimer();
}
/////////////////////////////////////

void Display::DefinePoolObject (Pool &PoolObject) {
        cout << "\nDefining the pool object";
        pPool1 = &PoolObject;
};

void Display::AddOfPoolObject() {
        cout << "\nPool1 points to " << pPool1;
};

void Display::GetStatus(){
static Status State;

        cout << "\nNow reading pool status";
        disable();
        State = pPool1->GetStatus();
        enable();
        if (State == On){
                cout << "\nState is ON ON ON ON";
        }
        else
                cout << "\nState is off";
        // end of if else
}

void Display::Run() {
int Num;
char bs = (char)8;
        while (! kbhit()) {
                cout << "\nDisplay Running\n";
                for (Num = 1; Num < 800; Num++)
                        cout << "*" << bs;
                Display::GetStatus();
        } // end while !kbhit
};
```

sends messages (SetStatus) to the pool object, RobotDataPool. These are collected from the pool object by RobotDisplay (using GetStatus). Note how pool accesses are guarded by disabling and enabling of interrupts – thus preventing simultaneous access (*mutual exclusion*).

The final item to look at is that of time delays. In a simple sequential program this could be implemented in software, using loop counting techniques. However, where accurate timing is required or multitasking is used, hardware-based methods are needed. One way to implement delays is to have interrupt-controlled delay objects (Figure 15.17(d)). Here, object 1 calls on the delay object to implement a specific time delay in its program. This is demonstrated in its very basic form in Listing 15.5. The code should be self-explanatory.

```
#include <conio.h>
#include <iostream.h>
#include <dos.h>

void interrupt LoopTimer(...);
void interrupt (*DosTimer)(...);

int Period = 20;
int ElapsedTime =0;

void main()
{
    cout << "\nProgram Delay1.cpp";

    /* Saving the original interrupt  */
        DosTimer = _dos_getvect(8);

    /*    Install the new ISR    */
    _dos_setvect (8, LoopTimer);

    while (! kbhit()) {
        if (ElapsedTime >= Period) {
            cout << "\nLoop Running";
            ElapsedTime = 0;
        }//end if
    } // end while


    /* Replace the original ISR */
    _dos_setvect (8,DosTimer );
}

void interrupt LoopTimer(...){
    ElapsedTime++;
    DosTimer();
}
```

Listing 15.5 Implementation of a simple delay, using timing provided by the standard DOS timer.

Review

On completing this chapter you should now:

- understand that there are many ways to view objects
- know what these views are, and what qualities they express
- appreciate the way the various views affect each other
- realize that the use of active objects has significant implications for the run-time software
- recognize that passive objects are much simpler to implement (than their active counterparts)
- see how system requirements are major driving forces in the structuring of multi-computer and multiprocessor systems
- perceive the value of taking a concurrency-first design approach
- understand the relationship between the multiprocessing model, the multitasking model and those which describe individual tasks
- recognize the need for, and value of, carrying out performance modelling
- see how the object DFD can help in deriving objects within a task

Exercises

15.1 The owner of a small filling station – single pump only – decides to replace his pump attendant with an automated system. Thus unstaffed operation is required. A new type of pump is to be installed. System operation is as follows.

With the nozzle in its housing, the system is to be in available mode. When a customer lifts out the nozzle, the holster switch is operated. This signals the owner in a remote cabin (by illuminating the 'service required' lamp) that a customer requires service. If the owner permits use of the pump (using a push-button switch signal, 'pump on'), operations can proceed. If this signal is not made, the customer will not be allowed to have fuel. It can be assumed that the customer will eventually tire of waiting and put the nozzle back in its holster. At that stage the system will revert to the available mode.

Assume the operation is permitted. The customer inserts the nozzle into the fuel tank, and squeezes the trigger. This operates the trigger switch, which turns on the fuel pump motor, thus pumping fuel into the tank. Pumping stops either when the trigger is released or when the nozzle float switch is operated by a high fuel level.

A flowmeter is fitted in the line. This generates an output proportional to the fuel flow rate. This information is used to calculate the amount of fuel delivered and its cost. Both items are displayed locally, on the pump housing. They are also transmitted to a remote display unit in the cabin.

When the pump is replaced in its holster, the system is put into a standby mode. In this state the pump is not available for use. This is cleared to the available mode by a second push-button switch in the cabin, the 'pump set' switch.

Produce a suitable object-based design for this application, including the following:

- object diagram
- object message diagram
- message trace diagram

Where appropriate, produce the object state diagrams.

15.2 A new microprocessor-based unit is to be designed for access control to a ski-slope drag lift. Its specification/description is given below.

The system consists of an access gate controlled by a card reader. Each card carries a bar code, embedded using magnetic strip technology. When a card is wiped through the reader, then, providing the code is valid, the gate is unlocked. A short beep is sounded and an 'access permitted' lamp is illuminated. The user enters the drag lift area via a turnstile. After this clicks on for one entry, the gate is relocked and the lamp extinguished. If the code is invalid, a long beep is sounded and an 'access denied' lamp is illuminated for 5 s. The system then reverts to normal.

A skier can summon assistance by pressing a 'help' button on the gate unit. This illuminates a lamp in the lift supervisor's cabin, adjacent to the gate area. To extinguish this the supervisor must press an 'acknowledge' button in the cabin.

The supervisor also has an unlock control for the gate. Pressing this button causes the gate to unlock. Releasing it relocks the gate. The locking mechanism is operated by an electrical solenoid. This is a two-coil unit, one coil for locking, one for unlocking. Valid codes are changed each day. Thus it is necessary to program the card reader with the day's code before operations begin. This is done by the supervisor.

When the system is powered up, it goes into standby mode. From this it can be put (by the supervisor) into ready mode or programming mode. The card reader can be programmed only when the system is in programming mode. While in standby or programming, a red 'not-ready' lamp on the gate unit is to be illuminated.

The ready mode is the normal operating condition of the gate, this being shown by a green indicator lamp on the gate unit.

(a) List all physical/electrical items in this system; group them together in their correct physical locations.

(b) Given the geographical aspects of this problem, partition the system into a sensible grouping of subsystems. Specify the method by which subsystems communicate.

(c) For the design, produce the:

- object diagram
- object message diagram
- message trace diagram

(d) Where appropriate, produce the object state diagrams.

16
Design example – chilled water controller:
An object-oriented design solution

We are now in a position to bring together, in one example, the various OO topics from earlier chapters. Specifically, it describes the design and implementation of software for the chilled water (CW) system detailed in Appendix A. The objectives of the chapter are to:

- take the reader through the complete design process, starting with a specification and finishing with source code
- identify the major stages in this process
- define the aims of, and the methods used in, these different stages
- show how concurrency, timing and interfacing aspects significantly influence the design

16.1 Setting the scene

The work described here begins with the assumption that the system and hardware designs are fully defined. Now the concern is to develop the matching software. In practice, software aspects often affect the hardware, possibly leading to design changes. However, for this exercise, the hardware is considered to be fixed (at a design freeze stage).

The approach taken here is to carry out the work in four stages (Figure 16.1):

- Stage 1 – Develop an ideal object model.
- Stage 2 – Extend this – by introducing concurrency, timing and interfacing issues – into a basic multitasking object model.
- Stage 3 – Fully develop a realistic object model.
- Stage 4 – Implement this in source code.

Central to the process is the concept of *elaboration*. That is, each succeeding stage may *add* to, but should not distort, earlier work. Full traceability is required; no 'magic' is permitted.

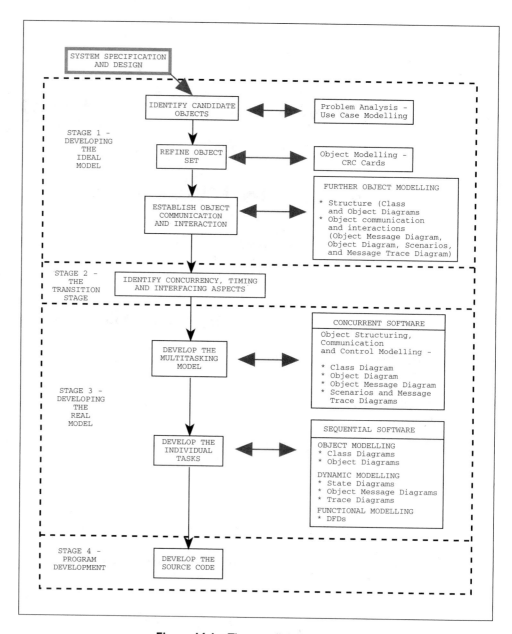

Figure 16.1 The overall design process.

The basic ideas are now described in some detail. However, for reasons already given, only major aspects of the development are shown. Much detail is omitted, although all important topics are covered in depth.

16.2   Stage 1 – developing the ideal object model

16.2.1   Introduction

The purpose of this first section of work is to establish the essentials of the design. In essence it seeks to answer the questions:

- What have we got in this system?
- What is the system *software* supposed to do?
- What sort of object model will satisfy these software objectives?

To answer the first question, it is *strongly* recommended that a context diagram such as Figure 10.1 (or something similar) is produced. Many OO techniques pay little or no attention to such aspects. Frequently design methods concentrate almost exclusively on software issues – system aspects are a sideshow (the word *myopic* springs to mind). Do not go down this dangerous, narrow-minded and unreal path. Remember, the context diagram presents an outside view of the software system. What it does is allow us to cross-check the software interfaces with the system and hardware structures.

The answer to the second question – *What is the system software supposed to do?* – can be found in the system design documentation. It may be that this also includes a detailed software specification. For the example discussed here, such a specification has not been produced. Thus the overall design process begins by evaluating the system specification and the **system** design documentation (Figure 16.1). From these we must:

- establish precisely what the aims of the software are
- identify *candidate* objects which satisfy these aims

These can be tackled in many ways. Here the chosen method is based on Jacobson's *use case* technique.

The next action is refinement of the candidate object set. Its purpose is to define a minimum, essential, set of classes which satisfy system objectives. Of primary interest is the development of classes and their relationships. Central to this is the application of the CRC object development method. The final part in developing the ideal model relates to object communication and interaction scenarios.

Note 1: In this chapter most of the design diagrams have been produced using the SELECT OMT CASE tool. This, however, does not *directly* support the full set of OO diagrams used here, specifically the trace and object message ones. These were generated using a free-form diagram editor.

Note 2: During the initial stages of the design, no particular distinction is made between objects and classes. Thus the words tend to be used interchangeably. The reason for this will become clear later.

16.2.2   Problem analysis – use case modelling

Use case modelling has its roots in business systems. Its basic purpose is to specify the requirements of a system *from the external point of view*. Those items which interact with – and are external to – the software system are called actors. The method aims to define and document the various ways in which actors use the system (hence the name). Normally it is carried out as a three-part process:

- First, identify actors and their roles.
- Second, generate an informal text description of the use cases.
- Lastly, define use case object interactions in detail using *Object Interaction Diagrams* (OIDs).

Note: here the production of OIDs is omitted.

These same ideas can also be applied to real-time systems. Here, though, the concept of an actor must be thought of in the widest sense – anything which interacts with the software. This includes people and equipment. Such information is held in the system design documents. Moreover, most (sometimes all) of it is contained within the context diagram. It must be reiterated, however, that use case modelling is aimed very much at extracting *system* requirements. Hence it would also be appropriate to apply it during the system design phase (Appendix A).

Identifying actors and their roles
In the chilled water system, the following actors exist:

- local operator
- remote operator
- the chilled water plant itself

For each actor, a brief but comprehensive role description is provided, namely:

(i) Local operator: the local operator is responsible for running the plant from a position in the machinery spaces. Functions include:

- resetting the plant on power-up
- starting and stopping the plant from the local position
- tripping the plant in abnormal circumstances

(ii) Remote operator: the remote operator is responsible for overseeing plant operation from a remote control position. Functions include:

- starting the plant once it is available to start
- tripping the plant
- monitoring plant loading and alarm conditions

(iii) Plant: the plant is required to deliver chilled water, at a controlled temperature, to the system air treatment units.

Informal text description of the use cases
The next step is to define how the actors use the system. In many cases there is a one-to-one link between actors and use cases. In other situations, particular use

cases may be associated with a number of actors. And, not surprisingly, one actor may be involved with numerous use cases.

One systematic way to proceed when producing the text description is to:

- Take an individual actor.
- Define all applicable use cases informally in text form.
- Repeat for another actor, until all are dealt with.
- Look for commonality amongst the use cases.

This is demonstrated in the following examples. These, of course, are only a few of the total number of possible use cases in the CW system.

(i) Plant

Use case – Put power on
When power is applied the controller:

1. Trips the motor contactor
2. Activates the master alarm
3. Activates the 'power failed' display
4. Sets the state display to 'Reset'
5. Sets the plant loading to 0%
6. Inhibits the low oil pressure alarm
7. Disables the temperature control loop

Use case – Generate alarm
When a plant alarm (excluding motor trip) occurs, the controller:

1. Trips the motor contactor
2. Activates the master alarm
3. Shows the cause of the alarm (the primary alarm)
4. Inhibits further (secondary) alarms
5. Sets the plant loading to 0%
6. Sets the state display to 'Reset'
7. Inhibits the low oil pressure alarm
8. Disables the temperature control loop

(ii) Local operator

Use case – Select start
When the local operator selects start, then if the plant is available (all alarms cleared down and the motor contactor reset), the controller permits energizing of the motor contactor.

(iii) Remote operator

Use case – Select start
When the local operator selects start, then if the plant is available (all alarms cleared down and the motor contactor reset), the controller permits energizing of the motor contactor.

The above is an example where both use cases are identical. This therefore translates to a single system use case.

Use case – Trip plant

When the remote operator selects 'trip plant' the controller:

1. Trips the motor contactor
2. Activates the master alarm
3. Shows the cause of the alarm (the primary alarm)
4. Inhibits further (secondary) alarms
5. Sets the plant loading to 0%
6. Sets the state display to 'Reset'
7. Inhibits the low oil pressure alarm
8. Disables the temperature control loop

It can be seen that `Trip Plant` is identical to `Generate alarm`. We can thus rename them both if we choose to. If we do, then the original use case names need to be amended. Here, for example, a new name, `Trip system`, is selected.

As the text information is generated, a corresponding use case diagram can be produced (Figure 16.2).

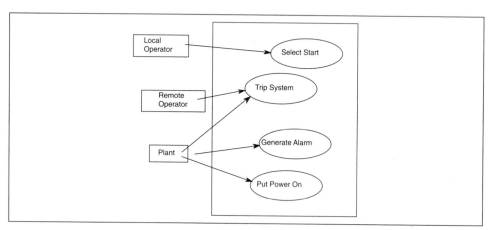

Figure 16.2   System use cases (part).

This is continued until the text descriptions and the use case diagram are complete.

One technique used to identify candidate objects is to extract significant nouns from the text descriptions. For example, in `Put power on`, we have `contactor`, `alarm`, `display` and `control loop`. This leads to an *initial* list of potential objects. For the design example the following were among those included in the initial list (derived from the use case `Put power on`):

- controller
- contactor
- alarms
- state display
- loading

The list is completed by extracting all suitable candidates from the complete set of use cases. This, however, is only the beginning: revision is always necessary. As a result, the process is an iterative one. Moreover, eventual choices are also heavily influenced by system specification and design aspects. Bear in mind that, by now, a great deal is known about the system and its requirements. Thus, for the experienced designer, selecting good candidate classes is not too difficult.

Many initial objects are quite detailed and low-level. Thus at this stage it may be better to subsume them (include them) in higher level objects. Be prepared for much revision, iteration and discussion when developing the class system.

For the CW design the following set of candidate objects were eventually defined:

- alarm and protection
- controller
- communication
- compressor
- display
- timer
- water
- valve

Be clear on one point. While it is possible to give guidance on class selection, the process cannot be automated. Design, by its very nature, is an intellectually challenging process. Further, as you may have already noted, the procedure is a highly subjective one.

16.2.3 Object modelling with CRC cards

The next step in the design process is to refine the initial object set. As noted earlier, CRC modelling techniques are invoked. The fundamentals of the method have already been described (see Chapter 12); if necessary re-read it now. An essential aspect is the use of CRC cards as part of an interactive (preferably group) design session. It isn't feasible to describe such sessions in this one chapter. Therefore only the final card versions are shown (Table 16.1).

Observe that the original card layouts have been extended to include timing information and external interfacing (I/O devices).

16.2.4 Establishing object communication and interaction

Using the CRC card information we can now generate the class diagram (Figure 16.3).

Table 16.1 CRC cards.

CLASS: VALVE	
RESPONSIBILITIES Energize De-energize Set initial state Control rate of loading ⟶	COLLABORATORS General – TIMER TIMER
TIMING DATA Rate of Loading – 1 s resolution 25% to 100% loading change – 1 minute min. 100% to 25% loading change – 1 minute min. No. 2 chiller valve – energize for 20 s on start-up	DEVICE I/O OUT: Chiller and loader valve signals IN: None

CLASS: WATER MONITOR	
RESPONSIBILITIES Compute required loading ⟶ Set loading demand ⟶ Set initial state Trip on <25% load demand ⟶	COLLABORATORS General – TIMER TIMER VALVE, TIMER ALARM
TIMING DATA Periodic, 1 s sampling	DEVICE I/O IN: Return water temperature Contractor on/off signal OUT: None

CLASS: REMOTE COMMS	
RESPONSIBILITIES Send data ⟶ Receive data Signal integrity check ⟶ Trip plant ⟶	COLLABORATORS General – TIMER DISPLAY TIMER PROTECTION
TIMING DATA Rx/Tx line data – μs region Update Tx data – 1 s rate Respond to Rx data – 1 s rate	DEVICE I/O OUT: Serial Tx data IN: Serial Rx data

CLASS: DISPLAY	
RESPONSIBILITIES Display alarm status Display loading status Display status (remote) ————▶	COLLABORATORS General – TIMER REMOTE COMMS
TIMING DATA I s update	DEVICE I/O OUT: Alarm and state display signals

CLASS: ALARM	
RESPONSIBILITIES Set initial state ————————▶ Handle plant alarms ——————▶ Define alarm state ——————▶	COLLABORATORS General – TIMER DISPLAY, PROTECTION TIMER DISPLAY

TIMING DATA
 	
0.5 s update
LOP alarm – 20 s override on start-up
	DEVICE I/O
	
	OUT: None
	IN: Plant alarm signals
	    Power supply signal
	    Alarm cancel command
	    Plant trip command
	    Contractor tripped signal
	    Contractor on/off signal

CLASS: PROTECTION	
RESPONSIBILITIES Trip plant Remove plant trip Enable plant start-up Disable plant start-up	COLLABORATORS General – TIMER
TIMING DATA 0.5 s update	DEVICE I/O OUT: Trip signal Permissive start signal IN: Contractor on/off signal

CLASS: TIMER	
RESPONSIBILITIES Provide time information	COLLABORATORS
TIMING DATA	DEVICE I/O

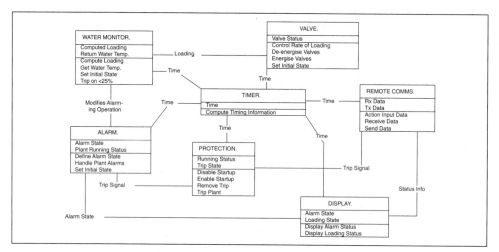

Figure 16.3   Class diagram (ideal model).

Following on from this is the development of the preliminary object message diagram (OMD) (Figure 16.4).

The OMD is one of the most important diagrams produced during software design; it is essential that it is thorough and correct. These factors can be verified to a very high degree by running through all known operational scenarios. Some typical examples are given in Figure 16.5.

Note that at present the timer object has only one purpose – to produce timing information.

16.3   Stage 2 – the transition stage (concurrency, timing and interfacing aspects)

The transition stage is the point at which practicalities are brought to bear on the ideal model. Specifically, the items to be considered are those of concurrency, timing and interfacing. Although these are separate issues, they are, in fact, very closely related. Thus it becomes essential to bring them into the design process simultaneously. Treat them as a collective item, not three isolated activities.

There is one major difficulty in OO design: the mismatch between the object model and the reality of software implementation. The ideal model implicitly assumes that objects are truly concurrent. However, to implement this, each object would need its own processor. Clearly such a costly and complex solution is not realistic when building real systems. In reality, most software is executed on single-processor designs. As discussed earlier, apparent (quasi-) concurrency can be provided by time-sharing computer resources – multitasking. Here, object concurrency can be attained by mapping each object to a task. Unfortunately, multitasking brings with it an overhead: it uses processor time and resources. The more tasks there are in a system, the greater the overhead. The implication of this is that implementing

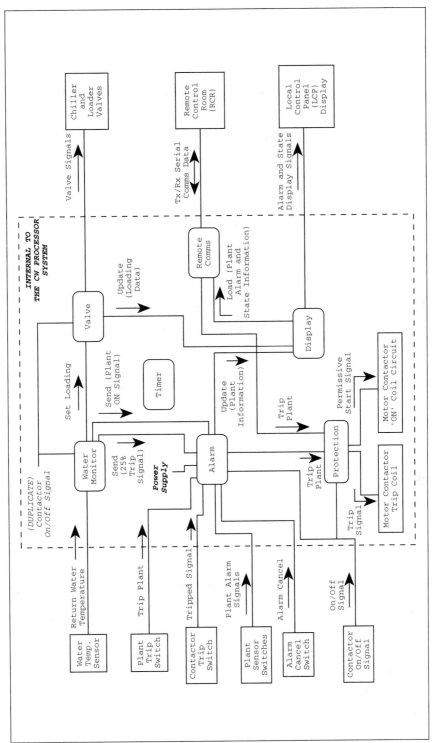

Figure 16.4 Preliminary object message diagram.

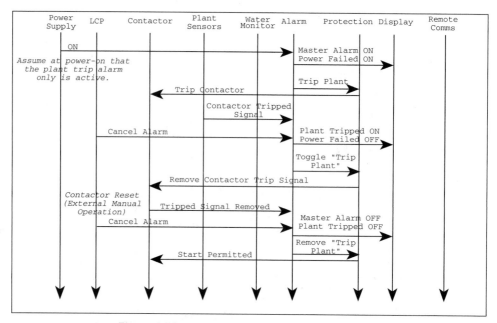

Figure 16.5 Example scenarios – preliminary design.

each object of the ideal model as a concurrent item may seriously affect performance.

From a performance point of view the less concurrency the better. One way to minimize the number of tasks is to form *groups* of objects from the ideal model; then map each group to a task (the aim being to devise a minimal task set). Both timing and interfacing act as significant drivers in the task reduction operation. Let us now consider these aspects.

Timing features fall into three categories:

- periodic tasks
- aperiodic tasks
- time delays

Periodic (also called synchronous) tasks are those which are run at fixed, regular intervals. Aperiodic or asynchronous tasks are those which become active ('arrive') at random times. Delays are self-explanatory. You may also find that some authors define a fourth category called *sporadic*. For simplicity it is here considered to be a special case of the periodic task.

Timing data for the CW system is given in Table 16.2.

Now consider the interfacing aspects. The Remote Comms object has to handle the serial data input. From the time response requirement it is clear that an interrupt-driven operation is essential. However, transmission can be dealt with under program control; interrupts aren't needed here.

Both the Alarm and Protection objects interface to switch input signals. These,

Table 16.2 Initial timing data.

Periodic		Aperiodic		Delay	
Name	**Period (s)**	**Name**	**Deadline**	**Name**	**Delay (s)**
Valve	1	Comms Rx	50 µs	No. 2 chiller	20
Water Monitor	1			LOP alarm	20
Remote Comms	1				
Display	1				
Alarm	0.5				
Protection	0.5				

by their nature, are asynchronous. However, by choosing to poll the signals, they can be transformed to a synchronous form. The decision here is to do just that, and poll at 0.5 s intervals. Thus the switch interfaces may be included simply as a component of an aggregate. Similar reasoning applies to the temperature data acquisition activity, and also to the output interfaces.

These factors help in developing detailed properties of the object set (Figure 16.6).

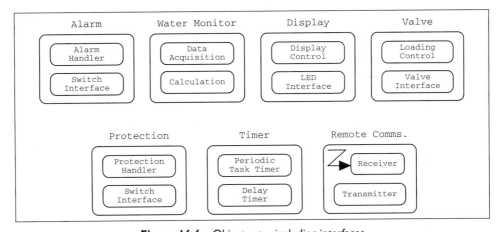

Figure 16.6   Object set – including interfaces.

We can now group together the various objects to form the tasks of the system. Here one task is designated as the `Periodic Task`, being run under timer control. Any others are interrupt-driven aperiodic ones. In this case the `Periodic Task` set comprises:

* `Valve`
* `Water Monitor`
* `Remote Comms` (non-interrupt driven object)

- Display
- Alarm
- Protection

These are collected together in the (new) collection object `Periodic Task`. It (the object) is implemented as a sequential program, individual component objects being executed at the required time intervals. To ensure that all works correctly, a scheduler object is added to the design. Here it is convenient to 'promote' the timer object to also act as the scheduler. The object `Periodic Task Timer` will be renamed as `Scheduler`. `Scheduler` must, of course, be provided with timing information in order to maintain correct time. Two choices are available. First, the task may be activated directly using a timer interrupt. Alternatively, the task could run in a continuous loop, using clock data to ensure timing compliance.

The run-time scheduling can now be dealt with in some detail. Rate groups (see Chapter 9) are organized as shown in Figure 16.7.

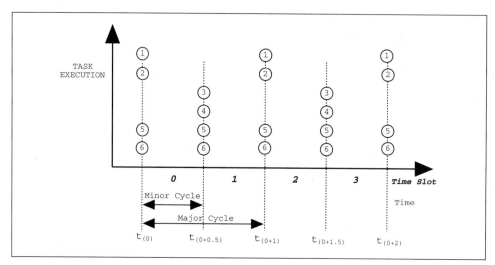

Figure 16.7   Periodic task object – rate groups.

Thus the STD for `Scheduler` is that of Figure 16.8.

The timing table information shows that the result of the computation (T MOD 2) produces a continuous 101010 sequence. Each time a timer interrupt occurs the calculation is performed. When a zero is produced, the objects in the even rate group are executed (slots 0, 2, 4 and so on). Otherwise those listed in the odd slots (1, 3, 5, …) are run.

Implicit here is the assumption that all tasks run to completion within their allocated time slot.

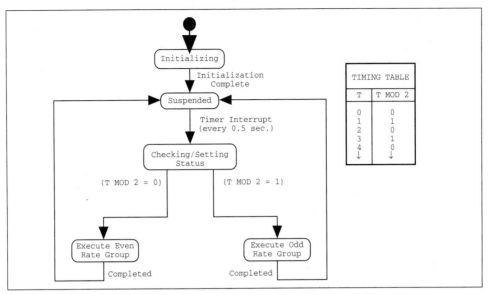

Figure 16.8   Scheduler object – basic state diagram.

16.4   Stage 3 – developing the real object model

16.4.1   Design for concurrency

At this point two primary concurrent objects have been identified: Periodic Task and Input Line Data Handler (note: at the tasking level of design the words object and task are used interchangeably). Using information gleaned earlier, the task level object message diagram can be developed (Figure 16.9).

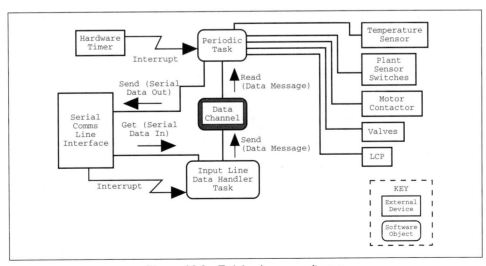

Figure 16.9   Task level message diagram.

Observe that a new object – Data Channel – has been included. Data Channel is a passive, container object used only as a tasking-level channel communications component. Its purpose is to decouple data transfer activities between the two concurrent tasks. Adding this to the task-level model is a *design* decision; a decision, however, which is driven by an important rule of multitasking design – always interconnect concurrent tasks using communication components (see Chapter 9). For clarity, plant data has been left off the diagram.

It can be seen that here the task level structure is quite simple. Thus there is little reason to produce a message scenario diagram.

It is recommended that a class diagram be produced for the task level model. Each task should be considered to be a composite class, having a set of components. It is then a straightforward operation to generate the class diagram for each aggregate. The alternative approach – a single monolithic class diagram – is likely to be highly complex and difficult to understand.

16.4.2   Sequential software – object structuring, communication and control

We move now to the design of individual tasks. It is important always to keep in mind that task software is sequential, not concurrent. One advantage of using a task-first design approach is that tasks can be dealt with individually (all others can be treated as external entities). The result is that software development poses fewer difficulties.

Let us start with the periodic task, its class diagram being that of Figure 16.10.

Observe that some regrouping of child objects has been done. The purpose is to improve the structure from an implementation point of view. In particular,

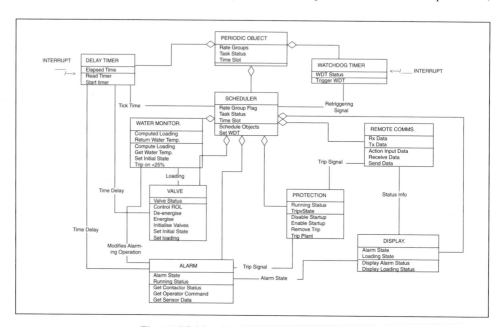

Figure 16.10   Class diagram – periodic task.

`Scheduler` has been defined to be the parent (assembly) class of an aggregation. This fits in more naturally with the revised scheduling scheme.

Concerning Figure 16.10, several points deserve a mention:

- All associations are one-to-one, which is unusual in object-oriented programming. However, bear in mind that here we are dealing with the application software. Design at the application level tends to generate classes which have single implementations only. Further, reuse is secondary to structure, performance, encapsulation, information hiding, coupling and cohesion.
- The wording used to define the associations places emphasis on relational aspects, not messaging, control and so on. For instance, the association between `Delay Timer` and `Valve` is the `Time Delay`. What the valve does to the timer (or vice versa) is not expounded on.
- Aggregation is used extensively; inheritance is absent. This also is a characteristic of application-level design in embedded systems. Do not, however, infer that inheritance has no part to play in such designs; far from it. But there always has to be a trade-off between its advantages (code reuse) and disadvantages (maintenance and stability). An anonymous quotation: 'What is best about inheritance is its power and flexibility. What is worst about inheritance is its power and flexibility'.
- A new object, `Watchdog Timer`, has been introduced. Once again we have an implementation-related decision. The function of a watchdog timer in a processor system is one of protection (usually with safety in mind). In general it is the last line of defence against program malfunction when all software guards have failed.

The next design step is to produce the final version of the object message diagram. Here it is fundamentally the same as Figure 16.4; developing it is left as an exercise for the reader. What follows next is the generation of the event scenario diagrams for the objects.

16.4.3   State modelling

At this point the dynamics of individual objects can be defined, using state transition diagrams. Input information for state modelling is provided primarily by the class, communication and event scenario diagrams. One workable method for developing the dynamic model is to:

- Choose one object.
- Note its inputs and outputs and the objects connected to these.
- Produce an event scenario diagram for the chosen object.
- Using this information, derive the object STD.

Figure 16.11 demonstrates the first part of the procedure, applied to the valve object.

The diagram, which is very much self-explanatory, helps in explaining the event/response behaviour pattern of `Valve`. Such behaviour is defined in the event trace diagram of Figure 16.12.

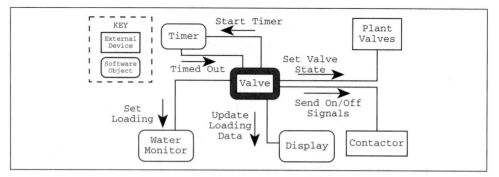

Figure 16.11   Valve object interactions.

Using the information contained in Figure 16.12, a top-level STD can be derived for `Valve` (Figure 16.13).

The state `Normal Running` is somewhat more complex than the others. Therefore it is refined into a set of substates, the substate diagram being that of Figure 16.14.

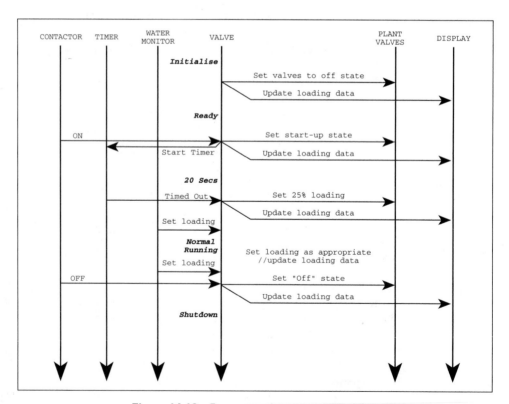

Figure 16.12   Event trace diagrams – valve object.

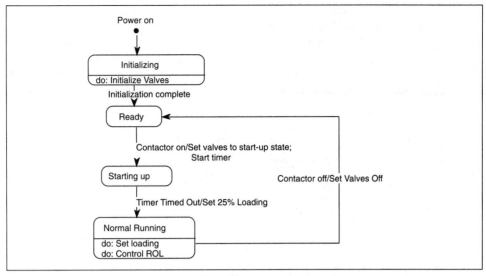

Figure 16.13 STD for the `Valve` object.

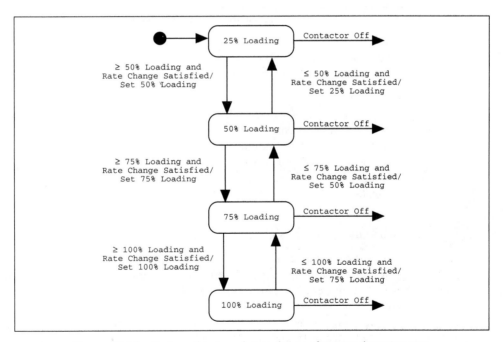

Figure 16.14 `Valve` object – substate diagram for normal running state.

16.4.4 Functional modelling

At this juncture the design is almost complete. Nevertheless the diagrams produced thus far have one weakness: they don't necessarily highlight the functional requirements of the design. Frequently such information is present, but is implicit or unclear. Efforts to remedy these problems by making the information explicit may only throw up new difficulties; design diagrams become complex and difficult to understand. At best the result is confusion; at worst it may lead to implementation errors. Fortunately, there is a ready way to deal with the problem; the use of a data flow diagram (Figure 16.15).

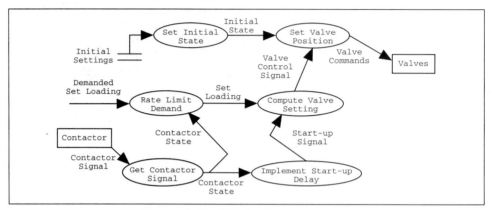

Figure 16.15 DFD for the Valve object.

The diagram describes clearly and explicitly what processing is carried out by the object. However, for completeness it must be augmented by descriptive text, as for example:

> When the unit is powered up, initialization is performed by the DT Set Initial State. This also includes setting the plant valves to the off state. Next the state of the contactor is read in by the DT Get Contactor Signal (on power-up it will be Off), the data being sent to the DTs Rate Limit Demand and Implement Start-up Delay. Rate Limit Demand ensures that Set Loading is maintained at <25% (the off state), irrespective of the demanded loading.
>
> When the contactor signals On, then:
>
> (i) Rate Limit Demand sets Set Loading to 25%.
> (ii) Rate Limit Demand now responds to the demanded loading signal.
> (iii) Implement Start-up Delay generates a start-up signal.
> (iv) Compute Valve Setting responds to both Set Loading and Start-up signal inputs, generating the appropriate Valve Control Signal.
> (v) Set Valve Position produces the output drive signals for the valves themselves.

In normal running the valve settings are determined by the input Demanded Set Loading signal (subject to rate limiting, of course).

When the contactor signals Off, Set Loading is set to <25%, the plant-off loading state.

16.5   Stage 4 – program development

16.5.1   Service software

The topic of 'service' software has been discussed earlier in Chapter 3 (re-read if necessary). Irrespective of the design technique adopted, the same basic ideas still apply. Perhaps the simplest way to identify a service class is to ask:

- Can it be developed without any knowledge of how it is going to be used?
- Will it be essential to the overall functioning of the application?

A 'yes' to both clearly defines a service class.

We may, of course, choose to refine such classes at a later stage, making them more application-oriented. Changes are normally made for reasons of speed and/or code efficiency.

The CW system service classes include:

- analogue data acquisition
- switch input signal handling
- switch output signal handling
- serial communication device control
- hardware (including watchdog) timer interfacing

Other candidate classes (but not applicable here) include:

- graphical user interfaces
- data store, disc and memory management
- signal processing and control algorithms

Figure 16.16 illustrates the overall structuring and relationship of the software in the system.

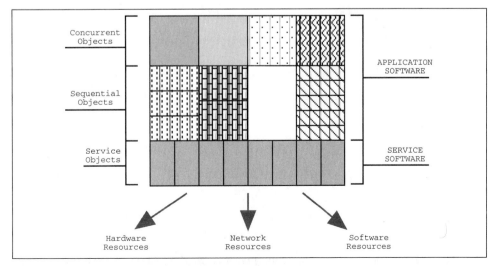

Figure 16.16   Software structuring.

16.5.2   Application software

Only part of the application software has been developed here. It does, though, illustrate the major aspects of translating diagram to code. Moreover, to allow readers to experiment, it has been designed to run on a PC. Consequently, it was necessary to structure the software taking into account the PC hardware and its operating system.

Listing 16.1 shows:

```cpp
#include <conio.h>
#include <iostream.h>
#include <dos.h>

class WaterMonitor {
public:
    void Run() {
        cout << "\nWater Monitor running";
    }
};
class Valve {
public:
    void Run() {
        cout << "\nValve running";
    }
};

class Alarm {
public:
    void Run() {
        cout << "\nAlarm running";
    }
};

class Protection {
public:
    void Run() {
        cout << "\nProtection running";
    }
};

class Display {
public:
    void Run() {
        cout << "\nDisplay running";
    }
};

class RemoteComms {
public:
    void Run() {
        cout << "\nRemote Comms running";
    }
};
```

Listing 16.1   Simple cyclic scheduling, using timing provided by the standard DOS timer to give a periodic time of 0.5 s.

```
//Global information for time management
void interrupt LoopTimer(...);
void interrupt (*DosTimer)(...);
enum Task {Run, Stop};
volatile Task PeriodicTask = Stop;
int Count = 0;
int TimeSlot = 2;
int RateGroup = 0;
const int Slots = 2;

void main()
{
Valve ValveObj;
WaterMonitor WaterObj;
RemoteComms CommsObj;
Display DisplayObj;
Alarm AlarmObj;
Protection ProtectionObj;

    cout << "\nProgram Listing 16.1 - CW_Sched.cpp";
    PeriodicTask = Stop;
    DosTimer = _dos_getvect(8);
    _dos_setvect (8, LoopTimer);
    while (! kbhit()) {
        if (PeriodicTask == Run) {
            RateGroup = TimeSlot % Slots;
            if (RateGroup == 0 ){
                cout <<"\n\nRun of first time slot";
                ValveObj.Run();
                WaterObj.Run();
                AlarmObj.Run();
                ProtectionObj.Run();
            }//end if
            if (RateGroup == 1 ){
                cout <<"\n\nRun of second time slot";
                CommsObj.Run();
                DisplayObj.Run();
                AlarmObj.Run();
                ProtectionObj.Run();
            }//end if
            TimeSlot++;
            PeriodicTask = Stop;
        }// end if PeriodicTask
    } // end while !kbhit
    _dos_setvect (8,DosTimer );
}//end main

void interrupt LoopTimer(...){
    Count++;
    if (Count > 20){
        PeriodicTask = Run;
        Count = 0;
        }
    //end if
    DosTimer();
}
```

Listing 16.1   *continued*

- implementation of the periodic task
- implementation of the Timer object
- coding of the Valve object.
- formation of rate groups in code

The source code, when compiled, can be run to emulate the periodic task object.

Review

You should now:

- understand the use of a four-stage design process
- know the purpose of each stage, and the detailed activities within them
- appreciate the interrelationship between the stages
- know where, how and why the following are used: use case modelling, CRC cards, class diagrams, OMDs, task-level diagrams, scenario diagrams, STDs and DFDs
- realize why concurrency, timing and interfacing features are important topics in their own right
- see the advantages in first developing an ideal object model, then developing it into a realistic one
- appreciate the value in developing the multitasking model as the first part of the real model
- understand the subsequent development of, and the interaction between, the object, state and functional models
- appreciate the need for and use of these different models

Appendix A:
Air conditioning – chilled water system

This appendix describes the system to which the software designs of Chapters 10 and 16 are applied. It is typical of many process plants, having control, protection/alarm and sequencing requirements. Such facilities are to be provided by a plant controller based on microcomputer technology.

The opening section explains the purpose and functioning of the system. Following this, system-level design is carried out, which defines the controller structure and function. It also delineates the boundary between hardware and software. The final section considers the design of the microcomputer hardware at block diagram level. It is at this point that software design commences. Chapter 10 describes a structured design solution, while Chapter 16 offers an object-oriented one.

A.1 Introduction

A.1.1 General description

Air conditioning within a building is provided by a series of air treatment units (Figure A.1).

These units are responsible for providing cooled, dehumidified air to the environment. They work on a heat exchange principle, recirculating the building air over chilled surfaces. Chilled water, derived from a chilled water unit, maintains these surfaces at the required temperature. Heat energy extracted from the air is transferred to the water, and hence back to the chiller. There it is removed (eventually) by compressor refrigerant action.

The system works correctly provided the temperature of the delivered water (Water Out) is within close bounds. To achieve this, some form of automatic control is needed. Chilling of the delivered water is altered in two ways:

- changing the compression action within the compressor (using sets of Loader valves)
- switching the coolers on/off, via liquid control (Chiller) valves

The degree of chilling produced is referred to as the 'loading' of the system. Table A.1 shows the relationship between the various valve settings and system loading (note: the compressor motor must be running for chilling to take place).

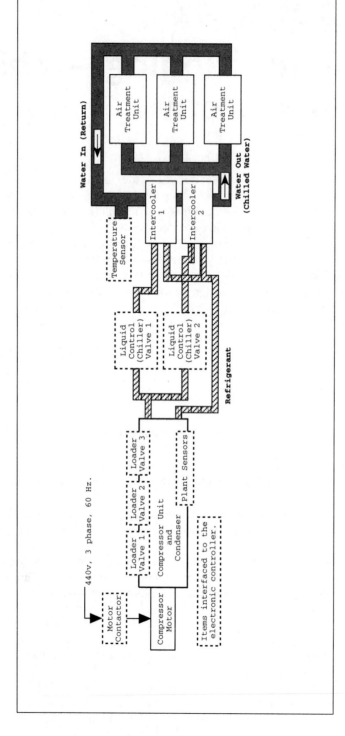

Figure A.I Air conditioning system – overall.

Table A.1

	Load				
	0%	**25%**	**50%**	**75%**	**100%**
Chiller 1	D	E	E	E	E
Chiller 2	D	D	D	E	E
Loader 1	D	E	D	D	D
Loader 2	D	E	E	D	D
Loader 3	D	E	E	E	D

E = energized
D = de-energized

A.1.2 Control requirement

It is required to control the Water Out temperature so that it lies in the range 7 to 7.5 °C. This is done indirectly by measuring the Water In temperature, and adjusting the loading accordingly. Such an operation is based on the assumption that the water flow is constant. The temperature controller is required to produce the loading schedule defined in Figure A.2.

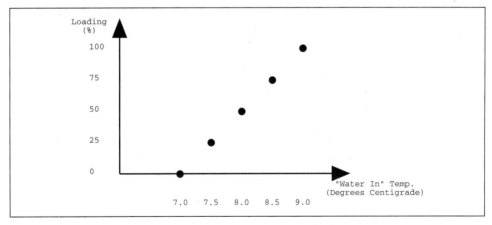

Figure A.2   Loading schedule.

It can be seen that the plant operates in a stepped, not continuous, control mode. Owing to system constraints, the rate of loading and unloading must not exceed a specified rate. In this case, the minimum time to go from 25% to 100% (and vice versa) is one minute.

A.1.3 Protection requirements

The plant is equipped with sensors to provide the following alarm (switch) signals:

- Low Suction Pressure
- High Discharge Pressure
- Low Chilled Water Flow
- Low Chilled Water Temperature
- Low Oil Pressure (compressor)
- Motor Trip
- Below 25% Loading (from temperature controller)

Should any alarm (except `Motor Trip`) occur, the compressor motor is to be tripped out.

When any alarm occurs, two system master alarms are to be activated; one local to the plant, the other at a remote location.

The alarm which initiates a `Motor Trip` is to be displayed (see MMI requirements).

An alarm cancel function is to be provided (see MMI requirements). When selected, the status of *all* alarms is to be displayed. If alarms are clear, then the master alarm is to be deactivated.

Note: the low oil pressure alarm is to be inhibited for the first 20 s after start-up.

A.1.4 Switching and sequencing requirements

This section is concerned with the operation of the compressor motor and the valves. In normal conditions, switching of the valves is a control requirement. However, this is subject to additional constraints, included in the following specification.

(a) The plant may only be started with the loading set to 25%. This is defined to be the reset condition.
(b) Start can take place only if the plant is in reset *and* alarms are clear *and* start is selected.
(c) Starting the plant is achieved by energizing the motor contactor.
(d) The No. 2 chiller valve is to be energized for the first 20 s after start-up. It then reverts to normal operation as determined by the controller.
(e) The plant may be switched off locally or remotely (see MMI details).
(f) Stopping the plant is achieved by tripping the motor contactor (thus it will require a manual reset before the plant can be once again started).
(g) If a running plant is tripped, it is to go automatically to reset.
(h) The contactor provides a switch-type signal to show whether it is on or off.

A.1.5 Man–machine interfacing (MMI) requirements

Provision is to be made to have both local and remote MMI interfacing facilities.

Local interfacing

It must be possible to operate the plant from an operator's position local to the plant. This MMI, called the local control panel (LCP) is to incorporate the following displays and controls (Table A.2):

Table A.2

Alarm indications	State indications	Switch controls
Master alarm	Plant reset	Alarm cancel
Low suction pressure	25% loading	Plant start
High discharge pressure	50% loading	
Low CW flow	75% loading	
Low CW temperature	100% loading	
Low oil pressure		
Motor trip		
Below 25% loading		

(i) alarm indications
(ii) state indications
(iii) switch controls

The first alarm which occurs (the primary cause of a plant shutdown) is to be displayed; all subsequent (secondary) alarms are to be inhibited. The local master alarm is to be activated (as also is the remote master alarm). All indications are to be maintained until the alarm status is accepted using the alarm cancel function. When cancel is selected, the status of *all* alarms is to be displayed. If alarms are clear, then the master alarms are to be deactivated.

Remote interfacing
It is required to be able to operate the plant from a remote control room (RCR). The remote operator will be able to:

- trip the plant
- monitor plant loading and alarm condition

Note that alarms *cannot* be cancelled from the RCR.

Design of this unit does *not* form part of the system under consideration. Communication between the plant controller and the RCR is to be done using a serial data link. This is to be implemented at the physical layer as a 1 Mbit/s RS422 half-duplex system. It is a point-to-point connection, the message structure being that of SDLC. All message protocols will be defined later in the project. It is a requirement that the integrity of the data link must be monitored. Any failure is to be brought up as an alarm at the RCR.

A.2 System design

A.2.1 Overall organization

The first step in the design process is to decide how the overall control system should be organized. In this case the structure shown in Figure A.3 is chosen as the most suitable one.

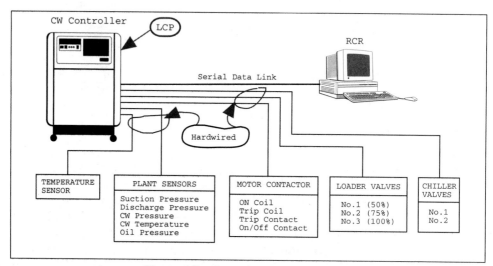

Figure A.3   Control system organization.

Here a unit – designated the chilled water controller (CWC) – is to house the embedded controller for the system. This unit is to be located adjacent to the CW plant. Local displays and controls are to be mounted on the front of the unit, thus forming the LCP. All plant components are hardwired to the CWC. Communication with the RCR is handled by the controller, the connection being made via a serial data link.

A.2.2 Control system specification

This defines the requirements to be met by the hardware and software of the system. There are three aspects to be considered: device interfacing, system operation and timing issues.

Device specifications
(i)   LCP displays: light-emitting diodes, 2 mA nominal current
(ii) LCP switches: push-button type, single contact, close on push
(iii) Plant sensor (alarms): single contact, close on alarm
(iv) Chiller and loader valves: 115 V single phase, 0.5 A rating
(iv) Motor contactor:

- On coil – switched by a 1 mA contactor control circuit
- Trip coil – as for the On coil.
- Overload sensor – single contact, close on overload
- On/off signal – single contact, closed when on

(v) Return water temperature sensor: This produces an analogue voltage output in the range 0 to 10 V d.c. as shown in Table A.3.

Table A.3

Water temperature (°C)	Sensor output (V)
0	0
10	10

The output is linear with temperature change.

(vi) Serial link: twisted screened balance pair, length 50 m. The signal levels are to comply with the EIA RS422 standard

(vii) Remote control room: no detailed specifications issued

System operation

There are two distinct aspects to system operation: temperature control and protection/alarm. Preliminary designs for these are covered in the following sections. The overall system dynamics are shown in the state transition diagram of Figure A.4.

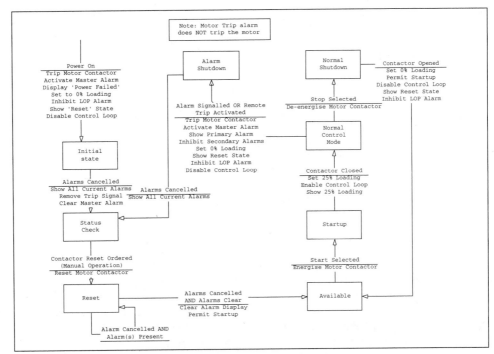

Figure A.4   Overall STD for the CW system.

Refer to this as necessary when reading later descriptions of system operation.

Alarm and protection
This block diagram of this subsystem is given in Figure A.5.

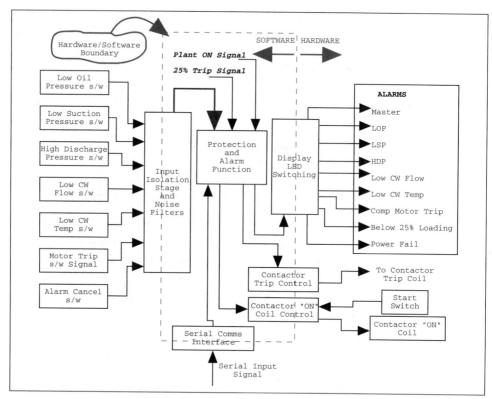

Figure A.5 Alarm and protection subsystem.

The major interfaces are:

- alarm input signals
- alarm display outputs
- motor contactor control

It is an operational requirement that should power fail, a motor contactor trip signal is to be generated automatically. When power is (re-) applied, the system is to stay locked out, with the trip being active. This lockout state is to be indicated by turning on a 'power failed' LED. Also, the master alarm LED is to be activated, to flash at a 2 Hz rate. The alarm cancel switch must be operated to reset the system and remove the trip signal. Only when the contactor is reset and all alarms are clear can a start be invoked. As far as the control system is concerned, this is a 'permissive' start. That is, starting is permitted, but not initiated, by the controller. This is achieved by activating the contactor coil circuit. If the start switch is now operated, the contactor coil is energized, closing the motor contactor. Switching the coil off de-energizes the contactor.

When the system is powered up, but the compressor motor is not running, it (the compressor) has zero oil pressure. Thus the low oil pressure alarm – which will be active – must be inhibited. Also, when the compressor is started, time must be allowed for the pressure to build up. Thus the alarm is to be overridden for the first 20 s of operation. The `Plant On` signal is used to indicate start-up of the compressor.

There are a total of eight alarms. All of these *except* `Motor Trip` must trip out the motor contactor. All are required to activate the master alarm. The first alarm to occur is to be displayed; all others are blanked. Until `Alarm Cancel` is selected, this condition is to be maintained. This ensures that the system cannot be restarted until alarms have been cleared. Note that when the plant is tripped the `Plant On` signal once more inhibits the low oil pressure alarm.

To reset the system, the alarms must be cancelled. If the alarm condition has been remedied, then pressing `Alarm Cancel` will clear the alarm displays. It will also remove the trip signal from the contactor. However, if alarms are still present, then *all* of them are displayed. The master alarm is deactivated and the contactor trip signal is removed.

Temperature control

A block diagram for the temperature control subsystem (including state indications) is given in Figure A.6.

Assume for the following description of operation that the `Water In` temperature is greater than 7.5 °C. Also, the complete system is initially powered down; thus the motor contactor is open. When power is applied, the control system responds to this combination of the temperature and contactor signals. The results are twofold. First, the valves are set to the 0% loading condition (Table A.1). Second, the plant reset LED is illuminated.

The system waits in this state until an 'on' signal is received from the motor contactor. As a result, the demanded loading is set to 25% and the control loop enabled. This now sets the valves to the appropriate condition (subject to rate of loading limits: Section A.1.2). At all times, current plant loading is shown on the LCP.

During normal running, water temperature is controlled by switching the chiller and loader valves. These settings are determined by the control law calculation section, based on the current water temperature signal.

Should the return water temperature fall below 7.5 °C then:

- a 25% trip signal is generated, and
- all valves are set to the 0% condition

This will (indirectly) cause the contactor to be tripped. When the contactor signal changes state, it causes the controller to revert to that described under power-on. It is now ready for a further start-up.

It is permissible for the operator to switch off (not trip) the plant using the local start/stop switch. This is detected by the contactor on/off signal going to 'off'. If this happens, the resulting action is as for power-on.

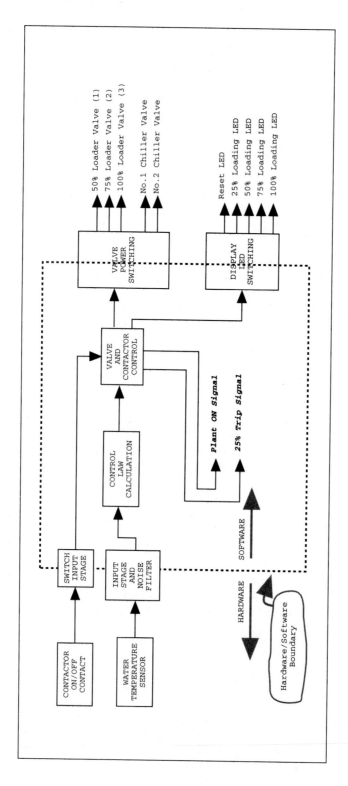

Figure A.6 Temperature control subsystem.

Timing issues

Preliminary studies indicate that the following timings should be complied with:

- control loop – 1 s sample rate required
- alarms – 0.5 s updating required
- displays – 0.5 s updating required
- loading/unloading time, 25% to 100% and vice versa – 1 min minimum
- starting up – low oil pressure alarm to be inhibited for 20 s. No. 2 chiller valve to be energized for the first 20 s
- remote control room information update – 1 s intervals
- response to remote control room commands – 1 s
- detection of failure of the serial data link – within 10 s

A.2.3 Controller hardware organization

Figure A.7 shows the initial design for the electronic hardware of the system. This is arrived at by taking into account factors such as:

- existing hardware
- existing software
- development costs
- manufacturing techniques and costs
- design risks

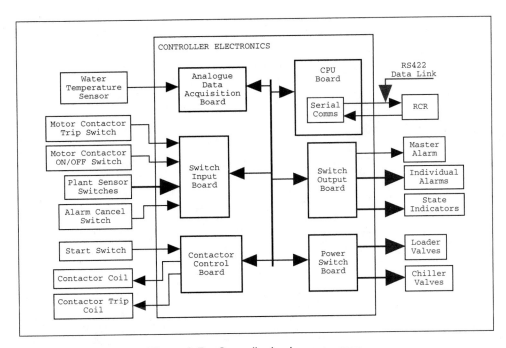

Figure A.7   Controller hardware structure.

- test and maintenance policies
- performance requirements
- staff availability (design team, drawing office and so on)
- delivery schedule
- customer preferences

There is no uniquely 'right' solution in situations like this.

Bibliography

Books – structured techniques

Goldsmith, S. (1993) *A Practical Guide to Real-Time Systems Development*, Prentice-Hall, Englewood Cliffs NJ.

Hatley, D. and Pirbhai, E. (1988) *Strategies for Real-Time System Specification*, Dorset Publishing House, London.

Jackson, M.A. (1975) *Principles of Program Design*, Academic Press, London.

Page-Jones, M. (1988) *Practical Guide to Structured Systems Design*, 2nd edn, Prentice-Hall, Englewood Cliffs NJ.

Yourdon, E. (1989) *Modern Structured Analysis*, Prentice-Hall, Englewood Cliffs NJ.

Ward, P.T. and Mellor, S.J. (1985) *Structured Development for Real-Time Systems*, Vols. 1, 2 and 3, Prentice-Hall, Englewood Cliffs NJ.

Books – object-oriented techniques

Booch, G. (1994) *Object-Oriented Analysis and Design with Applications*, 2nd edn, Benjamin/Cummings, New York.

Ellis, J.R. (1994) *Objectifying Real-Time Systems*, SIGS Books, New York.

Gamma, E. *et al.* (1995) *Design Patterns – Elements of Reusable Object-Oriented Software*, Addison-Wesley, Reading MA.

Jacobson, I. *et al.* (1992) *Object-Oriented Software Engineering – A Use Case Driven Approach*, Addison-Wesley, Reading MA.

Rumbaugh, J. *et al.* (1991) *Object-Oriented Modelling and Design*, Prentice-Hall Englewood Cliffs NJ.

Shlaer, S. and Mellor, S.J. (1992) *Object Lifecycles – Modelling the World in States*, Yourdon Press, California.

Wilkinson, N.M. (1995) *Using CRC Cards*, SIGS Books, New York.

Books – real-time systems

Allworth, S.J. (1981) *Introduction to Real-Time Software Design*, Macmillan Press, London.

Cooling, J.E. (1991) *Software Design for Real-Time Systems*, ITCP, London.

Gomaa, H. (1993) *Software Design Methods for Concurrent and Real-Time Systems*, Addison-Wesley, Reading MA.

Laplante, P.A. (1993) *Real-Time Systems Design and Analysis – An Engineers Handbook*, IEEE Press, New Jersey.

Schumate, K. and Keller, M. (1992) *Software Specification and Design – A Disciplined Approach for Real-Time Systems*, John Wiley, New York.

Papers and documents

Bliss, R. (1996) Unfinished business. *CrossTalk – The Journal of Defense Software Engineering*, **9(2)**, 32.

Booch, G. and Rumbaugh, J. (1995) Unified method. *Reference Manual*, Rational Software Corporation (http://www.rational.com).

Chen, P.P. (1976) The Entity-Relationship Model – toward a unified view of data. *ACM Transactions on Database Systems*, **1(1)**, March, 9–36.

Harel, D. *et al.* (1990) STATEMATE: a working environment for the development of complex reactive systems. *IEEE Transactions on Software Engineering*, **16(4)**, 403–14.

HOOD (1989) *Hierarchical Object Oriented Design, HOOD Manual*, prepared by CISI Ingenierie, CRI A/S and Matra Espace for the European Space Agency, Issue 3, 1989.

Kirk, B. (1994) A distributed architecture for real time, in *Oberon-2*, Proc. Conf. Joint Modular Languages, University of Ulm, pp. 325–66.

MASCOT (1987) *The Official Handbook of MASCOT*, Version 3.1, Issue 1, issued by JIMCOM.

Miller, G.A. (1956) The magical number seven, plus or minus two, *Psychological Review*, **63(2)**, 81–97.

Essential reading for everybody

Leveson, N. (1995) *Safeware – System Safety and Computers*, Addison-Wesley, Reading MA.

Neumann, P.G. (1995) *Computer Related Risks*, Addison-Wesley, Reading MA.

Wiener, R. (1994) *Digital Woes – Why We Should Not Depend on Software*, Helix Books, Reading MA.

Index

SELECT SOFTWARE TOOLS CD

The software provided with this CD is intended to provide students of software engineering with an overview of the capabilities of the SELECT product range, and some hands-on experience of using modeling techniques for software development.

The versions of SELECT OMT and SELECT Yourdon available with this CD are restricted functionality and designed for teaching and educational purposes only.

SELECT Software Tools offers special discounts and schemes for colleges and universities wishing to purchase SELECT's market-leading structured and OO modeling toolsets.

For more information about SELECT Software Tools or its products and services, visit the SELECT web pages on `http://www.selectst.com` or contact SELECT at the following addresses:

UK and International	USA
SELECT Software Tools plc	SELECT Software Tools, inc
Westmoreland House	1524 Brookhollow Drive
80–86 Bath Road	Santa Ana
Cheltenham	California 92705
Gloucestershire GL53 7JT	USA
England	
Telephone: +44-1242-229700	Telephone: 714-825-1050
Fax: +44-1242-229706	Fax: 714-825-1090

The SELECT Product Range includes:

SELECT Enterprise

SELECT Enterprise™ is a dedicated modeling toolset for building scaleable client/server applications. It provides modeling support for multi-tier architectures and integrated code generation and round-trip engineering for C++, Microsoft's® Visual Basic® v.4.0, Forté, Powersoft's PowerBuilder or Borland's Delphi.

SELECT SSADM Professional Workbench

The SELECT SSADM Professional Workbench provides integrated modeling support for the full range of structured techniques as described in the SSADM 4+ method. The modeling techniques are supported as part of a flexible framework within SELECT, enabling only the relevant techniques to be selected from the range available, for use on a new project.

SELECT Yourdon

Complete and rigorous support for the Yourdon method is provided in the SELECT Yourdon toolset. This approach enables developers to pick and choose techniques to suit their development approach. On-line help also provides context-sensitive assistance in using the toolset. SELECT Yourdon is easy to use, concealing a sophisticated underlying rule base. This provides developers with a powerful support environment for real-time development and an open multi-user repository.